Contemporary African Screen Worlds

Contemporary African Screen Worlds

Lindiwe Dovey,
Añulika Agina, and
Michael W. Thomas,
EDITORS

Duke University Press *Durham and London* 2025

Project Editor: Lisa Lawley
Designed by Courtney Leigh Richardson
Typeset in Portrait and Retail by Westchester Publishing Services

Library of Congress Cataloging-in-Publication Data
Names: Dovey, Lindiwe, editor. | Agina, Añulika, editor. | Thomas,
Michael W., [date] editor.
Title: Contemporary African screen worlds / Lindiwe Dovey, Añulika
Agina, and Michael W. Thomas, editors.
Description: Durham : Duke University Press, 2025. | Includes bibliographical
references and index.
Identifiers: LCCN 2024026658 (print)
LCCN 2024026659 (ebook)
ISBN 9781478031420 (paperback)
ISBN 9781478028208 (hardcover)
ISBN 9781478060413 (ebook)
ISBN 9781478094173 (ebook other)
Subjects: LCSH: Motion picture industry—Social aspects—Africa. | Motion
picture audiences—Africa. | Mass media and culture—Africa. | Mass media
—Social aspects—Africa. | Mass media—Political aspects—Africa.
Classification: LCC PN1993.5.A35 C658 2025 (print) | LCC PN1993.5.A35
(ebook) | DDC 302.23/43096—dc23/eng/20241214
LC record available at https://lccn.loc.gov/2024026658
LC ebook record available at https://lccn.loc.gov/2024026659

Cover art: Grainy texture. Courtesy Adobe Stock/Enzo.

Contents

Foreword

JONATHAN HAYNES

This fresh and wonderful book manages to feel adequate to the epochal shifts in media technologies over the last decades and to the equally dramatic transformations in Africa's mediated relations to the world. It explores what has grown through those changes: a dazzling explosion of creative energies, a plethora of humming new channels of communication, an outpouring of stories giving voice to an unprecedented range of African experiences.

The introduction to the book is ambitious, intellectually precise, and compelling in laying out the "screen worlds" framework. People enter a new field, or a new conception of a field, because their thoughts and feelings have changed about what work matters and would be exciting to do. This whole volume is singularly compelling in its human interest, running as it does on empathy and curiosity, and so should be influential in winning adherents to the screen worlds paradigm.

The book is kaleidoscopic, even more so than other collections with similarly vast geographic coverage, because it takes as its key subject and theme the interfaces formed by various kinds of screens—many kinds of interfaces, among film platforms, filmmakers, performers, and audiences. Different kinds of work are required to get at these relationships, including interpretative readings of film texts. But at the book's center are African people watching screens and the interview as a key heuristic and symbolic practice. There is no one world of African cinema, only a collection of many scenes and practices rendered vividly by a team of researchers with intimate local knowledge.

In her chapter, Elizabeth Olayiwola observes that the old cinema houses in Nigeria often became Pentecostal churches when the days of celluloid ended, and now Pentecostal churches are built to resemble cinemas because film has become so central to religious experience. Pier Paolo Frassinelli, in the hallowed precincts of screenings at the Pan-African Film and Television Festival of Oua-gadougou (FESPACO), observes that the audience won't turn off their phones. Solomon Waliaula shows us Kenyan housemaids watching Nollywood films. They do so while alone in their employers' homes, the families having gone out to school or formal-sector jobs. The housemaids use Nollywood's narratives to make sense of their own lives, which with distressing uniformity involve catastrophic dislocations and no clear path to possessing the kind of home in which they are left alone with the television—symbol of middle-class success, the regular reward for long-suffering Nollywood heroines.

The introduction celebrates the ethos of the level view that comes with participant observation and interviewing—or, better, *conversation*, a term that reduces the implied power imbalance. In her chapter, Lindiwe Dovey writes that her methodology "is feminist, collaborative, and conversational," and that it is crucial "that we continue to put ourselves in conversation with the people involved in the industrial screen worlds that produce and circulate those texts so that we can develop a clearer picture of how gender plays out in the practices of film labor behind the scenes."

This emphasis on conversation, as indispensable for capturing lived experiences and discovering the unforeseen, feeds into the volume's remarkable sociality, which I find moving and deeply attractive. The contributors were clearly prompted to put themselves into their story. This sometimes takes the form of identifying their subject position by race and so on, in the conventional contemporary way, but it extends to Temitayo Olofinlua's and Estrella Sendra's warm, cheerful admissions of their own fandom as they study how broadcasts spill into social media and spill again, vibrantly, into their own academic work—something like Plato's theory of the chain of inspiration in the *Ion*, only with cell phones.

The COVID-19 pandemic prevented much of the project's generous budget for workshopping and networking from being spent, but that side of the project was kept alive virtually, and the book has many traces of workshopping, shared reading lists, and a sense of common purpose and community, a shared expansive and expandable horizon. The kaleidoscopic fragments are not meant to add up to a totalizing whole, but they intercommunicate rhizomatically, just as the hugely complex and variegated media landscape is interconnected as never before, in ways and to an extent that define our age. The whole is greater than the sum of the book's parts.

It's time to say something about Lindiwe Dovey's role, while bearing in mind the contributions of her fine coeditors and other collaborators and her rather excruciating self-consciousness about her positionality as a white woman with an elite education occupying a position of relative power and therefore obliged to undo that power. Still: she had the vision, got the grant, established the community, provided intellectual and pedagogical leadership, and—ceaselessly driven and energetic—animated the whole with her magnificent generosity of spirit.

The project blasts open old divisions that have balkanized the study of various kinds of media, so we can see more. It's provincializing: suddenly a lot of previous (and current) work seems blinkered. And it's deprovincializing, urging (as some other scholars have been urging, notably Moradewun Adejunmobi and Carmela Garritano) that African film studies stop talking so much to itself and engage with what's going on around the world. The introduction sets a strenuous example of doing this. Alexander Bud's remarkable chapter is an example of importing a new kind of film studies that has been flourishing in the North—close attention to the materialities of film production—and marrying it with the volume's commitment to locality and to interviewing. He has talked to a staggering number of people working in Nollywood in roles no one thought to pay much attention to before: set designers, location scouts and agents, upholsterers, metalworkers, electricians, carpenters, and painters. His analytical categories are numerous and precise, but the objective finally is to blur the boundaries between the "real," material world and the filmed world of illusions. Bud drills down until the comedy of Nigerian life comes gushing out: wealthy women like the prestige that comes from having their homes used as film locations, but their husbands are willing to outbid the filmmakers to bribe their wives into maintaining the household's privacy; the builder of a new Lagos housing estate did such a good job of making it look like Atlanta or Houston that prospective Nigerian expatriate buyers suspected that the advertisements were a "419" fraud scam, so the builder was glad to have Nollywood films shot there to attest to its reality. This is research that swings.

As the editors point out in the acknowledgments, most of the contributors are based in Africa and are at early stages of their careers, and so are doubly deprived of academic resources and power. The project shows that excellent, original, inspiring work can be done with simple tools. The appropriate technology is their "firmly grounded, horizontal, eye-level positions," the "groundedness that allows many of our authors to approach their subjects with the deep knowledge, humility, ethical engagement, and empathy that—in our view—leads to rigorous, insightful, *rich* research."

The one explicit polemical target is the conception of "world cinema" that conceives of its subject as an ideal collection of masterpieces—feature films, needless to say—contemplated with gentlemanly connoisseurship from an invisible but implicitly air-conditioned, ideal, frictionless perspective that seems to float above the planet. No fieldwork is required; nothing fieldwork could teach would seem to be relevant. The screen worlds framework, in contrast, is about lived relationships to all kinds of media. In their chapter, Robin Steedman and Rashida Resario return to this polemic, pointing out that the subjects of their research would be invisible to "world cinema," arguing with some asperity for the absolute necessity of fieldwork and invoking Lizelle Bisschoff's cautions about overenthusiastic assessments of the potentials of digital technologies. They continue: "Infrastructural constraints remain highly relevant, but so too do human capital, social position, and skills. In order to understand the differing trajectories of film businesses in Ghana, we must be aware of the link between offline inequality and the ability to seize opportunities in digital spaces." Digital technologies enable nearly all the phenomena this book studies, but the researchers are too grounded in specific realities to be utopian.

Only a few chapters address the shapes of African film as they have been conceived in African film studies. Frassinelli's chapter about the FESPACO film festival's fiftieth birthday pays tribute to a noble tradition but notices the old unresolved tensions, including FESPACO's hostility toward the video revolution. The mood of anxious disquiet about the future that seemed to pervade the festival is strikingly different from the exuberant precarity of Lagos. The conflict between FESPACO and Nollywood parallels in some ways that between world cinema and screen worlds: the former has similar investments that are liable to be diminished, in practice, in the wider horizon; the role anthropologists played in establishing Nollywood studies gives it a family relationship with screen worlds.

But Femi Eromosele sees Nollywood and Nollywood studies as a problem, a hulking blockage that occludes other media forms such as music videos. To which I have two responses, one being that Nollywood was a genuine world-historical revolution and the stakes of the present and immediate future are enormous and require urgent attention. My other response is, yes of course: Nollywood certainly didn't come out of nowhere; in its classic form it has already begun to seem to belong to the historical past and shouldn't fill the whole horizon. One lesson this volume teaches, if we needed to learn it, is that things are changing so quickly that everything must be described as existing in a specific historical moment. I am struck by the fact that three of the leading American midcareer Nollywood scholars—Connor Ryan, Matthew Brown, and Noah Tsika—have written recent books that deal with Nollywood's prehistory on celluloid and television.

Moradewun Adejunmobi (2016) has pointed out that few of the most-cited Nollywood scholars have backgrounds in film studies—the plurality comes from literature and language departments and/or operates in an African studies framework. In Nigerian universities, film studies continues to be largely blocked by entrenched theater studies faculties—small-minded territorialism with enormous consequences. If one looks around or looks back, such disciplinary issues are formidable obstacles to doing the work of, or making a career in, screen worlds. But if one looks forward, things are perhaps not so grim. A number of the book's contributors are also filmmakers, or festival organizers, or something else. Joe Jackson, the author of the concluding chapter, works as a "media disseminator" for the African Screen Worlds project—a kind of job that didn't exist when I was a PhD student. This working across platforms will only increase as neoliberalism makes conventional academic careers rarer and harder.

African Screen Worlds is a vision of a disciplinary reconfiguration more than a new discipline; it's a plane of analysis of a new field of objects or, better, of a vast array of relationships. It's not a theory of how power works through media. On that score there is nothing like a party line among the contributors, and in fact perhaps there is a principled resistance to totalization: we're in a post-Foucauldian world where meaning, the making of meanings, is dispersed, though local struggles are linked. But this project comes with an ethics, and its perspective is democratic and democratizing, with a strong inclination to privilege the agency of ordinary people.

A few chapters focus on dramatic intrusions of transnational corporate power into the world of African media. Añulika Agina's chapter on Netflix and Elastus Mambwe's on M-Net's Zambezi Magic channel are both deeply ambivalent, appreciative of the resources the corporations provide but uneasy about other effects. In Zambia as elsewhere, M-Net seems pretty good on the score of supporting local languages, but I find its class politics chilling. According to Mambwe, "'The Zambezi Magic Commissioning Brief' (MultiChoice Africa 2015, 4) . . . states that the channel primarily targets the eighteen to forty-eight age-group, which it calls the 'upgrade generation,' a group of ambitious and aspirational people, from different socioeconomic backgrounds, who are trying to achieve economic success." Those not in this category wouldn't be able to afford the channel's subscription, so this is a rational business decision, but it excludes most of the population. Neoliberalism is widening class divisions in Africa, and the corporate media are thoroughly implicated.

A third parallel study—though it perhaps does not appear as such—is Temitayo Olofinlua's chapter about the television series MTV *Shuga Naija*.

The American MTV entertainment juggernaut mounted an NGO-type public health campaign across the continent to raise awareness of AIDS and in general to educate and empower young people about sexual matters. This chapter is emblematic of the volume in its account of the seamless integration of a television serial with a social media dimension and various real-life extensions. Olofinlua's fandom is infectious, and my values accord completely with the program's purposes. But—on reflection—is there anything to worry about here? MTV Shuga Naija seems to have been extremely skillful and effective in mobilizing African youth to reject crucial swaths of their parents' cultures and to seek to install northern standards of sexual behavior—a remarkable feat of social engineering. The faces, the agents, and the agency seem entirely African, but what is the American role, and who was actually running the show?

I don't mean to be paranoid, or protective of a reactionary African "authenticity," or to be anything but clear-sighted about political possibilities. During the "Arab Spring" of 2010–11, social media famously played a key role in organizing uprisings, and a powerful motive force was the desire of Arab young people to live in "a normal country," meaning the kind of society they saw on foreign television programs. Both these factors were also important in the "Occupy Nigeria" movement (2012) and the Nigerian #EndSARS (2020) movement. In none of these cases was either element enough to effect the desired revolutionary change, but we must keep hope alive, and the last dreadful decade has given many of us a renewed appreciation for the value of liberal democracy, even as filtered through capitalist media.

The dispersed, localized perspectives of this book cushion it from lurching between hope and fear on the macro level. But the Africa that emerges is marvelously lively and dynamic, the vast continent extending its life into the digital dimension. Olofinlua's term *mobile screens* acquires symbolic resonances as the book goes on: it names the little screens on our phones but also the ubiquity that defines the contemporary screen media era, and it suggests a mediated world in constant flux and motion. This whole project shows the way to a more mobile screen studies, one that goes everywhere we go, nimble and adaptable, adventurous and humane, capable of taking stock of a burgeoning world.

Acknowledgments

First and foremost, the editors would like to thank the European Research Council and the European Union's Horizon 2020 research and innovation program for the generous grant (grant agreement No. 819236—AFRISCREEN WORLDS) that funded the African Screen Worlds: Decolonising Film and Screen Studies project, through which this edited volume was created. The volume brings together the work of a new generation of African screen media researchers; many of the authors are early career scholars without the privilege of deep institutional power in higher education; many are based within African contexts where there are fewer financial resources for research than in the so-called Global North. And yet it is precisely this groundedness that allows many of our authors to approach their subjects with the deep knowledge, humility, ethical engagement, and empathy that—in our view—lead to rigorous, insightful, *rich* research. Using the word *poor* provocatively to describe the wealth that emerges from this kind of scholarly pursuit that has to work with the energy and creativity of *not* having access to many resources, Ngũgĩ wa Thiong'o writes: "Without the luxury of excess, the poor do the most with the least. Poor theory and its practice imply maximizing the possibilities inherent in the minimum. Poor theory may also provide an antidote to the tendency of theory becoming like a kite that, having lost its mooring, remains floating in space with no possibility of returning to earth" (2012, 2). Many of the authors unfurl multiple worlds from the contexts in which they live and work every day, meaning that they do not address them from vertical perspectives above the earth (might we use the more apposite analogy of the drone?) but rather from firmly grounded, horizontal, eye-level positions. After all, as Ngũgĩ continues, "Even in social life, *poor* means being extremely creative and experimental in order to survive" (3), and this is also in evidence across many of the fascinating screen media practices explored in this volume. It is to be found, for example, in what has been achieved by entrepreneurial Ghanaian film students, evangelical film movements in Nigeria, the craftspeople of Nollywood, filmmakers in Uganda and Senegal using YouTube to connect their films with the world, and "housemaids" in Eldoret using films for self-therapy. It is also apparent in the passionate labor of some of our non-African contributors, such as Stefanie Van de Peer, whose activist work to restore feminist North African films is exemplary.

Our methodology for developing this volume could also be described in relation to such inventiveness, somewhat paradoxically, since it emerged from a well-funded project. After circulating a global, open call and selecting in January 2020 drafts of the chapters that appear here, we had intended to bring all our contributors together for an in-person workshop in London in September 2020. The world had other plans, however, with the COVID-19 pandemic compelling us to shift our workshopping online, through four, intensive Zoom sessions and ongoing conversations with one another. Suddenly, the significant resources we had to run an in-person workshop were rendered useless, and although we of course regret not having had that chance to come together in embodied form, we have also been surprised at how being forced to work online and at a distance from one another—through the screen interfaces of our computers and phones—has introduced other benefits and insights. First, there was a certain sense of synchronicity created given that we were researching screen worlds and the relationships between people and screens. Furthermore, on realizing how easy it was to connect online (everyone managed to join the workshops despite the digital inequalities that divide the world), it made us wonder why we had not been connecting with one another more frequently in the past. Too often the rush and excitement of in-person events trumps the value of continuous, ordinary, regular conversation. The methodology behind this book has thus been slow, collegial, and conversational; working against the conventional process of putting an edited volume together, where one often does not meet the other contributors, let alone have an opportunity to read and discuss their chapters before the volume is published, we have attempted to put ourselves in dialogue with one another—even going as far as to think of ourselves as a choir.

We are extremely grateful to our publications partner, Carli Coetzee, whose own ethical work and collaborative values as the editor of the *Journal of African Cultural Studies* over many years have been a major inspiration for us. We are also indebted to our "keynotes" (Moradewun Adejunmobi, Alessandro Jedlowski, and Jonathan Haynes) for the special role they have played in helping us, as editors, to conduct our choir. Carli has been a constant support throughout the process, while the keynotes, especially Jonathan Haynes, devoted a great deal of time to reading this book in draft form and providing vital, critical feedback to help us improve it. We are also extremely grateful to the whole team at Duke University Press, in particular Elizabeth Ault for her constant engagement with and belief in us since the beginning of the project, and to Benjamin Kossak and Lisa Lawley for all their hard work and support. Swetal Agrawal, Georgia Thomas-Parr, and Susan Ecklund have provided meticulous copyediting help for which we are extremely grateful.

Tragically, during the process of creating this volume we lost one of our dear participants—Pier Paolo Frassinelli. However, his voice remains firmly in our choir, and we will always remember with great appreciation and affection his generous, spirited personality, his sparkling intelligence, and his enthusiastic contributions to our workshops. His passing is yet another reminder of how fragile human life is and that academia should not be seen as a competitive space divorced from the rest of our lives; we need to work with one another in solidarity and support, care, and collaboration.

We hope that you enjoy our songs in what follows.

Introduction

Exploring Screen Worlds

LINDIWE DOVEY, AÑULIKA AGINA,
AND MICHAEL W. THOMAS

In the past decade, digitalization and expanding internet usage have created an unprecedented form of global media synchronicity and convergence in which Africa and Africans are firmly embedded.[1] Despite ongoing digital divides and issues across Africa with internet connectivity and bandwidth, the high cost of data, and lack of online payment options, internet penetration throughout the continent has increased exponentially, and millions of people—and, in particular, the youth, who make up the majority of Africa's population—are engaged with digital platforms and applications used across the globe, such as YouTube, WhatsApp, TikTok, and Twitter (now known as X). Much of this engagement involves consuming, circulating, and communicating about audiovisual content through supersmall phone screens, and the ubiquity and everyday nature of such activity makes the days when Africans had to rely only on daily terrestrial broadcast television, rare film festivals, or even Nollywood films on VCDs to access screen narratives feel like a distant memory.

Indeed, it is this new global context of audiovisual narrative media practices that inspired us to propose the concept of "screen worlds" as a heuristic to encourage fresh avenues of reflection in our field of film and screen studies. Many scholars have argued that, in our digital and internet age, we need to move beyond consideration of cinema to embrace, think through, and explore screens in their entirety (Bruno 2014; Cunningham and Silver 2013). Cinema certainly is an element within screen worlds, but the latter also allows us to embrace a whole range of other practices and processes within screen production, circulation, and spectatorship that go beyond the purely cinematic. In this volume, the feature-length fiction film takes a back seat as it jostles and vies with a rich array of other audiovisual screen worlds for people's attention: episodic narrative series created and circulated both by large companies and by entrepreneurial individuals, and which are evidence of Africa's full participation in the global "televisual turn" (Adejunmobi 2015; Lotz 2017); short films and film skits that are uploaded to YouTube or distributed via WhatsApp; and the music videos of a new generation of Black creatives experimenting with visual and sonic registers in radical ways, and which are appreciated throughout the world and not only by Black fans. These screen worlds are dynamic, fragmented, interactive, and transnational; they sometimes make appearances at film festivals, but they are certainly not exclusive to festivals.

The concept of screen worlds asks us to pay attention to the screen as a material object (Wasson 2012) and to people's physical and emotional relations with screens—whether as filmmakers or film spectators. In the opening chapter of this volume, Temitayo Olofinlua helps us to theorize screens in these multiple dimensions through putting forward a key concept—"mobile screens"—which she explains as follows: "The term *mobile screens* encompasses the idea of screen as infrastructure and virtual environment in our contemporary world, but it specifically emphasizes the role of audiences in this mobility. In this sense, I am interested in how films and television shows 'move' their audiences and how they respond through social media. How does this engagement take spectators beyond being a 'viewing audience' to being a 'doing audience'?" In this way, Olofinlua suggests that mobility refers not only, quite literally, to newly mobile film viewers who carry their screens around with them in their laptop bags and pockets to watch films while on the move but also, more abstractly, to the mobility of people's emotions and the worlds that are created in the screen interfaces between audiovisual narratives and viewers—viewers who do not simply watch but who engage deeply with these stories and with other viewers of them in all the ways their screens allow them to. There is something undeniably liberating about this mobility when one considers that when Olofinlua was growing up "the media landscape . . . was one that existed largely within the home" and that "access to these [media] spaces was controlled" (Olofinlua, chapter 1). For many people mobile devices have freed screen worlds from more regulated spaces, such as the domestic arena or the cinema theater, where parents or exhibitors act as gatekeepers (for better or worse). They have also taken us beyond theories of a rather passive notion of the "haptic" in relation to the film medium and film spectatorship (Marks 2000) toward more active, and often communal, engagement.

Rather than screens existing as inert, rectangular surfaces that beam audiovisual narratives at us, they are increasingly becoming portals or prosthetic devices that almost seem to be an extension of our own bodies due to their ubiquity and mundanity. In this volume we dwell on moments in which screens seem to break because of the binge-watching demands of fans (Olofinlua, Eromosele) or in which audiovisual material seems to spill out of the screen or be sucked into the screen because of the viscerality of the screens themselves (Moonsamy, Grieve). Alexander Bud's chapter provides uncanny examples of real and screen worlds overlapping and intermingling, with a particularly hilarious moment in which a screen world of a film set / housing development is used as evidence to justify its actual existence to skeptical potential buyers. We thus concur with performance theorist Philip Auslander that "the idea of liveness is a moving target, a historically contingent concept whose meaning changes over time and is keyed to technological development . . . liveness describes a historical, rather than ontological, condition" (2008, xii–xiii). Far from being able to neatly separate out online and offline experiences, in today's environment (particularly given the widespread impacts of COVID-19), our screens live with us daily, and we treat them less like inanimate objects than as portals for live interaction with others. For many people today, losing one's phone thus feels like losing one's voice, one's connection to the larger world.

While we use the concept of screen worlds and not cinema here, we retain a focus on the cinematic insofar as our interest resides in the contexts and experiences of audiovisual narrative storytelling, and—while documentary is also of course a form of narrative-making—it is notable that all our authors focus on the production and circulation of fictional screen worlds of various kinds. In our neoliberal era of big data, algorithms, filter bubbles, casualized labor, and growing inequalities, human creativity and imagination as expressed through fiction and storytelling often exist against the odds, and there is thus political potency in focusing on this ingenuity and what threatens or sustains it. We are therefore collectively interested in the agency of contemporary Africans who contribute in diverse ways to audiovisual fictional storytelling—filmmakers, exhibitors, entrepreneurs, audiences, film restorers, and craftspeople. It is these African authors who bring to life the imaginative storyworlds that constitute African screen worlds.

As storyworlds have been defined by contemporary media scholars around the world, they are far more expansive, dynamic, and malleable than how "texts" have been conceived of through close analytic methodologies in the past. Warren Buckland, for example, emphasizes the diegetic worlds created through storytelling, through the interfacing of both storyteller and audience: "Narratives create worlds, not just a sequence of divisible events; each narrative text therefore implies a larger fictional world beyond the boundaries of (or distinct from) the manifest text. . . . Furthermore, a storyworld is not autonomous but depends on the audience's affective and emotional response—a type of aesthetic engagement that determines whether or not they can imaginatively inhabit that storyworld" (2020, 20). We are concerned with how Africans (as both makers and viewers) engage in such storyworld building through screens—where these worlds often end up exceeding the contained, bounded text, leading to a sense of spatial and temporal portals opening up beyond everyday life and allowing audiences to engage with, reimagine, or even escape their own lives. As Marta Boni notes, "Worlds—as imaginary territories and perennial, collectively built, semiotic realms—are necessary for the understanding of media creation and for the interpretive processes it stimulates" (2017, 9). We would like to add to this, from a decolonial perspective, that alternative world-making, where worlds become imaginary territories, have also long been a mode of survival for those who have been excluded from what Walter Mignolo and Catherine Walsh (2018) call the "North Atlantic fictions" that have tended to assume the prerogative to define the world in universal terms, despite the provinciality of these same fictions. This is what has led indigenous decolonial thinkers and activists to call for "proposals for a world of many worlds" (Blaser and de la Cadena 2018) in which people have the agency and the freedom to build their own worlds and not have to define themselves through the colonial matrix of power that has structured our planet for centuries (Mignolo and Walsh 2018).

A People-Oriented Approach

The focus of this volume is the passionate people who dream up, bring into being, contribute to, circulate, watch, fall in love with, share, comment on and discuss, and reuse and repurpose screen worlds. While being attentive to the effects and impacts of changing technologies on screen media production, circulation, and spectatorship, we adopt what we call a "people-oriented" approach and remain assertively anthropocentric in our attempts to understand what people *do* with films in their desire to create social meaning. It has taken engagement with diverse scholarly fields and theoretical and conceptual frameworks (not just film and screen studies), as well as a commitment to fieldwork, interviews, focus groups, and conversations, to bring the diversity of these contemporary African screen worlds and the people who create them into view. Foundational to us has been the vital work conducted by African popular culture scholars—all the way from Karin Barber's field-defining article "Popular Arts in Africa" (1987) to Grace Musila's edited collection, the *Routledge Handbook of African Popular Culture* (2022)—and the work of African media scholars, from many of the articles in the *Journal of African Media Studies* founded by Winston Mano in

2007 to Gilbert Motsaathebe and Sarah H. Chiumbu's groundbreaking book *Television in Africa in the Digital Age* (2021). We also want to pay tribute to the work of all the Nollywood and African video film scholars (such as Moradewun Adejunmobi, Carmela Garritano, Jonathan Haynes, Alessandro Jedlowski, and Onokoome Okome), who courageously challenged African cinema scholars to question their own hierarchies and understanding of quality and value, thereby revolutionizing our field. In addition, we want to acknowledge a key conference organized by Mahir Saul and Ralph Austen in 2007 at the University of Illinois Urbana-Champaign, the first to bring together African cinema and Nollywood scholars and thereby paving the way for our convergence.

Global creative industries scholarship that explores the difficulty and precarity of sustaining a living through creative work (McRobbie 2015), and the kinds of work involved in film production (Curtin and Sanson 2016) and spectatorship (Jenkins 2012), has also been crucial to our ability to bring to light the creative and affective labor that exists through and around screen worlds. While many of the pioneering African filmmakers had to make their capital-intensive celluloid feature films through irregular subsidies from Europe (often from France and its Bureau of African Cinema [Andrade-Watkins 1996]), many of the contemporary African filmmakers discussed here have to rely on diversified business strategies and creative "hustling" (Steedman 2023) to sustain their creative filmmaking work in today's competitive, capitalist, saturated, digital environment. Both environments—past and present—were/are difficult for creatives, and some of our authors are optimistic about the ways that digitalization has opened opportunities to African filmmakers who were previously marginalized, and particularly women (see Sendra; Steedman and Resario, both in this volume). However, as Robin Steedman and Rashida Resario show in their comparative analysis of two female filmmakers working in different parts of Ghana, the ability to access and benefit from digital opportunities is often dependent on one's location, social class, and connections as well as educational background. It is worth mentioning here that many of the early Nollywood filmmakers and distributors who worked with analog formats (VHS tapes, VCDs, and DVDs) in the 1990s were a rare example of those from the so-called lower social classes asserting themselves within the film industry; film scholars such as Ezinne Ezepue (2020) and Tejaswini Ganti (2012) are thus rightly concerned about the effects of gentrification on the ability of people with fewer resources to participate in film industries throughout the world, despite the democratization and affordances occasioned by the digital revolution.

Indeed, it would be irresponsible to engage in techno-optimistic discourses that lionize new mobile technologies without considering how, just as they liberate some, they exclude others. As Añulika Agina notes in her chapter in this volume about the impact of Netflix on the Nigerian screen media scene: "Inevitably, in every disruptive game, there are winners, losers, and those who maintain the status quo." The technology itself is neutral, but who has access to it and the benefits produced through and around it are subject to the same intersectional privileges or oppressions that affect human beings' lives. The effects of gender and class on the ways people participate in or are excluded from these new mobile screen environments are fully evident in the discussions across this volume. Just as we are excited about some of the ways that increased access to the internet in Africa has allowed for the circulation of new kinds of narratives and images about women and women's sexuality in particular (see Sendra, this volume), we are also deeply aware of how certain communities can become victims to digital inequalities. As Steedman and Resario note in their chapter, it often takes looking beyond feature fiction filmmaking to even *see* the work and labor of many African women screen practitioners, since women have mostly not had access to the resources to make capital-intensive films. Most (African) women have traditionally worked in film administration (for example, running film festivals) or have made television series, documentaries, and short films (see Ellerson 2000, 2002). By expanding our *objects* of analysis in this volume through our conceptualization of capacious screen worlds, we have thus also been able to expand our *subjects* of analysis, making African women's contributions to screen media-making, circulation, and spectatorship far more visible, exploring their work as entrepreneurs, leaders, mentors, spectators, and film restorers across this volume rather than in only one discrete part (see Olofinlua; Sendra; Agina; Dovey; Steedman and Resario; Waliaula; Van de Peer). In this way we are building on and extending the excellent work that has been done to date to document, celebrate, and analyze the work of African women filmmakers (for example, Bisschoff and Van de Peer 2020; Dipio 2014; Ellerson 2000, 2002; Garritano 2013; Kassahun 2018; Mistry and Schuhmann 2015; Steedman 2017, 2023; Tsika 2015).

While emphasizing human agency and a people-oriented approach, it is also our constant foregrounding of the role that technology plays in the ways that filmmakers, exhibitors, and audiences shape and experience screen worlds that distinguishes our work from an important edited collection that we see as a predecessor to ours, *A Companion to African Cinema* (2019). Although many of the chapters in that volume also engage with how technology is transforming African audiovisual storytelling (for example, in chapters by Moradewun Adejunmobi, Alessandro Jedlowski, and Robin Steedman—all of whom have also participated in this volume), this previous volume foregrounds "theoretical work on time, sound, genre, queering, and biopolitics" (11). The editors of *A Companion to African Cinema*, Kenneth Harrow and Carmela Garritano, position these "New Critical Approaches" to "African cinema" within a genealogy of African film criticism originating with Marxist revolutionary analysis in the 1960s and 1970s (1); then developing into postcolonial and cultural studies approaches in the 1980s and 1990s (8); and then broadening out, in our current era, into a "multiplicity of approaches" of "new poetics and new theoretical engagements" (11). Our volume contributes to this contemporary "multiplicity of approaches," but where many of the authors in *A Companion to African Cinema* analyze film texts and film directors, we tend to foreground the complex relationships among mediums, platforms, audiences, and the craft and entrepreneurship of different people who contribute to film (for example, set builders, video-on-demand platform founders, film producers, and film restorers). We are grateful that *A Companion to African Cinema* and the large body of previous scholarship on African film have enabled us to adopt a different approach here—one in which we do not feel that we need to rehearse histories of African filmmaking and the theories that have been applied to it; instead, this previous work has freed us to focus on the present moment and on specific case studies.

While the power and affect of screen worlds demand that we continue to analyze audiovisual narratives through the lens of representation (in other words, what is contained within their diegetic worlds), in this volume we are more interested in exploring how these narratives are made and circulated in ways that create interfaces between filmmakers, audiences, and others involved in the creation, curation, and consumption of screen worlds. We find David Trotter's distinction here between representational and connective media useful to our attempt to keep both of these dimensions within the purview of our analyses while privileging the latter:

> There is a useful though by no means absolute distinction to be made, where media are concerned, between the representational and the connective. . . . The axiom of representational media might be: two places at two times. . . . The principle or value articulated by media used to represent arises out of that double removal in time and space. Representational media, it could be said, enable us to reflect upon a reflection of our world. The axiom of connective (or "tele-") media, by contrast, is two places at one time. Their primary emphasis has always been on instantaneous, real-time, and preferably interactive one-to-one communication at a distance. (2013, 8)

Many of the chapters in this volume are more interested in analyzing the connective rather than the representational nature of narrative screen worlds in contemporary Africa, although we still see close film analysis as a vital tool, and a few of our authors use this mode as their main methodology in their analyses of diegetic screen worlds (for example, Moonsamy, Grieve, and Jackson). However, the majority of our authors situate diegetic screen worlds within the broader dynamics of industrial screen worlds—at the nexus of production, curation, circulation, consumption, and connection. Indeed, as Karin Barber says, "Connection . . . is the other side of the coin of access. No point in having access to internet space if you don't connect with users" (2022, xviii). But Barber goes on to lament, "We could do with more empirical investigation of what it is that audiences like, why they like it, how they get involved, how they discuss, remember and interpret it. 'Reception' (really the wrong term, considering what an active role many participants play in the constitution of popular expressive forms launched by others) is still largely uncharted territory in African popular culture studies" (xviii).

The spectators our authors describe or conjure in this volume are not always in the same space—often they are on the move—but they engage frequently with screen narratives and with one another through social media. The fervor with which some of the spectators studied here extend these screen worlds into new directions and dimensions means that, rather than seeing them as mere spectators, they can be viewed as fans, a term that is invoked across several of the chapters. These fans are indispensable to the imaginative construction of screen worlds, and it is through them that what is real and ideal, filmic and extrafilmic, frequently becomes blurred. Many of our authors (such as Waliaula, Olofinlua, and Sendra) even confess to coming to their own creative scholarly work via fandom and in their chapters describe in detail the ways in which fandom becomes a "labour of love" (Lothian 2015, 138; Sobande 2020, 9) that significantly contributes to "industrial production" itself (Lothian 2015).

Decolonizing Film and Screen Studies: Moving beyond Binaries

What insights do the chapters in this volume bring to the question of the decolonizing of film and screen studies, and the decolonizing of higher education in general, in line with the aims of the broader project within which it sits? One of the things that has become clear through the process of conversing with one another to create this volume is that, as much as decolonizing work involves challenging the status quo through antiracist and antisexist scholarship and activism, it is unhelpful to engage in binary thinking. In her chapter, Alexandra Grieve draws on Achille Mbembe's well-known concept of "entanglement," reminding us that Mbembe argues that "the postcolony encloses multiple *durées* made up of discontinuities, reversals, inertias, and swings that overlay one another, interpenetrate one another, and envelop one another: *an entanglement*" (Mbembe 2001, 14, cited in Grieve, this volume). The Kenyan popular culture scholar Joyce Nyairo has consistently asked scholars to avoid the temptation to downplay what Isabel Hofmeyr calls the "chaotic plurality of the post-colony" (cited in Nyairo 2015, 70), and in an especially radical moment in her book *Kenya@50*, Nyairo compares the popular songs of Joseph Kamaru, which she refers to as "a melting pot of practices" (65), with Ngũgĩ wa Thiong'o's arguments in *Decolonising the Mind* (1986) as follows: "While Ngugi's decision to write in Kikuyu was projected as a return, Kamaru demonstrates the difficulties of projecting contemporary experiences as if the colonial encounter never took place—without any traces of the grammar and practices of the colonizer's world. As Simon Gikandi posited, the epistemological shift Ngugi attempted was untenable because you cannot go back to something that is no longer sitting where you left it" (65).

Olúfẹ́mi Táíwò makes parallel arguments in his book *Against Decolonisation: Taking African Agency Seriously* (2022), in which he says his aim is to "point to ways in which the ex-colonised, at least in some parts of Africa, have domesticated (and not merely by mimicry) many ideas, processes, institutions and practices that are routinely attributed to colonialism, but are in fact traceable to modernity and other causes" (7). Many of the Africa-based, African authors in this volume are similarly uninterested in binary thinking—which is too often a result of distance, of a drone's rather than a grounded view—and dwell instead on the complexities and entanglements of what it means to live, work, and engage with screen worlds on an everyday basis in Africa and as an African. Temitayo Olofinlua, Añulika Agina, and Elastus Mambwe, for example, are all concerned with the potential contributions (and not only problems) that "foreign" players such as MTV, Netflix, and M-Net bring to specific screen media environments in Africa. Their work takes us beyond the simplistic dichotomies drawn in some of the scholarship concerned with media imperialism—and, indeed, in some contemporary decolonizing discourses—and into the daily realities and lived experiences of African film creatives.

However, unlike Táíwò, we do not feel that "taking African agency seriously" and *all* the work that takes place under the rubric of "decolonizing" need to be mutually exclusive. Rather than throw the proverbial baby out with the bathwater, we are instead interested in the extent to which—whether people like it or not—"decolonizing" has become a phenomenon so widespread (particularly within higher education institutions globally) that it merits deeper analysis. We feel that homogenizing "the decolonizers" in the abstract language of analytical philosophy, as Táíwò does throughout his book, does not help us to analyze the complexities and contradictions of work that calls itself "decolonizing." Instead, we are more concerned with empirical, grounded approaches that allow for both scrutiny of *and* engagement with "decolonizing" projects and initiatives, thereby recognizing failures *and* successes. To us, it is undeniable that the movements initiated at universities around the world in the wake of the 2015 Rhodes Must Fall movement in South Africa have brought about some significant changes. At SOAS University of London, where our African Screen Worlds: Decolonising Film and Screen Studies project has been based, for example, this movement led to a collaboratively authored decolonizing learning and teaching toolkit that has had an impact on curricula and pedagogy around the world.

Empirical, grounded approaches to analyzing what it means to "decolonize" are profoundly concerned with *who* is doing the work, *from where*, and *how*—questions that have been crucial for us to grapple with in a project like ours, based as it is *not* in Africa, but in the United Kingdom. "Decolonizing" activism gave us the tools and mandate to analyze the demographics of many Africa-focused projects run from Europe and North America and to decide that, in contrast, we wanted our volume to foreground as much as possible the work of African, Africa-based, early career researchers. Furthermore, we asked all our authors to reflect on their own positionality and lived experiences in relation to the research they were producing for this volume so that we would all be conscious about how our subjectivity inevitably influences our research and interpretations. Then there is also the question of research methods, particularly if one is not from or located in the place one studies. As Steedman and Resario note in their chapter, "While one can study world cinema without ever traveling to those regions whose filmmaking cultures are under examination (cf. White 2015), African film scholars have long argued for the absolute necessity of fieldwork in film studies to understand cultures of both production and consumption."[2] Rather than confine ourselves to textual approaches (although we see the deep value in those), many of us have drawn on conversational methodologies that include interviews, focus groups, and discussions, which have also allowed our research participants to speak back to us and challenge our ideas—another necessity of research that claims to "decolonize."

Decolonizing work, for us, also involves an end to Africa and Africans being viewed and treated as part of a separate planet, a different world (Dovey 2015b). In this sense, in his chapter, Femi Eromosele offers one of the best examples of decolonizing that we have, which is of the Nigerian musician Falz's music videos' exceptional global mobility *not* because of affinitive transnationalism (in other words, their popularity with diasporic Nigerians or Africans) but because of their attractiveness to audiences everywhere regardless of the music videos' Nigerian provenance. The diversification and mainstreaming of Nigerian screen worlds evidenced in this example raise questions about whether Nigerian filmmaking can continue to be seen as a "minor transnational practice," as Moradewun Adejunmobi argued in her influential article in *Postcolonial Text* in 2007. Whereas it took a long time for many African film scholars to acknowledge the energy and ingenuity of early Nollywood, Nigerian screen worlds are now so popular and dominant across many parts of the continent and beyond (Krings and Okome 2013) that it makes their general exclusion from much mainstream film and screen studies scholarship and teaching even more perplexing, and the case for decolonizing our academic field even stronger. Many contributors to this volume are Nigerian and/or focus on Nigerian screen worlds (Haynes, Olofinlua, Agina, Bud, Waliaula, Olayiwola, Eromosele, Adejunmobi, Jedlowski); what their scholarship collectively reveals is that Nigerian filmmaking practices have diversified to such an extent that any casual reference to "Nollywood" now requires qualification and specification. As our authors show, Nigerian screen worlds now embrace multiplatform television shows, commissions from Netflix, complex craft considerations for set building, fans in rural communities throughout Africa, evangelical film movements, and music videos circulating around the world. In this sense, this volume can be read as a call to scholars everywhere to acknowledge *heterogeneous* Nigerian and African screen worlds that are *at once* local, national, regional, and global.

We ask you to read this volume not only as a collection of grounded, African case studies but also as contributing to contemporary global debates and theorization around screen media, industries, makers, and fans. A vast amount of media studies scholarship has been produced in and about the so-called Global North and Asia in relation to changing audiovisual storytelling experiences and formations over the past decade—characterized variously through phrases such as "transmedia storytelling" (Boni 2017; Jenkins 2006; Khiun and Lee 2020), "media mixing" (Steinberg 2012), "intensified media swirl" (Vernallis, Rogers, and Perrott 2020), and "media crossroads" (Massood, Matos, and Wojcik 2021). However, the majority of this work continues to ignore the African continent, even as it may engage with issues of race and intersectionality. The African Screen Worlds project was designed to bring African and other regional screen media contexts and theorizing into conversation so we can chart and describe these dramatic global changes with greater accuracy and nuance. The indispensability of such dialogue and interaction has been extolled by Ngũgĩ wa Thiong'o as follows: "At the International Center for Writing and Translation, we took our motto of 'culture contact as oxygen' from Aimé Césaire's *Discourse on Colonialism*, where he writes 'that whatever its own particular genius may be, a civilization that withdraws into itself atrophies; that for civilizations, exchange is oxygen'" (2012, 2). While our preoccupation here is with African screen worlds, the conversations that resulted in this volume were informed by global theorizing, and we hope, in turn, that our theorizing here is seen to have value globally, not only for Africa. In *Global Screen Worlds*, a companion to this volume, we were also inspired by Eileen Julien's proposal that scholars should put "literary, film, and visual arts by Africans in dialogue with the work of artists from Asia, Europe and the Americas" so as to "recognize both African specificities and Africa's presence in the world" (2015, 26). That volume has thus explicitly brought into conversation African and other (mostly Asian) films and film scholars, thereby responding to calls by Paul Willemen (2005) and Mitsuhiro Yoshimoto (2013) for a comparative and collaborative approach to film and screen studies.

Structure of the Volume

This volume has been organized thematically, so that we can respect but also move beyond the national perspective that has been the framework for much previous rich (African) film scholarship. It has emerged out of many of our contributors' grounding in and deep knowledge of very specific (often subnational) local contexts in Africa but has also been inspired by our collective search for similar—as well as distinct—experiences across diverse African contexts (including diasporic contexts, as explored by Joe Jackson and by Michael W. Thomas and Asteway M. Woldemichael in their contributions) and by our desire to bring these experiences into pan-African conversation to transcend the dominance of the state or the nation as the only way of understanding and interpreting (African) screen media.

The first part of the volume contributes to global screen media research that explores the erosion between the categories of film and television in our contemporary era (Lotz 2017). Temitayo Olofinlua's chapter sets the tone for the whole volume by theorizing the concept of the mobile screen and moves deftly between analysis of the makers, marketers, performers, and fans of *MTV Shuga Naija*, a transmedia television series that also screens on YouTube. While the series has a social development goal—to improve sexual health—its audience engagement methods encourage agency rather than the kinds of unidirectional, patronizing messaging typical of how foreign nongovernmental organizations (used to) operate in African contexts. Estrella Sendra explores the women-led, Senegalese internet television series *Maîtresse d'un homme marié* (*Mistress of a Married Man*), showing how this screen world is brought alive by its avid fans all over the world (the show has had more than four million viewers per episode) who have actively engaged with and remixed it in fascinating ways. Añulika Agina's chapter explores the ways in which Netflix is shaping Nollywood's exhibition ecosystem by simultaneously disrupting existing industry operations and enabling newer modes of storytelling to emerge. Elastus Mambwe's chapter moves us from West Africa to an underexplored part of the continent where screen media is concerned. Here the "foreign" entrant under scrutiny is the South African satellite, pay-television platform DStv, and Mambwe balances critique of this company's dominance in Zambia with a tempered optimism that DStv's recently founded Zambezi Magic channel has had a positive impact on the film industry in Zambia.

In the second part of the volume we consider local stakeholder entrepreneurialism more broadly in the production and circulation of African screen worlds. Alexander Bud offers a fieldwork-informed study of house casting and crafting in Nollywood that is the first of its kind in our field and is inspiring in its expansion of which people are deemed worthy of study in film and screen studies. Dennis-Brook Prince Lotsu's case study focuses on entrepreneurial and enterprising Ghanaian film students whose work to get their own films distributed and viewed has seen them using social media platforms such as WhatsApp in creative and innovative ways that have even enabled them to transition into mainstream cinema. Lindiwe Dovey's chapter focuses on the South African film producer Bongiwe Selane and her "Female Only Filmmakers" slate, through which Selane produced twenty-six short fiction films led by female teams, thereby helping to rectify gender imbalances in the South African film industry both on and off the screen. Robin Steedman and Rashida Resario's chapter puts the spotlight on two entrepreneurial women filmmakers working in very different contexts in Ghana: the celebrated filmmaker Shirley Frimpong-Manso, who not only directs films and commercials but also runs her own video-on-demand platform (Sparrow Station); and Evelyn Asampana, an aspiring filmmaker who makes films in the Frafra language in Bolgatanga, in the rural Upper East Region.

The third part of the book continues the focus on gender found in the first two parts, but this time in terms of close textual analysis of on-screen representations of women, fieldwork-informed research on female film viewers, and the restoration of women's films. In their chapters, Nedine Moonsamy and

Alexandra Grieve analyze the work of male filmmakers, but their attention is on the complex gendered screen worlds crafted and fashioned by these men. These chapters explore the tensions among mobility, domesticity, affective labor, and worlds of work and love in African women's lives; static experiences of domestic labor connect Grieve's analysis of the fictional "housemaid" Diouana in *La noire de* . . . (an African cinematic classic from 1966 by Ousmane Sembène) with the "horror" of homes experienced by the female characters in the Ugandan filmmaker Dilman Dila's subversive contemporary rom-coms (which he uploads to YouTube). Solomon Waliaula's chapter complements Moonsamy's and Grieve's textual analysis of representations of women in domestic spaces by providing a particularly poignant case study of fandom, one in which the only type of mobility is the one created through the fantasies elicited through the relationships that "housemaids" in Eldoret, Kenya, form with the audiovisual narratives of Nollywood films playing on the television screens of their employers, and which they have to view secretly while working. Labor and leisure collapse into one another in this example, where film "becomes a medium that helps them transcend the limits of their situation and aspire to another, much more desirable world," thereby offering a form of therapy and self-help. The final chapter of this part suggests that, like the Sankofa bird in Akan mythology, we need to look back to be able to understand our contemporary moment and the future. In her self-reflexive work, Stefanie Van de Peer describes and analyzes her hands-on experiences of collaborating with others to restore particular North African films by women filmmakers. She encourages us to remember that the boundaries between what we consider old and new are porous and that superficial engagement with the "contemporary" might blind us to the hard work, solidarity, and collaboration of committed individuals who try to make rare (African) films accessible to us.

While cinema has increasingly moved onto the (super)small screens of televisions, computers, and phones, it continues to play on large "theatrical" screens as well—and, in fact, piracy of VCDs and DVDs has compelled many filmmakers in Africa to prioritize such theatrical screening as a way of both sharing their work with in-person audiences and achieving much-needed financial returns. However, as the chapters in the fourth part of the volume collectively show, the traditional "theatrical" modes of cinema exhibition and distribution—through cinema chains and film festivals—are in flux. The use of "theatrical" screenings is far more strategic these days, as Elizabeth Olayiwola reveals in her fascinating study of how evangelical filmmakers in Nigeria use church halls—and other means—to spread their films and their worldviews. How Africans approach "cinema" remains deeply embedded within other aspects of culture, as Michael W. Thomas and Asteway M. Woldemichael show in their study of the relationship among theater, performance, and cinema in an Ethiopian film screening for Ethiopian diaspora audiences in London. In their chapters, Alison MacAulay and Pier Paolo Frassinelli in turn explore how film festivals in different African contexts—Rwanda and Burkina Faso, respectively—are only one space among many diverse venues, platforms, and modes for exhibiting audiovisual narratives.

The fifth part of the book challenges us to rethink our fetishization of the visual in film and screen studies and to take account of hybrid audiovisual forms, and especially music videos, which have been particularly prevalent in the creative work of former generations of Black artists around the world as well as millennials. Femi Eromosele takes Falz's music video "This Is Nigeria" (2018) as his case study to explore "the place of technology in shaping filmic forms in the country as well as their insertion or otherwise into global networks of circulation." Joe Jackson also focuses on a music video as a case study—US-based filmmaker Kahlil Joseph's "Cheeba" (2010), which he argues creates a "crossroads" between continental Africa and its diverse diasporas, situated as it is within the broader work of Afrodiasporic filmmakers, musicians, and music video directors. Both authors attend to Carol Vernallis, Holly Rogers, and Lisa Perrott's call for a focus on "new audiovisual aesthetics" and even a new field of "audiovisual studies," which chimes with our expansive conceptualization of screen worlds: "Our project (and it can be yours) is to develop a field of audiovisual studies that's engaged with all media, and that's political. . . . The media swirl, audiovisuality and the digital turn—and the ways these interrelate and overlap—help describe today's aesthetics. The digital turn, for example, blurs the boundaries between sound and image, for both now share an ontological ground of being code. An adjustment in one medium can spur a modification in the other, and then back and forth again, nearly effortlessly" (2020, 7). But where the book by Vernallis and colleagues mostly analyzes the work of white, wealthy, male artists, ours is invested in a decolonial feminist framework and believes in the need to explore and parse the creative, often resistant, work of Black African artists who embrace different expressive forms but whose work is often overlooked in scholarship and curricula.

The volume concludes with two short afterwords on our work from two leading scholars in African screen media studies—Alessandro Jedlowski and Moradewun Adejunmobi. These reflections point to what is unique about our volume but also to areas that we have not been able to cover adequately. We recognize, for example, that studies of screen worlds must expand to encompass more diverse objects of study, and we hope Eromosele's and Jackson's chapters serve as a springboard for future scholars to explore more fully the relationship between the visual and the aural. Most important, echoing Adejunmobi, we hope that new generations of African screen media scholars will pay attention to how African audiovisual storytellers and audiences can continue to secure their creative autonomy and independence in the growing, often discriminatory, algorithmic environment of digitization.

NOTES

1   To take two countries of focus from this volume as examples: according to the *Digital 2020 Global Overview Report*, in 2023, internet penetration in Senegal stood at 58.1 percent, 17.4 percent of the population uses social media, and there are 20.13 million cellular mobile connections; in Nigeria, internet penetration is at 55.4 percent, with 14.3 percent of the population using social media and with 193.9 million cellular mobile connections.

2   Indeed, we wish to signal our strong preference for the word *fieldwork* here and to question the word *ethnography*, which—through the retention of the prefix *ethno*—carries with it the full weight of the racialized history of a unidirectional, white gaze in much academic research. If we are to liberate ourselves from these violent histories with their painful practices, we need to reconsider not only our methods but also the language that we use. As Linda Tuhiwai Smith (1999) reminds us, even the word *research* has negative connotations for indigenous peoples who have been subject to brutal abuses.

Part I

___

Mobile Screen Worlds and the Televisual Turn in Africa

1

We Need New Screens

MTV Shuga Naija, *Youth Sexual Agency, and the "Mobile Screen"*

TEMITAYO OLOFINLUA

This chapter focuses on what happens when audiovisual narratives become "unmoored" from the domestic space, turning into mobile screen worlds that people carry around in the palm of their hands and engage with in new ways. I argue that these screen worlds break the fourth wall between audiences and performers and build solidarity and community through social media engagement. Although the context I focus on is Nigeria, insights derived from this country are relevant globally, as screens everywhere become more mobile.

The history of film screens in Nigeria—from the late nineteenth-century peephole viewing devices to the mobile cinema vans of the 1950s, the proliferation of cinema houses in the 1960s to the video films of the 1990s—is tied to changes in technology. With the recent increase in internet use in Nigeria, there has been a gradual shift in people's engagement with film screens—from home videos viewed on television screens, and cinema screens, to mobile screens, ones that enable the viewing of films via phone or computer. Heidi Rae Cooley (2014) refers to mobile devices as mobile screenic devices in relation to their industrial design, how they fit in the hand, and how they enhance tactile vision—a kind of seeing that involves the eyes and the hands (see also Agina 2019; Larkin 2008).

Nanna Verhoeff (2012) uses "mobile screens" broadly to refer to different types of screens—even highway panoramas seen through car windshields—and their interaction with the moving eye. By showing how "visuality" exists in our everyday reality, she examines forms of navigation by assessing the historical evolution of screens. The idea of the unique space that mobile phones occupy, not only as viewing spaces but also as production spaces, is captured by Jan Simons when he refers to the practice as "pocket movies"—meaning "movies made with and for mobile phones" (2009, 2). While describing the versatility of the mobile phone as a device doubling as a camera and screen, Simons also captures its limitations (encouraging a short attention span, multiple distractions) as well as its advantages (immediate engagement, editing possibilities, animation software), concluding that mobile phones allow for hybridity and experimentation (14). However, many of the existing analyses of mobile screens have come from European perspectives and are focused more on the features of the devices than on screen audiences. In contrast, I conceptualize the idea of mobile screens here in relation to a specific screen media show—*MTV Shuga Naija*—and from an African perspective.

As in the rest of the world, internet usage in Nigeria is on the increase. The *Digital 2020 Global Overview Report*, a yearly global report of internet usage, states that Nigeria has 85.49 million internet users and 27 million social media users, while the Nigerian Communications Commission (2019) announced that there were over 141 million mobile internet users as of May 2020 (Okafor 2020). While it is not clear how many of these internet users actively search out film content online, the evolving nature of internet television in Nigeria seems to be creating a gradual shift in the film production space to address and engage these users. While academic study of the impact of technology on film production formats in relationship to audience engagement is still emerging, previous studies have paid attention to the impact of technology on African film productions in relation to new funding and distribution models (Dovey 2018; Ebelebe 2017; Pratt 2015) and as a means of enhancing new spaces for new voices (Ugor 2009). Pratt (2015, 82), for example, examines how video on demand is changing the flow of content and moving Nollywood films into new spaces, beyond Nigeria, and in the process creating new audiences, raising queries around piracy, tracking revenue, and measuring viewership. While the new technology has created new opportunities by increasing the films' circulation, it has also raised novel challenges that need to be addressed for the industry to grow.

While many former studies have examined the infrastructural benefits of technology to the Nigerian film industry, it is with reference to the peculiarity of mobile screen productions and the dexterity of social media audience engagement that I use the term *mobile screen* here. Yoruba people name forms of mass media according to their function in relation to the audience, and it is with explanations of media infrastructure-user engagement interaction in mind that I attempt a theorization of what this new screen is. Yorubas call the radio *èro asòròmágbèsì*, meaning "the one/thing who talks but does not wait for a response," drawing from the early days of radio when audiences did not engage with the shows but only listened. However, the nature of the radio in its early days was as a device that disseminated largely colonial information in a language that many people did not understand and could not engage with (J. A. Adejunmobi 1974). The television is called *èro amóhùnmáwòrán* in Yoruba, which means "the one/thing who brings voices and pictures," whereas the cinema is an adaptation of the English word, as *sinimá*. In a way, this also speaks to the nature of Yoruba society, in which everyone has a right of reply encapsulated in the proverb "A-gbéjó-ęnikan-dájó, òṣikà èèyàn," which means "He who decides a case after hearing only one side [is] the dean of wicked persons." Today, the radio and broadcast space in Nigeria draws on different forms of technology—including online streaming, call-in programs, as well as social media, yet the terms remain even though the nature of audience engagement now allows for response (Apata and Azeez 2019). For the Yorubas, the terms for these different mediums draw on what they *do*, on inherent features that they have as well as how they are perceived by the audience. Hence, my use of the term *mobile screen*s encompasses the idea of screen as infrastructure and virtual environment in our contemporary world, but it specifically emphasizes the role of audiences in this mobility. In this sense, I am interested in how films and television shows "move" their audiences and how they respond through social media. How does this engagement take spectators beyond being a "viewing audience" to being a "doing audience"?

This chapter builds on previous scholarship by examining MTV *Shuga Naija*, a television series targeted at youth audiences that embraces social media and audience engagement. I explore the tools MTV *Shuga Naija* uses to build online communities and the impact of these tools for sexual education messaging. I also examine how young people express their agency through MTV *Shuga Naija*'s social media pages and how these new engagements contribute to the idea of the mobile screen. Consequently, I draw attention to the evolution of mobile screens—and how they engage young audiences—in the age of the internet. I suggest that in different ways MTV *Shuga Naija* not only entertains and educates its audience but also engages audience members by making them part of the production process. I am also interested in how the changing media landscape is one in which screen media leaves homes and moves beyond the television into computer and telephone screens. This thus raises the following questions: What are the implications of this change for film production, consumption, and distribution? What happens when the "home video" is now in the palm of your hands and can be accessed anywhere—at home or in public? Does the virtual environment—the structure of the interface where the video is being watched, either on a social media page or on YouTube—have any effect on audience engagement?

"Screening" Sex Education in Nigeria: From I Need to Know *to* MTV Shuga Naija

These children have questions, if we don't address them, they will definitely learn from the wrong source.—CORPER YASMIN, MTV *Shuga Naija*, season 4, episode 4

When I was a child growing up in Nigeria in the 1990s, my parents did not tell me much about sexual reproductive health and rights (SRHR). When I became a teenager, much of what my mother told me was a warning—"If you let a man touch you, you will get pregnant." Many Nigerian parents of children who grew up in the 1990s used three tools when it came to SRHR: religion, silence, and fear. They believed that ignorance of sex would stop their children from being sexually active; however, several studies (Adepoju 2005; Ohia 2016) have shown that young people's ignorance made them susceptible to the wrong information and sexual abuse. Classroom education also did not achieve much, as sex education was reduced to science classes on "reproduction"; even today, the kind of sex education provided to students remains a source of debate in many Nigerian schools (Akwei 2017).

It was while living in this environment that shrouded sex in darkness that as a thirteen-year-old I stumbled on *I Need to Know*, a weekly television series on SRHR screened on the Nigerian Television Authority (NTA) network and several private television stations. Every evening, my siblings and I would sit glued to our television screen as we followed the stories of seven teenagers at different life junctures. Sponsored by the United Nations Population Fund (UNFPA), each episode was focused on an adolescent reproductive health issue—abortion, menstrual health, sexual intercourse, rape, and more. More than that, as our parents watched the series with us, it also provided them with avenues to speak about issues that they previously had been silent about. *"I need to know, if education is the key, then why do you deny it?"* goes the chorus for the series' soundtrack; in episode after episode, the series either educates on a sexual health issue or debunks an incorrect belief. However, is information *dissemination* strong enough to influence behavioral change? A survey conducted by UNFPA in 2000 showed that the television series was an effective tool for parents to broach conversations on reproductive health and sexuality with adolescents. However, the media landscape at the time was one that existed largely within the home, the domestic space—a radio, a newspaper/magazine, or television. Many times, access to these spaces was controlled. In the 1990s, the private broadcasting business in Nigeria was in its early days; hence, there were few television stations showing content, and the content that was available was quite heavily regulated, as a result of strict broadcasting codes. Yet, the content of sexual health educational series such as *I Need to Know* was likely effective for that time, as seen through the proliferation of similar television and radio drama series across the country. These included *Wetin Dey* on television; *Flava*, a radio production in pidgin English; and *Ya Take Ne*, a radio production in Hausa, all by BBC Media Action. About twenty million Nigerians had seen or heard of these shows, a 2009 BBC World Service Trust (2009) report states. Beyond distribution and with action-driven impact, a 2011 post-broadcast evaluation report indicated that the target audience acquired lessons from the shows.

While *I Need to Know* thus worked as a tool for SRHR education for a generation that had limited access to information, its effectiveness in today's world—one in which young people are inundated with all kinds of information across technology devices—is questionable. In addition to the increase in media stations and channels across the country, the growing use of social media has also led to more access to different forms of content, including age-inappropriate or inaccurate content. With the German online platform Statista showing increasing internet use in Nigeria, reaching over 185 million people in 2023, contemporary Nigerian society needs screen content that not only speaks about emerging issues but also engages its audience in innovative ways—something that *MTV Shuga* does.[1]

A Brief History of MTV Shuga

In 2009, I was a master's student at the University of Lagos, Nigeria; my laptop was my portal to different screen worlds either through films collected on flash drives or from the internet. In addition to my laptop, my internet-connected phone also kept me up-to-date with different things happening in the world. It was on one of those evenings, while crawling through the streets of the World Wide Web, that I stumbled onto MTV *Shuga* online. It was the first episode of the series, set in Kenya. Every week, once the episode was released on the internet, I watched it because it raised issues about sexuality—which are usually communicated in hushed tones, behind closed doors—that normally would not be seen on screens in many African homes. Eleven years later, the television drama series is in its eighth season and has moved from Kenya (two seasons) to Nigeria (four seasons) and South Africa (two seasons). Commissioned by MTV Network Africa in association with MTV Staying Alive Foundation, the series emphasizes responsible sexual behavior and has aired across more than seventy television channels across the world.

Despite the role social media has played in terms of the success of the series, many reports have not focused on this element of the show. Sarah Piot, Jack Okell, and Bar Hariely (2017) historicize the evolution of MTV *Shuga* production in Africa even as they show the progression of the television series from one part of the continent to the other. The movement of the production to different African countries speaks to the consideration of the uniqueness of youth experiences in the focus countries. For instance, in its South African edition, the show paid attention to lesbian, gay, bisexual, transsexual, and queer (LGBTQ) issues, showing that the producers understood South Africa as a country where same-sex relationships have been legalized. The project takes a 360-degree approach as it is disseminated through the following communication platforms: television series, website (www.mtvshuga.com), social media platforms, radio drama, MTV *Shuga* graphic novel, MTV *Shuga* music video, MTV *Shuga* tour, as well as the MTV *Shuga* peer education campaign. While in this chapter I focus on the television series in connection with its website and social media pages, it is important to note that the show exists in connection with several other products and activities, both online and offline. The 2017 report by Piot, Okell, and Hariely also provides further insight into how each season of MTV *Shuga* is conceived, packaged, and distributed. First, the MTV *Shuga* team review reports on focus countries in addition to on-the-ground studies; this enables them to discover the issues they want to engage and the best ways to communicate with their audiences. Second, they design a strategy—which includes the communication platforms mentioned earlier—that aligns with their findings. Third, the television series is created and then tested on some select audience members; feedback from this test is taken and used to rework what will become the final project. The fourth, fifth, and sixth steps involve different levels of engagement with the audience—audience sampling and university, celebrity, launch, and peer group events—in ways that influence not only their social media content but also future *MTV Shuga* series.

Previous studies on *MTV Shuga* have focused on the program's impact on its viewing audience, especially from the perspective of sex education. Abhijit Banerjee, Eliana La Ferrara, and Victor Hugo Orozco-Olvera (2019) offer an audience impact assessment of the television series across Africa. The research used the television series to show how much of an impact edutainment can have on its audiences, who can use the knowledge garnered from watching the show to take life actions and make decisions, such as to get tested for HIV/AIDS. The study also found that "*MTV Shuga* led to significant improvements in knowledge about and attitudes towards HIV and to less risky sexual behavior. Treated subjects were twice as likely to get tested for HIV 8 to 9 months after the intervention. We also found reductions in STDs among women" (Banerjee, La Ferrara, and Orozco-Olvera 2019, 32). This report aligns with previous scholarly studies that argue that mass media, especially television, plays a significant role in encouraging positive sexual behavior (Klein 2019; Nwaolikpe 2018; Obono 2011).

However, many of these reports do not pay particular attention to the significance of the television series' online activities, even though a Mann Global Health report (2016), citing an MTV report, foregrounds the significance of social media to the program's success: "*MTV Shuga* is aired by 179 broadcasters worldwide, the majority of which are in sub-Saharan African countries. The show's popularity has grown over time to reach an estimated 720 million viewers to date. Social media plays an important role in the 360-degree mass media campaign, with an estimated 118 million people reached through their online platforms such as mtvshuga.com, facebook, twitter, and instagram" (24).

Also central to the evolution of *MTV Shuga* has been its adaptive use of digital technology. More than being shown solely across linear television screens, the series has taken advantage of YouTube as well as social media to extend its message to a wider audience, at a faster pace. More than that, these changes have implications for the content format as well as audience engagement, which I will highlight in more detail later in this chapter.

In what follows, I will show the forms and means of engagement that occur, solely online, among *MTV Shuga Naija* viewers. First, I will analyze the content formats of one of its seasons and show how it is deliberate about its audience engagement. Second, by analyzing social media engagement on the series' website, Facebook page, and Twitter (now X) handle, I will show how it moves its audience to action. Third, I will examine audience responses on YouTube and social media.

Much has changed since the days of the series *I Need to Know*. In the social media space where several forms of content struggle for the attention of the same audience, MTV *Shuga Naija* builds a community of viewers by adopting several strategies, online and offline. In addition to screening on television screens across Nigeria (MTVBase, NTA), the series is also shown for free on YouTube; at this writing it has over 249,000 subscribers and its videos have been viewed more than twenty-eight million times. Besides the basic components of compelling storytelling, believable plot, and feasible action, MTV *Shuga Naija* takes deliberate steps to engage its young audiences, as the series' director Tope Oshin says in an interview:

> MTV *Shuga* is . . . not just entertainment, it cares about helping you make better decisions concerning sexual partners, your health, teenage pregnancy, preventing HIV/AIDS, planning your family, making the right decisions as young people and as their parents/caregivers/mentors. . . . These are some of the messaging points of MTV *Shuga*. It is way beyond just a drama show; it is a show that leaves your life changed. . . . I often call myself a filmmaker for change and this is because I believe that entertainment should not just be entertainment but should also change. . . . [W]e have loads of issues in the world, many problems . . . and while we are laughing and being entertained, it is good that we should talk about them.[2]

The first engagement tactic is aural, in the lyrics of the soundtrack that opens the series:

> We all got to make choices
> So you decide whatever side that you decide to play
> So do you want to be a player?
> Or wan siddon dey look? [Or you want to sit down and look?]
> Do you wanna be great?
> Or you wan siddon dey cruise? [Or you just want to sit down and cruise?]
> So you decide

With this soundtrack, performed by the Nigerian musicians Larry Gaga and Vector, the audience is invited as a participant into the "choice-making" that happens in several instances in the series, through the use of the second-person *you*.

While watching the series on YouTube, one of the first things I noticed was the use of the hashtag #MTVShugaNaija. Scholars have discussed the significance of hashtags, from their linguistic meanings (Shapp 2014) to their classification and dissemination of ideas (Goyal 2014) and their potential for community building and creating a sense of belonging, especially during key events (Gleason 2018). With the hashtag foregrounded throughout each episode of the series, it can be argued that it is a deliberate strategy not only to draw viewers into the online *MTV Shuga Naija* community but also to encourage them to participate by using the hashtag and disseminating the series beyond the YouTube space (Jenkins, Ford, and Green 2013). I go into more detail on audience engagement later in this chapter, but it is important here to elucidate this with a soundtrack-related example. One Twitter user, Nana, tweeted, "One of my favorite things about #MTVShugaNaija is its theme song. I've been searching for the name of the song for a long time and I finally found it." Through the use of the hashtag, Nana connected with other members of the ShugaFam, who provided an answer to her question about locating the theme song for the series. This is a form of community building in which community members, united by similar interests, provide help to one another.

In addition to the soundtrack and hashtag, each episode also includes a poll. In each poll, there is first an effort to create a sense of community with the audience through the use of "Hey ShugaFam!"—where the term *ShugaFam* refers to the *Shuga* audience—as the quiz for each poll is read out like a call to action. Second, the poll tests the accuracy of the audience's knowledge of sex education, with reference to the issue of focus—family planning, sexually transmitted infections, rape—in response to the story. For example, one poll asked audiences, "Is Mahmud's mum correct to think that Corper Yasmin's use of contraception will harm her chance of having children?" Third, the poll is an attempt to elicit action from the audience and measure their reaction to the act being displayed on-screen. Another poll asked audiences, "Both Simi and Tobi told their sexual partners about their STIs. Would you tell your sexual partner if you found out you had an STI?" In addition to the visual portrayal of polls embedded in the frames, there are also situations where polls are read out by the actors. Consistently, each episode also has an outro call to action that encourages viewers to call a toll-free number (a helpline available only in Nigeria) should they be dealing with any of the issues highlighted in the series. As such, the series encourages viewers to take immediate action after watching each episode, showing the significance of an intersection between online engagement and corresponding offline action.

The internet allows for ease of film production and distribution due to reduced production costs. As Paul Ugor argues: "Trailers of these films are often fired off to YouTube where millions of young men and women from all around the world seek daily information on the latest cultural resources of the twenty-first century" (2009, 398). In addition to enhancing distribution by cutting costs, the internet allows for more flexibility in content distribution. The fourth season of MTV *Shuga Naija* even featured something called the "aftershow"—a detached show hosted by the MTV television host Dadaboy. It includes behind-the-scenes shots, blooper reels, interviews with cast members, and #Shugawatch—a term for when cast members meet and watch the show with *Shuga* fans and experience their reactions while watching the show. Through #Shugawatch, the lines between performance and audience are blurred—actors become spectators as they watch the show, and the audience also become performers. This creates several layers of spectatorship and participation: first is the immediate audience behind the screen watching the in-screen audience who have now become performers; second is the in-screen audience watching the show along with the actors.

There are also short clips of the cast members discussing various issues in the series, thus generating conversations among their YouTube audience on specific topics. This aftershow can be said to be a strategy to engage the viewers beyond the actual stories on the screen. It also features visits to some of the "on-screen" sites where youth can get help when faced with real-life challenges. In the season 4 aftershow, Helena Nelson (who plays Diana) visited Hello Lagos, one of the care centers mentioned in the season, to provide more insight into the work done there. She says: "Pregnant, feeling alone and with apparently nowhere to turn? This is something that happens to many young women in real life. I am going to take you to Hello Lagos—a safe, confidential and accessible place for young women. Am I right? At Hello Lagos, they attend to young people from age ten to twenty-four where they assess mental health and sexual health services." This comment echoes Tope Oshin's words when Nelson says that the strategy was deliberate, that "we see them at those crossroads when they make the most important decisions in life—safe sex, family planning, female empowerment, teenage pregnancy. . . . Let us put them in the shoes of the characters." While at Hello Lagos, Helena meets the founder, who educates the audience further on the services the organization provides. She also meets Priscilla, who was in the same position as the character. In that moment of meeting another person who had gone through what Helena went through in the series, the gap between screen and reality is blurred. In a sense, this provides an avenue for the audience to walk through the center and see for themselves. In addition to providing an avenue to share more details on the show, the aftershow can also be described as a way of bringing in the Shuga-Fam, the audience, to get a better view of what the show is about behind the scenes. By meeting the interviewed members of the audience in their homes, where sexuality issues are discussed, the *Shuga* team further strengthens the bond between the two parties.

Through YouTube, then, the screen is broken as the barricade between audience and cast is eroded. This is seen in the way cast members communicate directly with the audiences, as in the case of Yakub Mohammed, who announces his arrival on the YouTube page as it streams. Members of the cast also engage in debates on different topics addressed in the series. For instance, in one of the videos, Timini and Bukola chat about gender-based violence and toxic masculinity, and this encouraged audience commentary and interaction on the issue. These deliberate strategies—using the soundtrack, polls, call-to-action outros, and aftershows—are ways through which MTV *Shuga Naija* moves beyond the contemporary idea of a television series and creates a new, interactive screen. The series employs an engaging format that not only draws viewers into the screen but also moves them to action by encouraging them to take immediate steps that may provide them with the tools to make the right decisions.

While examining how the internet enhances "spreadability," Henry Jenkins, Sam Ford, and Joshua Green (2013) show how, more than distribution, the internet enhances circulation; in certain circumstances, rather than creating an individual viewer, it creates communities of viewers, and rather than creating a viewing audience, it creates engaged publics. In this changing world, film production teams are continually creating strategies to engage audiences beyond the screen, through "transmedia" approaches that "assume that the gradual dispersal of material can sustain these various types of audience conversations, rewarding and building particularly strong ties with a property's most ardent fans while inspiring others to be even more active in seeking and sharing new information" (Jenkins, Ford, and Green 2013, 143). MTV *Shuga Naija* exists in this transmedia world through its website and its social media pages. The MTV *Shuga Naija* website (https://www.mtvshuga.com/naija/) has different sections including "News," which contains articles based on the show or other information around the cast; "Episodes," which features past episodes of the show; "Characters," which informs readers about the different characters on the show, especially through its "meet the cast" interviews; "Backstage," which gives viewers or readers a better idea of what goes on during recordings; "Questions," which is like an "agony aunt" column in which audience questions are answered; and the "Help" section, which features organizations through which audience members can get assistance when faced with any of the issues raised in the series. In a sense, the website acts as a "static home" for information on sexual health in a fast-moving space.

MTV *Shuga Naija* also makes use of shorter clips and pictures from the show to share its message beyond YouTube and enhance engagement among its audience on platforms such as Facebook and Twitter. For instance, a fifty-eight-second clip from season 4 shared on Facebook on child marriage and education in Northern Nigeria generated over 150 comments and is important because it not only touched on a sore issue in that part of the country but also revealed the significance of the series, as there were comments showing support for child marriage. The video was shared more than 250 times, with viewers adding their own comments. Jenkins, Ford, and Green call this kind of engagement "skilled labour" because the more these audiences share the content, the more potent the content's media properties, as audiences also disseminate the brand's messages: "They are deploying both media texts and brand messages as carriers of cultural meaning and as resources for everyday life. Indeed, companies are often profiting from this audience labor, but it's crucial not to paint this wholly as exploitation, denying the many ways audience members benefit from their willing participation in such arrangements" (2013, 128). Karin Barber calls such a practice "re-consumption" (1997, 359); yet, while it may be "re-consumption" for loyal *Shuga* fans, it may be the first level of consumption for new social media audiences. The internet allows this "re-consumption" to happen as it is shared across social media profiles.

In addition to using short clips to engage people on sex education issues, social media pages are used to organize competitions—for example, the #Eachoneteachonecompetition, whereby social media followers made short video clips on safe sex. The winners of the competition attended the premiere of the series and had an opportunity to meet the *Shuga* team. This competition is important for two reasons. First, it connects online activity with offline action. Second, in a sense, this online activity is connected to offline action because the participants in the competition were able to confirm their "Shuga-famhood" status. As Jenkins, Ford, and Green explain, fans not only spread conversations but also sustain them through curation and circulation in a way that may "help prepare them to take action around the issues being discussed. Since the public can only engage with content if they can find it among the plethora of available options, it's becoming increasingly important to use such texts as calls to action to gather such publics or else to develop material which can sustain or engage existing communities" (2013, 170). Consequently, the

MTV Shuga Naija audience is a producing one as well as a "using" one. This supports my idea that this new kind of screen not only provides entertainment or education but also moves viewers to do more—to engage and to provide content that will engage others. *MTV Shuga Naija* also leverages the social media power of its cast, as they share episodes in which they feature, and respond to, audience questions via their social media platforms, which, in turn, are shared on the *MTV Shuga Naija* pages.

These features of *MTV Shuga Naija*—community building on social media, use of hashtags, deliberate use of online campaigns, and more—made it easy for the series to adapt when the COVID-19 pandemic ravaged the world. Rather than being forced to shut down, like most other film production projects at the time, it was easy for the series to adapt through the creation of a spin-off season called *Alone Together*, which featured seventy daily scripts filmed throughout the lockdown in South Africa, Botswana, Ivory Coast, South Africa, Nigeria, Kenya, and the United States. A new episode was released daily, from the premiere on April 20, 2020, until the last episode on August 14, 2020. The short videos, usually lasting less than ten minutes, featured characters from the show who were dealing with different issues raised by the pandemic—for example, the pervasiveness of fake news as many struggled to understand the new virus, and the effects of lockdown on people.

Georgia Arnold, the executive director of the MTV Staying Alive Foundation, provides further insight into how the show adapted during the COVID-19 pandemic:

> The idea is that it is fully scripted but the actors are self-filming because they are in lockdowns. Our director is down the line on Zoom to make sure that we can direct the shots directly within their homes, so we can figure out where we should be filming with them, talk to them about clothes and hair and makeup but of course they have to do it themselves. A normal *MTV Shuga* series will take ten months from green light to getting the first episode on air. The first episode of *Alone Together* went on air three weeks after we agreed to do it.[3]

Technology was the glue that held the *MTV Shuga* team together across nations, even as they filmed. The *MTV Shuga* actors turned the cameras on themselves from their homes as they became more than actors—they were also mobile filmmakers, many of them recording with their (mobile) phones and handling the makeup, lighting, and filming. The actors also shared their private spaces with their audiences, as their homes became filming locations. In each episode, there were also instances whereby most of the characters communicated with one another via text messages, live videos, and memes. And, through the series streaming on YouTube, audiences were able to access it and connect with one another even during lockdown. While the world was literally grounded and domesticated, the series continued to move by engaging its audiences through these YouTube videos and through the use of hashtags such as #MTVShugaAloneTogether and #AloneTogether. Speaking about the significance of the series during the pandemic, Arnold states:

> COVID-19 is not just about hand washing and social distancing and lockdown, it is also about understanding the difference between isolation and quarantine, it is also understanding that for teenagers even though they may be asymptomatic, they can still spread it. It is talking about the mental health issues, the threat of domestic violence and addressing all the myths around it. We think we have found a format here that is really interesting, that is flexible and relevant and is not expensive compared with what we would normally produce. We are also looking if we can take this to any other continent as it is needed around the globe.[4]

Beyond the traditional media programming on how people could stay safe during the pandemic, the series addressed issues around relationships during lockdowns, maintaining positive mental health, sexual protection, making a living during lockdown, and more. Arnold emphasizes the importance of an engaged audience to the production and how it is accomplished: "We are doing lots of work on social media. We have a TikTok promotion going out tomorrow. They are taking a clip of the show and asking the audience to mimic what she is doing, then send it back and we are giving the first ten data [GB] of 5,000 naira. Being engaged with our audience gets them involved." While the series is streamed immediately, the urgency of the issues as they evolve in reality is also embedded in the narrative of each episode. As such, there is a cyclical relationship between the real world (from which screenwriters draw) and the screen world created by *MTV Shuga*. This relationship is pivotal to the content of the series.

We Need New Screens

In this chapter, I have explored what the internet has enabled through the example of *MTV Shuga Naija*. I propose the idea of the mobile screen as a screen that exploits the dynamic nature of the internet by describing its existence with three frames. In the first frame are the mobile screen's innate characteristics—ones that combine the features of earlier mass media forms but that also do more. This screen moves the audience to do something through embedded techniques that are part of the film production.

I also propose a second frame, which shows that filmmakers / content producers understand that much more than providing entertainment, they operate in a space—the internet space—where different kinds of content compete for the attention of the audience so there is a need for more strategies embedded within their film content to engage the audience beyond the diegesis of the story. For *MTV Shuga Naija*, this involves the use of polls and engaging social media content. The mobile screen filmmakers are continually challenged to be inventive in their creation of content that not only speaks to the audience but also connects with the audience in a world saturated with content. More than that, the connection with the audience transcends entertainment. As Barber notes, we have to study how "a text or performance addresses a public, and how people out there take up that address, selectively and for their own purposes . . . in their local and historical specificity" (1997, 353).

Finally, this is a screen that not only moves around but also moves people to do something—by commenting on YouTube, sharing on social media platforms, or responding to an issue that is raised. In this way, the audience members become content producers, users, and spreaders. The mobile screen audience is an equally dynamic one that moves between simultaneous screens—from the YouTube page to social media—sharing opinions about content it has watched and engaging with the cast of a film. It is in this confluence of roles that the meaning of the text extends far beyond its diegesis, and it is through this extension—which is seen through social media shares, commentary, and creations—that screen worlds bearing social meaning are generated.

NOTES

Please see www.screenworlds.org for images and further audiovisual materials that complement this chapter and other parts of this book.

1   "Number of Internet Users in Nigeria from 2018 to 2022, with Forecasts from 2023 to 2027," Statista, June 2022, https://www.statista.com/statistics/183849/internet -users-nigeria/.

2   Tope Oshin, "This Season Will Be the Biggest One Yet!," YouTube video, accessed January 15, 2020, https://youtu.be/C6kdB_PwprY?si=1069373MQSuPzRJj.

3   Arnold offers insights into the origins of the idea. See "Every Woman Every Child COVID-19 Expert Series: MTV Shuga Alone Together with Georgia Arnold," April 29, 2020, https://youtu.be/845gAHxw9Fo?t=757.

4   See "Every Woman Every Child COVID-19 Expert Series: MTV Shuga Alone Together with Georgia Arnold."

2

Maîtresse d'un homme marié

Retracing Womanhood in Senegalese Screen Worlds

ESTRELLA SENDRA

This chapter builds on the previous one by exploring how mobile screen worlds have created new forms of sociality and community in Senegal and beyond. From the late twentieth to the early twenty-first century, African audiovisual production and distribution have experienced remarkable changes (Sawadogo 2019); one of the most exciting of these changes is what Moradewun Adejunmobi (2015) has referred to as "African film's televisual turn," highlighting the growing number of African filmmakers who are turning their talents to television. This chapter specifically seeks to explore the ways in which *internet* television is transforming the screen media industry in Senegal, through a focus on the first two seasons of the women-led internet television series *Maîtresse d'un homme marié* (*Mistress of a Married Man*; launched in 2019, its last episode of the second season ended in July 2020), hereafter referred to as *MDHM*. Directed by Kalista Sy, *MDHM* is an intersectional and complex site of negotiation of feminism in contemporary Senegal. Its plot revolves around several strong women who together represent the various forms of everyday struggles embodied by women in Senegal, Africa, and the whole world. The success of this series, however, cannot be discussed without an attendant focus on how it was made widely accessible by Marodi TV, the first African online video platform to offer television channels the possibility of replaying their video content (*Jeune Afrique* 2013) and one of the largest video-on-demand (VOD) platforms in Senegal (Kifouani 2022). Importantly, this content is freely accessible to everyone in the world, online via YouTube and via a mobile application, which contrasts with the restrictions of many VOD platforms, which require registration via email or fees. Furthermore, Marodi TV centers its audience by allowing users "to comment on the content at any time: before, during and after their dissemination" (Marodi TV founding director Serigne Massamba Ndour quoted in *AfriqueITNews* 2013)—thereby creating fan communities, which also contribute significantly to the success of the series.

This case study foregrounds gender in the conceptualization of (Senegalese) screen worlds, questioning the extent to which the internet has enabled the production and circulation of screen media made by women. It also contributes to decolonizing existing scholarship on media fandom, which tends to define fans as "largely female, largely white, largely middle class" (Jenkins 2012, 1). *MDHM*'s multimodal distribution, where television and the internet meet, favors the formation of "social audiences," who differ from "spectators" in that the latter refers to "individuals who engage with a TV show but who may or may not do so with any sense of belonging to a larger collective of viewers" (S. M. Ross 2008, 7). In contrast, social audiences are those who imagine themselves as part of a collective, a fandom community, making the series "mean and mean again" (Dick Hebdige, cited in De Kosnik 2013, 105) through forms of active engagement such as remixing videos, commenting on social media pages, and blogging. On the one hand, *MDHM* invites commentary via social media, fostering a fandom community concerned with gender issues and locating Senegal at the epicenter of the discussion. On the other hand, through its strategic use of product placement, it allows for "window-shopping" among a wide range of local products that are coherent with the lifestyles of the characters featured in the series—thereby celebrating, and commodifying, all things "Made in Senegal."

Becoming a Fan of MDHM

The global outbreak of COVID-19 in 2020 greatly impacted the film and cultural sector (Banks and O'Connor 2021). During lockdown audiences had to move online, leading to increasing demand for screen media content (Rader-mecker 2021). On April 21, 2020, I read an article titled "The Series That Breaks Stereotypes about Senegalese Women," about MDHM (Justo 2020). Having conducted research in Senegal since 2011, I was fascinated to hear about the series and went directly to Marodi TV on YouTube to watch the first episode. A couple of weeks later, I was already on episode 39. I had become one of MDHM's fans and binge-watchers, and also a follower of various Senegalese shops featured in the series, which I visited virtually, via Google Maps, identifying their location to see how to get there from Liberté 6, where I tend to be based when I am in Dakar. Similarly, I found myself participating in MDHM's social media pages, commenting on the series and watching videos remixed by fans. I then sent a private Facebook message to the director, Kalista Sy, introducing myself and saying that I would love to write about this series that had accompanied my lockdown and moved me to Senegal at a time when traveling physically was not possible. She responded generously, and in June and September 2020, I conducted semistructured interviews with her, which have contributed greatly to this chapter's reflections on a woman-led screen world from a media industries perspective. Kalista Sy's voice further contributes to the production of knowledge on African feminisms from "the intersections of our everyday realities and solidarities" (Dieng 2021, 22). Such a perspective also required considering fans' voices, since "now more than ever, fannish love is an essential part of industrial production" (Lothian 2015, 138). It also required reckoning with how technological innovation and transnationalization are impacting on screen media (Sawadogo 2019, 4–5). I suggest that MDHM is an excellent example of the mobile nature of contemporary (African) screen worlds, since audiences—both in Senegal and beyond—tend to watch the series on their mobile phones.

Situating MDHM *in Screen Worlds*

The origins of MDHM are deeply entrenched within the role of social media as "a key site of consumer culture" and of "contemporary meaning-making" (Sobande 2020, 10). The idea started as a social media chronicle but was adapted to a television screenplay in 2016–17. People were hesitant to invest in the project, however, due to Sy being a self-taught writer. After some time, the screenplay reached the hands of Serigne Massamba Ndour, the founding director of

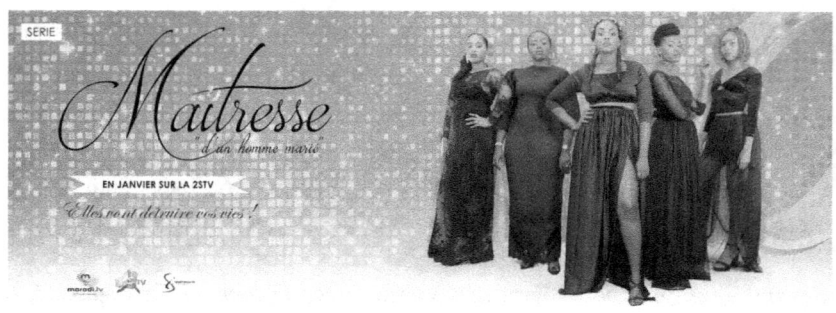

FIGURE 2.1. Promotional poster for the series *Maîtresse d'un homme marié*.

Marodi TV, who "was charmed by the project" (Kalista Sy interview, June 15, 2020). Five minutes were enough for Ndour to realize this was a project that "was going to revolutionize many things" (Sy interview, June 15, 2020), and he thus decided to become its producer.

MDHM was first released on January 25, 2019, as figure 2.1 indicates. The web series approaches womanhood in contemporary Senegal primarily through the experiences of its five leading women—Lalla, Marème, Djalika, Racky, and Dalanda—although there are also several strong secondary roles. The plot revolves around what happens when Marème has an affair with Cheikh, who is married to Lalla, thus becoming a "mistress." However, with its variable focalization, shifting from one character to another within each episode, the series brings diverse, parallel stories into convergence, all revolving around crucial themes such as women's sexuality and sexual freedom, intersectional forms of oppression of women, intimate and professional relationships, and mental health.

A week after *MDHM* was launched, the Comité de Défense des Valeurs Morales au Sénégal (Committee of Defence of Moral Values in Senegal) placed a complaint against the series for what it called its "shocking, indecent and obscene images," which the committee said was likely to harm the "preservation of cultural identities." A couple of months later, this committee would be joined by the religious nongovernmental organization Jamhiya'atu Rasheediyatul-Islamiyat (JAMRA) with its own complaints (*Seneweb News*, March 20, 2019). Following deliberations, the director of the Conseil National de Régulation de l'Audiovisuel (National Council of Regulation of the Audiovisual) confirmed the series could continue to show, as long as certain "corrective measures" were adopted (CNRA, March 30, 2019). According to Sy, "What concerned [them] was the fact of hearing a woman express herself freely about her sexuality" (Sy interview, June 15, 2020). *MDHM* overcame the initial controversy surrounding it, and its degree of popularity, with over four million viewers per episode for both seasons, has been compared by the international press to that of *Sex and the City* (Turkewitz 2019). Sy suggests that the increased audience numbers in the second season have confirmed that the success of the first season was not due to the controversy around the series. In 2019, the BBC listed Sy as among the one hundred most inspiring and influential women from around the world.[1]

Web Television and Mobile Screen Media in Senegal

In Senegal, the beginning of the twentieth century saw the emergence of various web television channels, with Sénégal TV and Carrapide TV among the first ones (*Au Sénégal* 2018). Today, these channels include Okayafrica, Leuz TV, Pikine TV, Lelewal TV, Warkha TV, Marodi TV, and, since 2021, Kalista TV, launched by Kalista Sy herself. It was on Kalista TV that the Senegalese director and producer released her second online television series, *Yaay 2.0*, on the theme of motherhood, and which in 2023 was screened at the Pan-African Film and Television Festival of Ouagadougou (FESPACO), where Sy was one of the four women honored during Celebrities Day on February 27. Marodi TV was the home of Sy's first series—*MDHM*, the subject of this chapter—and plays a key role in the streaming of Senegalese screen media, and especially series. However, as Lindiwe Dovey (2018) notes, the appearance of online television does not imply the end of legacy television but rather the convergence of old and new models; this is precisely how Marodi TV was created.

Marodi TV is a Senegalese start-up founded in 2012 by then thirty-year-old Serigne Massamba Ndour. As of this writing, it has forty-eight employees and twenty-three million views per month (Kifouani 2022, 85). It is a screen media production company that partners with a private TV channel in order to replay programs online once they have aired on broadcast TV. It aims to produce and provide access to multimedia content through different platforms, including web browsers, smartphones, tablets, and television screens, and is currently available as a downloadable mobile application for international users. The platform has built a large body of loyal consumers, mainly through the production and online exhibition of series that trigger public discussions of diverse opinions about social topics, "such as love rivalry, intimacy in couples, alcohol, drugs, rape, polygamy and sexuality" (Kifouani 2022, 83).

Born and raised in Senegal, Ndour received a scholarship to pursue his higher education in telecommunications and computer engineering at Télécom Paris Tech, where he graduated in 2008. While his initial plan of returning to Senegal changed, Ndour has nonetheless returned in a different way, through Marodi TV, whose legal structure is based in Paris but which also has offices in Dakar and Cameroon. The idea resulted from a holiday experience in 2011. "I felt that Senegalese people needed to watch their favorite television products in replay: those from the diaspora, due to the time change, and those residing in Senegal because they consume TV on demand," Ndour notes (*AfriqueITNews* 2013). Marodi TV's accessibility and specific focus on replay facilitate the creation of social audiences and fandom communities, since "rereading is central to the fan's aesthetic pleasure. Much of fan culture facilitates repeated encounters with favored texts" (Jenkins 2012, 69).

In 2013, Marodi TV won the VentureOut Challenge Award for the African continent, an award managed by the World Bank and the American nonprofit Civilian Research and Development Foundation. The prize consisted of US$10,000 and a six-month mentorship program to place the enterprise internationally. As figure 2.2 shows, Marodi TV prides itself on having beaten all audience records on YouTube, with a significant increase in numbers over the years (Dione 2019). The company is run by young people in their early twenties; as Sy notes, "Marodi TV is letting young people be responsible for the remarkable production of work, which, other than in Senegal, is appreciated all over the world" (cited in Sane 2019). During the first two seasons of the series, Sy highlighted the opportunity to collaborate with Marodi TV on the project, suggesting that she and Ndour had created "a union that allows the project to be accomplished in its full sense" (Sy interview, June 15, 2020).

While *MDHM* is also shown on broadcast television just before being released online, the audience numbers for the episodes on YouTube evidence the extent to which the series is followed online, through mobile phones—what Dovey (2018) has called the "supersmall screen." Senegal is a country where the number of mobile phone connections (18 million) is higher than the population (16.52 million). The number of internet users on any device is 7.6 million, which constitutes 46 percent of the total population, and of active social media users is 3.4 million, which constitutes 21 percent of the total population. The average speed in mobile internet connections is 23.22 Mbps. Following Google, YouTube is the second most visited website (*DataReportal* 2020). This context of increasing access to the internet has transformed access to film production, distribution, and reception in Senegal and across the world (Sawadogo 2019); it has favored adapting audiovisual content for smaller screens, where moving

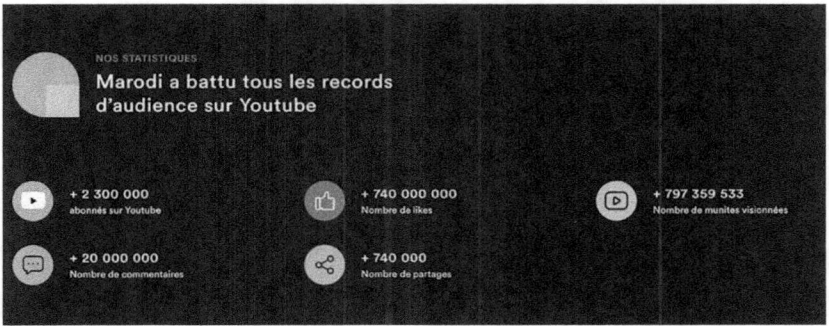

FIGURE 2.2. Audience numbers (2022) for Marodi from Marodi TV. Screenshot

image becomes streamed image, and where the realities on-screen are not arriving only from far away in the world but also from nearby. This is why, when speaking about the popularity of MDHM, it is essential to speak about its mode of production and reception as a form of *mobile* screen media. This term resonates with Alessandro Jedlowski's (2012) understanding of Nollywood as "small screen media," yet where the emphasis is on mobility, in line with Nicholas Rombes's (2017) point that "film itself is moving, because its screens are mobile" (84). But there is a further issue here, beyond the shift to smaller, more mobile screens. As Olivier Barlet argues, there has been a shift from cinephilia to seriephilia (2016, 349, cited in Sawadogo 2019, 5)—and the "televisual turn" Adejunmobi points to in Africa is also a global phenomenon. This turn to serial and episodic screen narrative forms is particularly relevant in a continent where a large number of cinemas have been abandoned or closed but where television is quite widespread (Adejunmobi 2015, 121). Adejunmobi thus calls for "frameworks for understanding how to position these popular audiovisual narratives in relation to television, on the one hand, and cinema, on the other" (120).

This volume's conceptualization of "screen worlds" allows us to keep both forms—film and television—under consideration. It also allows me to theorize "Senegalese screen worlds" as an inclusive concept not only in relation to audiovisual forms but also in terms of industrial formations, where a series such as MDHM can be said to be "locally configured as well as globally networked" (Ramon Lobato cited in Dovey 2018, 97). As I noted earlier, Ndour is Senegalese but based between Paris and Dakar. Sy is based between Rennes and Dakar. This mobility of the people behind the scenes of MDHM is reflected also in the characters' stories on-screen, where Marème and Mansoura have studied abroad, in France, before returning to Senegal. In this way, transnationalism becomes a feature of the industrial and diegetic screen worlds of MDHM while the series also respects that in West Africa "the audience not only connects more intimately with the films' images, but most importantly derives and constructs meanings from culturally proximate content" (Sawadogo 2019, 4–5).

MDHM: A Women-Led, Womanist Screen World

Since the late 1970s, African television screens have been home to imported, melodramatic telenovelas, particularly from Latin America, and these have been very popular (Jedlowski and Rêgo 2018; Moukouti Onguédou 2014). By 2006, twelve Latin American telenovelas had been broadcast in Senegal (Werner 2006, 443–44). Since the 2010s, however, television channels have increasingly favored local productions, such as *Pod et Marichou, Un Café Avec, Dinama Nekh, Mbettel, Idoles*, and *Wiri Wiri* (Dione 2019; Gueye 2019). These became very popular, since they were considered to be mirrors of everyday Senegalese lives, revolving around love and marriage (Diallo 2016). Very often, however, these experiences were portrayed through a hegemonic male gaze (Gueye 2019).

In contrast, MDHM is the first Senegalese women-led television series in which women are placed at the very center of the narrative. As Delphe Kifouani (2022, 80) notes, the fact that it is both written and coproduced by a woman is worth emphasizing. MDHM started from the perception that "women did not really have their place" in Senegalese screen media—let alone in society (Kalista Sy interview, September 10, 2020). As Sy told me:

> The exact definition of Senegalese woman is a woman who does not exist. Because when it is said that it is a woman who does not say much, who does not look much, who does not walk making much noise, who should be a virgin until marriage, these are the attributes of a nonexistent person . . . because a person who lives, must talk, necessarily. She expresses herself; she looks around to discover the world. She goes wherever she wants to, and she is not subjected to opposing people. She has quite a strong relationship with her intimacy, which is her sexuality, and she has the right to decide how she sees her sexual life, regardless of her religious beliefs. . . . What has disturbed some people, I think, is to listen to a person say that, that we [women] are free to decide about our sexuality. (Sy interview, September 10, 2020)

MDHM retraces womanhood from a Senegalese perspective; I use the term *retracing* because women have always played a crucial role in Senegalese society although, as has happened to women globally, they have often been written out of history. Sy thus says: "I needed to tell my story about women, the story of all women, and I think, first and foremost, of Senegalese women," and she feels that "every woman who watches this series" will see "an intimate part of herself" (Sy interview, September 10, 2020)

MDHM can be understood not just as a women-led screen world, then, but also as a womanist Senegalese screen world. The term *womanism*, which was coined by Alice Walker and Chikwenye Ogunyemi in 1982, contests the white bias in much feminist discourse (Kolawole 2004, 261–62). Understood from an intersectional perspective, it is an inclusive term celebrating Black roots and womanhood, with considerations of class, race, and sexuality and experiences of family, motherhood, and work (Kolawole 2004, 260–61). These various facets come together in *MDHM*. In previous publications, I have written about how the emphasis on women's sexuality serves as a way of asserting freedom and challenging hegemonic power (Sendra 2018b, 2020). I draw on scholarship that sees bodily performance operating as a form of struggle, as a subversive act against Western hegemonic constructions of Black African women's bodies (Bâ and Taylor-Jones 2012). In *MDHM* we see such bodily performance and reclamation of women's ownership over their sexuality, but what is impressive is that the women characters' "lives do not center exclusively on their relationships with men" (Diallo 2016). This focus on sexuality is perceived as a key component of decolonial feminism. As Rama Dieng puts it, "This feminism must promote an open and positive discussion on sexual practices and experiences in all shapes and far from the seal of the taboo" (2021, 212–13).

Unlike *Wiri Wiri*, where audiences had noticed that "no character was seen at work" (Diallo 2016), in *MDHM*, women are hardworking entrepreneurs and decision-makers at various enterprises, working on projects for the transformation of Senegal. Thus, the fact that *MDHM* was created by female screen media professionals is mirrored also in the representations of working women in the series. This is particularly evident in episode 22 of the second season, in which a female photographer attends a baby's baptism. Sy says her aim was to show women that "they are the ones who set their own limits, but . . . our own limit is ourselves and fearing or distrusting our abilities." She adds, "This woman appears as a photographer, well dressed, and charms everyone. I am sure that there is a woman somewhere who will now dare enjoy the fact that she likes photography and do her best to work as a photographer" (Sy interview, September 10, 2020). This bold move in the Senegalese context was very well received by audiences, whose attention on social media was firmly on

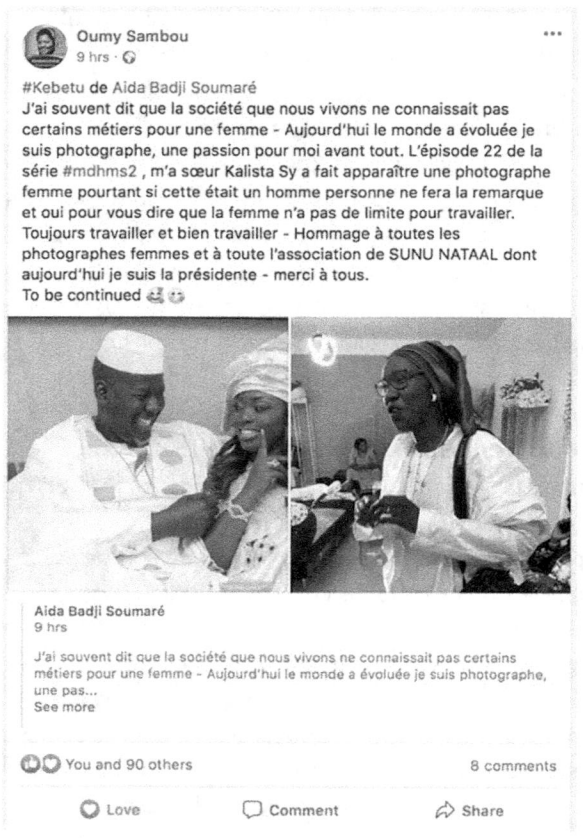

FIGURE 2.3. Facebook post celebrating the physical appearance of a female photographer. Screenshot

the photographer, smartly dressed in *tenue traditionelle* (traditional clothing). Oumy Régina Sambou, a young cultural journalist based in Dakar who plays the role of the lawyer, Régina, in the second season of MDHM, published a Facebook post about this, celebrating the visibility given to women photographers in the series (see figure 2.3). Furthermore, as Ndiaye Ciré Ba, who played the role of Djalika in the series, mentioned in a television interview, the series shows that "women are as good at an office as they are at home" (TV5 MONDE 2019). In this way, the series has allowed women in Senegal and beyond to think of their future horizons and fight to achieve their own goals.

However, MDHM also shows the continuous struggle women go through on an everyday basis and the psychological impact this has on their lives. In the series, women are "the embodiment of many other everyday heroines" (Kifouani 2022, 85). Within this context, MDHM has innovatively introduced the character of a psychologist, showing women daring to seek professional psychological help. As Sy says: "Today, the world is evolving at an incredible speed. In order to live in this world, it is important to keep one's values, but also to accept suffering and, in certain aspects, to modernize oneself. . . . What is wrong about accepting that our lives may not be perfect, and that even our sisters and brothers are going through difficult times?" (Sy interview, September 10, 2020). The psychologist is first introduced through voice-over, as a narrator sharing reflections on mental health issues, and eventually becomes known as Mamy's therapist. However, his clinic becomes a meeting point for several women in the series as they all try to deal with their own psychological issues. The series successfully demonstrates that it is precisely by acknowledging mental health issues and seeking professional help for them that these women become even stronger, moving away from representations of women as victims. Vulnerability, acknowledgment of our own imperfections, and self-care are also key in the social transformation sought by African feminisms (Dieng 2021, 213–15). In MDHM, this focus on mental health was, according to Sy, an important choice in an African society where there is the tendency to see a marabout (spiritual guide) when encountering problems. While acknowledging that really good marabouts do exist, she also notes that sometimes they can make a problem worse; there are no marabouts in MDHM, even if there are references to them. "To me, it is important to build something new and show people who may encounter problems which can be addressed and explained . . . and that the psychologist is there to help deal with them" (Sy interview, September 10, 2020).

Through her women characters of Lalla, Marème, Djalika, Racky, Dalanda, and Dior, among others, Sy offers a window onto the lives and experiences of Senegalese women, a reality accessible online to the whole world, but where Senegal is the continuous cultural reference and target.[2] Kalista Sy continuously stresses the Senegalese roots of her narrative: "I'm doing something very Senegalese. It's for Senegalese people first, then for the world" (quoted in Turkewitz 2019). The series is also a celebration of Black women's natural beauty, which contrasts significantly with the mainstream representation of beauty on television. According to Sy, "We are not going to follow the norm of Senegalese shows that primarily feature women who have lightened their skin. We want to show women in a way that audiences have not gotten used to seeing them on screen—focusing on natural beauty in all shapes, shades and sizes" (quoted in Kimeria 2019).

The notion of screen worlds also allows us to explore how diverse the influences on contemporary African audiovisual work are. Indeed, Sy says that MDHM is the result of a mix of influences, thanks to the possibility of being able to watch "everything" nowadays and to being open to the world: "We are very open and that shows in our country, but always remaining ourselves, considering our values. . . . I cannot make films like American people. I am not American. I like their cinema, but what they show is not my reality. . . . I can show a Senegalese modern woman, who is influenced by everything but who remains Senegalese, who goes back home at lunch time and eats her *cebbu jënn* [rice and fish, one of the main national meals], not hamburger or paella" (Sy interview, June 15, 2020). This openness to the world, while being rooted in Senegal, can be theorized via Kwame Anthony Appiah's (2006) concept of "rooted cosmopolitanism"—a concept I have applied to Senegalese cultural work in other research (Sendra 2018a; 2021). This concept becomes particularly important in understanding the identities not just of Sy and Ndour as the director and producer of MDHM but also of MDHM's audiences and fans.

MDHM's *Online Audiences and Social Media Fan Communities*

As noted earlier, MDHM's popularity has been significantly shaped by a context of technological innovation and transnationalization, which has also greatly contributed to the "boom in fan activity" (De Kosnik 2013, 98). As Francesca Sobande puts it, "Just as the development of television 'altered our world' . . . so too did the rise of the internet and WI-FI connections from the 1990s onwards . . . paired with the popularity of mobile devices which enabled some people to create and communicate online and while on the move" (2020, 2). The internet has also led to a "greater accessibility to one another" and, as a result, to "an expression of love and solidarity" among geographically dispersed communities (Dieng 2021, 139). The online distribution of MDHM via Marodi TV, through either the mobile application, the website, or the YouTube channel, plays a key role in the popularity of the series. Online serial narratives allow for binge-watching, and Marodi TV specifically encourages audience commentary through blogging, posting, and vidding. The international media coverage of the series resulted from such fan commentary as the YouTube reviews of the series by Khady, who created the blog *Senegalese Twisted*, where she introduces herself as "a multilingual Senegalese twisted girl that lives in the Netherlands but is (obviously) originally from Senegal, West Africa."

The *Senegalese Twisted* blog, featured in figure 2.4, and YouTube are two of the various forms of "emotional and intellectual involvement" that allow us to speak about a fandom phenomenon rather than simply watch television. For, as Henry Jenkins notes, "Watching television as a fan involves different levels of attentiveness and evokes different viewing competencies than more casual viewing of the same material" (2012, 56). When the last episode of the second season was aired on TV, fans recorded their television screens and shared these videos via social media, as fan communities who could only watch via the mobile application were impatiently waiting for it. The anticipation was palpable on the Facebook page "Si tu aimes les series sénégalaises" (If you like Senegalese series), which has more than 232,000 followers. As fans wait for the beginning of the third season, various YouTube remixed videos have appeared. As shown in figure 2.5, when some key cast members went to Abidjan on August 29, 2020, the pandemic did not prevent hundreds of fans from enthusiastically welcoming the protagonists of the series that would be screened in Ivory Coast through the channel A+ Afrique, dubbed into French.

The word *fan* has its origins in the Latin *fanaticus*, which has connotations of "orgiastic rites and enthusiastic frenzy" (De Kosnik 2013, 98). As Jenkins says: "The fan still constitutes a scandalous category in contemporary culture, one alternately the target of ridicule and anxiety, of dread and desire" (cited in De Kosnik 2013, 98). Sometimes fan activity is considered worthless, "insignificant and a waste of time," because it is the work of amateurs (98). However, if we turn to the origins of the term *amateur*, deriving from *amar*, which means "to love," fandom productions can be understood as a "labour of love" (Lothian 2015, 138; Sobande 2020, 9). As Abigail De Kosnik suggests, fan activity "should be valued as new form of publicity and advertising, authored by volunteers, that corporations badly need in an era of market fragmentation. In other words, fan production is a category of work" (2013, 99). Sobande (2020) sees it is a "form of (un)credited labour or, simply, an entertaining and enjoyable pastime" (9). What these scholars seem to agree on is that fans play a crucial role in the success of media productions, where "fandom is what completes and perfects the object" (De Kosnik 2013, 100).

Social media allows Senegalese women in particular to be at the heart of intersectional discussions on gender representations in *MDHM*. However, YouTube comments also evidence the popularity of the series *beyond* Senegal. In an interview with *Seneplus*, Sy said she had not foreseen such international success: "I just thought we were doing a production for Senegalese people and by Senegalese people. But it is true that both for the rest of the team and myself, it has been surprising to see how the series has been followed beyond Senegal"

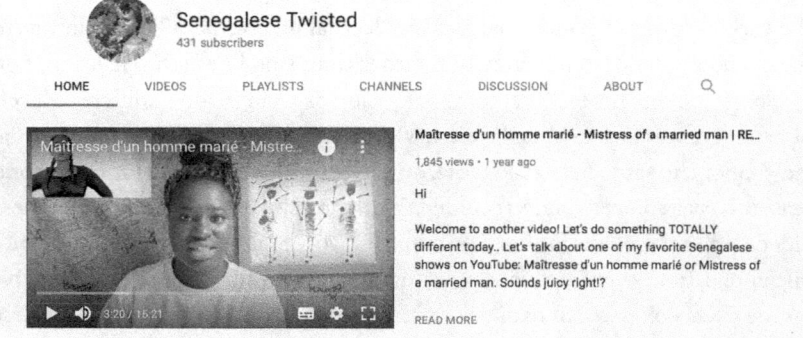

FIGURE 2.4. A video clip and description from the YouTube channel Senegalese Twisted. Screenshot

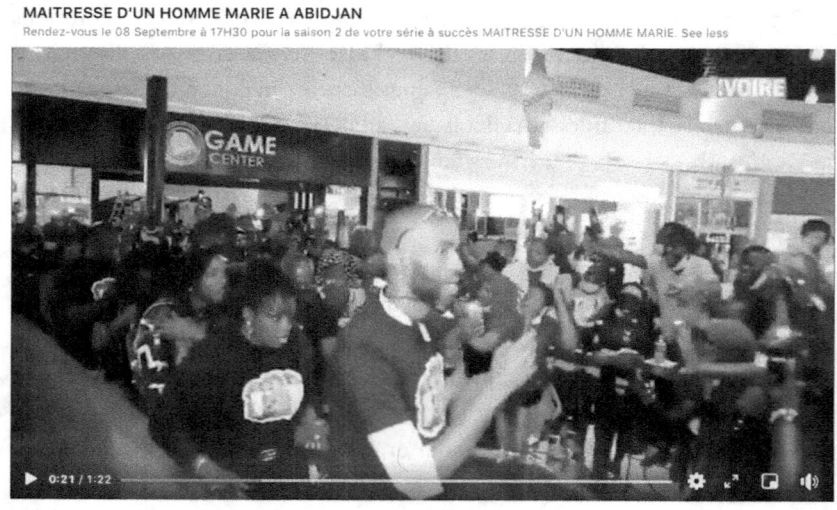

FIGURE 2.5. *Maîtresse d'un homme marié* actors astonished by the excitement of fans welcoming them to Abidjan, Ivory Coast, on August 29, 2020. Video posted to A+ Afrique. Screenshot

(Sane 2019). One YouTube comment by a woman with a Senegalese surname reads: "I have goose bumps, you are wonderful. You have really touched me, wonderful story, hats off. I have caught up with the first 50 episodes in a week, which I had just discovered. The actors . . . waw! They are all great. We have learned a lot. Thank you for this quality, this wonder! May it serve as a lesson, of better behaviours, of a better life." Another YouTube comment reads: "LOL, I love them so much! I am Congolese from DRC and I swear to you that this series has made me fall in love with Senegalese people and Senegal. What a beautiful representation of our continent and we learn many lessons from this series! And Wolof is music to the ears. I have to visit Senegal even!"

Beyond the enthusiastic YouTube comments, numerous references to the series populate the virtual space, with the creation of social audience or fandom communities through hashtags, Facebook pages, and fandom videos. Both Sy and a *New York Times* journalist who wrote about the series described teenagers, for instance, who were copying Djalika's hairstyles and fans who were joining "Racky Team" and "Marème Team" pages on Facebook (Turkewitz 2019). Online television makes it possible for newcomers who may arrive at different times to join such online community spaces to be able to watch multiple episodes and participate in the debates around the series. Sy argues that MDHM works because "today, social media offers speed to the product's life. It is more accessible. It is because of social media that people have been sharing, spreading the word" (Sy interview, June 15, 2020).

Because the series is freely available on the internet, audiences can watch it anywhere—on the bus or train, or in the gym or office. It can be watched alone, intimately, or with a chosen group. Telenovelas broadcast on linear television offer a space among family members "for experimentation with identities, especially among the young" (Werner 2006, 465). However, in online series, the forum happens beyond the domestic space, creating broader communities where women's experiences are discussed. As Sobande observes in her study of the digital lives of Black women in Britain, "People's identities and social relations are continually (re)produced as part of their engagement with on-screen images and media practices at different stages of their lives" (2020, 10). And as the Senegalese journalist Ibrahima Dione notes, "Television series fuel discussions in public places . . . [and] create strong communities of fans on the web" (2019). Just such communities—local and transnational, intimate and public—have developed through and around MDHM, through people's enjoyment of the series and through discussions around topics addressed in the series, such as womanhood, sexuality, sexual and mental health, entrepreneurship, and leadership.

Through its social media presence, Marodi TV has sought active engagement with the series. This is a common practice among TV professionals globally, who seem to be incorporating an awareness of such fandom activities into the shows themselves (S. M. Ross 2008, 4). By participating in social media discussions, audiences are also keen to access behind-the-scenes or insider information, "to learn how it was made and why it looks the way it does" (Jenkins 2012, 65). For instance, in June 2020, as the second season was coming to an end, Marodi TV posted a series of pixelated photos so that social media audiences could participate in a competition that consisted of identifying the character. Viewers responded to this call to tele-participate, a common practice among fandom communities (S. M. Ross 2008, 4).

The popularity of the series is not measured just qualitatively but also quantitatively. As Kalista Sy points out, "The digital technology makes it possible to measure the number of people reached. . . . Instantaneously, it is possible to witness its evolution, and the number of viewers across the world" (Sy interview, June 15, 2020). The data-driven nature of the internet also allows producers to know about viewing modes, for instance, by being able to know who stops watching and at what point in the series. Some VOD platforms, such as iROKOtv in Nigeria, have been transforming themselves to adapt to such uses (Haynes 2018, 22). This has confirmed to Sy that the success of the series was not *just* due to the controversy it raised, since the second season not only maintained audience numbers but increased them. This is also a determining factor for production funding, as it attracts advertisers, not just YouTube advertisements but also advertisements integrated within the diegesis (product placement).

Made in Senegal: Window-Shopping through Senegalese Screen Worlds

Kalista Sy was clear about the fact that offering a free product to the Senegalese and transnational population has a cost. This is why the financial sustainability of MDHM relies significantly on product placement, which Sy describes as the most viable "economic model to offer a free-of-access product to Senegalese viewers," although she says this is a temporary solution (Sy interview, June 15, 2020). Product placement is thus a way of enabling Senegalese screen worlds and is not strange for local television viewers, since advertisements have been appearing on Senegalese television screens for decades, and product placement is common in telenovelas too (Jedlowski and Rêgo 2018, 139). The reliance on product placement also inevitably commodifies the relationship between viewers, screens, and the screen storytellers as investors in the series aspire to earn revenue from turning spectators into consumers.

Product placement could be, and has been, perceived as disruptive by some viewers. In fact, in mobile screen worlds, such disruptive potential is greater, since online viewing allows for a multiplicity of windows and tabs to be opened at any time and for viewers to pause the series to buy something. In MDHM there is another dimension to all of this, as the products and companies are Senegalese, thus inviting viewers to use the series not only for free entertainment but also as a form of window-shopping, contributing to the Senegalese economy. This strategy implies that, if you want to look like a certain character, this is where you should buy your clothes, and these are the mobile apps you should consider installing. Of course, this raises questions about the status of MDHM—is it more advertisement for, or representation of, Senegal, or both? Sy acknowledges this, saying: "Beyond the series, we are also selling and exporting the label 'Made in Senegal,' with the landscapes, the location sets, but with costumes made by Senegalese designers. We contribute to marketing Senegal as a destination. All productions today have an added financial value for the country" (quoted in Sane 2019). An example of this product placement is the reference to the mobile application YUP (available in Senegal, Burkina Faso, Cameroon, Ivory Coast, and Guinea Conakry), which is used for transactional and business services, and loans and savings. Scenes feature dialogue between people of different generations, occupations, and genders, with one person explaining to the other how YUP works, implying its convenience as an efficient mode of payment. In another example, the product placement is of the series itself. In a conversation in which Moustapha/Tapha tells Racky he will be on time for dinner and to watch MDHM, which "seems to be a good series today," Racky warns him that the series "has very much opened the eyes of many women." This is a recursive scene that celebrates and acknowledges the devotion of audiences and fan communities. In other words, it is a form of celebration of the success of the series.

Conclusion

Maîtresse d'un homme marié is a very successful, female-led contemporary online television series whose production and distribution model contributes to the theorization of screen media not only in Africa but also more broadly amid the current global "televisual turn." The series reflects and creates a Senegalese world, on-screen and beyond, that is rooted in Senegal, made in Senegal, for Senegal, yet with a deep awareness of multiple forms of mobility—of national boundaries and affiliations, of moving images as they have become democratized through people's greater access to mobile phones, and of women's status in society. This Senegalese screen world is thus both indigenous and inclusive, foregrounding Senegalese people both behind the scenes and on-screen, yet also welcoming those beyond Senegal to enjoy and participate in its local environment. A result of the creative use of technological innovation and product placement, MDHM contests hegemonic global flows of cultural production and distribution, reclaiming these spaces first and foremost for Senegalese women in relation to stories about and for themselves, and becoming both a statement and a promotion (advertisement) of the value of what is "Made in Senegal." The work of Kalista Sy and her team has also been complemented by the (mostly female) fans of the series, whose "labour of love" (Lothian 2015; Sobande 2020) has no doubt helped make the series so successful. And since "fan cultures are not without connections to radical movements for racial, gender, and disability justice" (Lothian 2015, 144), it is likely that the promotion of gender equity within the diegetic screen world of MDHM is likely to also contribute to greater gender equity in Senegal and across the world.

NOTES

Please see www.screenworlds.org for images and further audiovisual materials that complement this chapter and other parts of this book.

1   "BBC 100 Women 2019: Who Is on the List This Year?," BBC, October 16, 2019, https://www.bbc.com/news/world-50042279.

2   The series was originally made in Wolof and French, with French subtitles. After the series' second season, the television channel A+ Ivoire bought the rights and dubbed it into French for dissemination in Ivory Coast.

INTERVIEWS

Sy, Kalista. Interview (WhatsApp video call), June 15, 2020.
Sy, Kalista. Interview (via Zoom), September 10, 2020.

3

Netflix

The Enabling Disruptor in Nigeria

AÑULIKA AGINA

Any study of screen worlds and the "televisual turn" would be incomplete without an analysis of Netflix, and this chapter thus contributes to this volume by exploring the relationship between Africa's most significant film-producing nation (Nigeria) and the world's largest subscription video-on-demand (SVOD) platform. Netflix means different things to different people. For a filmmaker, it is fame, transnational audiences, and money. For a cinema exhibitor, it is a respected enemy that is taking the food out of their mouth. For the local audience, it is a streaming service to be taken advantage of; one commentator on a WhatsApp group chat described her relationship with Netflix as follows: "Without giving them your money after all, what difference is my small money going to make to them?" For researchers, it is an enigma of sorts even if they do not acknowledge it themselves and someone else has to point it out to them. That was what Andrew Higson noted at a research workshop in which he stated that presenters were ambivalent about the cultural value of Netflix in the respective countries they studied. In his keynote titled "Netflix the Disruptor: Cultural Enabler or Cultural Enemy," Higson problematized the questions of Netflix's diversity, accessibility, and the construction of cultural taste to suggest that criticisms of the company in one context easily fade away in another for several reasons, not least because of its massive campaigns and investments in "local," non-American productions.[1] This is amply evident in Nigeria with the growing number of locally produced films on the streaming platform. In thinking about Netflix, Amanda Lotz (2020) cautions against lumping the streaming service with other SVOD platforms because of its distinctive technological, industrial, and multinational strategies, which make it a compelling site of study.

This chapter takes up the concept of disruption within a media industries framework to examine Netflix's relatively short presence in Nigeria and what it means for a film industry whose main problem remains distribution. Scholars have given some limited attention to digital delivery and streaming of films in the African context (Adejunmobi 2019; Dovey 2018; Miller 2016; Simon 2021), but none has given exclusive attention to Netflix. Of great interest here is whether Netflix's disruptive role can be applied to Nigerian film (hereafter Nollywood) producers, exhibitors, and audiences. Relatedly, how can we unpack the "enabling" influence of Netflix in the Nigerian context? Alessandro Jedlowski (2018) has questioned the sustainability of Netflix's major involvement with Nollywood through the acquisition of Genevieve Nnaji's *Lionheart* (2018), thereby alluding to the fact that streaming films on SVODs in Nigeria is an elitist practice, out of the reach of the majority. But the distribution problem he traces encourages Samuel Andrews (2020), a leading intellectual property professor, to interrogate the preparedness of Nollywood filmmakers who associate with Netflix in the face of Nigeria's lax copyright laws. Similarly, Añulika Agina and Vinzenz Hediger (2020) have reflected on the burgeoning relationship between Nollywood and Netflix, raising questions on what the alliance means for the industry in the long term, whether Netflix will face any competition from local and regional services (iROKOtv and Showmax, respectively) and the potential implications of what appears to be an unequal relationship (Agina 2021). This chapter therefore seeks to contribute to media industries' discussions about internet-enabled video distribution, with a focus on the largest SVOD platform in the world. The chapter makes no claims about putting these questions to rest, but it does reflect on the practices of several industry stakeholders, which might be losing or winning in Netflix's disruptive game.

The research presented here draws on fieldwork conducted in 2019 and 2020, the COVID-19 years in which a national lockdown enabled a surge in online spectatorship on Netflix and other video-on-demand (VOD) and SVOD platforms. Research methods involved observing the industry closely through the trade press, conducting formal and informal interviews, attending industry-related meetings, participating in social media discussions (on WhatsApp and Instagram) on the trajectories of the film industry, and following on Twitter (now known as X) and Instagram filmmakers who have films on Netflix. These methods have facilitated a deep understanding of Nollywood's perception of and response to Netflix. Following film industry people, including Netflix executives, on social media can reveal much more about their work and life than a one-hour interview could possibly yield.[2] The chapter thus contributes to global media and screen studies in an internet age. It reinforces already available information about digital transformation in Nigeria's screen media landscape (Adejunmobi 2019; Haynes 2017; Jedlowski 2017) and how that is altering consumption practices in spite of the perceived challenges articulated by Lindiwe Dovey (2018), Godwin Simon (2021), and Añulika Agina (2022). In the following sections, I examine four main subheadings: digital disruption, Nollywood before Netflix, Nollywood in a Netflix period, and consumption patterns on Netflix.

Netflix and Digital Disruption

Netflix does not refer to itself as a disruptor. According to the promotional description on its website, "Netflix is the world's leading streaming entertainment service with 208 million paid memberships in over 190 countries enjoying TV series, documentaries and feature films across a wide variety of genres and languages" (Netflix.com). Globally, it is the only digital media company that gives painstaking and exclusive attention to television and film, unlike other internet-distributed services that combine audio-visual content delivery with other businesses such as Amazon Prime (Lobato 2019; Lotz 2020; McDonald and Smith-Rowsey 2016). It is a multinational platform that offers professionally produced and curated content, all advertisement-free, for a monthly subscription fee. Netflix is the significant, suspicious, provocative, and elusive hybrid TV-cinema-digital media service that "performatively enacts its association with these media at different times and for different purposes" (Lobato 2019, 43–44; see also Alexander 2016; Lobato and Lotz 2020). In 2012, Dina

Iordanova reflected on the radical changes being caused by the technological bubbling that soon erupted to significantly alter the way mail delivery systems and the music, publishing, and cinema businesses worked. She identified important traits of digital disruption in film distribution to include disintermediation, transborder flows, new business models, and varying patterns of spectatorship, which have also played out in the clash between Netflix and the Nigerian film industry in dynamic ways.

It is important to qualify my use of *disruption*, a term borrowed from Andrew Higson and economic theorists. Higson's use of *disruption* was informed by the American economist and original theorist of the concept Clayton Christensen, who cited Netflix as the perfect example of disruptive innovation in the video distribution ecosystem. For Christensen, Michael Raynor, and Rory McDonald (2015), "disruption describes a process whereby a smaller company with fewer resources is able to successfully challenge established incumbent businesses" by servicing an overlooked audience through cheaper alternatives. The economists devised the theory of disruptive innovation as an explanation of Netflix's displacement of Blockbuster, a now-defunct American company established in 1985 that was involved in video rental and DVD by-mail services. This is not the case of Netflix in Nigeria; thus, my use of *disruption* simply refers to an emerging change of the status quo in the film industry regarding distribution and exhibition, acknowledged by industry heavyweights and consumers, as shall be discussed later in the chapter. Borrowing the term but not the theory for my purposes, disruption ruffles feathers, awakens nervous reactions, and is lucrative to existing, nonbenefiting players while irritating incumbent beneficiaries of the status quo. This idea of disruption is grounded in the Nigerian context with the unique traits of the nation's film industry for, as Lotz observes, "Studies about Netflix grounded in particular contexts offer much richer information" (2020, 2). Therefore, what and how Netflix disrupts or enables media industries vary among regions, and understanding the unique traits of Nollywood will reveal why the term *enabling disruptor* can qualify the burgeoning relationship between the streaming service and Africa's largest film industry without confusing it with Christensen's theory. Inevitably, in every disruptive game, there are winners, losers, and those who maintain the status quo.

Netflix is contributing to changes in the distribution and exhibition models in Nollywood (Agina 2021; Miller 2021). It did the same in its country of origin, as Ramon Lobato (2019) has pointed out. Writing about Netflix's effect, Kevin McDonald and Daniel Smith-Rowsey observed that, "in many ways [Netflix is] realizing long-held predictions of a future in which all media is available on-demand across multiple platforms—the major media conglomerates have been less appreciative of its aptitude for technological innovation, often viewing Netflix more as a disruptive interloper than as a savvy competitor" (2016, 3). These scholars' description resembles the Nigerian situation to an extent, extending the argument made by Moradewun Adejunmobi, in which she demonstrated that regional media companies were more of a threat to local productions than to global ones because of their capacity to "co-opt" rather than "suppress" the locals (2011, 67). Similarly, Netflix has entered the Nigerian market to co-opt both distributors and producers, thereby disrupting local distributors while enabling producers. The existing distribution companies are not enthusiastic about Netflix's direct relationship with producers but manage to maintain a respectful business relationship with the streaming service through content aggregation. In contrast to Jedlowski's argument that the "ongoing switch to intangible media distribution is favouring the progressive monopolization of [African screen media] sectors" (2017, 673) by France's Canal, this chapter claims that Netflix is unable and unwilling to take over Nollywood's distribution because of its own business strategies and the "increasingly variegated and contradictory whole of African screen media" (Haynes 2018, 5). Netflix is interested in doing business not with the masses but with elite producers such as Mo Abudu, Kunle Afolayan, and Genevieve Nnaji, as its recent original acquisitions have shown. And Haynes suggests that Netflix's entry at an opportune moment coincides with a shift (from tangible to intangible media formats) that fully prepared the industry for internet distribution. In other words, Netflix is riding on the back of the "success" established by local distributors DStv and M-Net (both owned by Naspers, a South African company), Chinese StarTimes, and especially Nigeria's iROKOtv.

Nollywood before Netflix and Nigeria's VOD Ecosystem

Nollywood's origin is inextricably tied to its distribution by electronics marketers in Nigeria's large markets, especially Idumota and Alaba, to mention the southwestern ones. Aided by technological advancements, the marketers' distribution of video films morphed from circulation on VHS cassettes to VCDs and DVDs. These businessmen gained a stranglehold on the industry and were able to informally regulate it from within in what resembled a cabal. They determined cast and crew fees, story concepts, and directors and actors (capable of guaranteeing the commercial success of a film), even up to placing a ban on actors who, because of their growing popularity among other reasons, started demanding higher fees. Within this distribution economy, piracy thrived because it was common knowledge that the marketers were also the pirates or at least controlled the subeconomy of piracy (Haynes 2017; Jedlowski 2017; Miller, 2016).

Before Netflix entered the Nigerian market, iROKOtv, established in 2011 by Jason Njoku, was the dominant subscription VOD platform through which Nollywood films were consumed. The evolution of iROKOtv has been sufficiently traced by scholars, notably Jade Miller (2016), Alessandro Jedlowski (2017), and Godwin Simon (2021). My concerns here are not about iROKOtv's history but, rather, whether it managed to disrupt film distribution in the way that Netflix appears to be doing. Njoku was able to wage a distribution war with Alaba marketers with whom he did business for a while, trying to formalize the informal distribution economy of Nollywood. Miller (2016) records in detail the battle between iROKOtv and the Alaba marketers, who also started uploading films on YouTube, in some cases illegally. But Njoku feared and resisted competitors when he increased his company's licensing fee from US$100 to US$3,000 and when he publicly declared that with digital migration of films and audiences, "the Alaba way will fade" (Miller 2016, 141–42). Apart from his fraught relationship with the marketers, iROKOtv's founder had a difficult time persuading filmmakers to sell their films to his company because what he offered at first was considered too little. Only films with low production values made it to the platform. In its first years, no theatrically released film was licensed to iROKOtv. This is one of the reasons Njoku's company went into its own production under the auspices of ROK Studios, which was founded two years after the launch of its online distribution company. In 2019, ROK Studios was bought by Canal+, a French media company. iROKOtv's disruption is unlike that of Netflix. The two companies have different visions, strategies, and capital bases that permit the latter to go directly to the top filmmakers while iROKOtv had to begin with midlevel to low-level filmmakers and then work its way up.

Like iROKOtv, Netflix is highly unlikely to solve the distribution problems that plague the Nigerian film industry, not least because the industry is dispersed; production is feverish, on different budgets, and with varying production values. Besides, different kinds of films appeal to different audiences. But Netflix's presence in Nollywood through time-bound licensing and acquisition of original productions will not go unnoticed. In recent times, emerging filmmakers have been asking established ones at public film events what the Netflix formula is because they hold aspirations of seeing their films on the platform.

As mentioned earlier, Netflix is focused only on conducting business with a small group of established producers in order to increase its subscriber base in Africa. But gauging the extent of Netflix's business in terms of subscriber figures or the profits derived from Nigerian subscribers is difficult because of password sharing and the fact that the company is not forthcoming with such information. On the one hand, Netflix's original acquisitions do not fall under the purview of the National Film and Video Censors Board (NFVCB) since those films and series were not premiered in physical locations within the country. *The Return of the King* (2021), *Oloture* (2019), and *Namaste Wahala* (2020) did not go through the NFVCB, for example. And Netflix aggregators from which it licenses films for two or three years would have addressed the NFVCB's requirements prior to the release of older films. On the other hand, it is not clear whether Netflix is paying taxes to the Nigerian government owing to its relationship with Spectranet, the local internet provider that hosts Nigerian films for Netflix on its servers. Prior to 2019, the profits derived from online activities such as movie streaming by nonresident companies were outside of Nigeria's tax net. To address this and other taxation irregularities, the Finance Act of 2019 came into full effect in February 2020. The Finance Act "introduced the concept of significant economic presence (SEP) to expand the scope of Nigerian tax on foreign companies deriving income from their activities in the country which hitherto were not captured" (KPMG 2020, 1). To remit tax to the Nigerian government, such a company must be determined to have derived ₦25 million annual gross turnover or its equivalent through streaming, downloading, transmitting data about Nigerian users, and a host of related activities. Unless the government mandates Netflix to disclose the revenue generated from the Nigerian market as governments elsewhere have done, it is unlikely, if not impossible, that the company will do so. Besides, given the nature of digital services and streaming in Nigeria, and the unlikely goal of attracting paying subscribers to the tune of ₦25 million, it is improbable that Netflix makes such profits from Nigeria alone. This requires further investigation, which the limited space here does not afford.

The "cabal" of cinema exhibitors and the incessant complaints by filmmakers about being underserved during theatrical exhibition are beginning to be upturned by Netflix. In this case, the biggest culprit according to aggrieved filmmakers and critics is Filmhouse Cinemas, even though FilmOne Entertainment's (owners of Filmhouse Cinemas) cofounder, Moses Babatope, has energetically refuted the claims, saying:

Yes, yes, it's very irritating and it keeps coming . . . from the crop of independent filmmakers [who] I expect to be a bit more discerning; I expect [them] to be a bit more intelligent in their breakdown of what they think the issues are. It's not enough to just say, Oh, FilmOne won't get back to you or they won't support your film. . . . Your content does it all. Your content gets my attention. Your content gets the attention of FilmOne. . . . If you don't have . . . compelling content, if you don't have the kind of content that gives us goosebumps and gets us out of bed every morning . . . we will find a way to manage how you feel because we don't want you to feel bad. We try to be careful so that we don't bruise your ego because you've spent time making this film. But, . . . if you have the right content, I will call you. (Moses Babatope interview, March 2, 2021)

Although FilmOne Entertainment is a progressive cinema distribution chain, severe criticisms against it have continued, including from the director Mildred Okwo. Okwo's film *La Femme Anjola* (2021) was removed from specific Filmhouse locations within its week of release, which caused a slew of verbal fireworks on Twitter.[3] FilmOne Entertainment was criticized for monopolizing the distribution and exhibition space since it has subsidiary companies that produce, distribute, and exhibit films. Okwo threatened to appeal to the government to enforce some regulation to prevent such a stranglehold on exhibition and distribution spaces because, given the limited number of screens available, FilmOne prioritizes the marketing of its own films at its Filmhouse locations. But with a direct release on Netflix, independent filmmakers have been saved from FilmOne's alleged monopoly.[4]

As discussed later in this chapter, Netflix is disrupting and bypassing FilmOne, although it is a partner for aggregating content (several cinema films on Netflix were originally distributed by FilmOne) in what Iordanova (2012) refers to as "disintermediation." This elimination of an intermediary in the supply chain is causing FilmOne to rethink its strategies to safeguard its business in Netflix's disruption game.[5] Other problems associated with theatrical releases that a direct release to Netflix is overcoming are fraudulent sales of tickets, dubious film promoters, and double taxation. Cinema-going audiences and filmmakers have reported the sale of tickets of films that were not requested by unsuspecting viewers at the box office. This is part of the wider attempt to promote films produced by cinema owners over those of independent filmmakers and is another hurdle overcome by online releases on Netflix (for the small but increasing number of films that have gone that route). When such customers notice they have tickets for a film that they have not requested, the box office staff reassure them this will not stop them from watching the film of their choice. Upon presenting the ticket at the entrance of the cinema hall, no questions are asked; the tickets are simply ripped into two pieces, with one half given to the customer. But the money and attendance for the viewer's preference are recorded in favor of another film. This phenomenon featured in all the interviews conducted with independent filmmakers like a recurring decimal, but the interviewees refused to disclose the perpetrators to avoid endangering future distribution prospects. Even if one disbelieved the filmmakers based on their anonymity and nondisclosure, listening to viewers (who have no business interests to protect) repeatedly describe the same situation lends a measure of credibility to the allegation.

Relatedly, dubious film promoters approach Lagos-based filmmakers who have no presence in big cities like Port Harcourt and Abuja with enticing proposals to promote their films for an agreed period prior to its theatrical release in those cities. Because the filmmaker is already concentrating his limited resources in Lagos, where there are more cinemas, he yields to the proposal. This would normally entail positioning roll-up banners at the entrance of the shopping malls where the cinemas are located and providing posters and handbills at strategic positions of the cinema building. The filmmaker then uses his personal network of friends, family, and fans to monitor the process, which might last no longer than one day, contrary to the informally agreed duration of two to three weeks. The loss accruing to such filmmakers could be up to ₦500,000 (Ekene Mekwunye interview, May 23, 2021). This, in addition to double taxation, contributes to depleting a filmmaker's budget. Operating under a registered production company, the film producer pays taxes or faces fines by the Revenue Board. When the film has had its run at the cinemas, and before any remittance is made to the producer, a further entertainment tax of 15 percent is taken, leaving him with a fraction of the 30 percent sharing formula agreed upon with the distribution company. Both loopholes of financial losses are checked on a Netflix deal if the film is released directly on Netflix, even for films that are not original acquisitions like Ekene Mekwunye's *One Lagos Night* (2021).

FilmOne is not the only concerned stakeholder observing Netflix's bold and disruptive steps. Another is MultiChoice, a South Africa–owned pay TV provider, operating in Nigeria since 1993. While MultiChoice is reacting nervously (Jedlowski 2018) to the streaming giant's inroads, iROKOtv is restrategizing operations. iROKOtv announced in 2019 that it was refocusing its business strategy to concentrate on diasporic markets (Adejunmobi 2019) after years of struggle with infrastructure in Nigeria (Miller 2016). There has been a long and mutually beneficial, even symbiotic, relationship between MultiChoice and Nollywood as revealed by Wangi Uzo-Mbaukwu, the channels director for Africa Magic (Wangi Uzo-Mbaukwu, interview, March 12, 2021), the company's dedicated channels for Nollywood films. MultiChoice has trained industry practitioners, from writers to screen editors, on a regular basis and even instituted an annual awards program, the Africa Magic Viewers' Choice Awards (AMVCA) to recognize Nollywood's distinctive talent. When MultiChoice started licensing Nollywood films in July 2003, filmmakers were happy at the prospect, but they soon began to complain about the disparity in the license fees paid to them and their South African counterparts—a situation that is being repeated in the Nollywood-Netflix relationships. This conflict is summarized thus: "One might in fact describe Nigerian film producers' contracts with DStv [the video entertainment company owned by MultiChoice] as a form of syndication, albeit a form of syndication where the producers do not reap the highest profits possible for a variety of reasons" (Adejunmobi 2011, 72).

Nollywood in a Netflix Period

Despite the various attempts at solving the exhibition- and distribution-related problems described here, they persist. That is why filmmakers are pleased with Netflix's presence, which affords them simultaneous transnational exhibition and alternative funding opportunities (Agina 2021). In turn, Nollywood filmmakers promote @netflixnaija (Netflix's Twitter handle) and @naijaonnetflix (Instagram) among fans on social media.

Ecstatic filmmakers are reaping huge financial benefits from Netflix's growing investments in the industry (Agina 2021; Agina and Hediger 2020). Filmmakers, content owners, creators, and aggregators are benefiting from the streaming giant, even if several others criticize it for paying African filmmakers much lower rates than filmmakers elsewhere. The popular actress Omoni Oboli, who has ventured into production and directing, insists quite obviously that with greater funding, which Netflix is currently providing through licensing deals and acquisitions, content quality improves, and so do cast and crew fees (Omoni Oboli, interview, January 26, 2022). With the exclusive release of his film on Netflix in May 2021, Mekwunye can corroborate Oboli's point. *One Lagos Night* cost Mekwunye ₦26 million to produce, but from Netflix, he received up to twice his production budget. This amount may be more than double. An industry that has built itself on personal savings, sporadic bank loans, intermittent government aid (Haynes 2017), product placements, brand ambassadorship, and corporate investments (Jedlowski 2017) based on celebrity status now has a fairly decent and steady source of income. Mekwunye

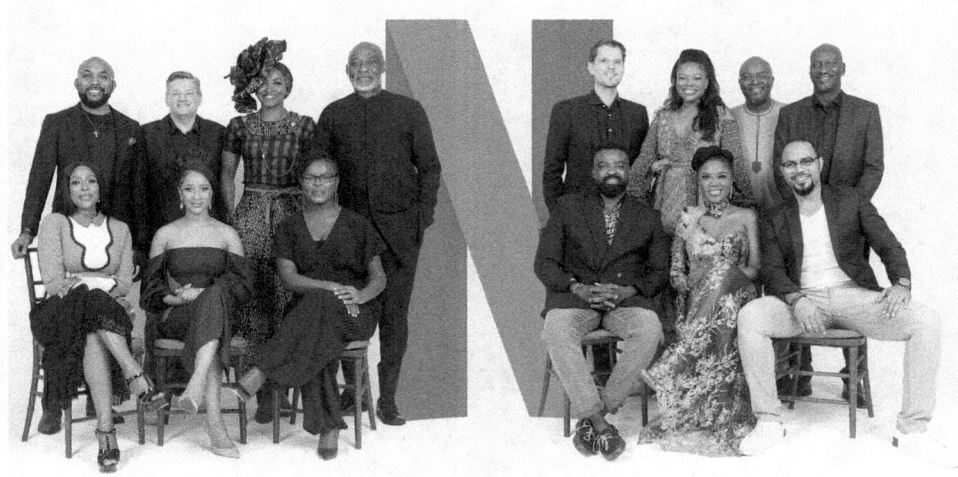

FIGURE 3.1. Netflix executives with Nigerian filmmakers and actors. *Back row, left to right*: Banky W, Ted Sarandos (Netflix chief content officer), Kate Henshaw, Richard Mofe-Damijo, Felipe Tewes (Netflix Italian and African Originals director), Kemi Adetiba, Ben Amadasun (Netflix African licensing director), and Akin Omotoso. *Front row, left to right*: Mo Abudu, Adesua Etomi, Dorothy Ghettuba (Netflix African Originals lead), Kunle Afolayan, Omoni Oboli, and Ramsey Noah. Source: https://theconversation.com/netflix-naija-creative-freedom-in-nigerias-emerging-digital-space-133252.

reminds us that even though Netflix's money comes in tranches, it comes "as certainly as dawn and dusk at the contracted time" (Mekwunye interview, May 23, 2021). Even local content aggregators like FilmOne and Blue Pictures are getting their share of Netflix's deals, but as shown in figure 3.1 (in which no exhibitor or distributor appears), taken in February 2020, Netflix chose to partner directly with filmmakers and actors.

FilmOne would have distributed the films of prestigious filmmakers like Kunle Afolayan (*Citation* 2020) and collaborated with Mo Abudu (*Oloture* 2019) as it has done in the past, but those functions have been taken over by Netflix, which has been approaching filmmakers directly, thus bypassing the local distribution company. Netflix, even though it got into the film industry through its relationship with Jason Njoku (Adejunmobi 2019) and later through Film-One, has found new partners in Golden Effects Pictures (owned by Afolayan),

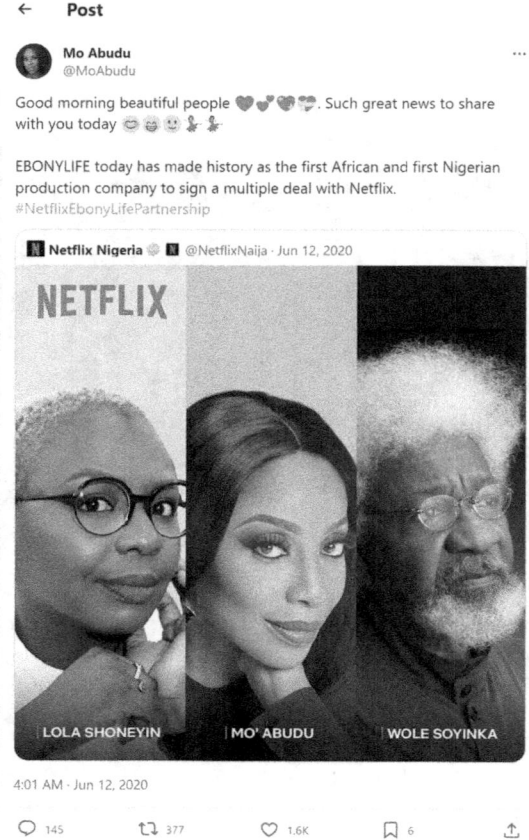

← Post

Mo Abudu
@MoAbudu

Good morning beautiful people 💚💕🖤🐦. Such great news to share with you today 😊😄🙂🕺🕺

EBONYLIFE today has made history as the first African and first Nigerian production company to sign a multiple deal with Netflix.
#NetflixEbonyLifePartnership

Netflix Nigeria ✅ @NetflixNaija · Jun 12, 2020

NETFLIX

LOLA SHONEYIN | MO' ABUDU | WOLE SOYINKA

4:01 AM · Jun 12, 2020

💬 145   🔁 377   ❤️ 1.6K   🔖 6   ↥

FIGURES 3.2 AND 3.3. (*above and opposite*) Personal tweets (from Twitter, renamed X in 2023) of Mo Abudu, owner of EbonyLife Studios. Screenshots

EbonyLife Studios (owned by Abudu), Inkblot Productions (co-owned by Chinaza Onuzo), and Kemi Adetiba Visuals, to name the prominent ones. In an article by Georg Szalai for the *Hollywood Reporter*, Dorothy Ghettuba, Netflix's lead for African originals states: "Netflix is proud to continue to invest in more original content from Nigeria. . . . We're also thrilled to grow our existing creative partnerships while forming new ones with Chinaza and the amazing Inkblot team who will now join the growing list of Nigerian partners" (Ghettuba cited in Szalai 2020). Filmmakers react with elation to this type of comment (Agina 2021). Chinaza Onuzo tweeted the Christmas card sent to him by Netflix along with the following words: "It still doesn't feel real mehn

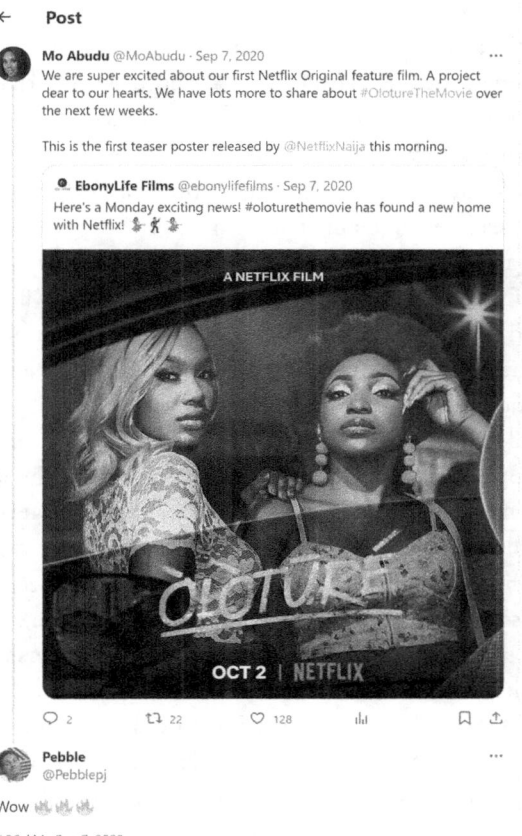

Mo Abudu @MoAbudu · Sep 7, 2020
We are super excited about our first Netflix Original feature film. A project dear to our hearts. We have lots more to share about #OlotureTheMovie over the next few weeks.

This is the first teaser poster released by @NetflixNaija this morning.

> **EbonyLife Films** @ebonylifefilms · Sep 7, 2020
> Here's a Monday exciting news! #oloturethemovie has found a new home with Netflix! 💃 🕺 💃
>
> A NETFLIX FILM
>
> OLOTURE
>
> OCT 2 | NETFLIX

♡ 2   ⇄ 22   ♡ 128   ılı   ⛶ ⬆

Pebble   ···
@Pebblepj

Wow 🔥 🔥 🔥

6:36 AM · Sep 7, 2020

[man], but bloody hell I'm a Showrunner on a Netflix Original Series. How did that happen?" (@IamSnazz, December 20, 2020). And Mo Abudu's tweeted celebratory comments are just as telling (figure 3.2 and 3.3).

These filmmakers share local and global aspirations of reaching transnational audiences while partnering with prestigious multinational companies. The streaming giant is meeting these aspirations with its numerous strategies for engaging with the Nigerian market outlined by Agina and Hediger (2020). The financial benefits achieved through partnerships with Netflix have ripple effects, as filmmakers themselves have recognized. Working with a global player like Netflix attracts other companies that, before Netflix, either were hesitant to do business in Africa or lacked confidence in the ability of African storytellers to attract global audiences. In an interview with Alex Ritman, Mo Abudu reports that this is the case with Sony; AMC (originally known as American Movie Classics), an entertainment company involved in independent film distribution among other related businesses; and other international corporations that are investing in the Nigerian screen media industry. According to Abudu, "Netflix are trailblazers. And no doubt the others will come and sign deals too. I've been going to MIPCOM for probably 10 years now. I go every year and I'm really excited about meeting all the big studios and pitching, and they always say there's never a bad meeting in Hollywood. Everybody always sort of listens to you politely, you have a glass of wine, you exchange cards. . . . And you come home, you're sending emails and you're not getting any replies" (cited in Ritman 2020). Furthermore, Netflix is changing the on-demand scene in Nigeria because it is hugely capitalized and therefore can withstand being snubbed by small markets like Nigeria, something that other emerging local VOD platforms can barely afford. The largest of them, iROKOtv, is now concentrating its business outside Nigeria for diasporic audiences (Adejunmobi 2019). IbakaTV, the second largest, is struggling to retain subscribers. Afrinolly launched in 2011 and Dobox in 2013, but both have folded for reasons outlined by Dovey (2018) and Simon (2021). FilmOne experimented with an online platform (myfilmhouseng) in partnership with Richard Signesky of Blue Sky Media in 2018 that lasted only two years. Even the prestigious EbonyLife media company owned by Mo Abudu launched its own VOD platform, EbonyLife ON, in 2017 but has failed to attract subscribers, thus licensing all its films and series to Netflix. EbonyLife ON's Twitter account has managed to attract only about 800 followers since 2017, and iROKOtv has had about 82,000 followers since 2011, while Netflix has over 100,000 followers in a Twitter account launched in February 2020. The point here is that internet distribution of premium content in Nigeria is not an all-comers affair even at the realization that cinema audiences are moving online. In my opinion, FilmOne and EbonyLife would rather license cinema films to the disruptive Netflix, and reap the financial benefits from doing so, than continue trying to sustain the capital-intensive VOD option, thereby rethinking their business models. Although a former employee of FilmOne revealed anonymously that myfilmhouseng failed because of numerous complexities, including the disproportion between the high costs of content acquisition and tech infrastructure deployed and the meager revenue from subscribers, Moses Babatope had a different view and revealed that myfilmhouseng is launching again very soon:

> We did venture into VOD and I'm glad to say we are still at it. I would probably not accept that it failed. I would just say we had to take a pause

and rework the modalities. We were too early in that phase. And at the time it made sense to do what we needed to do but the kind of infrastructural support and gateways were an issue for us for a while. We also needed some kind of flexibility with the studios in getting the kind of content that we needed for this market. Unfortunately, we didn't have the infrastructure on ground.[6] (Babatope interview, March 2, 2021)

The VOD ecosystem in Nigeria appears to be saturated with the likes of Scene-OneTV and countless others springing up on a regular basis, but the failure rates indicate that the road to viability without capital investments the size of Netflix's is tortuous in the complex business environment that is Nigeria.

The Netflix Audience

The challenges faced by media entrepreneurs offering digitally delivered content to audiences on their mobile devices in Africa have been well documented (Agina 2022; Dovey 2018; Simon 2021). As with iROKOtv, there have also been suggestions that most of the audience for Netflix will be from diasporic markets given the costs and related factors working against streaming in Nigeria (Miller 2016). In his discussion of Netflix's aspirations and performance in India, Ramon Lobato (2019) stated that Netflix was looking for a segment of elite Indians who are interested in American shows and can subscribe to its service. Although it has been indicated elsewhere that this is also true in Nigeria (Agina and Hediger 2020), it would be naive to assume that Netflix's investments in Nollywood do not reflect a desire for more than a segment of the elite Nigerian audience. Partnering with Spectranet, a local internet provider, to deploy servers to hold its growing content or negotiating with local telecommunication companies to check data costs and make offline viewing more accessible is not geared toward diasporic audiences. Netflix wants local audiences as well, and its main competitors for Nigerians at home are Showmax (the VOD platform owned by Naspers Group) and iROKOtv.

Cynical audiences who preferred Hollywood films to Nollywood are now taking the latter seriously, reasoning that if Nollywood films are on Netflix, they must have some international appeal, and since such audiences prefer foreign films, they get on the bandwagon (Babatope, interview, March 2, 2021). The audience for Netflix in Nigeria is among the elite and middle class—that is, viewers interested in premium Nollywood content who did not catch a film during its cinema run. Thus, Netflix is reopening access, choice, and convenience and is also profitably transnationalizing Nigerian screen worlds in a way previously unseen on any other platform. No prominent filmmaker has ever released a film directly on iROKOtv, something the industry is currently seeing more of. Rather, it was iROKOtv that began producing films partly because of its inability to secure premium Nollywood. Uzo, an acquaintance met through one of the WhatsApp groups in which Nollywood and Netflix are randomly discussed, is a banker who earns up to ₦15 million annually. She has a premium Netflix account (not Showmax or iROKO) that allows the other three members of her family simultaneous streaming of different content, to avoid viewing clashes. Uzo claims that when she is not in the mood to go to the cinema, she turns to Netflix, which also served her well during the COVID-19 lockdown from March to September 2020. Other Nigerians in Uzo's socioeconomic bracket would go to the cinema or stream on Netflix, indicating that Netflix is serving a specific, high-end clientele and gradually attempting to overtake Showmax, which has considerably more African content built on the back of MultiChoice Group's years of producing and licensing continent-wide films and series.

A basic Netflix subscription plan in Nigeria costs ₦2,900 (₦34,800 annually), which is the same price as for Showmax. The cheapest DStv package bouquet, a pay TV service requiring a purchased and installed decoder, costs ₦11,850 for the first month. Subsequent months cost ₦1,850 each, with an annual rate of at least ₦22,200. Therefore, a total of ₦57,000 is required for paid entertainment—something considered important but nonessential—in a country whose minimum wage is ₦30,000 per month. To consider a cheaper pay TV alternative at an annual rate of ₦6,200 would amount to ₦41,000 per annum for entertainment needs, primarily drama for women and football for men. This estimate does not factor in data costs. Therefore, we can see why Showmax leads in the VOD sector since its offerings include movies, series, news, music channels and live sports channels, not only films and series in the Netflix fashion. Hence, by the second quarter of 2021 in sub-Saharan Africa, Showmax maintained the lead.

To avoid the Netflix subscription cost, some viewers shared accounts, as described in the following scenario. Before Netflix canceled its thirty-day free trial, groups of friends sometimes signed up in turns to enjoy films and TV shows on the service. When one person's trial period was over, another would sign up using a different email ID. Belinda, residing in Lagos, shares her US-based sister's basic account through password sharing. Assumpta shares her cousin's basic account in the same way. Michael accesses Netflix through his sister-in-law's account, and Adaeze, residing in Philadelphia, shares one premium account with four siblings in the United States and parents in Nigeria. Whether these users, all of whom watch Netflix on smartphones and laptops, are streaming daily or weekly, they are not paying the subscription fee. It reminds one of L. U. Marks and Radek Przedpełski's

(2021) reproduction of a January 16 tweet of a Lebanese user: "Ya man there are only 2 Netflix accounts shared among half Lebanon people." These patterns indicate a desire among indigent or unwilling-to-pay users for the convenience of Netflix and are similar to the following comments randomly taken from an all-female WhatsApp group of over-forty-year-old, educated, middle-class users. The women's initials have been used to protect their identity. In other platforms, the comments range from IP masking via proxy servers to free virtual private networks that permit a host of unauthorized viewing of content.

NU: Most people on this group don't have the luxury to change used cooking oil. That's a fact, not to talk of maintaining Netflix for a year. How? We share with friends and family. . . .

CM: Netflix is the only one showing the best of *Naija* content now. It started showing *Naija* movies in America before *Naija* sef [itself]. In fact, do u know I canceled DStv just to have Netflix . . . but it's not possible for each family member to have a Netflix account. The highest subscription allows you to stream on 5 devices. What if you are more than 5 at home? Are you going to have two different accounts or what? No now . . . you share password.

AE: Netflix is about to stop acct sharing. They announced it some weeks back but I have not seen any action. 5 of us in 5 different states are using my brothers acct. They should allow us *biko* [please].

AA: So many of my American friends love *Naija* films on Netflix *o*. My friend said they love seeing movies with only black people. *Naija* films have gone mainstream especially in the US.

DR: . . . I love Netflix more than DStv . . . in fact I was using GOtv for my shop then, but I still love, not like *oooo*, Netflix so much.

JN: The catalog might be big but it's not everything that appeals to each individual. . . . For instance i used to watch local and foreign movies, i watched them all and there was no more content for more than 6 months i totally lost interest and stopped watching Netflix.

FF: They don't add new movies frequently . . . once you watch a movie, there are no new movies . . . you end up watching old movies, and that is boring. For some shows, Season 2 might take another 6 months to show up. So I just forget about them.

CZ: I know how long I have waited for shows to return. . . . I just moved on.

Audiences are confirming how streaming on Netflix is a desirable albeit nonessential means to access screen entertainment, with its added competitive edge over DStv even if subsequent installments are slowly, if ever, uploaded. Socioeconomic factors cannot be ignored when considering who has access to the streaming platform. But what is more interesting here is that Netflix is motivating the migration from DStv, a satellite television option, to its service, thus disrupting the equilibrium for DStv. This change is closely tied to socioeconomic status, since prospective users cannot afford both services even though DStv has a mobile option—DStv Now—that allows subscribers to either catch up on missed content or view new content. The comments from the WhatsApp group are indicative of audiences' movement between platforms, a point that suggests the inability of one platform to hold audiences' attention (and patronage) for a long time. In the keynote address by Higson mentioned at the beginning of this chapter, he stated that in spite of Netflix's diversified and huge amount of content, people like him tend to prefer the carefully curated content offered by the streaming platform MUBI, just as many on the continent prefer MultiChoice's Showmax to Netflix. Inevitably, audience tastes, which vary from one season to another, determine their migratory practices and streaming destinations. While Netflix has been criticized by scholars as being the evil embodiment of algorithmic culture, the datafication of storytelling, and the mathematization of taste (Alexander 2016), suggesting films and shows based on a previously viewed library and the top 10 content in a geographic location, audiences revel at such management of viewing preferences. Another WhatsApp user commented, "Imagine re-starting my film from the exact point I stopped . . . without me rewinding or fastforwarding no matter when I return to it. Forget, Netflix is in a class of its very own."

Conclusion

There is a lot to be said about Netflix's enabling-disruptive pattern not only in Nigeria but also in other parts of Africa, given its ongoing and ambitious project to reach all corners of the world. From media industries perspectives to regional discourses about the future of television and failures of media entrepreneurs, audiences, and questions of access, Netflix always seems to take center stage, not least because of its distinct growth strategies and investments on both the global and the local level. Precisely because of its success, and its ability to simultaneously enable and disrupt, Netflix attracts fans and enemies at the same time, thus confirming that digital disruption erodes traditional modes of distribution while democratizing spectatorship and liberating film from the tyranny of geography (Iordanova 2012).

Certain questions about Netflix's impact in the Nigerian film industry and the wider media ecology remain. In my opinion, the enabling disruptor has had and continues to have a far-reaching albeit *controversial* impact in Nigeria and in Africa at large. With larger investments among elite producers like Mo Abudu and Kunle Afolayan come bigger productions that create employment and career advancement opportunities for cast and crew, collaborations with other sectors of the creative industries like fashion and design, and more nuanced storytelling as seen in the miniseries *Blood Sisters* (2022). These collaborations create avenues for emerging producers and independent filmmakers to experiment with new modes of production. Furthermore, media celebrities like Chinenye Nworah (*Shanty Town*, 2023), the popular blogger Linda Ikeji (*Dark October*, 2023), and others are producing content for Netflix in ways that are growing new, impressive talent who go on to work on other film and TV productions. Netflix is also indirectly forging relationships between Lagos-based creatives and those in other parts of the country such as Enugu (Akah Nnani, male lead, *The Man of God* [2022]) and Kaduna (Toka McBaror, director, *Dark October* [2023]). The streamer's main strategy remains attracting box-office successes (films and talents) while giving little attention to award-winning films or critically acclaimed festival films. However, such desirable investments as Netflix's often result in a sort of meddlesomeness that irritates filmmakers. A highly acclaimed filmmaker recently revealed his unending correspondence with Netflix, which is interested in licensing a recent documentary of his, but the condition for signing on is the expungement of a portion of the film. His refusal has stalled the relationship as he is mindful of the new forms of censorship that trail global capital.

This chapter has examined Netflix's relatively new presence in the Nigerian market and how it is disrupting the status quo in a film industry that has struggled with funding, recognition, distribution, and infrastructure, to mention the most prominent concerns. While some sectors of the industry are reaping the bounty from Netflix's largesse—that is, producers and arguably audiences—others (mainly the exhibitors and distributors) seem to be losing out. The relationship is financially and professionally beneficial to Nigerian filmmakers and is continuously open to scrutiny and claims of exploitation by notable others. To such claims, Netflix's response is the same: we pay market rates. Relatedly, as filmmakers have claimed, creative autonomy on the part of Nigerian filmmakers is arguably giving way to newer forms of control as Netflix forms partnerships with local producers to create original content.

For some exhibitors, such as FilmOne and Blue Pictures, their losses, although significant, are mitigated by the fact that they continue doing business with Netflix as aggregators. But they are rethinking their business models by fully going into production or weighing their options for (re)launching VOD platforms. Blue Pictures has already gone into production with its first film, *Gone*, which premiered in December 2021. FilmOne is better insulated from Netflix's disruption because of its more progressive business strategies, international collaborations, and unrivaled position in the industry. This is in addition to its production company, which ensures that the traditional windowed release of films is still in place. But exhibitors like Genesis Deluxe Cinemas (GDC) are losing out and have only realized this rather late. Ope Ajayi, the executive director of GDC, remarks with hindsight that he wished his company had gone into film production of local content at the same time it began exhibition in 2008 (Ope Ajayi interview, March 6, 2020).

Netflix exists for audiences' eyeballs and credit cards. And because audiences' patronage cannot be taken for granted, since tastes and preferences change and competition is ongoing, the company consistently invests in strategies, such as the Netflix Party for film premieres and other uses, to increase its subscriber base. Content-hungry Netflix is interested in Nollywood to enrich its offerings for local and foreign audiences. The fact remains, however, that an average Nigerian cannot afford an annual Netflix subscription given competing, essential needs. To the privileged few who can, what does Netflix mean for the long term? Further research is needed to deepen the understanding of how Netflix is disrupting Nigeria's film industry, and how that is happening in other African contexts.

NOTES

Please see www.screenworlds.org for images and further audiovisual materials that complement this chapter and other parts of this book.

1 Indeed, the title of this chapter is informed by Andrew Higson's keynote address at an online research workshop organized by the Department of English and Related Literature, University of York, on April 23, 2021. Higson is the director of the Screen Industries Growth Network.

2 I resorted to this method after twenty-seven rejections and unanswered emails or phone calls.

3 Twitter rumors alleged that *La Femme Anjola*, distributed by Silverbird with fewer cinema locations than Filmhouse, was removed from Filmhouse Cinemas to make room for *Prophetess*, distributed by FilmOne. In the past, independent filmmakers have repeatedly called out FilmOne Entertainment for this practice.

4   As of 2020, Nigeria had 77 cinema locations, out of which FilmOne owned the largest number (12), followed by Genesis (10) and Silverbird (9) (FilmOne Entertainment 2020, 12).

5   In 2019, FilmOne Entertainment partnered with China's Hua Hua Media and South Africa's Empire Entertainment to attract film funds to inject into coproductions with local filmmakers (Vourlias 2019, n.p.). This move has funded films like *Quam's Money* (2020), *Kambili* (2020), and *Prophetess* (2021).

6   Moses Babatope left FilmOne, the parent company of Filmhouse Cinemas, in February 2024.

INTERVIEWS

Ajayi, Ope. Interview, March 6, 2020.
Babatope, Moses. Filmed interview, March 2, 2021.
Mekwunye, Ekene. Interview, May 23, 2021.
Oboli, Omoni. Interview, January 26, 2022.
Uzo-Mbaukwu, Wangi. Filmed interview, March 12, 2021.

4

Examining the "Opportunities"

*M-Net's Zambezi Magic Channel and the Emerging
Zambian Film Industry*

ELASTUS MAMBWE

This chapter takes the example of M-Net's Zambezi Magic channel (owned by the South African company MultiChoice) to analyze the "opportunities" the company claims to be offering to the small, emerging Zambian film industry. Building on the previous chapter, the key question here is whether the expansion of media firms from the Global South (in this case, from South Africa) into other countries within their regions or continent can be considered a form of cultural or media imperialism. Musa Ndlovu (2003) contends that oftentimes the continental expansion of southern-based media is taken only to indicate this media's potential to counter the domination of programming or content from the Global North or "West" that maintains a strong grip over global culture. These media companies are thus frequently assumed to be part of a regional response to cultural imperialism without considering how these expansionist media can also be a threat to local or national media.

Background

The Zambian media and cultural space has seen important changes since the country took a liberal turn in 1991 with growth in sectors such as radio, television, online media, and—more recently—filmmaking. The coming of private investment in the screen media space was a direct consequence of Zambia's landmark shift from the one-party regime of Dr. Kenneth Kaunda that year to the historic constitutional change and the coming of the new government of Frederick Chiluba and the Movement for Multi-party Democracy. Chiluba's government embarked on an ambitious reform program that included new broadcasting regulations that opened up the broadcast sector to private investment (Makungu 2004; Mambwe 2013). The new Zambian National Broadcasting Corporation (ZNBC) Act of 1994 established new licensing regulations that welcomed private applications for broadcast licenses. Since then, private sector investment in television became a reality. Compared with 1990, when there was only one television station run by the ZNBC, forty licensed television stations were listed by the country's Independent Broadcasting Authority (IBA) by the end of 2019 (Independent Broadcasting Authority 2020). Most crucially for the focus of this chapter is the fact that the IBA compels television stations to provide local content, which has stimulated local filmmaking activity.

MultiChoice was one of the earliest entrants into the newly liberalized Zambian broadcast market, and MultiChoice Zambia was established in 1994 as a joint venture with ZNBC.[1] Initially, the subscription company provided analog television in Zambia's major cities, but later it introduced its flagship satellite television service DStv.[2] MultiChoice's involvement in the Zambian media landscape has increased over the years. A recent economic impact assessment report by Accenture estimated the company's contribution to Zambia's economy between April 1, 2015, and March 31, 2019, to be over US$244.8 million.[3] This amount includes US$12.8 million dedicated to content development. However, a glossy corporate report such as this one prevents more nuanced, critical analysis of the company's impact on Zambian filmmakers themselves—the aim of this chapter.

Vital to drawing out such critical analysis is paying attention to the work of Zambian entrepreneurs and filmmakers before the arrival of M-Net's Zambezi Magic channel in 2015. For example, a terrestrial free-to-air channel called

Muvi TV was founded in 2002 by the Zambian entrepreneur Steve Nyirenda, demonstrating that there was intense demand for local stories on Zambian screens. Between 2004 and 2007, this terrestrial free-to-air station produced various dramatic and comedic television series under its director of programs, Angel Phiri, who recruited, trained, and led a team of mostly young creatives, many of whom would later become major players in Zambian cinematic arts. These include Frank Sibbuku, Henry Joe Sakala, Metrix Chipeta, and Chris Zulu. Shows such as *Constable*, a comedy that parodied the life of policemen working in a police post in a township in Lusaka, and *Banja*, a drama series that addressed various challenges in family and community life, were widely popular among viewers (Angel Phiri interview, June 27, 2018). Muvi produced most of its content in Nyanja and Bemba, the local languages most widely spoken in Lusaka, where the station broadcast to initially. Using local languages was key to Muvi's popularity among audiences (Banda 2009; Phiri 2010). By the time Muvi released *The Lawyer* (2008)—credited as being Zambia's first commercial feature film—the channel's production team had racked up a few years of experience in local, in-house productions (Phiri interview, June 27, 2018). Thereafter, Muvi went on to release films such as *When the Curtain Falls* (2009), *The Vanguards* (2010), *Street Circles* (2013), *LSK Heroes* (2014), and *The Red Bag* (2014). Muvi hired some of the best local talent to work on its productions and produced films for its channel and later its cinema franchise, Fresh View Cinemas.

Zambezi Magic launched in 2015 as an entertainment channel targeting MultiChoice's Southern African subscribers with content produced from countries in this region. Apart from showing South African archival content previously unavailable elsewhere, Zambezi Magic was also supposed to help spur the development of homegrown regional productions, including films; this, according to then MultiChoice Africa CEO Tim Jacobs, would strengthen the firm's links to the "burgeoning entertainment industry in Southern Africa" and strengthen its role in "developing and supporting African production companies" (Ferreira 2015). Zambezi Magic is currently available to DStv subscribers in Zambia, Zimbabwe, Botswana, Namibia, Malawi, and Swaziland. So far, the channel has differentiated itself as one that provides content that tells local stories on a platform that has been dominated by Western content, and African content from South Africa and Nigeria. Initially, South African soap operas such as *Generations* and *Isidingo*, as well as films and lifestyle content, were broadcast, but these were eventually phased out as more of the channel's prescribed regional content was developed or sourced. Figure 4.1 is an example of one of the channel's print and social media advertisements emphasizing its growing local production portfolio of shows and characters.

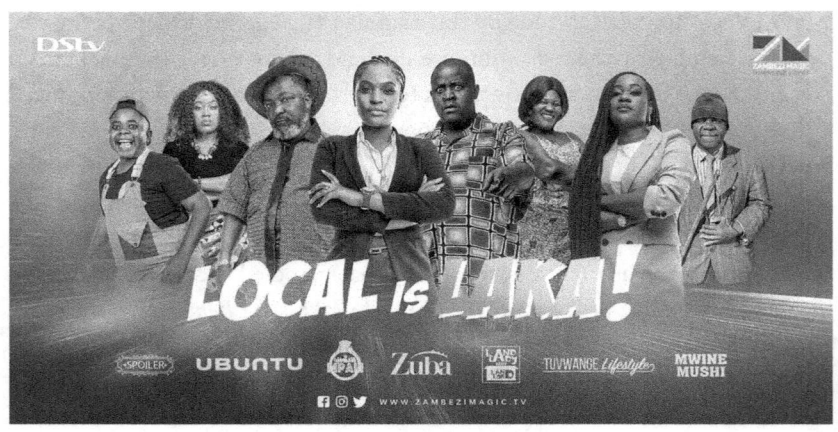

FIGURE 4.1. DStv promotional poster for the Zambezi Magic television channel. *Laka* is a Zambian version of the Afrikaans word *lekker*, meaning "good."

In its self-promotional discourses, the channel has maintained its commitment to localized productions that tell stories in local languages that are reflective of everyday life as experienced by the channel's audience. This suggests an appeal to "lower-class" audiences who are more inclined to watch local-language programming as provided by channels such as Muvi TV. However, the "Zambezi Magic Commissioning Brief" (MultiChoice Africa 2015, 4) seems to veer away from this assumption when it states that the channel primarily targets the eighteen to forty-eight age-group, which it calls the "upgrade generation," a group of ambitious and aspirational people, from different socioeconomic backgrounds, who are trying to achieve economic success. This explanation of the "upgrade generation," though vague, easily aligns with a "middle-class" to "upper-class" viewership, one that is more likely to be able to afford to subscribe to the DStv package that carries Zambezi Magicambezi Magic follows long-established M-Net guidelines for content proposals.[4] MultiChoice, through M-Net, accepts both solicited and unsolicited proposals for content. Producers sending unsolicited proposals get feedback on receipt and initial interest. Pitching sessions are also organized for proposals that seem viable and attractive to the channel. All productions are expected to meet technical and editorial standards set by the channel and as stipulated in the production agreement. These guidelines tend to emphasize visual or technical quality.

The channel follows three financing models: coproductions in which both MultiChoice and the producer jointly fund the production; broadcaster-funded productions in which MultiChoice commissions and funds the production; and producer-funded productions in which the producer funds the production but enters into a copyright licensing agreement with MultiChoice. When MultiChoice commissions a film and pays for it, the company will own all copyright relating to the production, "including, without limitation, rights to re-runs, the on-selling of programs to other broadcasting service licensees, the exploitation of secondary rights through other platforms such as DVDs or merchandising, and rights to make the programs available for research, and broadcast archival" (MultiChoice, 2015). For Zambian filmmakers, the coming of Zambezi Magic has thus seemingly provided a solution to two of the main challenges that have plagued the film industry in their country: the lack of funding for production and the problems with distribution that filmmakers previously faced. The channel has also helped with marketing and with the development and promotion of local talent. However, this is just one side of this Janus-faced issue. The other side is the concern over the various policies that govern how content is acquired as well as how much power the corporation wields over local production companies that are desperate for income.

In order to provide a nuanced, multidimensional, critical analysis of Zambezi Magic, I draw on interviews I have conducted with the filmmakers Lawrence Thompson, Owas Ray Mwape, Maynard Muchangwe, and Henry Joe Sakala; Angel Phiri, a filmmaker and director of programs at Muvi TV; Mwiza Nanzila, a spokesperson for MultiChoice Zambia; and Professor Dickson Mwansa, an academic, playwright, and cultural commentator. In addition, I had the privilege of making three visits to the set of one Zambezi Magic production, *Mpali*, a popular local soap opera that has become the flagship of the channel; I also interacted with the series creator and producer, Frank Sibbuku, and several members of the cast and crew.

Looking at Zambezi Magic from Multiple Angles

The collapse of Zambian filmmaking in the 1980s was the result of declining economic conditions that made the financing of film production difficult. Even with liberalization in the 1990s, described earlier in this chapter, financing for filmmaking remained elusive. Underground Zambian filmmakers who made low-quality, early-Nollywood-style films in the first decade of the twenty-first century produced their films with small budgets; as a result, few of these films managed to get mainstream interest. The films were, however, popular in the poorer, high-density communities where they were mostly distributed.

For years, even the state broadcaster ZNBC did not finance the production of fiction narratives for its channel. According to Angel Phiri (interview, June 27, 2018), ZNBC's policy required independent producers to pay the station to have their productions aired. Sometimes ZNBC would obtain the content and only pay the producer if a sponsor for the production was found. If no sponsor was found, the show would be aired without benefit to the producer. Lawrence Thompson, who created and produced Zambia's first soap opera, *Kabanana* (2001–2004), observed that this arrangement made it difficult for filmmakers to produce content for ZNBC. Thompson recalled how he once ended up in debt because he had to meet all the overheads for production on his own (Lawrence Thompson interview, July 11, 2019). For him, Zambezi Magic helped reshape the attitude of local broadcasters toward financing or purchasing productions by demonstrating that it was indeed possible. In 2019, Thompson, through his production company Centripetal Media, produced the drama series *Turn of Fortune*, which he licensed to Zambezi Magic. This was his first major drama production since *Kabanana*. In 2021, *Makofi*, another drama series developed by Thompson, premiered on Zambezi Magic. Both series were produced to cater to audiences from different socioeconomic classes, and both of them included the use of local languages.

The filmmaker Frank Sibbuku notes that the funding made available through Zambezi Magic has helped raise the quality of his productions. In an interview on the set of his Zambezi Magic *Mpali*, Sibbuku pointed out that his production company, A-List Media Works has been able to "up its game" in terms of quality and staffing (crew members) (Frank Sibbuku interview, June 25, 2019). This, he argues, has been made possible by the financial resources gained from his partnership with the media giant. Sibbuku, who had previously worked for Muvi TV, acknowledged that the visual and technical quality emphasized by MultiChoice also helps to distinguish his recent productions from those he previously produced while at Muvi.

The two perspectives provided by Thompson and Sibbuku convey a positive narrative about Zambezi Magic as far as financing is concerned. However, it is important to recognize that part of what makes it possible for the channel to achieve this has to do with the massive financial capacity and influence that MultiChoice possesses and injects into content acquisition. It is simply not possible for local stations such as ZNBC and Muvi to compete. Further, the financial possibilities brought by MultiChoice to local production have created a somewhat overly optimistic and unrealistic sense of what filmmakers in Zambia can earn or do. If we were to remove the media giant from the picture,

Zambian cinematic arts would revert to Zambezi Magic conditions. Unfortunately, only a handful of filmmakers get to share in this financial power. The rest must contend with the same challenges that have burdened Zambian filmmaking since the 1970s.

While distribution is a challenge for filmmakers worldwide (Lobato 2010, 345), African films face even more problems. In many African countries, cinema owners would still rather show Western films that they know will earn them profits, and there still are very few companies that distribute African films for local or international audiences. In view of this, several local filmmakers see Zambezi Magic as an avenue through which they can distribute their films and recoup some of their investment. For instance, Owas Ray Mwape, an award-winning director and actor, observed that "it is much easier and quicker to make money" by selling a production to an international broadcaster than selling on DVD (Owas Ray Mwape interview, August 10, 2018). In this sense, Zambezi Magic seemingly presents filmmakers such as Mwape with an avenue through which to reach the market far more easily. Mwape's film *Chenda* (2015) was one of the first Zambian films to be aired on Zambezi Magic. *Chenda* explores romantic relationships, family life, infidelity, and loyalty as experienced by ordinary Zambians. In the film, the desire of the housewife Chenda (played by the Malawian actress Flora Suya) for a happy family life is shattered after she learns that her husband, Kel (played by Mingeli Palata), has been unfaithful through a relationship with a younger woman (played by Dambisa Lunda). The tense situation in the house is further compounded when Chenda falls in love with Kel's attractive and spirited friend Emmit (played by Mwape), who comes to stay with the family. The themes that *Chenda* explores are present in several other Zambezi Magic offerings, perhaps because they are relatable across the cultures in the countries where the channel broadcasts and are appealing to a wider audience. Other common themes across the channel include witchcraft, polygamy, inheritance, cultural clashes, land disputes, and the negotiation between tradition and modernity.

Zambezi Magic is no doubt capitalizing on the fact that local filmmakers have long bemoaned the nature of the terms and conditions they have to contend with from traditional distributors. For instance, some distributors require that the filmmakers sell exclusive rights to the film, and some digital platforms only pay the filmmakers based on how many people watched the film. According to Maynard Muchangwe, another filmmaker, this scenario "was difficult because we couldn't monitor how many people watched it [our film]" and therefore could not challenge the low payments the filmmakers received

(Maynard Muchangwe interview, July 11, 2018). Zambezi Magic quickly became a preferred distributor because incomes and audiences were guaranteed and determined from the beginning.

Zambezi Magic created a platform for local producers not only to showcase their productions but also to make a reasonable income in the process when they licensed their films to the channel. Creatives such as Henry Joe Sakala and Frank Sibbuku, who previously worked for Muvi, have enjoyed a successful relationship with Zambezi Magic, collaborating on popular productions such as *Njila: The Phase* (2016–19), *Mfuti* (2019), and the widely popular and channel flagship, *Mpali* (2018–). *Mpali* follows the story of a wealthy farmer named Nguzu, who is married to seven wives and has to balance his life among the often-feuding women, his children, and his farming business. According to Mwiza Nzila, a MultiChoice Zambia spokesperson, *Mpali*'s take on polygamy, landownership, and family wealth has resonated with the station's target audience across the various countries, and the show has developed a consistent and loyal audience (Mwiza Nzila interview, March 3, 2020). However, it must be noted that no official audience figures have been made publicly available to document this claim. Aesthetically, *Mpali* employs soap opera/telenovela visual elements that include a "realist illusion" meant to reflect real life as much as possible (S. Gibson 2018, 98). *Mpali*'s producers often depend on cinematography, mise-en-scène, and production design to achieve this. The use of wide-angle shots to establish the scenes on the farm and of close-ups during melodramatic dialogue is common. Settings are designed to complement the narrative and enhance viewers' understanding of each character or location. For instance, each of Nguzu's wives has a house that has its own look that is influenced by the particular wife's character. The main house is grander and has spaces with darker colors and tones and is dressed with props that are intended to reflect Nguzu's character and experience within the world of the series. Further, *Mpali* embraces local languages (Nyanja, Tonga, and Bemba) even though the channel is broadcast to countries where these languages are not spoken. To address this, MultiChoice has put in place a subtitling unit that works with the scripting team to cater to non-Zambian viewers. This approach makes the story accessible for viewers in the region and speaks to MultiChoice's involvement in ensuring that narratives on the channel cut across geographic boundaries for maximum profit.

For Mwape and others, Zambezi Magic has also eased the burden on filmmakers by taking on the marketing of their films. Zambezi Magic has leveraged the power of social media to generate conversations about *Mpali* on Facebook and Twitter by promoting the hashtag *#MpaliZM* and running advertisements.

Such marketing work has also been supplemented with the sponsoring of artist awards ceremonies. For example, in the years following the launch of Zambezi Magic, MultiChoice went on to sponsor the 2016 and 2017 editions of the annual Zambia Film and Television Awards, with a sponsorship package valued at approximately US$50,000 in both years. The awards honor twelve outstanding individuals in film and television and are an initiative of the National Association of Media Arts, a voluntary association affiliated with the National Arts Council of Zambia that was established to promote the development of media arts and represent content creators such as filmmakers (Miselo 2017).

From the perspectives and experiences presented here, it may seem that Zambezi Magic is solely a positive force in the Zambian film industry. The opportunities related to funding, distribution, promotion of local talent, and industry support would appear to be welcome developments for a small and growing film market, such as that in Zambia. However, a few issues call for caution and concern—for another, more critical angle of analysis. One area that raises concern is that of filmmakers' awareness of and aptitude for the business side of film. The Zambian scholar and veteran playwright Dickson Mwansa suggested that while the gestures by MultiChoice may be welcome, there should be caution on the part of local filmmakers when it comes to making business transactions. Mwansa's call for caution emanates from the possibility that local filmmakers could be shortchanged, or they could lose out from such arrangements due to the intricacies of the business of film and television that they may not fully understand or be aware of. Mwansa therefore argued that "there is need for agents to handle business deals for artists so that they benefit appropriately from their works" (Dickson Mwansa interview, November 20, 2019).

Related to being aware of the business of film, Mwansa also suggests that filmmakers in contexts such as Zambia must take a keen interest in understanding intellectual property as it relates to television rights. This recommendation stems from the sad reality that content creators, and by extension audience creators, sometimes unintentionally lose the rights to their creations as they offer them for broadcasters simply because they do not understand the details of the various agreements. A recent legal battle between Luckie Chiyowele of Powermedia in Zambia and MultiChoice over the ownership of the music competition show Dreams Music Talent (created by Chiyowele) exemplifies this concern. MultiChoice is alleged to have offered predatory contracts and coerced Powermedia to sign them with a promise of renegotiation thereafter.[5]

Another reason for caution relates to arguments raised by Moradewun Adejunmobi (2011) about the potential co-opting of and subsequent loss of autonomy by local producers to regional corporations, which can present an even greater threat to local media production than global media corporations. Adejunmobi's observations follow her examination of the Nigerian film industry's association with DStv's Africa Magic channels. Africa Magic, launched in December 2003, is arguably one of MultiChoice's primary and long-standing contributions to screen media production on the continent. Through the Africa Magic channels, more Nollywood productions have reached consumers across the continent through licensing agreements and commissions. These channels have been instrumental in showcasing African-produced films and creating a continental awareness of films that would otherwise not be viewed anywhere except their country of origin. However, in creating Africa Magic, MultiChoice also exploited the popularity of Nollywood, with Adejunmobi suggesting that the company took over "important portions of the Nigerian film industry" (2011, 76).

Most filmmakers in Zambia view the relationship with Zambezi Magic as an important one because it exists as a key source of income—perhaps the only one, and a sharp contrast to the Nigerian or South African scenario. Coming from a situation where DVD/VCD sales networks were not as widespread and entrenched as in Nigeria, and where filmmakers everywhere must contend with high levels of piracy, it is no surprise that Zambezi Magic is seen as a crucial opportunity for the industry. However, there is still a fear of loss of autonomy in creative decision-making that may come with a dependence on Zambezi Magic. Zambian filmmakers are eager to generate an income, and they may be willing to accept any offer simply because it is better than nothing, even if it is less than what other creatives received in other markets.

The filmmaker Henry Joe Sakala argues that there is a "scramble" by filmmakers to get deals with Zambezi Magic (Henry Joe Sakala interview, June 8, 2018). Angel Phiri of Muvi goes so far as to suggest that this scramble is the result of filmmakers, for the first time, having a high earning potential in the country thanks to Zambezi Magic's willingness to license or commission content (Phiri interview, June 27, 2018). At the same time, Phiri claims that the desperation among local filmmakers has given Zambezi Magic leverage to negotiate even lower rates than those in other markets. In the absence of other large content corporations showing interest in Zambian film, Zambezi Magic is enjoying a dominant position. Furthermore, according to Phiri, MultiChoice in Zambia pursued this co-opting strategy (Adejunmobi 2011) years before Zambezi Magic even began—for example, through trying for years to co-opt Muvi onto its DStv platform. (Muvi resisted by arguing that it had its own channels.)

Although Muvi has remained as an independent broadcaster, the station has lost much of its viewership following the digital migration switchover and increased competition. Muvi was a victim of its own policy when it implemented a satellite-based digital transmission system (Digital Video Broadcasting - Satellite—Second Generation [DVB-S2]) as its solution for the switchover to digital television, ahead of the national program. The Zambian government, however, chose to implement a digital terrestrial television (DTT) system (Digital Video Broadcasting—Second Generation Terrestrial [DVB-T2]) that was significantly cheaper for the consumer, compared with Muvi's satellite solution. This process, together with increased competition from MultiChoice, which also introduced its own cheaper DTT solution (called GOtv) and later launched Zambezi Magic, significantly undercut Muvi's subscription revenue, which the station had hoped would help finance production.

Another potential area of concern relates to national identity and ownership. While the locally produced Zambezi Magic films and television programs are said to be Zambian productions, the involvement of foreign capital and labor in these productions, without which some would not exist, cannot be ignored. The question then arises: Are they still Zambian productions when the capital injection and some of the technical expertise hails from South Africa? Further, can we say for certain that these productions hold to a Zambian cultural identity, bearing in mind Nolwenn Mingant and Cecilia Tirtaine's argument that "defining the nationality of a film and program may, in some cases, be further complicated by the cultural identity they convey" (2012, 2)?

While the Zambezi Magic originals are clearly transnational, the reality is that the Zambian film sector continues to benefit greatly from this transnational flow of capital and expertise. Beyond the money, the transfer of knowledge and skills is key. This certainly has been the experience of Frank Sibbuku in the production of *Mpali*. Various MultiChoice appointees and technical consultants (mainly South African) have been attached to the show to assist in various departments to complement the capacities that are still lacking in Zambia. The media giant also emphasizes stories that cut across the region at which the channel is targeted.

Another point of concern over the coming of Zambezi Magic has to do with how the channel has brought about an increase in the cost of local filmmaking to a level that is challenging for other local channels. This argument can best be explained when Zambezi Magic is again contrasted with Muvi. Muvi has been producing films and television series at much lower costs than the larger Zambezi

Magic productions. It often works with smaller budgets, in-house production teams, and community-based locations, frequently relying on personal relationships and goodwill. Films have gone on to become successful despite having been produced within this context (Phiri interview, June 27, 2018). The coming of Zambezi Magic, while beneficial, has significantly raised the cost of production, especially as it relates to labor and resources, to the extent that remuneration expectations for on-screen and off-screen crew members are now higher. The various talent and crew members, such as scriptwriters, editors, directors, and others, are now demanding Zambezi Magic rates, being well aware that they can earn more working with the M-Net channel. It is not surprising that there has been a mass exodus of personnel from channels such as Muvi to Zambezi Magic funded projects. There is significant evidence to suggest that many former Muvi staff members are now attached to a Zambezi Magic production in one way or another, as seen with Sibbuku and Sakala. Muvi has been forced to maintain its model of using mostly in-house resources and talent for its productions. The station's 2019 feature film, *Mushala*, involved collaborations with both old and new crew members but was financed entirely with locally sourced funding. Produced and directed by Angel Phiri as Zambia's first historical feature film, *Mushala* tells the story of the eponymous freedom fighter, politician, and rebel Adamson Mushala, who ran a militia that challenged President Kaunda's government in the 1970s (Mambwe 2021). The film explores Mushala's complex motivations for the rebellion and details the national response to the uprisings, suggesting that, as scholars, we need to remain alert to how more critical diegetic screen worlds may be enabled by independent organizations such as Muvi.

Conclusion

The discussion in this chapter has examined the impact of the Zambezi Magic channel on the film industry in Zambia. The chapter has endeavored to analyze how the expansion of media firms from the Global South (in this case, from South Africa) into other countries within their regions or continent has affected local industries. I have explored the Zambian film industry and its interaction with the MultiChoice group and its entities or brands. This discussion is critical to our understanding of indigenous African screen worlds, which have long been in tension with Western corporations that fund large-scale production and distribution and contribute to cultural imperialism. The continental and sometimes global rise of media firms from the so-called Global South represents a counter to this historical reality. However, it is critical to consider the impact this expansion has on local industries.

The Zambia case discussed here has highlighted how MultiChoice, through Zambezi Magic, has contributed to helping the local film industry surmount various long-standing challenges in financing and distribution. However, the chapter has also outlined the opposite impact of such expansion, particularly on local firms such as Muvi TV and other independent producers, whose participation and place within the local screen worlds sphere are threatened. While the countering of the West's stranglehold on global cultural production is welcome, we must be cautious about regional commercial alternatives that may similarly be driven by expansionist motives that in the long run may create a vicious cycle of dependency and subjugation of local industries. Furthermore, we can argue that MultiChoice's entry and growth in the region and continent are an extension of South Africa's cultural power and its power to shape consumption preferences. There is a need for emerging film economies in Africa, such as that of Zambia, to explore trajectories that embrace the value brought by regional corporations but that are also responsive to empowering local industry players. This balance, it seems, will be essential for African screen media industries both in the present and in the years to come.

NOTES

1 MultiChoice's expansion into Africa has followed a joint venture model that sees the company partner with either state broadcasters or local business owners in the respective countries to establish local MultiChoice companies (Teer-Tomaselli, Wasserman, and de Beer 2007, 139). These local MultiChoice firms are supported by MultiChoice's technological and corporate infrastructure from regional centers and the headquarters in South Africa. The joint venture model was adopted as a way around the many differences in broadcasting operating environments across the continent (Ndlela 2013).

2 DStv is a direct-to-home digital satellite service launched in 1995 and operated by MultiChoice Group, an entertainment company owned by Naspers, a media, entertainment, and internet corporation with interests across Africa and the world. Naspers, founded in 1915 as De Nasionale Pers Beperkt (National Press Ltd.) in South Africa, grew from being a publisher and printer of newspapers, magazines, and books to launching the pay television channel and company M-Net in 1986. MultiChoice was founded in 1993 as MultiChoice Limited to manage the analog subscription service operated by M-Net. Although MultiChoice has undergone realignment several times within Naspers, the firm is essentially both a publisher of broadcast content and a subscription television operator (Teer-Tomaselli, Wasserman, and de Beer 2007). M-Net currently provides a diverse range of programming,

including Western-produced content and a growing amount of popular African programming, offered through a selection of channels sometimes referred to as M-Net Channels. Over the years, the company has developed several channels, such as Africa Magic and Mzanzi Magic, for exclusively African content it has licenced or commissioned. The channels are delivered on various subscription "bouquets" that are differently priced for different income groups. These packages are primarily distributed throughout Africa on DStv, and more recently on GOtv, the group's digital terrestrial television platform, which is available in only a few countries. MultiChoice also operates an internet-based subscription video-on-demand service called Showmax which has a sizable catalog of foreign and South African film and television content (Dovey 2018; Teer-Tomaselli, Wasserman, and de Beer 2007).

3   The MultiChoice report (which was published on December 3, 2019) gives details about MultiChoice's business in Zambia over a period of time.

4   The M-Net Commissioning Protocol has been adapted for Zambezi Magic commissions and is available on the channel website. DSTV Zambia, "Commissioning Protocol," Zambezi Magic, June 9, 2016, https://www.dstv.com/zambezimagic/show/ten-tamang-street/season/1/commissioning-protocol/news.

5   Luckie Chiyowele, "M-Net (Zambezi Magic) Scandles (Criminal Contracts)," Facebook, accessed October 23, 2021, https://www.facebook.com/luckie.chiyowele/posts/10225727832285921.

INTERVIEWS

Muchangwe, Maynard. Interview, July 11, 2018.

Mwansa, Dickson M. Interview, November 20, 2019.

Mwape, Owas Ray. Interview, August 10, 2018.

Nzila, Mwiza. Interview, March 3, 2020.

Phiri, Angel. Interview, June 27, 2018.

Sakala, Henry Joe. Interview, June 8, 2018.

Sibbuku, Frank. Interview, June 25, 2019.

Thompson, Lawrence. Interview, July 11, 2019.

Part II

———

Crafting the Production and Circulation of African Screen Worlds

5

From Infrastructures to Treehouses

Circulations in Nollywood Distribution, Locations, and Craft

ALEXANDER BUD

For fifteen years, a landscape of circulations, movements, flows, and networks has dominated Nollywood studies (Adejunmobi 2007; Jedlowski 2012; Miller 2016). While such approaches have appeared in multiple forms, the most influential contributions have come from Brian Larkin in "Degraded Images, Distorted Sounds" (2004), *Signal and Noise* (2008), and "The Grounds of Circulation" (2019). At the heart of Larkin's analysis is the concept of infrastructure: material networks that organize the movement of goods, information, and people between nodes, thereby constituting "the skeleton of urban life" (Larkin 2008, 5). These networks serve as conduits of domination and provide a substructure that undergirds and shapes "softer" social phenomena such as modes of leisure. In these terms, Larkin interprets the development of Nigeria's wired radio, film, theater, and video distribution systems. Crucially, Larkin argues that Nollywood grew out of an "infrastructure of piracy" that evolved through a "corruption" of the official infrastructure and involved the illicit replication and distribution of foreign films. In this regard, he makes a further contribution by showing that circulating films are not fixed but are in a state of flux, shaped by the technologies of replication that transformed their sounds and images through the addition of noise (Larkin 2004).

While the emphasis on circulations, the agency of distribution technology, and the role (or lack) of state involvement yield valuable contributions, *Signal and Noise* has had a rather double-edged effect on Nollywood studies. By arguing "that the roots of all Nigerian film" lie in the infrastructure of piracy, the work has aggravated a preexisting tendency to overplay the role of distribution systems, both historically and in contemporary industry dynamics (Larkin 2008, 230). This impact has been so profound that subsequent studies—including my own—naturalized the idea that the technologies and structures of distribution play a determining role in the sector (Bud 2014; Lobato 2010; Paulson 2012).

The point here is not quite that there has been too much emphasis on distribution per se, but to argue that there has been a certain synergy between industrial functions and scholarly biases. Sir Peter Hall's observation that the movie industry brings together "large-scale marketing and small-scale batch production" has correlates in academic studies that engage in systems-level analysis of the former and cultural-historical studies of the latter (Hall 1998, 516). In this vein, distribution studies, especially in Larkin's rendition, have had a tendency toward hegemonic structural explanations and various forms of determinism, leaving behind such themes as skills, labor relations, social histories (which Larkin eschews for genealogy), and culture as an active force.[1]

Perhaps even more seriously, Larkin's work has encouraged an archetype of circulation formed in the image of media distribution. The fundamental components of his rendition of "infrastructure" are limited to cultural texts, on the one hand, and the material systems that transmit these texts, on the other (Larkin 2019, 106, 113). As the anthropologist Alan Barnard (2000) points out, such a schema eschews all concern for processes of origination and making and, as such, is a close analogue of the doctrine of diffusionism. Larkin's so-called material approach therefore reveals itself as strangely immaterial. In this notion, films operate as movable units of information that come into existence ex nihilo. The entire filmmaking process is in fact reduced to "an aesthetic choice," in contrast to the "technical" construction of infrastructure (Larkin 2019, 108). Films here are more akin to signals and speech acts than to complex fabricated products.

The approach thus completely loses sight of the kind of relationships evoked by John McCall in his early Nollywood ethnographies, such as the description of a 2002 Enugu film set reimagined as a kind of factory: "The filming of *Ebube* required the services of more than 100 people. The costumers' area hummed with activity as women with Chinese foot-treadle sewing machines fit costumes on the spot. Make-up artists and hairdressers put the finishing touches on chiefs, native doctors, and warriors. Set builders erected a traditional village, complete with elders' meetinghouse, while teams of technical specialists fiddled with cameras, booms, and mixing boards" (McCall 2004, 101–2).

In order to offer an alternative interpretation of circulations in Nollywood, I am inspired by an older and somewhat neglected approach proposed by Karin Barber in *The Generation of Plays* (2000). It might seem absurd to suggest that Barber's work has been underappreciated in Nollywood studies, with concepts such as the "African popular arts" and "entextualization" having become so influential. However, the actual methodology and overall project of her magnum opus have had a surprisingly partial impact on the field. Central to Barber's book is her "generative materialism" program. The approach is based around the ethnographic and historical exploration of three processes: the emergence of cultural milieus and their publics, the professional life histories (and the associated skills and modes of working) of local cultural workers, and the stylistic development of local performance genres. The perspective emphasizes the contingent nature of Nigerian theater and, by extension, all cultural industries. Every fabricated cultural form is a "living growth point" that develops within a "productive field of potentialities" (9–10). Such a level of contingency reflected the artisanal mode in which the craftsmen-turned-actors found ways of adapting their practices in the face of unpredictable resources, the constantly changing tastes of audiences, and the flexibility of a genre that could be added to from a multitude of sources.

Despite the kaleidoscopic nature of Barber's work, its focus on theater does result in certain limitations. The camera is peripheral to her approach, and the aesthetics and craftsmanship of set construction were unimportant to the particular style of her theater company. I therefore turn to Birgit Meyer's (2010) work on "aesthetic formations" in the Ghanaian film industry, an approach that resonates with Barber's but adds a specifically filmic dimension. Meyer conceives of chains in which material pictures (including video frames) are internalized and assimilated to form mental images, and then externalized to form new physical pictures. These pictures can be embodied by any material medium, ranging from films to architecture to clothing and home furnishings. In Meyer's concept, the camera lens plays a particularly important role as it enables a "special kind of superior vision" (2015, 139).

In the 2005 conference Creativity and Cultural Improvisation and the edited volume of the same name, Barber, alongside Elizabeth Hallam and Tim Ingold (2007), attempted to build a higher-level theorization of these approaches. According to their performativity-orientated view, processes do not have beginnings or ends. The creation of a film, for example, does not start with the director's vision and end with the audience switching off the television; instead, each performance is shaped by previous performances and goes on to shape subsequent ones so each one "is just one moment in a work's concrescence" (Ingold 2007, 50). In this view, each work comprises the trail of its performances—it is a copy of a copy of a copy—and therefore every original is a copy of a previous instantiation, and every copy is an original for future performance.

Ingold (2013, 2015) has since developed this perspective into a fully integrated model that he terms *meshworks*, in distinction to the infrastructure/networks metaphor (figure 5.1). While infrastructures are made up of connected dots (nodes and links), meshworks lack such nodes. Instead, they consist of threads that sometimes tangle around each other to form knots. There are two principal advantages to this model. First, it replaces the idea of beginning and end points with ongoing "lines of becoming" that trail into the past and extend into the future. Second, it eschews the implication that the connectors (links) and the things they connect (nodes) are qualitatively different, self-contained objects. In the latter regard, Ingold uses the imagery of the spider "whose web is spun from materials exuded from [its] own body and are laid down as [it] moves about. You could even say that [the line of the web] is an extension of its very being as it trails into the environment" (2008, 210–11). The new approach facilitates a more dynamic processual concept of circulations, which now includes the "trails along which life is lived, which include histories, stories and trajectories that are full of loose ends and are always on the move" (Klenk 2018, 316).

In order to think about the kind of flows that constitute the Nollywood meshwork, it is helpful to first identify several key groups of actors. These include filmmakers (producers, actors, and location managers), house owners who make their homes available for filming, house owners in the wider community who incorporate filmic images into their houses, fabricators working on film sets (set designers, carpenters, painters), and fabricators in the wider world (such as architects, interior decorators, and furniture makers).

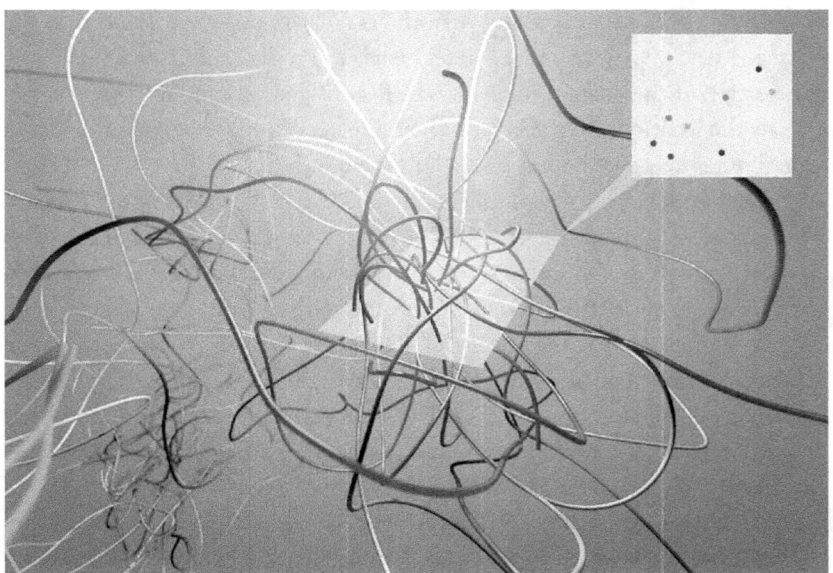

FIGURE 5.1. Meshwork as an encounter of lines of becoming rather than as a network of nodes and links. Artist: April Brust

This chapter traces five types of flow between the different sectors of creative production (film workers, housebuilders, carpenters) as well as between these producers and "tasteful" consumers in the Nollywood meshwork. The categorization of these flows contrasts with that of the "infrastructure" approach, which focuses on the circulation of media products (complete films) through physical and broadcast networks, specifically at the stage of distribution. Following Barber, Meyer, and Ingold, the flows in my approach are more contingent and less directed and occur at every stage in a film's life cycle. I therefore look at how different types of flow "leak out" from the film world, including both during production and after distribution.

I first examine location filmmaking in Igboland, exploring the flows through a scene populated by film producers, location managers, homeowners, and housing estate managers. Location production is the older filmmaking form—going back to Nollywood's earliest days—but has also continued on its own trajectory into the present. The flows in this arena reflect the convergence of the filmmakers with the everyday residential environment. We shall see the world of filmed onstage performance flow into the nonfilmed world; as filmmakers shot in new residential locations, they transformed these quotidian buildings into spaces of wonder. Second, in a sort of mirror image, there was a flow of off-duty crew and performers from the onstage world into the offstage world of private houses, hotels, bars, and restaurants. The final flow in this section of the chapter relates to the flow of pictures and images, as viewers saw the locations on-screen and then rematerialized them by building and redesigning their own houses in a "Nollywood style."

I then explore the recent phenomenon of studio production in Lagos, which arose around 2004 and has become increasingly important in the years since. The flows in this domain reflect its factorylike nature: more enclosed than location production, widely and deeply skilled, and materially productive. I therefore explore the flows of skills accumulated and redeployed by the set designers and a wide variety of craftsmen (carpenters, painters, upholsterers, welders, and aluminum and glass workers) who operate across studio-set construction and home furnishing fabrication. We also see material flows of the fabricated set elements, which have their own "afterlives," as well as of the pictures and images of these sets, resulting in various new forms of fabrication.

This chapter is based on fieldwork conducted in Lagos and Igboland between June 2015 and June 2017. The research in Igboland covered Enugu, Asaba, Onitsha, Nnewi, Abiriba, and Umuoji and included an ethnography with the Creative Designers Guild of Nigeria (CDGN). My key research participants included location managers, who played the central mediating role between filmmakers and owners of houses and hotels. I also carried out fifty interviews with homeowners, film producers, architects, "set and prop men," and other CDGN members. The Lagos leg comprised ethnographies with two leading set-building teams in Nigeria: Mr. Bedford's firm at Ultima Studios and Leo Spartani's team at MNET studios. It included eighty interviews with other set designers and craftsmen, including carpenters, upholsterers, painters, metalworkers, and electricians.

The Nollywood House Scene in Enugu

Since Nollywood's emergence in the early 1990s, a few cities have been used for location shooting, with the epicenter moving around various sites. From 1992 to around 1998, Lagos was the main shooting center, with Enugu (the former Eastern Region capital) and its environs leading for the following decade (Steve "Ajebo" Eboh personal communication, June 8, 2024; Azuka "Ulzee" Odunukwe personal communication, June 3, 2024). During this period of Enugu's dominance, there was a brief period of competition from Aba as well as shooting in the "rural towns" around Onitsha (Haynes 2016, 142; Kenechukwu Okafor interview, December 22, 2015).

A dynamic relationship between filmmakers and homeowners lies at the heart of these phenomena. Before exploring this relationship, it is helpful to recognize that houses held a special significance in Igbo culture long before the advent of the film industry (Bud 2019, 44–52, 71–85). This significance is closely bound up with the events and aftermath of the Biafran War (1967–70). Prior to the war, many Igbo families had lived in other parts of Nigeria and had built homes in such towns as Lagos, Kaduna, and Port Harcourt (D. J. Smith 2005; Uduku 1996). After the war ended, families who had previously owned property outside Igboland were often left with compensation of just twenty pounds. Properties that had previously been owned by Igbos were seized by local people or state governments. A notorious case was the appropriation of much Igbo property in Port Harcourt, which received legal sanction through the Abandoned Property Decree (Chukwuezi 2001; D. J. Smith 2017, 110). These experiences contributed to the popular belief that "no one can make that mistake [of building outside Igboland] again" and great social pressure to concentrate capital in house building back home (D. J. Smith 2005, 38).

This historical experience intersected with other cultural logics related to the generation of wealth. Barber suggests that these sensibilities were awakened in Nigerian society during the oil boom in which people suddenly came into huge fortunes, as if by magic. She identifies two cultural archetypes of wealth: the first is built up through the toil of "real work," and the second is an illegitimate or illusory form of wealth, gained through stealing the hard-won fruits of someone else's labor using witchcraft, deceit, and "fake work" or even not really existing at all (Barber 1982, 44–50).

Within this calculus, a house in one's hometown is an incomparable sensational form for proving real wealth. As one up-and-coming big man who was about to embark on building his own house reflected: "How do I know how successful you are in Brooklyn or London? How do I know? You can come back in Christmas with a bit of money but . . . if I come to your home . . . ok you're doing well" (Buffy Okeke-Ojiudu interview, April 20, 2017).

Proving real wealth is not just about showing that the money was not made up, but also about showing that it was generated and used in a moral way. By merit of their location, hometown houses involve sharing with the community—whether in terms of beautifying the village or contributing to the East in general. Furthermore, they operate as stages for welcoming local residents for festivities, further demonstrating the communal stake in the property. These practices prove that the owner is loyal to his people, and that he can be relied on because he remembers "that home is home" (Ifeanyi Ene interview, December 22, 2015). The sentiment is reflected in several popular aphorisms, including

"Aku ruo ulo, amalu onye kpatara ya" (When your wealth reaches home, we know the bread behind it).

The welcoming of film crews by Enugu homeowners from the mid-1990s can be understood as an extension of these logics (Bud 2021, 32–33, 35–37). The homeowners valued the ability of Nollywood to picture their houses—opening them up and projecting them to a wider audience. By accommodating film productions, they could thus enhance the sense of authenticity around their properties, accrediting themselves as respectable and their wealth as legitimate. They argued that this openness highlighted that they had no need to be corrupt and showed that whatever they were doing was not out of financial necessity. The latter motivation was reflected in my interview with Benson Okonkwo, a homeowner, who wanted to show that he came from a moneyed background and was not working out of desperation. As he recalled: "[I wanted to show that] I was born with a silver spoon, I wanted them to come [inside the house] and see my background and know that I'm not acting because it's my last option to make ends meet" (Benson Okonkwo interview, May 5, 2017).

Houseowners valued Nollywood's ability not only to picture their homes but also to enhance the communal celebrations that were essential in establishing the house's authenticity. They hoped these shared consumption events would be embellished by the actors, whose fame was described as a kind of "realness" that could imbue the occasions (Chijioke Jonas interview, May 19, 2018). Here, the homeowners were less concerned with the filming per se than with the actors' off-duty activities. The phenomenon illustrates how film "production" flowed beyond the confines of shooting to include the long waits before going on camera or relaxing after a day's shoot.

To understand how such relationships developed, it is helpful to explore location managers' procurement processes. Most often, the location manager would make direct contact with the homeowner's wife, who was usually both the organizer of the festivities and the primary gatekeeper to the house. Mrs. Chiamaka Okorie, a leading location manager, described a common negotiating scenario: "Some of the wives will go straight [to the point] . . . and want to know 'Who and who is coming to my house?'" (Chiamaka Okorie interview, May 19, 2017). Once everything was arranged, the hostess would theatrically welcome star actors into her home, prepare meals free of charge, and invite friends to come and join in. Some locations came to be valued not just for their filmic affordances but also for the quality of their hospitality. Mrs. Remi Ajibua-Ajayi, another location manager, noted an example of a house prized by film directors due to the exceptional food and hospitality offered by the hostess, Mrs. Folake Egbage. (Remi Ajibua-Ajayi interview, May 27, 2017).

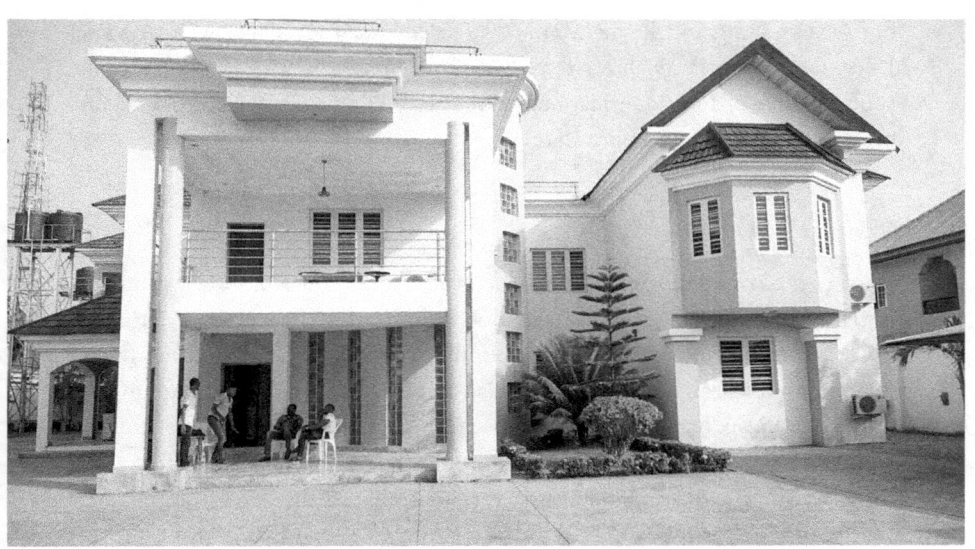

FIGURE 5.2. Nollywood House with column-and-pediment structure with balcony.
Source: *Asaba*, December 2015

The growth of location shooting in Enugu led to an unintended consequence: the emulation of the location houses' styles, with "Nollywood Houses" starting to pop up throughout Igboland. This tendency can be understood as part of a "detailed, appearance-centered mode of watching" (Meyer 2015, 105). Meyer developed this concept after observing similar practices of emulation in Ghana. She was at first surprised that spectators were "not really willing to engage in deep discussions about how to interpret a movie" (104) but rather were interested in using the films to get style tips for their own clothing, interior furnishings, and hairstyles. In the case of Nollywood Houses, some viewers copied the locations from the films' still frames; others contacted the location managers, who would give them more detailed pictures or the architect's contacts. This emulation practice was especially prevalent among prospective homeowners living abroad who wanted to build a village house in a befitting style.

These practices were so ubiquitous that some of the film locations' features came to be widely incorporated into the local architectural vocabulary, with Nollywood Houses mushrooming throughout Igboland. The proliferation of one architectural feature in particular—the front-column-pediment structure with balcony—was strongly linked to the films (figure 5.2). The location manager, Piccolo Oye, illuminated this phenomenon by reflecting on the use of a big Asaban bungalow in the film *More Than a Widow* (Piccolo Oye interview, December 20, 2015). Within a few years of the movie becoming a hit, Piccolo spotted three or four identical bungalows sixty kilometers away in Awka and others elsewhere in Anambra state.

Crisis in the Enugu House Scene

Despite the complementarities between the houses and Nollywood filmmaking, an impasse developed around 2008, leading to the severe restriction of house access in Enugu and the surrounding rural towns. By the time I conducted my research in 2015–17, politician house owners in Enugu had universally withdrawn from the scene, and their properties were now considered "no-goes" (Okorie interview, May 19, 2017). Some owners behaved almost fearfully, "dashing" location managers—or becoming aggressive—just to make the Nollywood people go away. At other times, husbands would outbid the filmmakers—offering their wives up to twice the amount proposed by the producer, just to get rid of the filmmakers.

Instead of authenticating homeowners' wealth, the interaction with the film industry seemed to have had the opposite effect, as long-standing ambiguities around houses were aggravated by Nollywood's own uncertain status. One problem was that Nollywood house owners had expected the films to project a sense of wealth, but their activities came to be viewed as moneymaking schemes indicating desperation. The concern partly reflected an awareness that Nollywood was transforming from a semi-artistic student endeavor into a profitable business. This development was surprising to me as I had expected the primary concern to be the risk of appearing ostentatious. I was enlightened by Benson Okonkwo, who described the logic of his father, the owner of a Nollywood house:

BENSON: [My father] is a Big Man, so he feels like it's a shameful thing for them to be using his house for locations

AB: Is that because it's not good to look too opulent . . . ?

BENSON: [interjects] No! [It's not good to look] too poor! He feels his house should be his privacy, and that the money is not big enough for him, and that he's bigger than that. (Okonkwo interview, May 5, 2017)

A second problem was that the film industry itself had an occultic association that threatened to imbue the houses (Bud 2019, 96–100). The miraculous rise of superstar actors echoed the mysterious ascent of the petro-naira billionaires to the extent that Nollywood was seen as another "get rich quick scheme." In the public imagination, this phenomenon was quickly linked to actors' uncannily deep knowledge of juju (Haynes 2016, 18). Actors and filmmakers fueled these rumors themselves. The director Kenechukwu Okafor, for example, argued that there was "a whole lot of competition in the industry, so some people will [turn to the occult] to be above other people and rise to stardom" (Kenechukwu Okafor interview, April 23, 2018). Simultaneous with the actors' off-set activities, the scenes within the movies were also considered troubling. Some films explicitly linked *ogwu-ego* (blood-money) with the big houses. Many depicted blood-money rituals taking place in secret parts of the houses—a plot element that Haynes describes as Nollywood's "hallmark" (2016, 25).

Mobility in the Nollywood House Scene:
Relocation to Asaba and Other Igbo Towns

In response to the difficulties in Enugu, the Nollywood House scene became mobile, relocating to other regional cities and beyond. Around 2008, many film producers started moving their productions to the Delta State capital of Asaba. By the time I commenced my research in 2015, an estimated 50 to 60 percent of all Nigerian productions were using Asaba locations (Baloebi Bedford interview, June 10, 2015; Haynes 2016, 215). Indeed, there seemed to be a special affinity between Asaba's civic culture and the movie industry, with Nollywood Houses soon taking root there even more successfully than in Enugu. The location managers recognized the "special appreciation" and "love" that Asaba's big men had for the industry and their greater enthusiasm about getting publicity than those in Enugu.

To assess Nollywood Houses' resonance with Asaba, we may acknowledge how the town's political culture contrasted with that of Enugu. Unlike Enugu, which had been a regional capital since the colonial period, Asaba (and its elites) was relatively new—the state and its capital had only been created in 1991. The Asaba homeowners may therefore have seen the welcoming of film actors as a unique way to connect with a global, cosmopolitan world, in contrast to their worldly Enugu counterparts who had more varied possibilities. Some location managers expressed this sentiment more negatively: that the Deltan house owners were less educated and more "bush" than the sophisticated Enugu elite (Bedford interview, June 10, 2015). Local munificence toward Nollywood was further encouraged by a state government policy to support the film industry under Governor Emmanuel Uduaghan (2007–15). This official sanction may have reduced the personal risks to Asaban politicians of offering their houses for filmmaking, and they therefore did not exhibit the same reticence shown by their Enugu counterparts toward the industry.

While Nollywood had a special attraction for Asaba homeowners, Asaba provided distinctive benefits to Nollywood filmmakers. Nollywood had a constant need for fresh houses as film directors did not like to repeat locations and were always on the lookout for new ones (Chinedu Arinze interview, December 15, 2015; Okorie interview, May 19, 2017). This was fed by fear of "Star House syndrome," in which locations were so overused that they became instantly identifiable (Oye interview, December 20, 2015). As a result, the stock of location houses in any given area is exhaustible. Asaba had the advantage of being able to offer vast numbers of new locations because its status as a new state capital had stimulated a building boom that inflated the supply of big new homes as the plentiful land on the city's outskirts was rapidly built on by wealthy Onitsha merchants (Sylvan Ugwumadu interview, April 25, 2017). As the town was hardly used for filming before the middle of the first decade of the 2000s, these new houses constituted fresh, previously unseen filming locations.

Emergent Spaces in Lagos

The higher end of location shooting moved even farther afield, with new housing estates springing up in Lagos that closely integrated Nollywood into both their forms and business models. These were entirely new types of spaces that melded aspects of film studios and living residences in novel ways (Bud 2021). Amen Estate, established in 2008, is a cutting-edge example that has taken this integration to new levels (figure 5.3). In Amen, film crews are allowed to shoot and lodge in houses until they are sold, before adding more location houses to the development. As inputs into Nollywood production, these estates offer a high-end ambience at a relatively low price and often with free electricity.

Amen's version of the Nollywood House represents a highly distinctive sensational form. Before the estate's linkup with the film industry, Amen's owners struggled to market the house plots. Interested clients, many of them in the diaspora, were suspicious of the reality of the estate. Even when the proprietor Babatunde Gbadamosi sent pictures of the houses, they alleged that the estate was a fraudulent fabrication: "[They] write us back insulting us, say fraudsters, Nigerian fraudsters have come again, 419" (Babatunde Gbadamosi interview, May 30, 2017). One prospective owner, thinking he

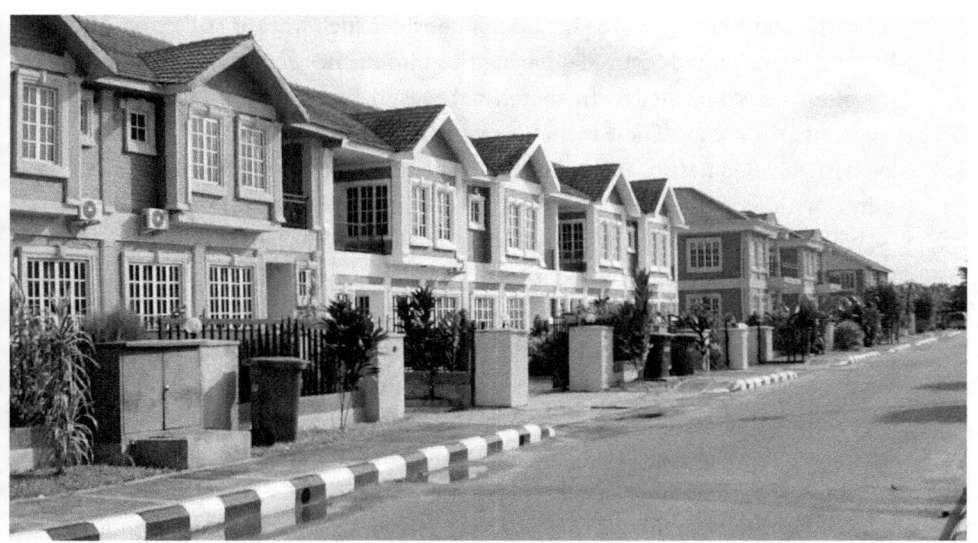

FIGURE 5.3. A street in Amen Estate, Lagos, May 2017. Photo by author

had caught Gbadamosi out, claimed that he recognized one of the houses as being in Atlanta, Georgia.

Allowing Nollywood productions to film proved a pivotal moment in the history of the estate. Surprisingly, it added a sense of concrete reality to the houses: "Getting Nollywood and the music industry to come shoot their movies and their musical videos here was our way of getting people to realize that actually you know what ... this is actually real ... you know, these houses are actually there and it's actually in Nigeria!" (Gbadamosi interview, May 30, 2017).

Counterintuitively, it had been necessary to create a Nollywood fantasy world in order to prove the authenticity of the estate. The phenomenon recalls Birgit Meyer's concept of the camera lens enabling a "special kind of superior vision" that provides insight into what is real beyond the capacity of the naked eye. While the effect in part relied on Nollywood's imaginary worlds, the intrusion of an anchoring reality into the frames was also a key ingredient. Mr. Gbadamosi explained how he comprehended the importance of the latter by accident after allowing a music video production and two films featuring Yomi Gold and Iyabo Ojo onto the estate. He noted that in these first productions, the intrusion of visual cues from the environment helped to subconsciously reinforce the Nigerianness of the scenes. He gave the example of a scene with a simple clothesline in the background, which he described as

"Nigerianism right there!" as he did not consider such lines as still typical of Britain or the United States. Following this finding, he orchestrated (without the filmmakers' knowledge) further visual cues to accidentally on purpose intrude into the scenes. These included cars with Nigerian license plates to drive by or "female domestics" to walk past in the background, making the viewer think, "wait a minute, that's not the average English pedestrian!"

Nollywood's relationship with Amen also had a striking effect in remolding the form of the houses. The decor in all Amen properties had originally been in beige and neutral pastel shades. However, acting on the advice of the entrepreneurial location manager Mrs. Remi Ajibua-Ajayi, Mr. Gbadamosi agreed for the location houses' interiors to be redecorated. The formerly subdued interiors were thus transformed with new paint jobs in bright, distinctive colors with matching duvets, sheets, and soft furnishings (figure 5.4). This contrast benefited the films' storylines by providing immediate visual cues implying that the action was unfolding in separate places. Unexpectedly, the innovation was a hit not only with filmmakers but also with prospective homeowners coming to see former location homes. As a result, Mr. Gbadamosi soon decided to apply this style to all the estate's houses.

Fabrication of Interiors for Studio Sets

Amen Estate reflects the growing trend of the adaptation of interiors for filming. This phenomenon has reached new heights with the emergence of a full-fledged studio system based in Lagos. While the kind of productions in the new studios are not necessarily ones that would previously have been filmed in the East, the developments reflect a common dynamic of industry concentration and—related to this—the sense that traditional locations are increasingly inadequate.

Several large studios have emerged since around 2008. The leading facilities are Ultima in Lekki, MNET in Ikeja, ROK in Kosofe, and EbonyLife in central Victoria Island, with other prominent examples including Rapid Blue, Royal Roots, Koga, Ten 'O' One, and Nigezie Studios. Filmmakers have been somewhat slower than their television counterparts to adopt studio production, but they are moving in this direction. Over the past decade, the country's most successful film production team of the director Kunle Afolayan and the art director Pat Nebo has made extensive use of temporary studios for their big-budget productions. Moreover, the dividing line between film and television is both blurred and permeable in the Nigerian landscape. The hugely popular studio-shot television show *Tinsel*, for example, is in many ways a successor to

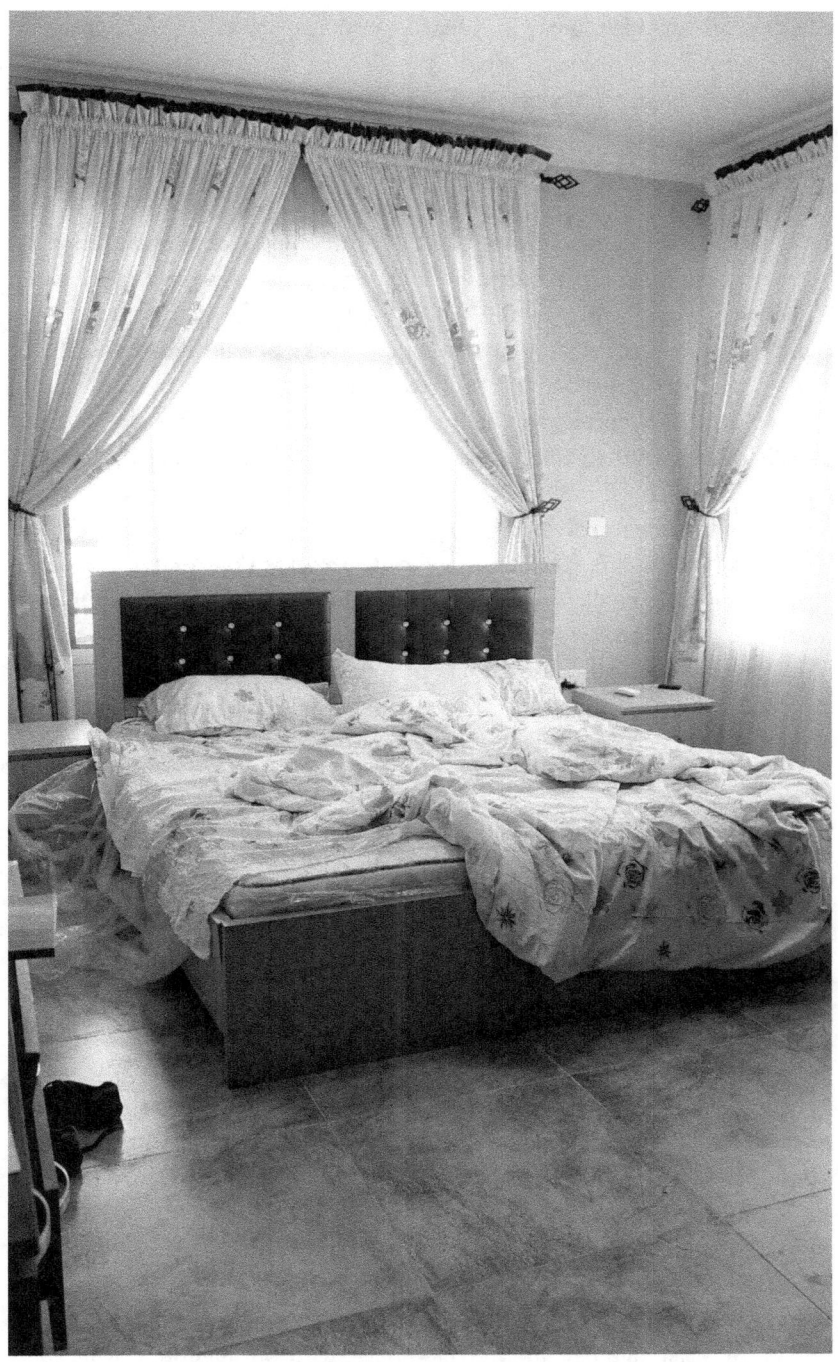

FIGURE 5.4 A color-coordinated bedroom with matching duvets, sheets, and soft furnishings in Amen Estate, Lagos, May 2017. Additional images at www.screenworlds.org.

earlier genres of video-film, which have recently declined in the face of significant concentration in the industry.

The dynamic in creating the studio-set world has been almost the inverse of that of the locations. Whereas the location film world emerged through filmmakers entering real-life houses, the studio-set world emerged through real-life architects, designers, and craftsmen entering the filmic space of the studio building. The set designers were usually professional architects, interior designers, or fine artists with degrees from federal and international universities. Their employees were generally skilled craftsmen in carpentry, upholstery, painting, and metalworking who had completed traditional apprenticeships or higher national diplomas at local polytechnics. This dynamic contrasted with that of location shooting, in which the small number of "set and prop men" usually came into their roles having been aspiring actors rather than professional fabricators.

While the set workers had brought skills into the studio from their outside work, the studio's specificity soon came to mark their practice in meaningful ways. The challenge that perhaps preoccupied the set builders most was building sets to have a specific quality, which we might term *filmability*. Whereas conventional house carpenters were replicating mediations (such as from catalogs), these set carpenters were also originating them. The house carpentry process simply involved copying furnishings *from* pictures (in catalogs), but set carpentry also involved producing furnishings *for* pictures. The set craftsmen were fascinated by this specific challenge of creating furnishings not for the immediate needs of the eye but, rather, for those of the lens, strongly echoing Meyer's concept of the camera's "superior type of vision." This imperative led to the application of new techniques and significant skill upgrading. The resulting filmability aesthetic comprised a heightened degree of precision, the creation of illusions, new color schemes, and soft and shiny materials (figure 5.5).

A curious development of the new set aesthetic has been its reproduction in *off-camera* arenas—for regular (nonfilmed) domestic interiors and farther afield. The mechanism for reproducing this aesthetic can be categorized according to three types of flows: those of materials, pictures/images, and skills.

Turning to material flows, furnishings created for film/TV sets had an afterlife as they were disseminated, usually as home furnishings. Some set designers chose to keep a store of props and furnishings in their houses and lease them out. Both Mr. Bedford and Hilary Patricks engaged in such leasing businesses, and there was a high demand for the service, with Mr. Bedford leasing some of his furnishings five or six times. It also became common for a production's

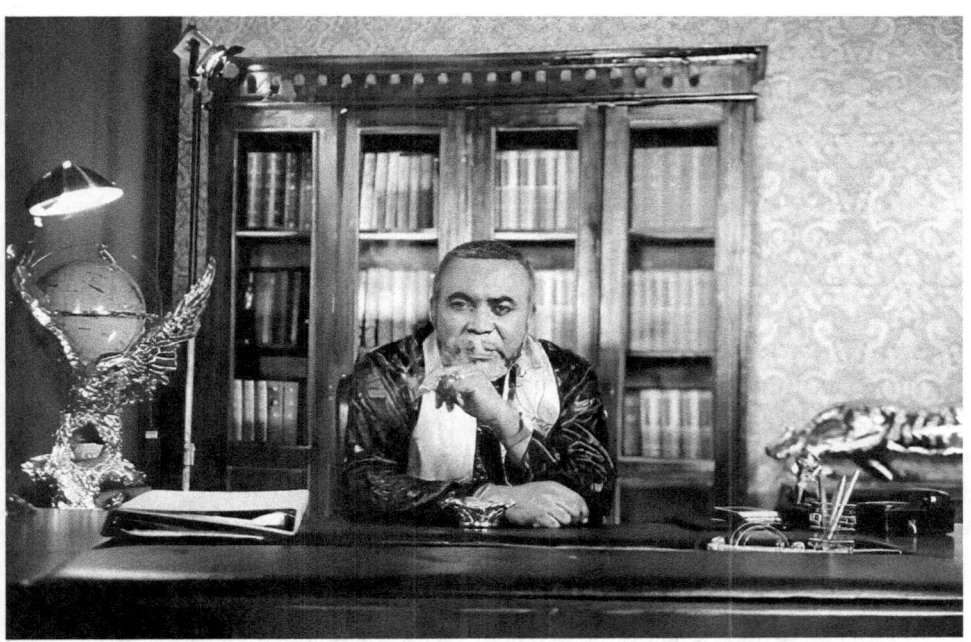

FIGURE 5.5. Hilary Patricks used illusion to construct a "book cabinet" from boxes and printed paper for *Casino*. Additional images at www.screenworlds.org.

crew to bid—sometimes very competitively—for the set and props once the show had finished.

In other cases, the aesthetic was reproduced through the flow of pictures and images leading to renewed fabrication. Third parties who saw the sets on-screen would independently re-create them as domestic interiors. Before he started working on sets, carpenter Moses would watch the sets with a keen interest and would "cram it in my [Moses' own] head" before reproducing it for clients. This practice was widespread: Mr. Bedford, for example, noticed that the furniture and bedspreads he created for the show *Project Fame* regularly became the popular style for the following year's interiors. During my time with him in 2015, he found examples at the Alaba International and Airport Road markets in a near-identical style to those he had made for the previous year's show.

Third, the filmability aesthetic was reproduced through a flow of skills as set workers diversified into—or returned to—interior furnishings. This process could occur through the "push" of the set man's independent entrepreneurial decision to reapply his skills. For example, set-designer Opejemi Daniel described how "as a set man, I now have the flair for colors, the eye for colors and qualities, and how to place things. . . . I do the same for sets, homes, boutiques, for a small hotel" (Opejemi Daniel interview, June 9, 2015). Similarly, Hilary Patricks described how he applied his set aesthetic to use motor parts, frosted glass, and a chrome fill to create a desk for a singer in Ikeja (Hilary Patricks interview, June 8, 2015). In some cases, these ventures were systematically organized as an entire studio-set team would transplant itself to work on home furnishing jobs in a private capacity.

Alternatively, the set designer could be "pulled" into home furnishing by market demand. These cases encompass an entwined flow of images and skills. Members of the public who had seen the set worker's creations on-screen would contact him to produce something similar for a domestic interior. The set man Sean Israel described this experience: "[In one movie] I created a shop—called Caroline Shoes. I had a printed banner. I put my phone number on the banner, so . . . every day, recently, I keep getting calls, they see the number on the banner—they want me to build that shop" (Sean Israel interview, December 23, 2015). Often these third parties would reach the set worker by first approaching the studio, whose social media managers would pass the inquiry on to the relevant carpenter. In this sense, the studio would act as a kind of agency for the carpenters.

In a variant of the "pull" factor, the carpenters—who otherwise struggled for visibility—benefited from their own professional brands being imbued with the studios' aura. Customers impressed by the carpenters' association with top shows would seek them out, even if they were not interested in a specific set. For example, Yemi, the *Project Fame* upholsterer, described how he benefited from his Ultima Studios connection, with potential clients asking around for "the one that do all the *Project Fame* shows!" (Bayemi Akinola interview, August 6, 2015)

Conclusion

In this chapter, I have offered a new interpretation of Nollywood's circulations, with reference to the concept of the meshwork. We saw early in the chapter that Tim Ingold proposed the meshwork approach partly due to his objection to the category of nodes. As an alternative, he has suggested the notion of knots, which are points at which the meshwork's lines entangle with each other. Unlike in a node, these knots are not static junctions at which the lines terminate but temporary comings together as "every line overtakes the knot in which it is tied. Its end is always loose, somewhere beyond the knot" (Ingold 2013, 132). In this regard, I sketch out six genres of house, each of which represents a distinctive knotting together of different threads.

The first two of these "houses" reflect the knotting together of the flows of performance and residential living. In the "location house" where filmmakers shot their movies, the world of filmed performance flowed into and imprinted the property. In parallel, the "movie-scene house," where the off-duty filmmakers lived or socialized, reflected the flow of nonfilmed off-stage lived performance into the home. Both of these circulations left an aura around the houses, which remained after the performances had circulated through them.

The next two houses reflect the flowing together of the living residences with the chains of pictures and images. In the "fan house," movie lovers took inspiration from houses they had seen on-screen by rematerializing them in their own homes. Then, in Amen Estate, we saw the "fantasy house," in which the flows of pictures and images combined with those of not-yet-living residences to produce the astonishing result of transforming these residences into fully living ones. After the pictures of the buildings were broadcast, this flow looped back toward the very same houses that were being depicted, imbuing them with a sense of reality to the extent that they were purchased by customers.

There are also two houses that constitute entanglements related to fabrication. The "studio house" was a house-like environment in which controlled shooting took place. This house involved the flows of materials as well as skills from carpentry that were adapted to meet the needs of filmability. Lastly, in the "designer house," set workers reapplied their skills to interior design and home furnishings projects beyond the film world. The carpentry skills that had originated in the living residences and had flowed into the studios were now running back into the residences, imbuing them with filmability even though no filming was taking place.

As a final thought, I return to the theme of materiality. The infrastructure model proposed by Larkin encompasses a network of immaterial flows through or within solid material structures (cables) or carriers (videotapes). Ingold, by contrast, proposes a model in which "materiality" is not assumed to connote "solidity" but also encompasses fluidity. Here materials do not constitute the infrastructure that undergird flow; rather, they *are* the flow (Ingold and Simonetti 2022).

At first glance, houses—conceptualized as bounded objects providing the stages for filmmaking and other human activity—constitute an archetypal example of infrastructure. This orientation has even been extended to the whole of the material world, so that "the furniture of the earth [is] like the furnishings of a room" (J. J. Gibson 1979, 78). Ingold, however, suggests an extraordinary inversion of this metaphor. Extending the organic model of meshworks, he draws a parallel with "the tree," which is seemingly also a very solid isolated object. Yet trees have no clear boundaries with the rest of the living world: their bark is inhabited by millions of tiny insects burrowing inside, and their branches are full of birds building their nests. The metaphor of the tree also foregrounds the house's fluid historical development rather than the designs of architects or intentions of political actors. Its very form—the configuration of the tree's branches, the lines in its trunk and knots in its wood—embodies the unfolding of flows that occurred throughout the "entire history of its development from the moment it took root" (Ingold 1993, 168; 2010, 4).

The point is that rather than conceptualizing the natural world as a house, we should instead see the house as a tree: "The real house is never finished . . . indeed not unlike the tree, the real house is a gathering of lives, and to inhabit it is to join in the gathering" (Ingold 2010, 5). In this sense, the Nollywood Houses are treelike in nature. There are no clear distinctions between the knotted threads of houses, filmmaking, socializing, and carpentry. Instead of classifying the Nollywood House as an infrastructure, it can therefore be rechristened as a "treehouse."

ACKNOWLEDGMENTS

I offer sincerest gratitude to the research participants who welcomed me with great openness to the Nollywood community. I received outstanding support from advisors, friends, and research assistants Peggy Ekene Godwin, Victoria Okpara, Stephen Ikeogu, Bedford Baloebi, Gerald Uloneme, Williams Omolu, Leo Spartani, Peter Eze, and Kennechukwu Okafor; the Creative Designers Guild of Nigeria; and host families Taiwo and Banke Lawal and Stephen and Theresa Oshilaga.

The following academics gave helpful advice and generously shared their work: David Wield, José-María Muñoz, Paul Nugent, Giles Mohan, Ola Uduku, Françoise Ugochukwu, Chinwe Sam-Amobi, and Alessandro Jedlowski. I also thank Lindiwe Dovey and the African Screen Worlds team for their industry and helpfulness in editing this chapter.

The following key informants generously contributed to this project: location managers Chiamaka Okorie, Sylvan Ugwumadu, Chimeze Bright, Chinedu Arinze, Piccolo Chidese Oye, Toni Ikechi, and Remi Ajibua-Ajayi; hoteliers Anthony Okeke-Ojiudu, Martins Onyebuchi Onyemaobi, Julie Obiagele Okenwa, Michael Adigwe, Buffy Okeke-Ojiudu, Michael Amadi, Boniface Uchechukwu, and Anthony Okoli; homeowners Babatunde Gbadamosi, Benson Okonkwo, Shiela Egemonye, Alex Egbonike, and Mary Ukaego Odili; marketers Steve "Ajebo" Eboh and Azuka "Ulzee" Odunukwe; and set designers Pat Nebo, Opeyemi Daniel, Hilary Patricks, Odejemi Oluwa Seun, Sean Israel, Bayemi Akinola, and the set construction teams at F4D Productions and MNET Studios.

NOTES

Please see www.screenworlds.org for images and further audiovisual materials in color that complement this chapter and other parts of this book.

1 Such a claim may seem surprising given that Larkin intersperses his argument with the language of culture and affect and elliptical references to "historical layering of networks" and "reciprocal engagement" (Larkin 2008, 6, 252; P. N. Edwards et al. 2011, 1400). However, in the actual implementation of his arguments, the cultural practices convene *around* the infrastructures and are essentially complying with or reacting to the technological or disciplining forces. The infrastructure of piracy, for example, "*imposes* a particular experience" of powerlessness and marginality through infrastructural breakdown (Larkin 2008, 233). In his recent work, Larkin similarly gestures toward "culture" by invoking Lindiwe Dovey's work on film festivals as examples of "cultural infrastructure" (Larkin 2019). But here he hollows out the cultural so that film festivals are reduced to technological "formats" and curators become passive entities who merely respond to the requirements of the system. In so doing, he obliterates Dovey's concept of "liveness" that encapsulates the moments of spontaneous multiauthorship entwining curators, filmmakers, and audiences (Dovey 2015b).

INTERVIEWS

Ajibua-Ajayi, Remi. Interview, May 27, 2017.

Akinola, Bayemi. Interview, August 6, 2015.

Arinze, Chinedu. Interview, December 15, 2015.

Bedford, Baloebi. Interview, June 10, 2015

Daniel, Opejemi. Interview, June 9, 2015.

Eboh, Steve "Ajebo." Personal communication, June 8, 2024.

Ene, Ifeanyi. Interview, December 22, 2015.

Gbadamosi, Babatunde. Interview, May 30, 2017.

Israel, Sean. Interview, December 23, 2015.

Jonas, Chijioke. Interview, May 19, 2018.

Odunukwe, Azuka "Ulzee." Personal communication, June 3, 2024.

Okafor, Kenechukwu. Interview, December 22, 2015.

Okafor, Kenechukwu. Interview, April 23, 2018.

Okeke-Ojiudu, Buffy. Interview, April 20, 2017.

Okonkwo, Benson. Interview, May 5, 2017.

Okorie, Chiamaka. Interview, May 19, 2017.

Oye, Piccolo. Interview, December 20, 2015.

Patricks, Hilary. Interview, June 8, 2015.

Ugwumadu, Sylvan. Interview, April 25, 2017.

6

Entrepreneurialism and Enterprise

Film Students Redefining Ghana's Creative Landscape

DENNIS-BROOK PRINCE LOTSU

Building on Alexander Bud's study of craft and creativity in relation to Nollywood "treehouses" in the previous chapter, this chapter focuses on the craft and creativity of film students in Ghana, particularly through mobilizing new technologies (such as WhatsApp) to distribute their own screen worlds to broader audiences. Drawing on popular genres such as comedy and romantic comedy, young filmmakers such as Peter Sedufia have found widespread fame, with millions of viewers appreciating their films on digital platforms such as YouTube.

Since 2010, film and media education in Ghana experienced liberalization, just like the film industry. The National Film and Television Institute (NAFTI), Ghana's premier film school, lost its monopoly not only to traditional universities running film, media, and television programs but also to film schools such as the GH Media School, the Accra Film School, the Multimedia Institute of Ghana, Insite Media College, and Doxa Open University (Abro Media Campus).[1] These film and media training institutions annually churn out graduates, many of whom settle for mainstream radio and television employment due to the lack of available jobs in the film sector. The challenge for these institutions thus becomes equipping students with entrepreneurial and vocational skills to create their own work in the film sector.

My encounter with this task and the question of graduates transitioning into mainstream media and other ancillary professions instead of making films occurred in my film producing class in 2012, a year after I joined NAFTI as a staff member from a mainstream public relations and advertising company.[2] To address students' posteducation employment anxieties, I introduced, as part of the producing curriculum, film proposal package development for independent film financing. During the semester, we explored pitching, budgeting, project management techniques, and leveraging new media affordance for branding and social engagement. For me, it was just an exciting pedagogical encounter of sharing ideas, strategies, and some of the experiences I have gained in the private sector; but that was not the thinking of these enthusiastic students, as we shall see in the coming sections.

A significant development of this era was Ghana's rising smartphone, internet, and mobile data penetration, at this writing pegged at 83.9 percent (National Communications Authority 2020). With this came increased subscription rates and purveyance of social media platforms, such as Facebook, Twitter (now X), Instagram, WhatsApp, and Snapchat. The total number of Ghanaians accessing social media via smartphones, as of January 2020, was said to be 6 million (Kemp 2020). Furthermore, the introduction of WhatsApp messaging technology in 2009 has significantly transformed interpersonal communication and redefined the performance and enactment of relationships in Ghana (Yeboah and Ewur 2014). Its gradual proliferation in Ghana by 2013 has remarkably impacted commerce, education, and the creative industries. As I shall discuss, the penetration of mobile phones and social media applications has rapidly altered the consumption of media content. Nevertheless, these same conditions have also "created new opportunities for movie consumptions in places people would never have guessed a few years back" (Kozlowski 2012). One such opportunity is the development of a "supersmall screen" phenomenon (see Dovey 2018), which has reconfigured the distribution, circulation, and promotion of films through the use of social media applications on phones, which allows for the distribution of video films from a sender to a single recipient or multiple recipients. The young filmmakers explored here capitalize on these current technological affordances to offer an alternative distribution and exhibition model while also seeking to participate in mainstream filmmaking.

The Interface of Pedagogy and Experimentation: Kofi Asamoah and Peter Sedufia

In 2013, a group of NAFTI students, led by two of my directing students, Kofi Asamoah and Peter Sedufia, audaciously embarked on the production of skits and short films as part of practicing their craft outside the confines of the classroom. The series, *Boys Kasa: The Adventures of Kalybos*, follows the comic escapades of Kalybos (Richard Asante), a wannabe rich braggart who tries to impress and woo the beautiful Ahuofe Patri (Priscilla Opoku-Agyeman).[3] Shot with portable DSLR cameras and a microphone, the videos were edited and circulated among students and teachers of NAFTI via the WhatsApp messaging platform. Due to their positive reception, the duo, with the assistance of other students, began making more of these videos and distributing them more widely through WhatsApp. By relying on the broadcast functionality of WhatsApp, which allows subscribers to create end-to-end broadcasts to send to multiple recipients, these budding filmmakers disseminated the skits to their contacts, who in turn rebroadcast to others in a cartelized distribution manner. To deepen the reach of these videos, Asamoah and Sedufia established virtual distribution channels consisting of the actors, production crew, and friends outside the chain of production who champion the redistribution of the videos to their contacts. Through this methodical process of distribution, the videos were circulated in a multiplex-like flow within this chain of distributors. Snowballing gradually, this model of video dissemination gained popularity as the videos became accepted forms of entertainment among students at the various university communities. The success of the *Boys Kasa* series marked an important interface between film pedagogy and practice, as students from other film training institutes and universities soon joined this new film culture by not only helping with the distribution of contents emerging from the NAFTI campus but also producing their own.

Notwithstanding the high cost of data and slow bandwidth transmission challenges, these videos registered huge successes for several reasons. The epoch's ever-dwindling volume of quality English-language feature films for predominantly local-language (Twi) movies, popularly termed *Kumawood* (Yamoah 2014), made these skits staples beyond the university communities. *Boys Kasa*'s characteristic blend of English and Twi, spiced with the quotidian romantic and sociocultural experiences of the urban youth, made these videos wildly popular and positioned them at the intersection of the everyday and personal, as they became transportable objects of entertainment. With the country's 43 million mobile connections and 50 percent internet penetration, these videos witnessed an explosion among 89.3 percent of Ghana's internet users and garnered an estimated viewership that ranged between 25,000 and 1.2 million on YouTube.[4] The main characters (Kalybos and Ahuofe Patri) soon gained popularity and instant celebrity status, with endorsement contracts with Airtel Ghana Limited (a telecommunications company), iTel Mobile (from 2017 to 2018), Dropyn (a local rideshare company), and Read More GH (an online bookstore).

The experimentations of these filmmakers paid off, particularly for Peter Sedufia, who graduated from skits to other formats within a short time. Relying on the support and expertise of his fellow students and deploying the same distribution frameworks mentioned earlier, Sedufia ventured into the production and dissemination of short films, *Percher* (2013) and *Hi-MUMMY* (2014), via WhatsApp and YouTube. The reception of these films on YouTube, however, fell far short (between 109 and 3,234 views) of the explosion witnessed with the *Boys Kasa* series. Perhaps the low patronage in this case stemmed from Sedufia's switch to the paranormal genre instead of the romantic comedy with which audiences have associated him.

Recognizing the audiences' distaste for the paranormal, Sedufia returned, in 2014, with another short film conceived purposely for film festivals and conceptualized within the realms of romantic comedy. *The Traveller* (2014), which recounts the unsuccessful attempts of an itinerant musician at a romantic relationship, is a heartwarming tale of unrequited love and the desire for companionship; after extensive circulation through festivals, it was later released on YouTube. Told by the musician, the narrative is heightened by the self-reflexivity and emotional authenticity of the character. Aesthetically, Sedufia's cinematographic approach invokes the visual tone of the classic Ghanaian film *Love Brewed in the African Pot* (dir. Kwaw Ansah, 1981), bringing nostalgic appeal. Through its warm golden patina of visuals, the film transports the viewer on a meditative journey to experience the hope and loss of the characters. With its limited dialogue but philosophical and lyrical narration, coupled with a soundscape that heightens phantasmagorical sequences, the success of *The Traveller* at international film festivals came as no surprise. At the 2015 edition of the Pan-African Film and Television Festival of Ouagadougou (FESPACO), the film won the Special Jury Prize while also winning Best Film at the Emergence Africa Film Festival (2015) and second prize at the Accra Francophone Film Festival (2015).

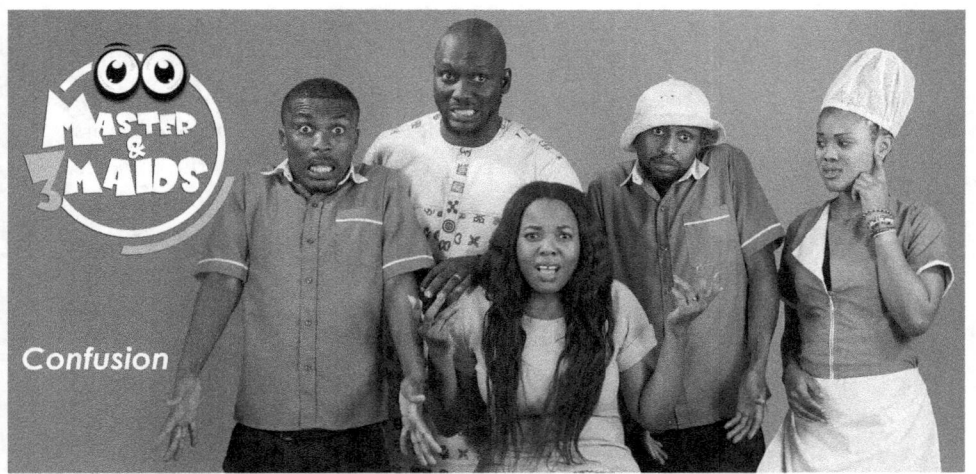

FIGURE 6.1. Promotional poster for *Master and 3 Maids*. Courtesy of Peter Sedufia.

Following *The Traveller*'s successful exhibition via festival circuits, Sedufia ventured, yet again, into the production of another comedy, *Master and 3 Maids* (2016) (see figure 6.1). This sitcom charts the humorous schemes and devices of three maids (Suarez, Zeenab, and DJ) as they navigate the never-ending ploys of their stingy master to terminate their employment because of their constant buffoonery. While the master's wife, madam, manages to recognize the schemes of the maids, the master, at every turn, falls victim to the maids' witty, comical remarks and orchestrations. With every sequence spiced up with situational humor, the first season of the family-oriented series received over 3.4 million views on YouTube. Although this level of viewership may seem insignificant by global standards, the release of the series at a time when many stakeholders were lamenting the dearth of locally produced films signaled Sedufia's bold and decisive move to transform his filmmaking.[5]

Although *Master and 3 Maids* was initially conceptualized as a web series for circulation on YouTube, the success of its first season propelled Sedufia to national prominence and earned him, three years later, television broadcast and theatrical release deals with Multimedia Group's Joy Prime Channel and the Silverbird Cinema, respectively. At the launch of the sitcom for television broadcast in 2018, Nana Yaa Serwaa Sarpong, the manager of Joy Prime Channel, observed: "*Master and 3 Maids* is close to our hearts, and it explores the usual Ghanaian life in a comical, yet creative way" (cited in Mortey 2018). This sentiment was echoed by Ken Fiati (who portrays the master in the sitcom) at the launch when he acknowledged that "there is too much political and religious voice all over. This is what we need for relaxation. It's a family program with hilarious moments fused with laughter" (cited in Mortey 2018). While some viewers praise the sitcom's young and versatile ensemble of actors (Ama Ablorde, Stacy Mawuse Afful, and Nii Addy), particularly the comedic actor Clemento Suarez, others celebrate its didactic values and focus on Ghana's cultural and social relations. Ghanaians' reception of the sitcom points to a heightened audience appetite for accessible, transportable, and short narrative forms that are devoid of the period's "Pentecostalite social imaginary" (Meyer 2002, 81), "occult forces," and fantasy style narratives (Meyer 2015, 176).

The period's rising penetration of internet, mobile, and smartphone technology created opportunities that Asamoah and Sedufia availed themselves of, to market themselves and distribute their experimental projects to audiences in formats that are downloadable, sharable, and accessible.[6] In fact, what started as experimentation with skits and short films cascaded and influenced other students and filmmakers who exploited the digital affordances of social media and social networking sites to distribute short films and web series, including *What's Up* (dir. Horla Manuvor Jr., 2016), *Dzigbeza* (dir. Eyram Adorkor, 2016), *Kejetia and Makola* (dir. Louis Lamis, 2017), *Forkboyz* (dir. Isaac Agyapong, 2019), *Inside Life* (dir. Horla Manuvor Jr., 2021), *Hashtag Series* (dir. Cheif Imanuke and Bismark Idan, 2021), and *Camouflage* (dir. Horla Manuvor Jr., 2021). While some of these commenced distribution via WhatsApp, like the pioneering *Boys Kasa*, others circulated solely through YouTube. The mobile phone, tablet, and laptop screens of audiences have, through these inventive strategies, become synonymous with mini-theaters, as their high-definition resolution, color display, and wide stereo playback functionalities enable Ghanaians with mobile connections on smart gadgets to stream videos on the go (Kemp 2021). This model thus presents a platform through which distribution and exhibition converge while cultivating new cinema audiences. As most of the new cinema audiences fall within the youth demographic, the contents of these skits and web series soon dominated conversations among students, bloggers, and tech-savvy netizens on social media platforms.

From Experimentation through Social Media to Mainstream Filmmaking

While still widening their visibility in the burgeoning moviemaking sector and charting the experimental model described earlier in this chapter, Asamoah and Sedufia have also made mainstream cinema fare with their debut feature-length films, *Kalybos in China* (2015) and *Keteke* (2017), respectively. *Kalybos in China* is a romantic comedy, a spin-off of the *Adventures of Kalybos*, in which the protagonist travels to China for greener pastures but encounters misfortunes. In *Keteke*, a comedic period drama, we witness an expectant couple (Boi and Atwe) attempt to catch a train from their village to the city to have their baby delivered. At a time when film production in Ghana was deemed unprofitable or narratives were criticized for being filled with visions of blood, sex, and money (Meyer 2003), the release of these films marked the beginning of experimentations with new aesthetic strategies and models of exhibition and distribution. The appeal of *Keteke* and its connection with both a local and a global audience, for instance, stem from the simplicity of the narrative and its seamless progression. Like Sedufia's earlier work *The Traveller*, *Keteke*'s tungsten-veneered visual aesthetic creates a nostalgic aura that transports audiences into 1980s Ghana with a single infrequent rail line commute connecting different towns and villages to the capital city, Accra. The narrative offers humorous and suspenseful moments that help sustain the interest of the viewers and heighten audiences' identification with the characters' appearance and scenarios. Boi's signature Afro coiffure and classic faded leather jacket over baggy trousers, and Atwe's plaited hairdo and wax print dress, evoke the 1980s' vibrant fusion of traditional and contemporary men's high-life styles and the loose-fitting, empire-waisted Ankara maternity dresses of expectant mothers, respectively (see figure 6.2). The historical identification instigated through costume and makeup is further complicated via humorous dialogue that leaves local viewers in stitches. For instance, upon hearing the approaching train, Boi dashes for the tracks and yells out to his wife, "Run! Do as I do, run. Hurry, hurry," momentarily oblivious to the conditions of his pregnant wife, who follows suit with much difficulty.

At the same time, Sedufia's films speak to the younger generation of cinephiles through serious subtexts. In an interview about *Keteke*, Sedufia says:

> With a lot of films nowadays, there is an assumption that if you are making a love story it [must] be showing sex. With *Keteke*, there is a demonstration of love but not through sex, and when the film came out it seemed what Ghanaians have been yearning [for]. I thought it was important to make it satirical and give audiences something to laugh about. But while they laugh, I also wanted them to look at the subtext and reflect on that. One thing I didn't want to do was satisfy a European fantasy of what an African film should be. (cited in Osei-Bempong 2017)

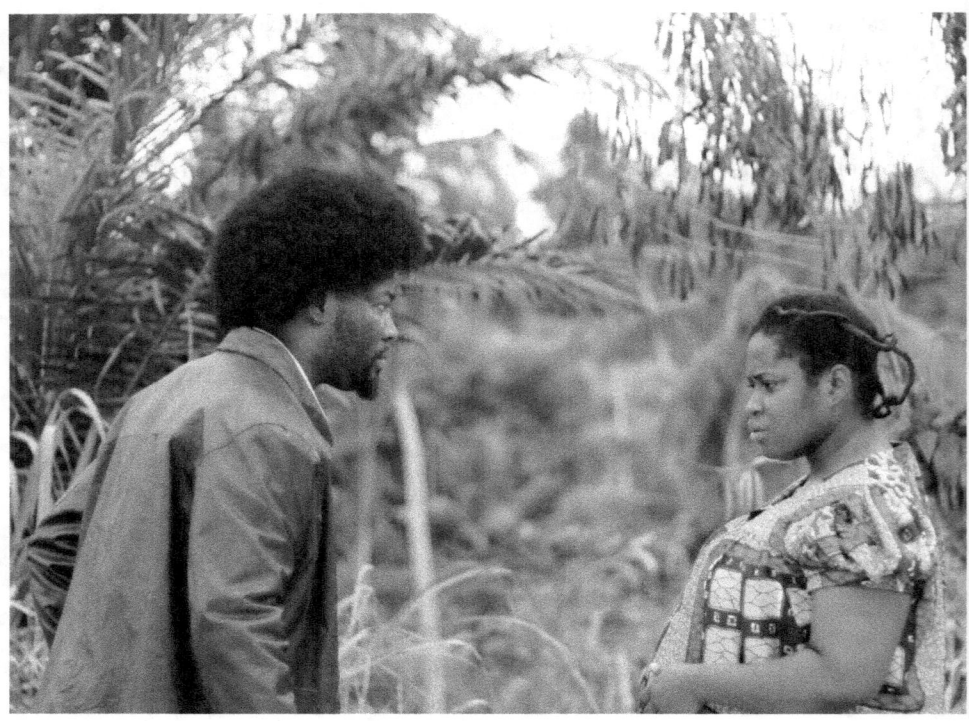

FIGURE 6.2. In this scene from *Keteke*, Boi scolds his expectant wife, Atwe, for making them miss the last train. Image courtesy of Peter Sedufia.

This film shot Sedufia to fame through its winning of several national and international awards, such as Best Film at the Festival International du Cinéma et de l'Audiovisuel du Burundi (2017), Best Editing and Best Sound at the Golden Movie Awards (2017), Best Actress at the Africa International Film Festival in Nigeria (2017), and the Best Jury Prize at the Luxor Africa Film Festival in Egypt (2018).

Subsequently, Sedufia produced *Sidechic Gang* (2018), featuring an all-female pseudodetective team comprising Pokuaa (Nana Ama McBrown), Baaba (Lydia Forson), and Fela (Sika Osei) and coproduced with Kofi Asamoah, and *Away Bus* (2019)—a story of two sisters who get involved in a highway bus robbery to save their dying mother (see figure 6.3). The business of the trio, who investigate infidelity in *Sidechic Gang,* commences when Pokuaa chances on the philandering husband of her friend and reports him to the wife. Out of appreciation for delivering the heartbreaking news, the team receives a hefty

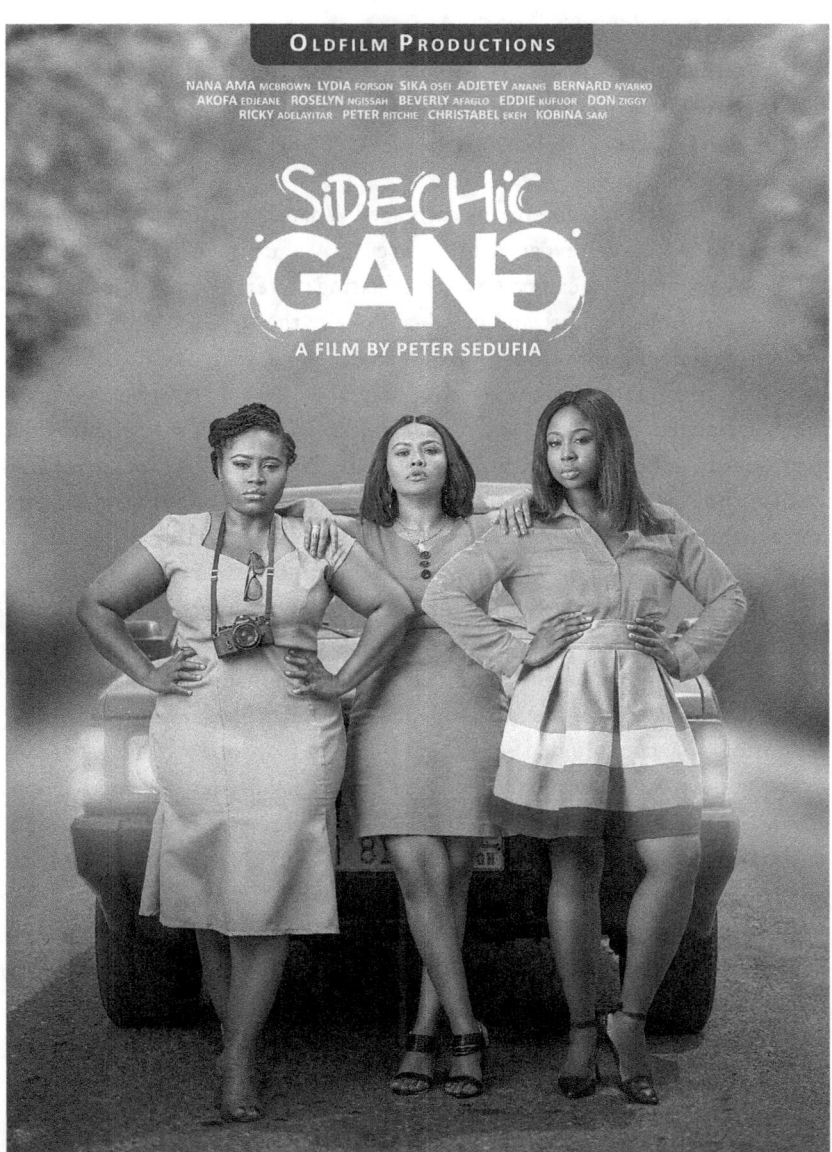

FIGURE 6.3. Promotional poster for *Sidechic Gang*. Courtesy of Peter Sedufia.

reward, which becomes the startup money for the detective agency. The modus operandi of the lady detectives is reminiscent of the exploits of Botswana's first-ever female detective, Precious Ramotswe, in BBC One's *The No. 1 Ladies' Detective Agency* (2009), a show based on the novels of Alexander McCall Smith.

Relying on social media and the cartelized WhatsApp distribution channels used with their earlier experimental projects, Asamoah and Sedufia pursued aggressive promotional campaigns by circulating posters, trailers, and endorsement videos from the cast and crew—a strategy that enabled them to make reasonable box office revenues, for the Ghanaian context. For instance, Kofi Asamoah's second feature film, *Amakye and Dede* (2016), sold 9,581 tickets, grossing an estimated US$49,557 via theatrical release. The narrative chronicles the escapades of two friends (Amakye and Dede) who fall in love with the same woman (Emefa) while each pretends to be someone they are not: a politician and a mechanic. *Keteke* and *Sidechic Gang* sold 2,853 and 7,642 tickets, representing total grosses of about US$43,103 and US$60,345, respectively. Asamoah's third feature, *John and John* (2017), however, dropped in theatrical admittance (6,556) due to accusations of plagiarism.[7] While it is important to acknowledge that these revenues are really not much by international standards, especially after cinemas have taken their commission, the duo made gains that surpassed renowned Ghanaian filmmaker Shirley Frimpong-Manso's *Potato Potahto* (4,611 tickets), which was released in the same year (data from Silverbird Cinema, Ghana, 2018). The inadequacy of revenue gains explains why these filmmakers need a multipronged strategy. For instance, after the theatrical release of their films at the Silverbird Cinemas in Accra, the filmmakers embarked on nationwide tours through major towns and cities, screening these films for audiences in makeshift venues such as town halls, university auditoriums, hotel conference rooms, and church auditoriums. They thus deploy exhibition models akin to the cinema-van strategy of the colonial and early postindependence era (Rice 2016) not only to cultivate their audience base but also to expand the reach of their films and generate interest in cinema. Sales of DVDs, which were a mainstay during the early video-boom era but were bedeviled by piracy, have become the last resort after filmmakers have exploited all other exhibition and distribution options. And during the 2019 edition of the Black Stars International Film Festival in Accra, Ghana, Sedufia revealed that although he does not gain financially from the practice, he is pleased to get his craft known by releasing skits on YouTube and WhatsApp, which is very fulfilling because it enables him to stay relevant in the filmmaking business (Peter Sedufia interview, August 17, 2019).[8] Thus, even after making his way to the big screen and the mainstream, winning awards, and gaining popularity, Sedufia continues to release skits between feature-length film projects.

Although these filmmakers commenced at the periphery of mainstream film praxis, their clever use of technology has propelled them into the limelight, as they have instigated new consumption patterns. Of particular interest here is that they have adopted and created "unofficial" (Adejunmobi 2007), private, and "unstructured" (Dovey 2015b; 2018) circuits of exhibition and distribution. They continue to seek new screening opportunities, such as through airlines and VOD platforms. For instance, *Keteke* was selected for in-flight entertainment platforms (such as on KLM, Emirates, Qatar Airways, Ethiopian Airlines, Royal Air Maroc, Rwandan Airways, Kenyan Airways, Tunis Air, Air Mauritius, Delta Airlines, and Air France) and has also been screened via online platforms such as CongaTV and Kwesé.[9]

As part of deepening audience engagement with *Keteke*, Sedufia also initiated a movie poster challenge that invited the public to design and submit their poster designs for the film. Winners in the competition were later invited to intern with Sedufia's OldFilm Productions as designers. Others would seem to have taken inspiration from Sedufia's and Asamoah's strategies. One example is the feature directorial debut of Ramesh Jai Gulabri, *Bad Luck Joe* (2018), a hilarious dramedy steeped in the appreciation of being Ghanaian.[10] The film explores the intricacies of family, marriage, love, and relationships as it takes the audience on a journey with Francesca and Beatrice, the two wives of Mr. Patapaa, who battle over the property of their husband. Prior to the premiere of *Bad Luck Joe*, Gulabrai engaged in a Facebook promotional campaign. First, the director's cut was screened at a private event for selected film and media instructors, journalists, and filmmakers. After the private screening, the views and reactions of attendees were recorded and packaged as testimonials that were deployed as promotional materials on Facebook. These strategies thus created opportunities for the audiences to be part of the film project before and after the opening weekend.

These strategies, whose developments are linked to globalization and its attendant proliferation and convergence of media technologies, influence how contemporary Ghanaian filmmakers appropriate digital and new media affordances in marketing films. Right from film ideation stage to production and exhibition, these new filmmakers deploy well-structured and coordinated publicity plans and marketing strategies to boost audience engagement. Unique movie identifiers and social media handles are created and used to disseminate targeted information to the audience to augment traditional media promotional efforts of the film. The stars also usually bring their celebrity status and visibility to bear on the promotion of the films. Short testimonials and endorsements are filmed and shared via either the actors' social media or designated platforms for the films. Even before the films screen in cinemas, then, marketing and promotional campaigns in the forms of testimonials, trailers, and behind-the-scenes materials have already intensified via social networking sites such as WhatsApp, YouTube, Twitter, Facebook, and Instagram.

In 2020, Sedufia released a third feature-length film, *Aloe Vera*, in collaboration with Canal+ and Gravelroad Distribution of South Africa.[11] The theatrical run of this film, however, was cut short with the closure of cinemas at the beginning of the COVID-19 pandemic. Sedufia told me:

> The continued closure of cinemas is hindering the furtherance of distribution. Our intention for *Aloe Vera*, for instance, was to submit it to internationally recognized film festivals to get some mileage to leverage good distribution deals from buyers. Unfortunately, because of the pandemic, most of these festivals are either called off or postponed. Although we already have a distributor, the disruption of the festival circuits is also affecting distributors. They, like us filmmakers, are not able to participate in festival circuits where they can network with potential buyers. The pandemic's impact on film production is frustrating, but there is little we can do now but hold onto our contents and hope they are good enough on their own to enable us to get distributors. (Peter Sedufia interview, February 18, 2021)[12]

The pandemic has thus shown that, despite the many innovations of this new wave of Ghanaian filmmakers, the new forms of filmmaking continue to interact and overlap with older forms of production, distribution, and exhibition in ways that invoke Henry Jenkins's (2006) pioneering concept of convergence culture.

Conclusion

New strategies have positively reconfigured the film production landscape in Ghana, contributed to the growth of new cinema audiences, and instigated a renewed interest in cinema-going. Located within this creative economy are inventive practices and an entrepreneurial impetus that fuel not only the development of context-driven genres and aesthetic approaches but also exhibition and distribution synergies that allow both the old and young, the experienced and student filmmakers to cohabit, share knowledge, and create content for both traditional and new media platforms. In this chapter I have foregrounded how film students' creativity and craft have allowed them to integrate into the film sector. Future studies could examine how this work has also led to opportunities for reflective practice and the development of innovative film and media pedagogy grounded in entrepreneurship, authentic learning, and creative assessment in Ghana and elsewhere.

NOTES

1 The primary mandate of NAFTI, at its establishment in 1978, was to train film and television creatives for the Ghana Broadcasting Corporation. It is a degree-awarding institute that trains students in film and television directing, cinematography, editing, art direction, film sound design, multimedia production, and animation. Through an act of Parliament, NAFTI was, in 2020, subsumed under the University of Media, Arts and Communication Act (Act 1059) that merged the Ghana Institute of Journalism, the Ghana Institute of Languages, and NAFTI into a single autonomous university.

2 My transition from mainstream visual and strategic communications to the film and television industry was serendipitous, to say the least. Growing up in a household full of cinema-related literature that belonged to an uncle who was a lecturer at NAFTI, I began my journey with film early with weekly readings, film screenings, and discussions. This induction whipped up my interest in the creative industries and my subsequent application to NAFTI's bachelor of fine arts (film directing) program. Although NAFTI's admission offer came when I was enrolled in a bachelor of arts program in another university, I found myself, eleven years later, at NAFTI as a lecturer after my MPhil program. I have since worked as a fixer, production manager, and producer of some commissioned projects, and as executive producer of *Aloe Vera* (2020).

3 The *Boys Kasa* series was chiefly engineered by Kofi Asamoah and his KOFAS Media company but with tremendous input from Peter Sedufia, Richard Kelly Doe, Vivian Ben-Adjetey, and other NAFTI students.

4 See Statista (2021) for country-specific data on internet penetration and usage. For instance, between 2021 and 2022, Ghana recorded 8.2 million and 8.8 million active social media users, respectively, compared to 2023 and 2024.

5 While opinions are divided on this issue, many veteran actors and media practitioners, like J. O. T. Agyemang, Pascal Akah, Kevin Ekow Taylor, and Gifty Andrah, held the opinion, at different times in Ghana's cinematic history, that the industry was dead. See J. O. T. Agyeman, "Who Killed the Ghana Film Industry? JOT Agyeman Speaks," PeaceFmOnline, October 22, 2013, https://www.peacefmonline.com/pages/showbiz/movies/201310/178023.php.

6 Statista (2021) reports that between 2017 and 2021, Ghana's WhatsApp users surpassed Facebook's 8.9 million subscribers to reach 83.9 percent of the country's internet users, which as of January 2021, was pegged at 15.7 million.

7 *John and John* is an action comedy about two guys who, charged to deliver money from a deal to their boss, fall into a series of misadventures. The film's release was

marred by a viral video alleging Asamoah plagiarized the South African award-winning film *Skeem* (2011). Although Asamoah still maintains that he sought permission from the director of *Skeem*, it is not clear in which form these adaptation rights were granted.

8   The Black Stars International Film Festival was founded in 2015 by Juliet Asante. The annual festival offers filmmakers on the continent a platform to make global connections through film and to share film expertise and business development ideas. It aims to bridge the gap between global cinema production dynamics and filmmaking in Africa through its film market and film development and financing plenaries.

9   CongaTV is a subscription-based streaming platform, while Kwesé TV was a pay TV service. Kwesé has been defunct since August 2019.

10 Ramesh Jai Gulabrai is an alumnus of NAFTI and the CEO of Apex Advertising and Post-Production, a brand activation, promotion, and advertising company that has been influential in Ghana's advertising scene. Although a trained filmmaker, Jai was most successful in the advertising scene until *Bad Luck Joe*. He was also the producer and executive producer of Nicole Amarteifio's *Before the Vows* (2018), director of the short film *Life* (2017), and, over the past two decades, the writer and director of scores of TV commercials for companies like Vodafone Ghana and Airtel.

11 When two feuding communities (the Aloes and Veras) that live as neighbors collide in *AloeVera*, it takes the love between their son (Aloewin) and daughter (Veraline) to unite them. Sedufia's transnational partnership with Gravelroad and Canal+ facilitated the dubbing and release of the film in more than ten Francophone African countries.

12 *Aloe Vera* streamed on Netflix, Amazon Prime, Canal+, DSTV Box Office, and over ten in-flight entertainment platforms on KLM, Brussels Airlines, Emirates, United Airlines, Saudi Airlines, Ethiopian Airlines, and Kenya Airways. It was subsequently dubbed into French and screened in selected cinemas across Francophone West Africa.

INTERVIEWS

Sedufia, Peter. Interview, August 17, 2019.
Sedufia, Peter. Interview (telephone), February 18, 2021.

7

South Africa's Female Only Filmmakers Project

From On-Screen to Calling the Shots

LINDIWE DOVEY

It is critical that female perspectives are communicated, be it through the eyes of a character or the storyteller. Film and television [have] the ability to embody dreams and aspirations, to create role models and smash stereotypes—music, art, film and television have at times been the catalysts that have brought about bigger societal change than politics or legislation.—NFVF, *Gender Matters in the South African Film Industry*, 2018

This chapter and the five chapters that follow it return to many of the questions posed by Estrella Sendra in chapter 2 of this volume, exploring the gendered nature of diegetic and industrial screen worlds and seeking out women-led, womanist screen worlds in terms of production, circulation, curation, and spectatorship. The first global research project into gender representation within film industries was published in 2014 and revealed that women are severely underrepresented in key roles, such as writing, directing, and producing (Smith, Choueiti, and Pieper 2014, 6). It also provided a stark, yet unsurprising, picture of how women are represented on-screen, often in hypersexualized ways that fetishize their appearances and do not afford them speaking roles to the same extent as men. The study did not include any African countries, and South Africa appears to be the only African country to date that has commissioned similar research into gender inequalities in its own national film industry. In 2009, the National Film and Video Foundation (NFVF)—South Africa's statutory film organization, which operates from within the Department of Arts and Culture—published research on the workforce behind the fifty-five South African feature films produced between 2000 and 2007; it revealed that only six were produced by women, six directed by women, and nine written by women (NFVF 2018, 8). In 2018, the NFVF published a more in-depth report, "Gender Matters in the South African Film Industry," in partnership with the advocacy group Sisters Working in Film and TV (SWIFT) (NFVF 2018). Very little appears to have changed across the decade between these two reports, with South African women filmmakers surveyed noting that "behind the scenes it is still very much a man's world, with white men, in particular, in key roles as heads of departments" (29), and that "the more senior a role, the less chance of it being held by a woman, and by extension, the less chance a woman has of being hired for it" (11). In addition to this important work conducted by the NFVF and SWIFT, many African women filmmakers, film professionals, film scholars, and activists across the continent have attempted to inspire awareness of and to redress gender inequalities in the film industries in Africa (Bisschoff and Van de Peer 2020; Ellerson 2000, 2015, 2016, 2020; Kassahun 2018; Mistry and Schuhmann 2015). There are certain trailblazers in diverse African countries whose passion and labor have contributed to bringing about necessary transformation, for example, the female filmmakers in Kenya who have led the film industry there (Dovey 2025; Steedman 2017, 2019, 2023).[1] One of these dynamic African women is the South African film producer Bongiwe Selane, and this chapter focuses in particular on the Female Only Filmmakers project (as it is popularly known) that she ran upon being awarded slate funding by the NFVF.[2] This chapter is complemented by, and should be read in conjunction with viewing, a one-hour documentary film I have made titled *From One Woman to Another: The Screen Worlds of Bongiwe Selane* (2023), which can be freely accessed on the Screen Worlds website (see figure 7.1). The importance of making research *films* about women filmmakers is summed up very well in the motto of the Geena Davis Institute: "If she can see it, she can be it"; the

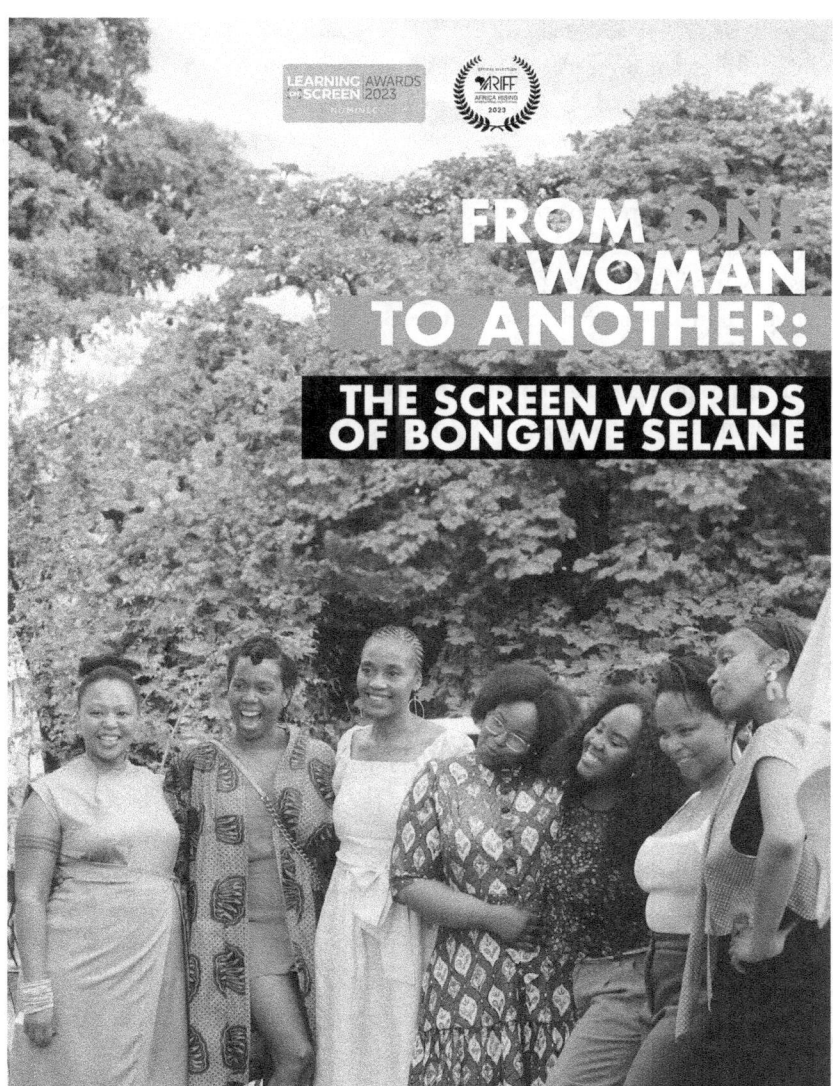

FIGURE 7.1. Promotional poster for the film *From One Woman to Another: The Screen Worlds of Bongiwe Selane* (dir. Lindiwe Dovey, 2023). Selane is third from left. Image courtesy Neo R. Paulus.

film allows Selane and many of the women who participated in the Female Only Filmmakers project to speak about their work in their own voices, something I am unable to do in writing.[3]

The Female Only Filmmakers project has become a regular, if not annual, opportunity on the South African film landscape and the only current one that devotes resources to upskilling women filmmakers—and particularly writers and directors (NFVF 2018, 10). Selane was the first producer to be awarded this slate funding from 2013 to 2016 to support women (particularly those from marginalized backgrounds) to make the leap into more creative central roles in the film industry. As she told me, "Most of it was just to give people a calling card, just to give them an opportunity to say, 'I have my name on something that was made that's professional'" (Bongiwe Selane interview, July 1, 2019).

Through eight months of support from professional mentors and experienced film personnel with the development, production, and postproduction of their films, each successful participant completed a twenty-five-minute film. Selane's involvement in the project saw twenty-six short films through to completion—many of which have been screened at film festivals, broadcast on the national South African free-to-air channel SABC 1, and screened on the South African video-on-demand platform ShowMax. In my filmed interview with her while making *From One Woman to Another*, Selane told me:

> It's probably the highlight of my career so far. And what's important to note also is that it promoted me as a producer because I'd never produced before. So . . . as much as I was in this space of nurturing female writers and directors, the NFVF was also nurturing me as a producer, making sure that I had a company [Selane set up her production company, Blingola, in order to produce the films], that that company was sustainable within that three years to make sure that those films were developed and made. And it's very exciting now to see some of the talent that is out there right now that are females that are really thriving in the industry, making films, working as head directors in drama series and telenovelas, and making film festival films. (Bongiwe Selane interview, April 29, 2021)

Thus, just as Selane was supporting and mentoring other women film professionals through this project, she was being given her first opportunity by the NFVF to work as a professional film producer. She attributes this to the affirmative action of the project, saying that "because it specifically targeted women and there was no space for any men to apply for it, I got it" (Selane interview, July 1, 2019). Selane came into the project from a background in broadcasting at South Africa's pay-television channel M-Net, so she did have experience in producing, but in a television rather than film capacity. It was while working in broadcasting that Selane developed her passion specifically for producing films; she says she enjoys the "enabling part" of producing, and that from the corporate structure at M-Net she learned how to package, pitch, and sell ideas (Bongiwe Selane interview, September 10, 2020). Given the vital role that film producers play in bringing films to life, it is remarkable that in film and screen studies so little attention has been paid to people occupying this role, with "auteur" studies of film directors dominating. This oversight has in part inspired my interest in researching Selane's work.

Negotiating Spaces

The theme of the female-only slate of film projects that Selane produced was "Negotiating Spaces," with applicants asked to think about how women negotiate their position as mothers, wives, daughters, career women, and professionals in a dynamic society. According to Selane, specific areas that applicants were encouraged to explore were family (responsibility and expectations); taboos (cross-cultural); love; life lessons (lived experiences and how they mold us); and the heroine inside and outside the family. In a country that has a history of acute racial and gender oppression (Gqola 2010; D. Lewis and Baderoon 2021), and with a film industry that has been male-dominated, South African women filmmakers collectively lament the often stereotypical, sexualized, and demeaning representations of women on-screen, also emphasizing that "Black women are the most incorrectly represented" (NFVF 2018, 30–31). It must be noted that their complaints chime with those of the UNESCO-funded global research project into gender bias in the film industries (S. L. Smith, Choueiti, and Pieper 2014) and are a reminder of how pervasive and universal these inequalities are, both on-screen and behind the scenes.

The films that emerged out of Selane's Female Only Filmmakers project, in contrast, reprogram representations of (South African) gender relations on-screen in refreshing, subversive, and sometimes humorous ways. Because I do not have the space to analyze all twenty-six of the films that Selane produced for the project, I have chosen to focus on three: *The Groom's Price* (2017, written and directed by Mmabatho Montsho), *Panic Button* (2014, written and directed by Libby Dougherty), and *Mmino wa Modimo* (*God's Hymns*; 2017, written and directed by Nozipho Nkelemba). My reasons for selecting these films for analysis were that I found them particularly engaging and that for each of them I managed to secure an interview with Selane and/or the writer-director so as to better understand the context around the film's making. In the course of my research, what has also struck me about the three writer-directors of these films is that they are all women who have come from acting backgrounds and for whom the Female Only Filmmakers project was a rare opportunity to reveal their writing and directing talent. The theme of female actors becoming stuck in front of the camera when they also aspire to take on leading roles behind the camera is a common theme in the NFVF's 2018 *Gender Matters in the South African Film Industry* report.

Mmabatho Montsho, the writer-director of *The Groom's Price* for the Female Only Filmmakers project, is one of South Africa's best-loved female actors, having starred since she was in her early twenties in popular television and soap opera series such as *Generations* (1993–) and *Jacob's Cross* (2007–13). Selane first met Montsho when she was cast as one of the leads for a major film Selane was producing—*Happiness Is a Four-Letter Word* (2016). But Montsho also had aspirations to write and direct films, and she decided to submit her own film idea to the Female Only Filmmakers project. In *The Groom's Price* we find the female protagonist Meme (played by Tumie Ngumla) offering lobola (bride-price) to the family of her fiancé, Musa (played by Wandile Molebatsi), rather than the other way around, as is traditional in South Africa. Not only does the gender reversal in the diegesis here flip conventional gender relationships in surprising ways, but so too does the direct, tongue-in-cheek address by Meme to the audience, which breaks the fourth wall.[4] The film is shot with a glossy filter that gives it a lighthearted tone; from the first shot the audience is primed to be entertained by the film. The comic performances, physical humor, smart writing, jokes, and code-switching all contribute to a film that makes its audience laugh out loud (confirmed when I showed excerpts from it at a conference in Cape Town in 2019). But beneath the sugarcoating, the film has a very serious message about the implications of tradition for gender equality, as indicated in the opening voice-over, delivered over a moving shot of framed images of weddings and family portraits hanging from a tree: "It's a concept 90 percent of us lean on for a sense of identity, dignity and guidance. The die-hard concept of tradition. But how many of us know exactly where the traditions we defend tooth and nail come from? And if we knew, would they still be as precious?" Selane says of Montsho: "She's incredibly talented as a performer, so just for me, what was really amazing with *The Groom's Price* and seeing her on set was just that relationship between understanding performance and character being translated into making a film." But she also notes that Montsho is "incredibly conscientious and conscious about the type of films that she wants to make in terms of really punctuating herself as a Black woman and her history" and that, since making this short film she is now "more behind the scenes than in front of the camera" (Selane interview, April 29, 2021). Since 2017, Montsho has been directing television series, such as *Thula's Vine* and *Emoyeni*, and in 2019 she jointly won the SAFTA Golden Horn for best achievement in scriptwriting for the latter.

Libby Dougherty is a white South African filmmaker who made *Panic Button* as one of the first women to work with Selane on the Female Only Filmmakers project in the 2013–14 class. Like Montsho, she comes from an acting and performance background; her first love was theater, and she initially attended drama school at the University of Cape Town. After a one-year master of arts degree in film and television at Bristol, however, she returned to South Africa and started working as a writer in television. She also aspired to direct but, other than directing a little on the *Zone 14* drama series, did not get many opportunities. *Panic Button* was thus her "second or third directing project," and she notes how "tremendously exciting" it was to be selected for the Female Only Filmmakers project and how it gave her a chance to realize her own vision as a writer-director. She emphasizes that she has "always loved collaborative processes" but that "when you're working in television drama and soap opera, it's easy to lose your voice." Nevertheless, the *process* toward finding her own voice in *Panic Button* was communal, in both the writing and the production phases. Selane organized two, five-day workshops, which were run by Thandi Brewer, an industry veteran, and attended by such celebrated filmmakers as Akin Omotoso, and which Dougherty describes as "very rich and collaborative" (Libby Dougherty interview, June 7, 2021). Dougherty also points out how professional the process was, with all the women who penned scripts being paid R20,000 for their work. When it came to the production of the film, she was particularly struck by how Selane assembled an almost all-female team, from the director of photography to the production team, and said she has never experienced that subsequently.

Dougherty is aware of her "very privileged background" as a white South African (Dougherty interview, June 7, 2021). In *Panic Button*, gender and race intersect in startling ways that bring to life on-screen Homi Bhabha's (1994) theory of the fear and desire that accompanies the "Othering" process in (post)colonial cultures. The protagonist is Jenny (played by Shelley Meskin), a middle-aged, white South African woman who lives on her own in a house in a gated community in Johannesburg, and who writes romance novels. Paranoid with fear, she takes to hailing the Black security guard for the community, Tshepo (played by Yonda Thomas), by pressing her remote-controlled panic button, even when nothing is happening. Tshepo is kind and gentle to her, and

Jenny starts to fall for him, using him as a muse for her novels and exploiting her panic button to invite him around for tea and a meal. The film cleverly shifts between two genres and two worlds—the brightly colored, breathless, floral world of Jenny's romantic imagination (accompanied by sentimental music) and the dark, eerie world in which Jenny's unfounded fears subsume her, usually at night (accompanied by haunting music that sounds like twisted nursery rhymes). Sometimes these worlds overlap—for example, in the opening close-up shot of a pink, dew-bejeweled rose coming into focus, but where we know that all is not well because of the use of the haunting, unsettling musical leitmotif. Indeed, we know from these first few moments of the film that we are ultimately *not* viewing a romance story and that there will be no happily ever after. In a deft and devastating final twist, the film reveals that what is most dangerous are Jenny's racialized and gendered fears. At one point she summons Tshepo because she is afraid of two Black men outside, who Tshepo tells her are the gardeners; in the end, she ends up shooting Tshepo dead when her feelings for him are unrequited.

Nozipho Nkelemba, like Montsho and Dougherty, was an actor before she had the opportunity to write and direct the film *Mmino wa Modimo* for the Female Only Filmmakers project. Nkelemba began auditioning and acting at a very young age, and this is what exposed her to the various professional roles on film and television sets. As soon as she came to understand that the director was the person "putting all these different elements together to form one big overall message," she realized this was what she wanted to do. However, Nkelemba says that when the call for female filmmakers came out, she was "still trying to figure out what it was that [she] could do outside of acting" (Nozipho Nkelemba interview, June 11, 2021). It was Thandi Brewer—whom Nkelemba had known since she was a child—who put her in touch with Selane and told her about the project. At first Nkelemba was hesitant to apply, though, because she did not think of herself as a writer. Nevertheless, she went ahead. She recalls:

> There must have been twelve of us, or nine of us, and she was there, Bongi, she sat through all of those [writing workshops]! I can just imagine how painful it must have been. She sits in with a bunch of girls who are half her age, whatever, and she helped engineer every one of those stories in the year I was there. And once we had a skeleton then she kind of disappeared to produce—do what producers do, make sure things are ready by the time we get there for output. And her team was just chicks, *bra!* . . . I was like, oh, we can do this thing, *mos!* These guys don't have to

keep sidelining us! Like all we're good for is production because we pay attention to detail. We had to engineer all these things from start to finish. (Nkelemba interview, June 11, 2021)

Like Dougherty, Nkelemba also notes how professional the whole process was. She was astounded that the women were all paid to write their scripts, even though the NFVF was also completely covering the cost of their films being produced. She was also surprised, once the NFVF had signed off on her script, that she was then required to pitch to direct her own story. She continues to describe the process, and how female-centered it was, as follows:

And now this pitch to direct my own film . . . mimics exactly what would happen if I was contracted to somebody to do this whole process. It was scary, scary. As well, in the room, more chicks. . . . Thandeka Zwana [business manager at the NFVF at the time]! And now you're like sitting there in front of Thandeka and you're like, *yo, yo, yo*—this is hectic, *bra*! This is hectic. These are the chicks they speak about in the textbooks, right? . . . Her, Bongi, Thandi—you know, Thandi, bless her heart, she was like my mother—she had heard the story a thousand times, but still she held my hand, made sure we reached the outcome that we wanted. (Nkelemba interview June 11, 2021)

The "outcome" was *Mmino wa Modimo*, a striking and poignant film that centers on a sibling relationship where a brother tries to take over his elderly, ill father's church despite the father's wishes that his daughter succeed him as the first female reverend. As with *The Groom's Price* and *Panic Button*, the actors' performances are strong and convincing, revealing how these women bring their experience with acting to bear on their directing. And, like Dougherty, Nkelemba praises the Female Only Filmmakers project for giving her the opportunity to learn to write and direct a film of her own, which is now an important calling card in the industry. She says she "still had a hard time breaking in after that" but that she "could use that film to get [her] foot through the door because [she] had something to show" (Nkelemba interview June 11, 2021). And, as a result of getting her foot through the door, she has come into contact with other female South African television, film, and advertising directors who have become important mentors to her, such as Catharine Cooke and Cindy Lee.

All the women I have interviewed thus far as part of the larger research project of which this chapter forms a part emphasize the value of projects such as Female Only Filmmakers that are trying to bring greater gender equity to screen industries. Dougherty says: "I really think it's so important. Even if you come out of a process like that and you never want anyone to see the film! It's just such a wonderful process to be involved in. [Because] it's just so hard to make your own work. Unless you are of a type—and they do exist—to go out there with your cell phone and film your story and edit yourself and put it out there and whatever. For me it was [an] incredible opportunity" (Doughtery interview, June 7, 2021). And Nkelemba says:

> I think we're in a good place where there are a lot of bodies and organizations that are pushing for that work. Like "Free the Work," where a third of the pitches should be heard by women, even in advertising, to even that playing field. We should continue on that trajectory, creating opportunities for women over men—sorry, but you know what I mean!—because they have those opportunities at their disposal. So we definitely need to keep pushing on that same trajectory to push the business open completely so that it's normal. (Nkelemba interview, June 11, 2021)

While female friendships in film clearly play a vital role in helping to secure gender equity (Bisschoff and Van de Peer 2020, 88–108), leadership and mentorship of more junior women by senior, experienced women in the industry—such as Selane—are paramount.

Continuations

There are no final "conclusions" here, then, only the need for continuing the important work that Selane and the NFVF began with the Female Only Filmmakers project. For me, as a researcher, this idea of continuation also coheres with the methodology I am using to produce this ongoing research, which is feminist, collaborative, and conversational. While it is vital for scholars to continue to analyze the diegetic screen worlds of particular films and thus understand gender dynamics in textual representation, it is equally important that we continue to put ourselves in conversation with the people involved in the industrial screen worlds that produce and circulate those texts so that we can develop a clearer picture of how gender plays out in the practices of film labor behind the scenes. As revealed in this chapter, as much as Mmabatho Montsho, Libby Dougherty, and Nozipho Nkelemba may be passionate about their work as actors, they have also had a particularly difficult time asserting their dreams to be defined by more than their on-screen performances and to showcase their writing and directing talent behind the camera. It was the Female

Only Filmmakers project and Bongiwe Selane's mentorship that gave them the opportunity to start redefining themselves as those also "calling the shots."[5]

NOTES

1 I have made a film about one of these Kenyan women filmmakers titled *Out of the Box: The Screen Worlds of Judy Kibinge* (2023). It can be accessed at www.screenworlds .org.
2 Officially, the NFVF program is known as the Female Filmmaker Project.
3 See www.screenworlds.org to watch *From One Woman to Another: The Screen Worlds of Bongiwe Selane* (2023) as well as the other films our team has made as part of the ERC-funded African Screen Worlds: Decolonising Film and Screen Studies project. Readers might also find it useful to read this chapter in conjunction with an article I have written about the value of such research filmmaking in academia that also gives some insight into my process of making the film about Selane (Dovey 2023).
4 This innovation seems to have taken place simultaneously with Phoebe Waller-Bridge's television series *Fleabag* (2016–19).
5 See also the academic project Calling the Shots: Women and Contemporary Film Culture in the UK, for which Shelley Cobb was the principal investigator and Linda Williams the coinvestigator (see https://womencallingtheshots.com).

INTERVIEWS

Dougherty, Libby. Interview (via Zoom), June 7, 2021.
Nkelemba, Nozipho. Interview (via Zoom), June 11, 2021.
Selane, Bongiwe. Interview (via Skype), July 1, 2019.
Selane, Bongiwe. Interview (via Zoom), September 10, 2020.
Selane, Bongiwe. Interview (via Zoom), April 29, 2021.

8

Female Film Entrepreneurs in Ghana

Shirley Frimpong-Manso and Evelyn Asampana in Focus

ROBIN STEEDMAN AND RASHIDA RESARIO

Filmmakers in Ghana are currently in a major period of transition in which the move to digital modes of production and spectatorship has fundamentally disrupted the way they run their businesses and bring their content to various screens—cinema, television, and computer and phone screens. Filmmakers, seasoned and newcomers alike, are fighting to survive as well as profit from this transition. That technological transformation could dramatically reconfigure the filmmaking landscape comes as no surprise to scholars and lovers of African film. We only have to think of the seismic shift brought about by Nollywood's video film model to modes of film production and consumption to establish the role of technology in the fluctuating nature of filmmaking (see Saul and Austen 2010). What these old debates remind us of, though, is the importance of technology in shaping filmmaking practice and filmmaking businesses, something that is ever more important as various kinds of digital innovations offer new opportunities, as well as challenges, for filmmakers and film audiences.

But what are women's experiences within this digital transition? Women have been making films in Africa for decades, and yet their participation has not been adequately acknowledged in scholarship, which has a tendency to focus on film waves and canonized directors (Bisschoff and Van de Peer 2020; White 2015). More women make more television and video than film, and focusing on the technology of production—looking at film rather than more holistically at screen media—has contributed to the undervaluing of female filmmakers' work in African film industries (Bisschoff 2012, 159; Bisschoff and Van de Peer 2020, 17). Examining the working conditions of female filmmakers as well as *all* their screen media output is vital to understanding *any* of their work (Steedman 2023). In this chapter, we focus on Shirley Frimpong-Manso and Evelyn Asampana, two entrepreneurial Ghanaian women filmmakers who are navigating the digital film world but operating in very different places and spheres of filmmaking. Through this comparison, we add nuance to discussions of digital film production and distribution today and about the kinds of filmmakers and film businesses that are surviving and thriving in this environment.

Contextualizing Film Entrepreneurship in Ghana

Survival in the world of business depends largely on an enabling environment that complements the daily, as well as visionary, efforts of entrepreneurs. Most workers in Ghana are self-employed or employed in the informal economy (Steel 2017), and government support for entrepreneurs in Ghana has largely been on an ad hoc basis, with no clear policies to support individual initiative (Adom 2016). Like entrepreneurs in other sectors, filmmakers in Ghana cannot rely on government support.

In the immediate postcolonial period, the Ghanaian government did promote and support the film industry. President Kwame Nkrumah nationalized film production in 1957 and created the Ghana Film Industry Corporation (GFIC); however, the success of the GFIC in creating a sustainable film industry was limited, and between its founding and when it was sold in 1996, it produced only fourteen feature films (Garritano 2013, 54, 93). In recent times, successive governments have begun to recognize the potential of creative industries for sustainable economic growth. Nana Akufo-Addo's government has invested in promoting the film industry through infrastructural and policy measures, including establishing the Interim Creative Arts Council in 2016 and the National Film Authority in 2019, and by passing into law in December 2020 the Creative Arts Bill, which establishes a creative arts fund to support creative producers. Given how recent these initiatives are, however, it is too early to judge whether they will have a major impact on the film industry.

Cycles of collapse and regeneration are a constant feature of film production in Ghana, and technological change has been vital to these cycles. Celluloid filmmakers in the 1980s had to support their practice by taking out bank loans while living in constant hope that their films would generate enough income to repay them. Still today, attracting formal investment is difficult, and filmmakers are considered high risk for loans, meaning accessing formal finance can be very difficult. As testing as the economic situation was during the 1980s under the military regime (Garritano 2008), filmmakers in Ghana were presented with an opportunity to revive their businesses with the introduction of video technology as a replacement for the more expensive celluloid. The opportunity offered by video technology in the 1980s and early 1990s is captured by Carmela Garritano's observation that "the erosion of state support for and control of filmmaking coupled with the ready availability of video technology allowed individuals situated outside of the networks of official cultural production, first, to import and exhibit pirated copies of imported films and television programming, and, later, to produce their own features" (2013, 62). Video was embraced because of its accessibility and the possibility it offered to filmmakers to survive in the face of a dearth of funding (Meyer 2015). Importantly, the shift to video film also allowed women to enter the industry as "no Ghanaian women had directed or produced a documentary or feature film before the advent of video movies" (Garritano 2013, 17). The shift from celluloid to video technology was quickly followed by a shift from cinema screenings to watching home videos in the mid-1990s. There was yet another shift from the technology of "Betacam and VHS to digital video, as a result of which producers could make use of digital editing programs, such as Adobe Premiere" (Meyer 2015, 67).

Digital technology has had complex and often contradictory effects on filmmaking in Ghana. In much of Ghana, digital cameras certainly enable production, but by the same token, digital distribution mechanisms have devastated parts of the industry, principally because consumers no longer buy DVDs due to the accessibility of films on digital platforms such as YouTube and on the massive number of TV channels enabled by the transition to digital television. Lizelle Bisschoff notes: "Whereas Nollywood films were initially primarily distributed on DVD and VCD (video compact disc), improved broadband and Internet streaming technology means that these films can now be downloaded or watched on multiple VOD (video-on-demand) platforms online, in Africa and internationally" (2017, 262). Such innovation is distinctly beneficial to *spectators* of various kinds of African film as they have access to a much wider range of content. However, this change has had quite different effects on *producers* of African film, which is what we focus on in this chapter. We therefore are interested in how women filmmakers engage with digital technology and how geographic location and other factors play key roles in their ability to thrive in the new digital ecosystem.

To try to answer these questions, we interviewed fifty filmmakers (in a variety of positions, but mostly directors and producers) in four locations across Ghana (Accra, Kumasi, Tamale, and Zuarungu) between January and March 2020. We interviewed thirty-three filmmakers individually and held a focus group in Zuarungu with a further seventeen. Accessing the different screen worlds of Ghanaian filmmakers requires such in-depth fieldwork. While one can study world cinema without ever traveling to those regions whose filmmaking cultures are under examination (cf. White 2015), African film scholars have long argued for the absolute necessity of fieldwork in film studies to understand cultures of both production and consumption (cf. Dovey 2015c; Steedman 2023). Our decision to expand our research contexts to include the fourth location of Zuarungu in the Upper East Region happened by chance when Evelyn Asampana—whom we interviewed in Kumasi—mentioned that she makes films in the Frafra language and is part of a community of filmmakers operating near Bolgatanga. We had never heard of this filmmaking configuration before and needed the serendipity of fieldwork to do so.

Our interviews helped us broadly understand filmmaking in contemporary Ghana, and for the purposes of this chapter we want to zoom in on two very different cases of female experience in Ghanaian filmmaking. We are not concerned here with the aesthetics or thematics of contemporary Ghanaian movies; there is already rich scholarship on this topic (see, for example, Jonathan Haynes's [2010] comprehensive literature review). We seek to examine industrial conditions—the intertwinement of production and distribution—and how these have shaped the business decision-making of two Ghanaian female filmmakers.

Shirley Frimpong-Manso

Shirley Frimpong-Manso is one of the most well-known Ghanaian filmmakers, and, not surprisingly, her films have received attention from several film scholars (Garritano 2013; Kwansah-Aidoo and Owusu 2012, 2017). The story of her business offers an illuminating case of a film entrepreneur navigating the digital transition and being radically innovative with her approach to both production and distribution. She is the CEO of Sparrow Media Group, based in Accra, which includes Sparrow Pictures, through which she produces her own films; Sparrow Station, which is her online platform; and Sparrow Studios, through which she produces advertisements, documentaries, and branded content (for example, for major brands such as Coca-Cola, Nestlé, and Standard Chartered).[1] Running these three related businesses is a balancing act, and Frimpong-Manso carefully plans her year so that she can film movies with Sparrow Pictures, but she has to prioritize Sparrow Studios because, if she does not, those contracts "will go away and may never come back." The ethos of each business is different: "Where we get very personal with Pictures, and we are all wound up in our own creative process, at Studios, it's very business. We have to wear that cap where it's like, it's not about you, it's about the client."

Frimpong-Manso studied directing at the National Film and Television Institute (see Lotsu, this volume), during which time she started a small production company and bought the franchise to organize the Miss Ghana pageant. Like other film students seeking careers in highly competitive industries (Mehta 2017), during her time in school she hustled in a future-oriented way to establish herself in the business of filmmaking. In her case, she did this through producing the Miss Ghana pageant for five years so that she could develop professional networks with important brands—the sort of companies she would need to know to start producing movies and series telling "progressive African stories" that focused, in particular, on the kind of women she knew. At the time she began filmmaking, she says, "on screen . . . it was a very sad image of this African woman basically at the mercy of society, and the mercy of men and stuff, and I wanted to change that narrative." This is a familiar motivation for African female filmmakers (Bisschoff 2012, 168; Bisschoff and Van de Peer 2020; Thackway 2003).

What makes Frimpong-Manso's work particularly exciting is that she has experimented with different forms of screen media production and distribution, including a "cinema series" called *Adam's Apples* (2011). At the time she had been releasing only one or two movies a year, but then she and her team decided that "instead of doing ten unique movies or twelve unique movies that we will release every [month] because that would be hugely expensive, what if we attempted to do a series? Because we also got to realize that Ghanaians loved the continuing story style. . . . The TV stations had introduced all these Mexican soaps that people were following religiously, and we were thinking, what if it was a Ghanaian series?" So the team made a ten-chapter cinema series, releasing a chapter each month in the cinemas (each was roughly 105 minutes long), and before the release of each new chapter, they would release a DVD of the previous chapter. Here we see her entrepreneurialism in action and clear parallels with African female filmmakers elsewhere who fluidly shift between formats and modes of production as part of the hustle to keep working (see Steedman 2023).

Frimpong-Manso makes relatively large-budget movies, and this makes international distribution a necessity. She describes herself as someone who makes Ghanaian movies but not only for Ghanaian audiences, which is evident in her distribution strategies, which target audiences with internet access and buying power. For the simple reason that there are not enough cinemas in Ghana, capturing the dramatically larger Nigerian cinema market is a requirement for her success. Making money through the international distribution circuit is a slow process: "You will need to give me three years to be able to make my money back because, first off, I have to use this one cinema to be able to outdoor the movie in Ghana. Then I have to go to Nigeria. Then afterward I have to . . . go to M-Net, and then I will have to use my distributors to, you know, be able to sell to the airlines and be able to sell to other VOD platforms. It takes time." Her current method of production is to focus from the outset on creating a marketable product. She has experimented with different genres—for example, she made the thriller *Potomanto* (2013) about an organ-harvesting enterprise, but the film had a poor showing in cinemas. She has found, over time, that "Africans and Ghanaians especially seem to love more romantic comedy-dramas" as opposed to "the serious stuff," and she focuses on this genre now. Once she has created a "good story," the next step is to find investors and talk to her distributor so they can assess whether or not they can sell it. "First off, you have to find out whether there's market interest," and, crucially, these conversations happen before she has spent any money on production. *The Perfect Picture: 10 Years Later* (2019), for instance, took two to three years to make. It cost USD 150,000 to USD 200,000, about 40 percent of which was spent on marketing. In comparison, most Ghanaian movies cost on average USD 30,000 to USD 60,000 (Garritano 2013, 174). Brands have to be approached a year in advance, and Frimpong-Manso had to plan for premiering in the United Kingdom and Nigeria and deciding which Nigerian actors to cast so that the film would travel. She even has "conversations with the likes of Netflix" before production begins to make sure that the film she plans on making will be commercially successful. Marketing is planned in preproduction, which, for her, means creating distinct plans for Nigeria and the United Kingdom.

According to Frimpong-Manso, in terms of distribution platforms, currently cinemas are the most lucrative, followed by VOD, pay TV, airlines, and then traditional broadcast TV. As of 2023 she had two films on Netflix, with *Potato Potahto* (2017) arriving on the platform in 2019, followed by *The Perfect Picture: 10 Years Later* in 2020. However, her only film on Netflix as of 2024 is *Potato Patahto*. She had previously been approached by Nollywood distributors about bundling her content with theirs to pitch to Netflix, but she waited "because we wanted to be able to present ourselves as this production company that was capable of doing original content for them as well. We needed to have our own voice."

Despite cinemas currently being the most lucrative distribution outlet, Frimpong-Manso feels that VOD will be the most lucrative in the future. At the time of our interview, Sparrow Station was in its fourth year and was "where all our content eventually ends up." But she wants to develop the platform into a "mini-Netflix" that would host productions she specifically created for it. In her view, an online platform as the "final resting place" for content makes sense in a context where "the DVD market is dead." Within five years, she would like to make 80 percent of her revenue through Sparrow Station and to rely less on cinemas. She says: "On a platform like that, it cuts your marketing cost into half. So, when you have created a platform where you have a waiting audience that are waiting to pay for it and watch it, it is the easiest way to make up your money compared to having to rely on cinemas. . . . What we expect to do is to be able to get investments, be able to create content, be able to lock down people in subscription and begin to grow the platform." The current audience of Sparrow Station is "mostly in America," which is unsurprising given the difficulties of accessing online streamed content in many African contexts. As Lindiwe Dovey writes, "Experiences of internet television for the majority of Africans on the continent are vastly different from those in the wealthy West, including for members of the African diaspora who have access to desktops, laptops, and high-speed internet" (2018, 97). Frimpong-Manso, however, is optimistic that her customer base will change as internet service becomes cheaper and more accessible in Ghana and she can convert Ghanaian fans into paying VOD customers. Moradewun Adejunmobi argues that cinema and streaming platforms are tightly interlinked: "Cinema currently matters for streaming platforms dedicated to African content as one of several possible means for designating content with premium value on the platform and thus generating additional subscriptions" (2019, 222). Running a profitable and sustainable online distribution platform in Africa is no easy task (Dovey 2018); however, the cinematic quality and cinematic distribution of

Frimpong-Manso's films may help her achieve her ambition of a lucrative and sustainable streaming platform, which would then also help to raise funding for her to keep making her films.

Evelyn Asampana and the Frafra Filmmakers of the Upper East Region

Evelyn Asampana is a filmmaker and administrative assistant at a private school in Kumasi. At the time of our interview she had made three movies, all with a focus on her Frafra culture, and she had a fourth waiting to start production. She has aspirations of becoming a full-time filmmaker, something that is not currently possible because filmmaking is not sufficiently profitable in the Upper East Region where she makes her films. She says: "Currently I'm working in a private school. It's not all that good but I'm managing. It's better than sitting at home doing nothing. But all my prayer is [that] when I get funding somewhere, I will establish my own film business. Then I will move 100 percent [to] filmmaking." She has to work her filmmaking around her job, and she shoots her movies during school vacations. Her company, Family Entertainment, has only made movies so far, something she hopes to change in the future. She would like to shoot advertisements and to create a TV show: "I want it to be [a] TV series in [the] Frafra language because in Ghana no one has ever done [a] TV series in [the] Frafra language, so I'm trying to start and see how it will go." In essence, she is hoping to create a diversified media business—a strategy other filmmakers have used to thrive, as in the case of Shirley Frimpong-Manso.

Accra and Kumasi have long been the epicenters of film production in Ghana, though filmmaking also has a fairly long history in the northern regions, albeit at a much smaller commercial scale (Young 2019). The domination of the South in movie production comes as no surprise considering that Ghana has a stark North-South divide in terms of development outcomes (Al-Hassan and Diao 2007; Hilson, Amankwah, and Ofori-Sarpong 2013; McKay and Osei-Assibey 2017). The Frafra filmmaking economy in Bolgatanga in the Upper East Region of Ghana, just south of the border with Burkina Faso, can best be described as emerging. The local filmmakers' association has about thirty members, many of whom are part of local drama groups that began by staging plays and only more recently moved into film production. Making Frafra film is difficult, but filmmakers like Asampana are passionately devoted to the task. She writes her scripts, directs her movies (with the support of one or two other directors), and produces them, a situation that is common for African female filmmakers (Steedman 2023) and even for the most high-budget filmmakers in Ghana, such as Shirley Frimpong-Manso. Asampana's business is a microenterprise and does not have fixed assets such as filmmaking equipment or permanent employees. She rents the equipment in Kumasi and brings it north for each production. She is looking for partners but has not yet found any (a situation that is extremely common across Ghana). Her audience is primarily in the Upper East Region because of her use of Frafra, although she subtitles the films to make them more accessible.

Asampana's films are entirely self-financed. Her last movie, *Anamkena* (2019), had a budget of GHS 9,000 (USD 1,550), which would cover only the cost of hiring "two or three stars in Accra or Kumasi," and one that is on the very small side for Ghanaian movies. She did not pay herself to direct, and the location was free, having relied on connections through her mother. The total cast and crew consisted of seventeen people who "were paid small"—something that is standard in the region and elsewhere in Ghana (for example, in Tamale oftentimes actors will not be paid at all for their work, or will have only their transportation and refreshments covered by the producer). The profit margins on Asampana's films are slim, but she is making money, something whose value cannot be underestimated in Ghana's current film economy (for example, we found in our research that many established Kumasi film producers are currently operating at a loss). She made GHS 10,500 (USD 1,810) from the movie, with a profit margin of GHS 1,500 (USD 260), but she was quick to note that in her mind "it didn't go well" because the GHS 1,500 (USD 260) she made in profit was not enough to cover her in-kind costs.

After production, the trajectory is to premiere the film, either at Catholic social centers in Bolgatanga or at the Kumasi Cultural Centre, and then to distribute it on VCD. Having a good premiere or "launching" is essential. Asampana does not sell tickets to the launch, as would happen at a Kumasi or Accra cinema premiere, because people will not buy them. Instead, she invites Bolgatanga-based actors and gospel musicians to perform and shows the trailer of the film. She invites "big people" to the launch in the hope that they will then contribute financially. As she explained, "The big men, those who are in Kumasi here, when they come you will give the person a chair and you will say, 'Ooh Evelyn has produced a movie, and Evelyn needs your support, so what do you do for Evelyn so that she can also produce another movie again?' Then someone will say, 'I will give Evelyn GHS 100 [USD 17] in the form of a donation.' At the end of the day you will get something small." Because launch parties rely on voluntary contributions, attracting the "right kind" of people is essential to their success. Another Frafra filmmaker, Godwin Abongo, said that most people who come to a launch will not have a *cedi* to support the film;

however, because he is a teacher as well as a filmmaker, his network is filled with people who are more affluent because they have a constant state salary.

For VCD distribution, Evelyn will start by making five thousand VCDs, and then, when the distributors need more copies, she produces more, up to ten to fifteen thousand total. She works with a variety of distributors across the country, since it is common for distributors to sell within a particular area rather than nationally. Her VCDs retail for GHS 5 (USD 0.86), which is a constant price for VCDs agreed on and maintained by distributors across most of Ghana, and of that GHS 5, she collects GHS 3.80 (USD 0.65). Selling movies on VCD is common, but filmmakers were quick to complain about this system and how VCD sellers exploit filmmakers by pirating their movies and pocketing the profits. Peter Awane, a filmmaker and pastor, reckoned if he gave copies of his movies to ten shops, only two would be honest and not pirate the movie. Of course, these numbers are impossible to verify, but the perception that the VCD model of distribution does not favor filmmakers and is not working as a mode of profitably leads to the conclusion that selling films is still important. Allegations of distributors cheating producers by not correctly accounting for the number of films sold has been a constant feature of the Ghanaian movie market since at least the early 1990s (Garritano 2013, 100), and this theme came up repeatedly in our interviews, especially in Tamale, Kumasi, and Bolgatanga—where VCD is the de facto mode of distribution.

The current distribution system in Bolgatanga thus exists mostly outside of the circuits of digital distribution. Asampana has created a YouTube channel for her company, Family Entertainment, but she has not yet succeeded in raising any revenue through the platform. Many of the filmmakers in our focus group spoke about not knowing "how to use" YouTube to make money and the difficulty of finding adequate training for navigating filmmaking distribution circuits. As we saw with Shirley Frimpong-Manso's situation, successfully navigating digital distribution depends to a great extent on connections—and being able to develop these connections often turns on one's class and educational background and one's location. In the wider field of research on digital skills and digital inequality, it has been shown that not having access to the right networks with adequate expertise increases digital inequality (Courtois and Verdegem 2016, 1523). Similarly, navigating the market on YouTube often requires the use of an intermediary to professionalize and monetize content so that it is competitive and lucrative in a saturated landscape (Lobato 2016). Third-party intermediaries such as multichannel networks ensure that their affiliate channels are managed in a way that is profitable to both parties. Without such networked affiliation, it is impossible for individual content creators with little knowledge about YouTube optimization and visibility to actually make money from the platform. Despite these difficulties of navigating the online distribution world, filmmakers like Asampana forge on based on their passion for making films and the small returns they receive through local consumption of their movies. The Frafra filmmakers we spoke to particularly emphasized their drive to promote and document their culture, with one filmmaker—Peter Awane—saying that making movies "is about maintaining our tradition, our culture and everything. That's why we still keep to it even [when] we don't get profit. If we leave it, we will lose a lot."

Conclusion: Ghanaian Screen Worlds

The screen worlds presented in this chapter contest the parameters of the "world cinema" paradigm. Neither of the entrepreneurs we have profiled here would usually fit within the world cinema category—Shirley Frimpong-Manso would likely be critiqued as "too Western," and the VCD and YouTube market used by Evelyn Asampana would likely never be found (except by empirical researchers doing fieldwork). Furthermore, neither of these filmmakers participates in the international film festival economy, a key gateway to "world cinema" (Stringer 2001).

Frimpong-Manso speaks of the importance of creating a marketable product, which runs in contrast to the pervasive discourse that artistic creation is first and foremost the product of an inner vision of the artist and a form of self-expression (Negus and Pickering 2004). Of course, creativity and the market are deeply intertwined in cinematic production, even in the sphere of "art cinema" where Romantic discourses of creativity are most pervasive (de Valck 2014). Similarly, Asampana did not express herself in the language of auteurism; rather, these two filmmakers explain their passion for their craft in terms of a relationship with their audience. They recognize that this relationship needs to have commercial elements if it is to exist in the first place. Similarly, as scholars we must be attuned to the entrepreneurialism of female filmmakers and how they experiment with different technologies of production and distribution as they attempt to build sustainable businesses and careers.

Christopher Chávez and Ashley Cordes enthusiastically argue that "online platforms have given [Ghanaian] producers the capacity to cultivate niche audiences while gaining access to distribution channels that extend far beyond the nation state" (2018, 193–94). However, as we have shown by contrasting two very different filmmakers, seizing these opportunities requires a constellation of resources and competencies that are unevenly distributed. Lizelle Bisschoff offers a word of caution to temper overenthusiastic assessments about the potential of digital technology: "The democratizing potential of digital technology should not be overestimated on a continent that is still on the wrong side of the digital divide" (2017, 262). Infrastructural constraints remain highly relevant, but so too do human capital, social position, and skills. In order to understand the differing trajectories of film businesses in Ghana, we must be aware of the link between offline inequality and the ability to seize opportunities in digital spaces (Dy, Marlow, and Martin 2017; van Deursen and van Dijk 2014, 521).

Ghanaian filmmakers use digital technology in different ways and with different motivations. Evelyn Asampana is hopeful that digital technologies will build her audience and one day allow her to become a full-time filmmaker. Shirley Frimpong-Manso, on the other hand, has already succeeded in reaching a global audience (or at least the possibility of one) through distributing two of her films on Netflix, and she is looking beyond Netflix to grow her own independent platform. Because of her networks, education, reputation, and business savvy, she has been able to exploit contemporary digital opportunities more successfully than perhaps any other Ghanaian filmmaker today. The digital space enabled by technology thus offers opportunities for filmmakers, but the unequal distribution of the technology and the knowledge needed to navigate this environment poses a particular challenge for filmmakers located outside Accra.

NOTE

All quotes of Shirley Frimpong-Manso are from her interview with Robin Steedman in Accra on February 16, 2020. All quotes of Evelyn Asampana come from her interview with Robin Steedman in Kumasi on February 16, 2020. Quotes from Godwin Abongo and Peter Awane are from a focus group with Zuarungu filmmakers conducted by Robin Steedman on February 29, 2020.

1 One example is the show *Yelo Pèppè* for Maggi (Nestlé), which is shot in both French and English with international actors so that it can be distributed across the continent. It is digital-only and broadcast on YouTube and Facebook.

FOCUS GROUP

Focus group with Zuarungu filmmakers (quoted filmmakers are Godwin Abongo and Peter Awane). Conducted by Robin Steedman, Zuarungu, February 29, 2020.

INTERVIEWS

Asampana, Evelyn. Interview by Robin Steedman, Kumasi, February 16, 2020.
Frimpong-Manso, Shirley. Interview by Robin Steedman, Accra, January 28, 2020.

Part III

Engendering Screen Representation, Spectatorship, and Curation

9

Domestic Disturbance

Afro-Feminist Poetics in Dilman Dila's Ugandan "Horror Romances"

NEDINE MOONSAMY

African filmmakers took to Third Cinema as a means of correcting the filmic gaze through which "Africa" and "Africanicity" emerged as powerful "simulacra" emanating "from the margins of African contexts" (Mudimbe 1988, 176). These early artistic ambitions realized themselves as political in order to reframe African existence in ways that fortified the Afrocentric consciousness of the burgeoning postcolony. Narratives of female liberation also formed part of the revolutionary agenda and led to representations of "strong women characters, powerful and positive matriarchal cultures, and a critique of tyrannical, patriarchal cultures—whether colonial, neo-colonial or postcolonial" (Dovey 2012, 18). For some, however, the legacy of a "profoundly feminist" (18) African cinema has been compromised by the arrival of the video film.

While video films have significantly democratized the market, encouraged experimentation, and allowed for global reception, they are continually plagued by perceptions of poor quality, vulgar consumerism, and the caricature of African life where women are now "marked by a new grammar of the political that would seem to be distant from its liberationist beginnings" (Harrow and Garritano 2016, 244). Because these films seek to entertain rather than educate, many dismiss these formulaic narratives as entrenched in increasingly Western and capitalistic aspirations that reinforce patriarchy and make "no attempt to broaden the roles or portrayals of the predominantly middle-class women in the films" (Harding 2007, 12). Yet interpreting popular culture as a mindless reproduction of the status quo overlooks how African video films have a remarkable "capacity to recontextualize and localize forms and styles associated with global mass culture" (Garritano 2013, 12) in critical and subversive ways. Western modes of cultural production thus come to serve as malleable screen worlds in the African context that also facilitate "expressions of desires for future alternatives, for emergent possibilities" (Newell and Okome 2014, 4) in contemporary society. Turning to two short films by the Ugandan filmmaker Dilman Dila—*How to Start a Zombie Apocalypse* (2017) and *Cursed Widow Blues* (2017)—I explore how African filmmakers make use of video films to tease out the various limitations and desires embedded in local popular imaginaries that are central to the negotiation of contemporary and urban Afro-feminist identity politics and ideals.

Dilman Dila is an author, filmmaker, and social activist—an amalgamation of portfolios that intimates at a desire for creative control over his storytelling processes. Ostensibly embracing what Dominica Dipio describes as an "'imperfect' cinema" (2014, 6), Dila works as an independent artist; his films are clear reflections of creative and sociopolitical integrity at the cost of high aestheticism and financially lucrative distribution deals. Dila thus prefers the short film because it is conducive to his smaller budgets, sourced through grants and online funding platforms, and requires fewer crew members—both factors allowing for greater artistic autonomy. In addition, he obviates the frustration of seeking formal distribution by sharing his films directly to YouTube. Despite these B movie features, Dila's films are receiving increasing acclaim for their imaginative and poetic rendition of African life where otherworldly technology and fantastic creatures are realized through local customs, cultures, and concerns. More recently, his short stories have been shortlisted for the Nommo Awards and the British Science Fiction Association Awards (2019, 2020). He also won Film of the Year (Best Director) at the Uganda Film

Festival (2014) and was a nominee for Best First Feature at the Africa Movie Academy Awards (2014).

Through the simultaneous experimentation with science fiction, horror, fantasy, and romance, his filmmaking practice attests to how "genres coalesce and cross borders" (Dipio 2014, 8) in local popular imaginaries and demonstrates that Western generic distinctions are often too narrow for the narration of African existence (Dipio 2014, 10; Haynes 2016, xxv). Dila's films are thus witty citations of generic expectations that confound the ideological certitudes they portend, and his creative conception of the "horror romance" in particular allows for the realities of Ugandan womanhood to emerge on-screen with refreshing humor and clarity.

The rise of the video film coincided with and benefited from rapid urbanization across the African continent and captures the immediate aspirations and anxieties of this environment, which are all too often projected onto the bodies of women. As Dipio argues, "While a man's exposure to modernity is admired, this is not so for the woman" (2014, 116), and though these films portrayed women in various economic and romantic pursuits, they occupied standardized, if not stereotypical, roles like the "good-time girl" or the "doting mother/wife" (see Dipio 2014, 18). The reliance on the Madonna/whore dichotomy is a clear indication that these roles are more symbolic than substantial: "images fixed within male fantasy" (Dipio 2014, 18) that project "anxieties and desires" (Haynes 2016, 76) about the extent to which modernity disrupts the reach of patriarchal control. Consequently, Dipio argues that African women "seem to be trapped in fiction" because these representations "are far removed from the complex, real woman" (2014, 18) whose urban experience is governed by much greater ambivalence. Understanding this cinematic paucity as a global phenomenon, Kara Keeling argues that it is incumbent on filmmakers "to reveal that which had been hiding in the image by rediscovering 'everything that has been removed to make [the image] interesting' or by 'suppressing many things that have been added to make us believe that we were seeing everything.' Both operations are important political processes because the realm of visibility—what can be retained from each image's appearance to an eye—is conditioned in advance by common sense" (2007, 18).

Keeling's methodology is a compelling intervention in popular culture, showing how the genericism of cinematic images can, in fact, be made complicit in its deconstruction. Filmmakers should, she suggests, use commonplace images to unhinge the ease with which we read them. This is salient to Dila's films, where images of contemporary Ugandan women confound our historically informed ways of seeing. In *How to Start a Zombie Apocalypse*, we are introduced to a married, heavily pregnant woman who fears her husband may be having an affair, and *Cursed Widow Blues* captures the anxiety of a widowed woman who tries to find new love but is sabotaged by the ghost of her dead husband. Both films are set in a domestic space and capture the anxieties around security and romance that the suburban, heteropatriarchal household has come to symbolize. Yet through the enmeshment of the horror romance these women do not disrupt the domestic in ways we would expect. Arguably, this allows for the surfacing of the mundane complexities of Ugandan womanhood and their Afro-feminist modes of resistance that often go unacknowledged because they do not necessarily resemble those of Western feminism.

According to Jonathan Haynes, one of the early attractions gleaned from Western films is that of the romance and how it is realized through "the mutually reinforcing ideologies of Christian companionate marriage, the limited household as a unit of capitalist accumulation and consumption, and the modern family as a foundation of the state and molder of citizens" (2016, 79). Yet given that the nuclear family is a fairly new phenomenon in the African urban context, Haynes opines that audiences remain curious, suspicious even, about its functioning and success, meaning that many plots are "devoted to scandal mongering," "revealing hidden secrets" and "sexual infidelities" (79) in and around the household. Hence, rather than feed into the idealism of romance, African video films are much more intrigued by how the model of Western monogamy goes awry in local contexts, which bears much stronger correlations to Western soap operas and chick films. Similarly, Frances Harding also notes how many African video films are infused with "rumours and counter-rumours of relaxed bar talk or intimate, intense talk of close friends" (2007, 15). This indigenous style, known as *fabu*, sustains the pleasure of secretive and intimate conversational dynamics that segues into the more feminine modes of narration usually deployed in chick films.

According to Suzanne Ferriss and Mallory Young, chick culture's connection to its predecessors is always "an ironic one" (2006, 3) because numerous subversions result in the dissolution of romantic and courtly ideals. In comparison to the nineteenth-century novel of manners and the Harlequin Romance, the chick genre "does not always offer its readers the satisfaction of a "happily-ever-after" (Guerrero 2006, 93). Unlike the romantic bildungsroman that is structured as a quest narrative that ends with meeting the "right" man, chick films often revel in the adventurousness of sexual relationships that lead to a series of joys, sorrows, and comedies (Mabry 2006, 200). Chick films reflect the lives of young women who struggle with everyday challenges like their romantic relationships, parents, friends, sexuality, body image, and consumerism (Harzewski 2011; Van Slooten 2006) and bring to light the complexities of modern women who are forced to navigate various conflicting experiences and social double standards that simultaneously empower and oppress women (Harzewski 2011, 8). Hence, unlike romance, where third-person narration usually inscribes its female characters as passive objects of romantic attention and "reinforces the heroine's position as the (often literal) object of a (primarily male) gaze" (Tania Modleski cited in Mabry 2006, 196), chick films heighten the experience of subjectivity through first-person focalization. For example, in the *Bridget Jones* films and the *Sex and the City* television series, it is always women's "desires and motivations [that are] the focus of the story," thus providing "authentic, in-depth accounts of women's experiences" (Mabry 2006, 196). These genres thus rely on styles that "explore the internal and emotional life of women" (Benstock 2006, 255), and akin to the confessional mode used in genres like memoir and autobiography (256), they give "the sense of being inside the mind of each character and watching her or his perceptions unfold" (Wells 2006, 66–67). The narrative consciousness inspires intimacy and identification with the women they portray and "also offers at least a temporary escape from the feeling of constantly being watched or controlled by a male-dominated society" (Modleski cited in Mabry 2006, 196) by advocating for women's modes of perception as the primary focal point of the narrative.

Despite being written and directed by a man, Dila's films nevertheless deploy many chick film features. For example, *How to Start a Zombie Apocalypse* opens with a young, heavily pregnant woman who is ironing laundry. She then folds over in pain—as viewers we anticipate that she might be going into labor—but she quickly recovers and resumes her chores. Her lover enters the room, and he presents her with a gift bag with the words "happy birthday" on it. There is nothing showy about their romance, and the scene plays out as an illustration of domestic and romantic ease. Yet this is interrupted when the man's mobile phone rings and he retreats slightly to answer it. After some whispering in the woman's company, he walks out of the house to continue with his call. The camera does not follow him and remains positioned over her shoulder for us to bear witness to the manner in which her eyes follow him out of the house. She turns around again, and the viewer sees her crestfallen expression. Without dialogue or melodrama, we remain aware of the lingering temptations of urban life that threaten her domestic sanctuary and empathize with the betrayal and maternal vulnerability she feels. *Cursed Widow Blues* also highlights a woman's difficulty in holding on to a lover. The film opens with a nervous suitor standing outside a woman's house, and once the female protagonist spots him from her bedroom window, she fixes herself to greet her lover, but a note suddenly slides out from underneath the bed. It has a message on it, warning her that she should not be seeing other men because she is a married woman. From this, we ascertain that the ghost of her dead husband lingers in the home. It appears to ward off new suitors and keeps his wife chaste in the realm of the living. Anxious and slightly flustered, the woman takes great pains to appease this ghost by performing a ritual and then removing her wedding ring. The ritual involves burning a photo of the once happy couple. Making some form of a cameo appearance, the husband in the photo is Dilman Dila, who is, arguably, the masterful ghost attending to everyone's actions in the house and the scene. This cheeky acknowledgment reads as a clever way of drawing attention to himself as a male director of this female-centered narrative and allows us to pause and question our level of comfort with that fact. When the woman finally opens the door, her suitor is on bended knee and presents her with a ring. Elated, she drags him into her bedroom. After sex, she goes to the kitchen to prepare a meal. When she returns, her new fiancé is missing—the ghost of the dead husband has killed him. The woman is bereft and left to bury her new suitor in the backyard.

Dila's female protagonists highlight the affective and psychological labor involved in keeping and capturing men in a tumultuous urban dating and marriage economy. Yet despite capitalizing on the humor and irony of the chick film to expose the perils of heteronormative romance, both films eschew the liberating effects of its overt sexual politics. For in stepping away from romance, chick films embrace womanhood as a messy terrain that is inherently ambiguous and contradictory. This allows for the negation of traditional gender roles that usually prevent women from pursuing sexual gratification. Chick films make the freedom of sex and sexuality permissible by inscribing it as self-exploration and the contemporary configuration of one's womanly identity. Yet despite their romantic disappointment, the protagonists in *How to Start a Zombie Apocalypse* and *Cursed Widow Blues* do not pursue socioeconomic independence and sexual emancipation, nor do they escape the domestic realm in any significant way.

In line with Lawrence Ekwok's assertion that "the tendency of using a radical feminist orientation in depicting womanhood in African movies often conflicts with African audiences' reading or reception of the films" (2017, 73), it becomes easy to interpret the feminist plot resolutions of Western chick films as not only alienating but also highly implausible in relation to Ugandan social realities. Yet, Lynda Gichanda Spencer takes this argument further, suggesting that critics need to be cognizant of the fact that the chick genre in Africa is informed by entirely "different feminisms" (2019, 157). With a specific focus on Ugandan and South African chick lit, she opines that these authors "resist, undermine, renew and rethink mainstream chick-lit" (159) in an active attempt to place "focus on the everyday of women's lives" (166). By illustrating how the concerns and lives of ordinary women are markedly different from those expressed in Western chick lit, Spencer's astute observation points out how African authors are not failing at genre fiction but, rather, are participating in chick lit in ways that inscribe Afro-feminist agendas as central to its realization on the continent.

Given that Afro-feminism involves "getting rid of those parts of Western feminism that were uncritically adopted and to reconceptualize the struggle for more meaningful and contextually relevant ways of addressing the marginalization of women" (Tamale 2020, 40), it becomes important to acknowledge that sex and sexuality are not universal concepts and certainly do not find the same expression in the Western world and a country like Uganda. For example, Florence Kyoheirwe Muhanguzi notes that "while women's agency of sexual expression is acknowledged, overt expression of this experience remains outlandish for many women" (2015, 64) in Uganda. Her study outlines how Ugandan women communicate their sexual desires in heterosexual relationships in accordance with carefully constructed social limits around the articulation and performance of sexual needs and pleasure. These women understand that men are still the primary initiators and beneficiaries of these sexual relations. In addition, though sex is an intimate act that occurs in the domestic space, the patriarchal demand of female silence is systemically reinforced by various government institutions. According to Prince Karakire Guma, Ugandan feminists are dismayed at the "increasing panic regarding the short-lived successes, the fading optimism, and perceived resignation of the feminist movement" (2017, 144). Despite significant change in the late 1990s, he notes an institutional "counteraction to women's 'increased independence'" (144); a backlash of new "prohibitive attitudes and perceptions that women's 'proper' place is in the home rather than in [the] public sphere are increasingly re-emerging" (144). For example, he points to the conservative Anti-Pornographic Bill (2013), which Ugandans have since nicknamed the "Miniskirt Bill" because of its interest in policing women's bodies and behavior and suppressing "women's assertion of their sexual rights and freedoms" (143). Given this context, it is unsurprising that the women in Muhanguzi's study were unanimous in stating that the emphatic and public expression of sexuality must be tempered to avoid being labeled a "good-time girl." Hence, by acknowledging these limits on women's sexual expression, we come to understand that Afro-feminist sexualities find alternative means of expression to prevent one's identity from lapsing into commonplace stereotypes that may invite harm.

Arguably, Dila grapples with this challenge in his horror romances by transmuting the sexual economy of the chick film into a haunting effect; the female protagonists do not make a radical break from the domestic order; instead, horror begins to seep *into* it. In comparison to chick film, horror holds a more clandestine potential for exploring women's sexual expression, making the horror romance a clever context-specific way of navigating with Afro-feminist intent. Similar to Alexandra Grieve's discussion in this volume of how Ousmane Sembène uses noir elements to expose the "carceral topography" of the home in *La Noire de . . .* (1966), Dila's portrayal of the domestic space belies the perception of home as a nurturing environment for its female protagonists. By turning to horror, Dila unearths the ambivalent desires that govern women's relationship to the domestic, thereby showing how women haunt and are haunted by it.

The appeal to the supernatural is, in fact, an ingrained feature in African cinema (Haynes 2016, 109), and, as in Western horrors, it tends to be "highly gendered" (107). Cosmic forces, usually in the form of women and witches, tend to disrupt the dynamics of the nuclear family by unearthing hidden "domestic tensions" or "emotional structures" (107). Although the supernatural in African cinema is reflective of an animistic worldview in which man communes with a relatively neutral, if not mischievous, spiritual realm, the rise of Pentecostalism on the continent has led to its increasing formulation as evil (Böhme 2013, 331). As a result, more contemporary films align with the moral attitudes of Western horror where the unknown is experienced as a threat to be purged and ultimately makes for "a conservative genre that works to justify and defend the status quo" (Jancovich 2002, 13). The pleasure of horror is thus twofold; it titillates the viewer through the spectacle of monstrosity but then also placates through its destruction. In psychoanalytic terms, the monstrous is seen as a manifestation of the subconscious that, when surfaced, can threaten the stability of the status quo. The ability to reinforce preexisting power structures has made horror particularly susceptible to bourgeois and masculinist sensibilities that use the spectacle of monstrosity to allay fears of the other, who must remain repressed and oppressed in the interest of identity and the retention of power. Feminists have long since noted how horror has rendered women as abject bodies in order to reinforce heteropatriarchal logic. For example, Cynthia A. Freeland notes how "the fates of monsters and women get strangely paired on the side of the spectacle" (2018, 158). For in bearing witness to how the feminine can overwhelm and destroy masculinity, the male psyche turns to horror to ritualistically deny and expel this realization in efforts to separate and sustain itself.

Feminist approaches to horror have thus sought to reinscribe the abject as "a potentially subversive critique of the social world" (Jancovich 2002, 21) by illustrating the extent to which women come to identify as or with monsters because of their similar status in the patriarchal structure (57). For example, Grieve's analysis of Majolie and Chouchou in Jean-Pierre Bekolo's *Les saignantes* in this volume highlights this affirmative use of women's monstrosity that disturbs and even overturns the civil and domestic order. Because women are second-class citizens in a patriarchal world, it is common for female characters to have an affinity with monsters who mirror and even champion their struggle for greater emancipation. Yet given the colonial history that informs the portrayal of femmes fatales as "dangerous, monstrous and violent women of color" (Caputi and Sagle 2004, 90), the translation of globalized representations of female monstrosity requires further consideration in an African filmic context.

Critics of African cinema are often affronted by the abundance of themes like witchcraft and horror because it reinforces a historical imaginary of Africa as a superstitious and illogical place, thereby constituting "a clear setback to the emancipatory politics" (Krings and Okome 2013, 2). Similarly, "femme noire stereotypes are often read as confirming women's base inferiority, immorality and monstrosity and can inspire hatred, scapegoating, and retaliation" (Caputi and Sagle 2004, 109). The grammar of conflating black bodies with animal bodies—hypersexualized, irrational, unintelligent, and lacking self-awareness—has consistently served to inscribe white masculinity as the primary subject of ontology. The assertion that a more embodied animal/magical identity is a progressive affirmation of black female bodies is thus a ruse that only serves to sustain the continual dehumanization of black and African women (see Bisschoff and Van de Peer 2020, 157; Keeling 2007, 83; D. Lewis 2011, 207).

Consequently, Desiree Lewis notes that "in refusing the stereotype, certain writers might have shied away from exploring African women's sexuality altogether" (2011, 207), and she insists on the need to address this oversight in both popular culture and academic scholarship. Thinking about what an Afrofeminist approach might entail, Lizelle Bisschoff and Stefanie Van de Peer suggest that representing African women's bodies in cinema "should not lead to an uncritical or romanticized celebration of the power of female sexuality"

(2020, 176) but to a more sustained awareness of how "African systems of relation have a different ontology to which psychoanalytical approaches are not necessarily applicable" (156). They opine that Western feminist cinema is historically informed by psychoanalytic theory and is entirely unsuitable for the representation and study of African women in cinema, which makes it necessary to reevaluate the nature of the monstrous in relation to the African psyche and social imaginary.

Contrary to Western expectations of dark and supernatural forces, Chimaraoke O. Izugbara uncovers how "indigenous supernatural beliefs surrounding sexuality in traditional Africa were driven primarily by the need to minimize chaos and promote general good conduct" (2011, 537). The appearance of the supernatural in African social structures was a narrative strategy for the modulation of the status quo rather than that which provided expression for a human psyche grappling with its sense of inherent dualism. This is made abundantly clear in a classic film like Kunle Afolayan's *The Figurine* (2009) in which the supernatural travels into contemporary urban settings and is ultimately exposed as a man's narcissistic attempt to control the woman he desires. It is possible, then, that in taking to popular genre film, African filmmakers, like Dila, will draw on this earlier indigenous configuration of the monstrous to reflect on the realities and confinements of the institutionalized patriarchy of modern domesticity.

After making love to her new fiancé in *Cursed Widow Blues*, the woman admires her new ring in the kitchen mirror and giggles with girlish delight while peeling plantains for lunch. The camera zooms in to show the knife cutting through the tough skin of plantain after plantain, whose phallic shape foreshadows the later revelation of the many lovers she has had and buried before. While she cooks, the film cuts back to the bedroom, where the satisfied man is resting on the bed. He is shocked when a note slides out from underneath the bed. Seeing as this is how the ghost of the dead husband communicated with his wife, we assume the note is coming from the same source. He reads the note, and it informs the new fiancé that the woman he is sleeping with is still married. He then hears a noise in the cupboard, and when he opens it, he is utterly confused by the sight of the woman who is supposed to be in the kitchen. This version of the woman, however, holds a knife out to murder him. When the woman returns to the room, her lover's body is missing, but her murderous doppelgänger now attempts to stab her. Yet, the ghost, who seemingly controls this murderous version of her, prevents it from killing his wife.

Like most horrors, this film plays with our expectation of dual—and dueling—identities. The doppelgänger looks exactly like her, but the female protagonist experiences alienation rather than an affinity toward it. Given the extent to which the monster seeks to exert control over the protagonist's behavior, we come to understand that the "monstrous feminine" is not a liberatory doppelgänger but a patriarchal henchman who does the dark bidding of the dead husband's ghost. The monstrous is thus a manifestation of an inescapable, patriarchal conservatism that annihilates any threat to the dead husband's dominion over the household and reinstates the status quo of a "faithful wife." In an understated but revolutionary manner, the protagonist refuses identification with a monstrous, bad or evil woman, thereby underlining that there is nothing deviant about her sexual experiences and behavior. Though the appearance of the monstrous feminine may seem normative, Dila collapses the potential for it to find interpretation as the repressed subconscious of the female character. Rather, the monstrous exposes the material and social forces of patriarchy as covert and ominous, lingering and haunting the lives of women. This film thus offers a crucial awareness of the pervasive and discursive nature of patriarchy for, somewhat tellingly, the monstrous is not dealt with "either by rejecting and if possible annihilating it" but rather by "rendering it safe and assimilating it, converting it as far as possible into a replica of itself" (Wood 2002, 27).

The film ends with a scene outside, at night; the woman is digging a fresh grave for her dead fiancé. She seems distant and resigned to her task, unfazed by this part of the "Cursed Widow Blues" that she repeatedly sings. The woman seemingly accepts her haunted house and understands that survival means living among ghosts and monsters, and she makes no drastic attempt to leave—but she also refuses to be dominated by these entities. Just as her husband's ghost haunts her, she continues to haunt him by not letting his ghost rest in peace. She persists in having lovers and then blithely buries them in her backyard. Furthermore, she is not murdered for her sexual engagement; the victims are all male, and the revelation of the many deceased lovers is treated with humor. In fact, one could argue that the cycle of sin and repentance enhances the sexual pleasure for the character. This clandestine awareness of sexual pleasure and the covert manner in which it is pursued illustrate how African women can, in fact, negotiate their way around patriarchy without necessitating a complete overhaul of the domestic realm. She lacks interest in inflicting a radical form of violence toward patriarchal constraint—for how does one kill an omnipotent ghost?—and functions with a level of ease without necessarily escaping its clutches. The portrait is thus not heroic, and we may not consider it feminist because it does not offer alternatives that would minimize her suffering, but it champions the mundane and covert methods that women adopt in relation to patriarchy to ensure space for themselves within a heteropatriarchal domestic order.

In comparison, *How to Start a Zombie Apocalypse* uses a different set of horror tropes to illustrate how the romantic idealization of domesticity is, in itself, rather monstrous. When the man answers his phone, the woman feels deeply betrayed and is again struck by a sudden bout of pain. A pixelated ominous black figure appears, revealing a digital alarm with her face on it, and when the alarm starts to beep, she collapses. As viewers of horror, we are familiar with the manner in which women's bodies are used as sites for monstrosity, a conceit that only intensifies when applied to the bodies of pregnant women who become examples of "embodiment run amok" (McReynolds 2005, 150). The black figure watches impassively as blood pours down her leg, suggesting a miscarriage, yet she does not summon her lover and soon dies. When she suddenly wakes up next to her own dead body, the black figure quickly atomizes her and traps her in the screen it carries. From the screen, she watches in horror as her own dead body reawakens as a zombie, awaiting the return of her lover. The zombie woman leaps forward and kills him by taking a bite out of his neck. He also then atomizes and joins her in the screen dimension. They are reunited in this digital world but then watch in horror as their zombified bodies roam freely in their home while they are stuck in the claustrophobic dimension of the screen. The overt reference to the screen is alienating and draws attention to the narrative artifice of the romantic domesticity that we have been engaging with thus far. In her detailed analysis of family law in contemporary Uganda, Sylvia Tamale states that "the law carefully places the institution of the family on a pedestal, upholds the sanctity of a hetero-patriarchal marriage and idealizes its functions. Ugandan family relations were reshaped and transformed by British colonialism. At the centre of these changes was the emergence of a new domesticity, geared to align Indigenous households to the capitalist exploitative system" (2020, 290–91).

Though traditional family structures were not necessarily less patriarchal, they were significantly looser arrangements that could be negotiated among individuals to suit their needs. Tamale argues that colonialism ultimately shaped the need and desire for nuclear domesticity, as it made men more directly dependent on the state for economic survival and women more directly dependent on men, since they were pushed out of the public economic sphere and into the home. The nuclear family is thus an imported fantasy that racial capitalism perpetuated and enforced in Africa in order to profit from exploitative labor demands on local communities. Seen from this angle, Dila's evocation of the zombie is chillingly apt.

Although its origins are in Haitian voodoo culture, the zombie is, in fact, "a white fantasy figure" (McReynolds 2005, 151) invented to quell the anxieties of the early twentieth century, white American psyche regarding the emancipated and self-governed Haitian population. Contrary to what one might assume, the zombie is a placatory figure—a wish fulfillment of "a docile (black) labor force that would never revolt, never demanded better working conditions, were insensitive to pain, and that could work day and night devoted entirely to carrying out the wishes of the zombie master" (151). By conforming to the eternal master-slave relationship, the zombie distills fears around race and revolution and keeps the logic of imperialistic capitalism alive. The early voodoo zombie drones on mindlessly, possessing no desire to reconfigure power, labor, and race relations; it is the plantation worker par excellence. Phillip McReynolds goes on to describe how the zombie figure is later appropriated by postmodern popular culture to represent modern man, trapped in the circular logic of capitalism; seduced by consumerism, he drones on about repetitive activity that promises neither vitality nor easy death.

Unsurprisingly, the zombie has also been used to explore the roles of women in modern society. McReynolds states that in early zombie films, the victims were mostly women who would "become mere automatons whose existence is exclusively defined by their subservience to their (male) zombie masters" (151). This aspect finds literal representation in Dila's film where the title slate reads, "How to start a zombie apocalypse," and cuts directly to a young woman ironing, which enforces a connection between the repetitive nature of women's domestic labor and zombification. The woman's cheery disposition while she is ironing is unnerving, and the extent to which she epitomizes the cliché of "happy, barefoot, and pregnant" injects satirical force into the scene, convincing the audience that she must be operating under a delusion or spell. Yet more compellingly still, the husband is also zombified during the course of the film, and the dark figure begins to resemble a zombie master who entraps them both in the screen world. Dila thus uses zombification to excavate the capitalistic underpinnings of the Ugandan heteropatriarchal household that, as described by Tamale, placed both men and women in positions of direct dependency in relation to the state. Somewhat significantly, the zombie master is a strange cross between a ghoul and a cyborg—an evocation of both old and new technologies that speaks to the longevity and reproducibility of capitalism across the ages. Overall, this is a relatively sympathetic representation of African masculinity, and it is possible to interpret this as part of the complexity of an Afro-feminist acknowledgment that men are also—though not equal—victims of colonial and neocolonial oppression.

In *How to Start a Zombie Apocalypse*, it becomes increasingly uncomfortable to watch the grotesque conversion of the couple's home into a zombie's cave filled with blood and stagnation. They remain trapped in the digital realm, and the manner in which their zombified bodies continue to roam freely around the home provides some cheeky commentary about how monogamous domesticity requires a level of brainwashing and "unnatural" or dehumanizing behavior from its participants. Moreover, the self-conscious reference to screens and screen culture makes us aware of our hermeneutic desperation for cinematic wish fulfillment. As Keeling argues, it is necessary to think about the emotions and desires we bring into the cinema because "affective labour is necessary for capitalism, it is what we use to produce and sustain common sense images" (2007, 97). Dila accordingly intimates that we—like zombies—have bought into expectations and fantasies of heteronormative romance. The film's ending is a discomforting reminder of the extent to which the "happily ever after" of global screen worlds has permeated contemporary Africa and how our engagement with global popular culture does, to some extent, make us complicit in the ideological and social reproduction of neocolonial capitalistic structures.

Yet, as I have shown through the close reading of Dila's two horror romances, the tone of these critiques is comic and playful, making them exemplifications of how African popular culture utilizes techniques of syncretism (Barber 1987, 12), sampling (Wendl 2007, 3), and bricolage (Böhme 2013, 332) to entertain as part of the continual process of negotiated meaning in contemporary African society. By bringing together the chick film and the horror romance, Dila has shown how "reconfiguring and re-articulating the global flow of images for new local audiences" (Wendl 2007, 3) can allow for the complexities of Afro-feminist concerns to emerge on-screen through the portrayal of women's domestic disturbance. As I have shown in this chapter, these women are exonerated from the burdens of monstrous representation, which allows us to explore the extent to which they are both haunted by and haunt the realities of heteropatriarchal domesticity. Through the reconfiguration of the monstrous that instead draws attention to the lingering ghostly effects of colonialism and patriarchy, we learn more about how women navigate contemporary domesticity by leaving the door open for the expression of their ever-evolving desires.

10

Fashioning African Screen Worlds

La noire de . . . *and* Les saignantes

ALEXANDRA GRIEVE

In *Surface: Matters of Aesthetics, Materiality, and Media*, Giuliana Bruno posits an alternate approach to the study of fashion in film, arguing that a "superficial" awareness of materials—layers, barriers, and textures—allows for the radical re-apprehension of costume and film as materially entwined, "fashioned as a matter of surface" (2014, 30). Although Bruno does not explicitly apply this schematic to the politics of film production in Africa, I consider her aware-ness of the material traffic between costume and cinema a generative ana-lytic rubric to bring to bear upon the notion of African "screen worlds," past and present. In this chapter, I put a pioneering film of African independent cinema in conversation with a more recent example, namely, Ousmane Sem-bène's *La noire de . . .* (1966) and Jean-Pierre Bekolo's *Les saignantes* (2005). Both filmmakers—particularly Sembène, who is lauded as the "father of African cinema"—are broadly emblematic of the prominence that male sub-Saharan African filmmakers have enjoyed at the expense of female voices in African filmmaking since the 1960s.[1] Against this backdrop, I suggest that a fuller engagement with dress and the "fashioned" surface of the screen is useful, as it opens up our cinematic analysis to a wide range of embodied and material techniques through which screen worlds have been fabricated—often in powerfully gendered ways. Specifically, I draw attention to the value of practices of "self-fashioning" (Jaji 2014, 116) in these films, where creative invocations of "contemporary" fashion by the films' female protagonists are enlisted into a critique of the colonial relegation of the non-Western Other to a state of temporal alterity. Just as Karl Schoonover and Rosalind Galt suggest that "every film constructs a world formally [and] has the capacity to recalibrate its own perimeters" (2016, 25), so too, in these instances, is fashion a transgressive modality of "world-making" and a means of mapping alternative futures for the African postcolony. In this way, I suggest that Sembène's and Bekolo's works yield an insight into the material "fashioning" of African screen worlds as well as the crucial role of women's embodied praxis in this process.

In her chapter in the book *Fashioning Africa*, Victoria L. Rovine reminds us that "garments, unlike other commodities, are very literally embodied; when they travel, they serve as shorthand referents to the people and cultures with whom they originated" (2004, 189). Following these lines, my aim in what follows is to stress the relationship between cinema and dress as a means of fashioning the self, an embodied habitus, or situated practice (Bourdieu 1994) through which postcolonial African subjectivities have been constructed. This notion of dress-as-habitus is rooted both conceptually and etymologically in the principle of "*habitare*, dwelling" (Bruno 2014, 31) and thus speaks aptly to the ways in which spatiality, dress, and social positionality are interconnected. Consequently, in making this argument, I consider it vital to reflect on my own situated positionality through which I am encountering and describing these embodied practices, as a white South African researcher with a European educational background. In attempting to reflect on the unequal power structures and the biases I might sustain in my methodology, I want to carefully consider the implications of African dress practices and, in particular, avoid the reproduction of analytic categories which may sustain universalist, ahistorical preconceptions about fashion.

To this end, it is important to assert that fashion and attitudes surrounding it have historically been implicated in the production of imperial regimes of geopolitical power. Even the juxtaposition of the words *fashion* and *Africa* is a problematic illustration of this. Foundational studies of fashion (Simmel

1973; Veblen 1970) framed it as a phenomenon that emerges exclusively from the processes of Western modernization and capitalist expansion, and consequently, as Jean Marie Allman writes, located "the motor of history squarely in Europe" (2004a, 2). There are notable echoes of the phenomenon that Johannes Fabian (2014) famously identified as anthropology's "denial of coevalness," whereby geographic distance is compounded with the demotion of the non-Western Other to a stage of "primitivity." Of course, fashion has never been hermetically sealed off or teleologically determined. Giorgio Agamben's sketch of fashion in "What Is the Contemporary?" (2009) affirms this; in its thrall to the urgency of the new, the substance of whatever is "in fashion" must, by necessity, mutate constantly, displacing the hegemony of the cultural moment that preceded it. In *La noire de . . .* and *Les saignantes*, I explore how this mutational potentiality has been harnessed to give expression to moments of uncertainty and social change. On the one hand, Sembène's film is an unflinching investigation of black domestic labor in France, undergirded by the rigid material arrangement of (neo)colonial domestic space and the corresponding fashioning of Black female bodies as docile, convenient amenities. However, *La noire de . . .* also indexes the cross-cultural encounters that invigorated African women's fashion in the 1960s, citing a self-possessed, thoroughly modern African sensibility in line with an emerging landscape of colonial resistance. In a like manner, *Les saignantes* alludes to an imperative of social transformation, with a strident voice-over insisting that "the country must change." However, in his dystopic, eclectically fashioned vision of Cameroon in 2025, Bekolo appears skeptical of this possibility. The "time of fashion," as Agamben writes, "constitutively anticipates itself and consequently is always too late" (2009, 48), and it is precisely this ambivalent oscillation that is at the heart of Bekolo's indictment of Western techno-capitalism and the notion of futurity more generally. What is clear, however, is that where the institutions of African filmmaking have historically relegated African women to the margins, fashion—in both *La noire de . . .* and *Les saignantes*—makes highly visible the role of women in the production of changing cultural paradigms. In both films, the fashioned female body, like the cinematic screen, becomes a materially dimensional site "in which different forms of mediation, transfer, and transformation can take place" (Bruno 2014, 3).

La noire de . . .

Set in 1960, after Senegal had gained its independence from France, and adapted from his short story of the same title, Ousmane Sembène's *La noire de . . .* is feted by film historians as the first independent feature film by a sub-Saharan

African. Given that it was an important interruption of the steady stream of films made in Africa by Westerners with little investment in the conditions of African life, it is easy to see why *La noire de . . .* occupies a singular position in African cinematic history. I would suggest, however, that one of the film's most striking innovations is its expression of an African postcolonial cinematic voice in distinctly textural terms, mediated through the embodied experience of a young Black woman. Fashion, as I have suggested, must be regarded as a materially and spatially situated process, a habitus that connects the individual and the social world. An uncompromising confrontation with neocolonial exploitation, dress, in *La noire de . . .* , is figurative of a much wider textural apparatus of power, acutely entangled in notions of conquest and the domestic consolidation of imperial space. Nevertheless, it is also through appeals to the discourse of fashion, in *La noire de . . .* , that alternative ways of being are imagined and liberating zones of cross-cultural contact are assembled. Emerging in the period when a network of media forms such as cinema, glossy magazines, and popular music had begun to sketch "modern," newly independent African identities as a conscious project of black female self-fashioning (Jaji 2014, 21), fashion, in *La noire de . . .* , can also be connected to a wider project of independent identity formation during a period of radical political change.[2] Through this lens, *La noire de . . .* brings into view a crucially gendered aspect of postcolonial identity construction.

The story follows the life of a Senegalese woman, Diouana, who is employed as a domestic worker and childminder for a petit bourgeois French couple. The film begins as she embarks on a cross-continental journey from Dakar, exhilarated by the thought of starting a new life with her employers in the Antibes, which unfortunately proves to be a crushing disappointment. Diouana is confined to a small apartment and subjected to months of abuse at the hands of her employers, who overwhelm her with demeaning chores. By anchoring the narrative in Diouana's journey from the postcolonial periphery to the metropolitan center, *La noire de . . .* effectively debunks the myth of European cosmopolitanism and renders the Antibes a thoroughly oppressive and intolerant space. More specifically, though, it is via the home of the French couple that this oppressive atmosphere is spatially configured, and Sembène becomes the intrepid explorer in reverse, a critical dissembler of the material world of the colonizer. In a manner akin to the domestic disorder of Dilman Dila's *No Letting Go* and *Cursed Widow Blues*, where the home becomes a site of profound ambivalence rather than comfort and familial security (Moonsamy, this volume), the space of the Antibes apartment in *La noire de . . .* offers a revealing view of the evident insecurity of the French couple's cultural position in the postindependence moment.

Occupying a somewhat diminished position on the global stage, France's self-image was undergoing significant changes in the 1960s. France's decline in colonial influence, somewhat paradoxically, coincided with a steady rise in domestic growth and prosperity. Following an influx of newly affordable consumer goods in the postwar economic boom, the space of the French home became particularly amenable to material expressions of renewed prosperity. Kristin Ross interprets these historical developments as follows: "With the waning of its empire, France turned to a form of interior colonialism; rational administrative techniques developed in the colonies were brought home and put to use side by side with new technological innovations such as advertising in reordering metropolitan, domestic society" (1995, 7). As Ross would suggest, even in the decade that witnessed many hard-won African liberations from France, the techniques of colonial governance and rationalization continued to enjoy a rich afterlife in the French interior. *La noire de . . .* uses the language of materiality and dress to highlight this doubled movement, tracing the tension between the former colonizer's purportedly broadened cultural horizons and, simultaneously, the hollowness of the promise of cultural assimilation.

To see this dynamic at work in the Antibes apartment, we can begin by noting that, on the one hand, the home is clearly tinged with modernist, colorful expressions of "cosmopolitan" French tastes. In the living room, we find abstractedly pattered cubist drapes and soft furnishings, straw woven chairs, and various African masks with feathers and beadwork. This decor highlights the legacies of cultural exchange that link Africa and Europe and, superficially at least, would appear to affirm the "worldly" sophistication of the Antibes couple. However, there are plainly additional operations at work here: in Sembène's novel on which the film is based, the room is described as offering its entrants "the impression of penetrating a hunter's den" (Sembène 1974, 84). As this would suggest, the room also points more critically toward the predatory commodification of African art into "material" (in the sense of pure expendability) for Western consumption. As the narrative unfolds and the reality of Diouana's exploitation becomes apparent, so too do the open horizons of the metropole appear to shrink and take on an increasingly carceral quality. "France: it's the kitchen, the living room, my bed," is how Diouana summarizes the scenario in her voice-over narration. Something of this carceral topography is also inscribed in Sembène's scenario, which configures Diouana's imprisonment in indisputability material terms: "Le territoire du pays se limitait *à la surface* de la villa" (Sembène 1961, 98; emphasis added), translated by Len Ortzen as "the whole country contracted to the boundaries of the villa" (Sembène 1974, 75). This arrangement of domestic space is, as I suggest, connected to the disciplinarian fashioning of the body, through which an imperial habitus (Bourdieu 1994) is "architexturally" molded in the Antibes.[3]

Correspondingly, with this sense of the flattening of space comes an altered sense of Diouana's subjectivity, which is discursively and materially flattened into an inorganic entity. The figure of the housemaid is one that often ambivalently straddles the categories of worker and household commodity. She performs essential reproductive but socially maligned labor, at the uneasy intersection of the domestic and commercial worlds. In Diouana's case, such tensions become particularly evident at a lunch during which her mistress instructs Diouana to serve her friends a traditional Senegalese dish, *riz au mafé*. After the lunch is served, the houseguests are overheard praising the food: "True African cuisine served by *la bonne* [the servant]." Much like the dish that she is tasked with preparing, Diouana, in this instance, is refashioned into a domestic amenity, yet another objectified emblem of her mistress's "urbane," cosmopolitan tastes. We might also consider that the label she acquires, *la bonne* (which typically designates a female live-in housemaid), needs only to be pluralized to become *les biens*, "something someone possesses, which has financial value and can be an object of property."[4] When a male guest insists that Diouana embrace him because he has "never been kissed by a black woman before," it serves only to crystallize the extent of this—evidently explicitly gendered and racialized—depersonalization at the hands of the French.

Diouana's eerie slippage from "someone" employed to "something" owned, yet another domestic comestible, is further inferred by Sembène through the language of dress as a "situated practice" through which imperial power is articulated (Entwistle 2000, 36). On the same day as the luncheon, Diouana is presented with an apron, which her mistress insists that Diouana wear over her lively polka-dot dress (figure 10.1). Diouana has been wearing this dress since her first day in the Antibes, along with a set of oversize floral earrings and a beaded necklace. With the imminent arrival of her guests in mind, Diouana's mistress reproaches her for this sartorial excess: "You're not going to a party." In a later sequence, we see Diouana removing the more appropriate items of clothing her mistress has lent her to wear as a replacement. As she sets aside a plain collared blouse and pencil skirt, Diouana laments her mistresses' tantalizing initial promise: "You'll see Diouana, there are lovely shops in France." Her voice-over narration continues: "Did she bring me here just to shut me

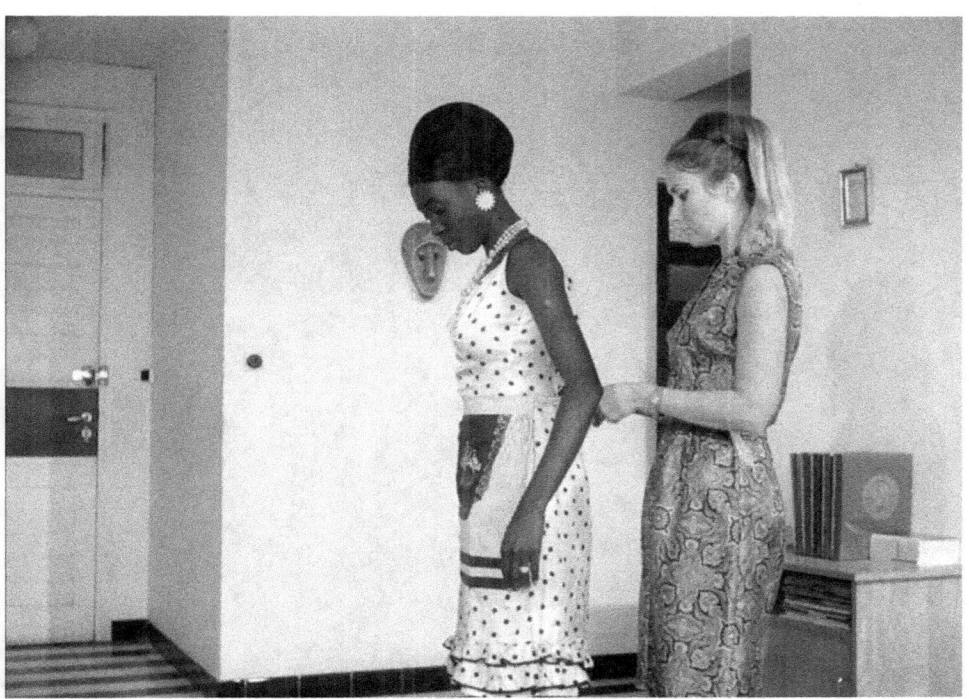

FIGURE 10.1. Diouana receiving the apron that her French mistress insists she wear over her lively polka-dot dress on the day of a special luncheon. Film still from Ousmane Sembène (dir.), *La noire de . . .* Courtesy of Alain Sembène.

in? That's why she was so nice in Dakar, giving me her old dresses, her old slips, her old shoes." The shoes, in particular, prove to be a sore point. Later, Diouana is again reproached by her mistress for dressing in a pair of black kitten heels, of which Diouana was especially fond (figure 10.2). When Diouana enters the living room to begin another working day in the heels, her mistress practically barks: "Take those off! Don't forget you're a maid. The kids are here, the picnic's over." Diouana obeys the instructions and begrudgingly continues barefoot.

Each of these incidents highlights a conflict over Diouana's identity in a rapaciously materialist context and demonstrates how fashion has strategically been deployed to inscribe Western, patriarchal codes of civility. Here, dress is not available as a mode of expressivity on equal racial and gendered terms; nor is it merely a generic assertion of taste or acculturation. As Allman (2004b) has shown, a lack of appropriate bodily concealment by clothing was deeply imbricated in the cultural production of racist and imperialist notions of

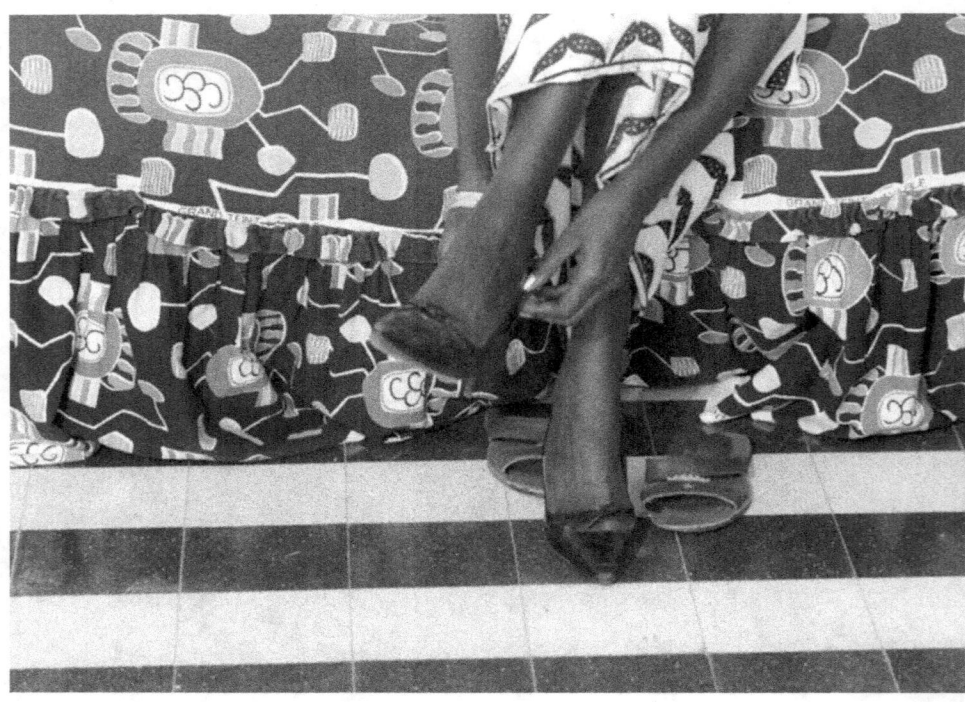

FIGURE 10.2. Diouana's kitten heels that her mistress demands she take off while working. Film still from Ousmane Sembène (dir.), *La noire de . . .* Courtesy of Alain Sembène.

"primitive" African societies and was viewed by colonizers as a source of moral concern. The sartorial "gifts" imparted to Diouana can be seen to replicate these historical patterns by enforcing more "productive" modes of bodily comportment upon her and enclosing her body within a colonial regime of propriety and modesty. The effect of the uniform as a means of encoding particular sexual values, "conveying certain attributes of femininity—modesty, neatness, demureness," as Jennifer Craik (2003, 130) writes, is important, particularly in view of the rhetoric surrounding African women's supposedly "uninhibited" sexuality. By stripping Diouana's body of "inappropriate" adornment and imposing a more modest style of dress her mistress resurrects these stereotypes and ensures Diouana's depersonalized status as "an object in the midst of other objects" (Fanon 2008, 82)—*la bonne* is firmly secured.

Nevertheless, *La noire de . . .* does not remain exclusively beholden to fashion as it has been instrumentalized in service of the colonizer. On the one hand, it is not likely that Sembène himself placed much stock in the subversive power of dress, given his harsh criticism of what he considered to be a materialist, image-conscious "new African class" emerging in the postindependence era (Sembène and Hennebelle 1998, 13). On the other hand, however, it is also via dress that Diouana's individual agency and private desires are repeatedly indexed. During a moment of respite during a lunch service, for example, Diouana draws up private plans to visit Cannes and Monte Carlo, which unspool in the form of a virtual fashion shoot: "I'll buy pretty dresses, shoes, silk undies, and pretty wigs. I'll get my picture taken at the beach, and I'll send it back to Dakar, and they'll all die of jealousy." Although fashion and dressmaking are necessarily enmeshed in circuits of consumerism, it is clear that for Diouana, as well as for her companions in Senegal, these are deeply consequential preoccupations, connected to expressions of personal distinction. It is also worth considering the highly assertive, self-possessed spirit through which Diouana exhibits her interest in dress before she departs from Senegal. A scene in which Diouana and her boyfriend take an afternoon walk through the Place de l'Indépendance in Dakar illustrates this well. Dressed in a black-and-white-striped wrapper and her heels, Diouana twirls her skirts and indulges a street photographer by agreeing to pose for snapshots. On the way home, the pair purchase a copy of the French fashion magazine *Elle*, which they page through enthusiastically as Diouana makes plans for her life abroad. While this latter gesture might be explained as Sembène's condemnation of Diouana's aspirational view of French culture, this reading too quickly dismisses the generative possibilities, in Diouana's case, of fashion as a rare means of self-expression. To understand this, it is helpful to revisit why, precisely, her French employers consider Diouana's embellished appearance to be inappropriate.

Assessing the polka-dot dress and heels, Diouana's mistress remarks that Diouana's outfit is better suited to someone at a party or a picnic. This comment is revealing; it suggests that the root of Diouana's sartorial transgression goes back to the Eurocentric biases encircling the term *fashion*, in short, the complications Diouana poses to the distinctions between work and pleasure, nature and culture, European modernity and staid African "pastness." Diouana's dress sense is troubling precisely because it enacts the collapse of the distinction between fast-paced European capitals, "birthplaces" of modern style, and the colonies, implicitly conceived of as disconnected from the passage of time. Diouana's style, by contrast, makes a bold claim to urban culture and the contemporary. Through her eclectic material assemblage of wigs, French magazines, jewelry, and patterned dresses, Diouana consolidates a fluid, transitional moment in the postindependence era, in which, to borrow from David Scott, "old social and political formations and their corresponding frameworks of value [were] being discordantly displaced by new ones" (2014, 801). In the fragmented aftermath of colonialism, it is not yet fully clear how previously colonized subjects might construct new ways of life; however, Diouana's vibrant dress sense asserts that such possibilities exist and that the meaning of the commodity is indeed contestable by both its producers and its consumers. The material objects that float in virtuality, in Diouana's voice-over—"pretty dresses," "shoes," "silk undies"—are, in this sense, not merely the ventriloquisms of consumer capital but an invitation to access an extradiegetic space of imaginative reinvention in which Diouana's exploitation is no longer the condition on which such glamorous fantasies depend. Such a possibility is even bitterly inscribed into Diouana's suicide, in which she ritualistically gathers her clothing and repacks the suitcase with which she had originally transported her things from Senegal. She declares: "Never again, 'Diouana, take off your shoes.' Never again, 'Diouana, wash Monsieur's shirt.' Never again, 'Diouana, you're lazy!' Never again will I be a slave. I did not come to France for this apron or this money." With these last rites, Diouana asserts that she will no longer be beholden to propriety ("take off your shoes") or to the imperative of colonial productivity ("you're lazy"). Her reference to the apron, too, is highly relevant—Diouana refuses to again be objectified into the form of a domestic amenity, voiceless and passive. Climactically, Diouana then chooses to end her life by slitting her throat in the family bath, unclothed. This particular choice, too, is symbolically charged, not least of all because of the colonial imbrication of clothing with the mission to civilize "primitive" African peoples. Entwistle observes that dress attempts "to transform flesh into something recognizable and meaningful to culture; a body that does conform, that transgresses such cultural codes, is likely to cause offense and outrage" (2000, 8). By refusing to sheath her body "appropriately," Diouana again declines the invitation to the culture that her apron and hand-me-down clothing offered and instead becomes directly threatening to colonial codes of demureness and propriety. Via dress (or, rather, the lack thereof) Diouana makes a final claim to independence and the right to "fashion" her identity autonomously.

Echoing Tsitsi Jaji's illuminating work on African vernacular modernisms, Diouana's suicide resonates poignantly with the practices of self-fashioning through which African women of the early postindependence era "[inserted] themselves into a coeval field of cultural action as an intentional challenge to the othering function of time as space that Johannes Fabian outlined" (2014, 14). In this sense, *La noire de . . .* invites reflection on the political relations between African cloth and screen, as phenomena that have materially shaped the spatiotemporalities of the African postcolonial order. The film confirms that *fashion* is far from a neutral cultural signifier in an African context, nor universally empowering; nevertheless, it can still interrupt the smooth articulation of colonial, patriarchal domination across the screen's surface.

Les saignantes

Fashion in *La noire de* . . . plays the critical role of reckoning with the future of the African postcolony. Staying with this business of African futurity, I turn here to *Les saignantes* (2005). Promoted by Jean-Pierre Bekolo's production company as "one of the first science fiction films to come out of Africa" (Quartier Mozart Films 2005), *Les saignantes* echoes the pioneering spirit that distinguished *La noire de* . . . , although *Les saignantes* eschews any emancipatory paradigm into which this progress might be plotted. The film begins with intertitles that underscore this, self-reflexively admonishing its viewers: "How can you make anticipation in a country that has no future?" Casting aside the arguably didactic modes of storytelling associated with Sembène (Harrow 2013, 31) and early anticolonial filmmaking movements, in this idiosyncratic, style-conscious film, no unilateral vision of revolutionary emancipation wins out. Immersed in the ludic joys of dressing up, the heroines instead embody a transgressive fashioning of African femininity that serves no trends or master narratives. As in *La noire de* . . . Bekolo's miniskirted, glamorous protagonists Majolie and Chouchou fashion themselves eclectically, where, like Diouana, the binary categorizations of "tradition" and "modernity," Europe and its "others" are destabilized. Also as in *La noire de* . . . , *Les saignantes* links dress and gendered resistance, in this case, via dress practices that highlight the transgressive powers of African female sexuality. However, by staying with the erratic temporalities of fashion, Bekolo's critique goes somewhat further than that of Sembène, to imagine a feminist African future that both satirizes and reinvigorates the very notion of change itself.

Set in Yaoundé in 2025, the story concerns two sex workers, Majolie and Chouchou, coping with the fallout from the death of one of Majolie's clients, the secretary-general of a tyrannical political regime. After the pair realize that the "accidental" death occurred as a result of Mevoungu, a cosmic force unleashed by the women's bodies during sex, the pair become embroiled in a plot to thwart the corrupt Cameroonian government. Marked by its investment in the prosthetic (Langford 2018, 185), the film foregrounds the interventions of artificial intelligence and mechanical technology in the daily lives of Majolie and Chouchou, such as voice-activated cars, video cell phones, and harnesses that allow the pair to perform elaborate acrobatic routines. The women themselves are also fashioned quasi-bionically, statuesque in high platform heels with multicolored hair and electric blue contact lenses. The landscape in which they operate, however, seems a mismatch. In contrast to Majolie and Chouchou's futuristic glamour, the Yaoundé cityscape is dilapidated, cloaked in darkness, and populated with abandoned buildings. This disjuncture is particularly evident during an early sequence in which we travel with Chouchou, in a modish pinafore and strappy wedges, on her way to meet Majolie. Bekolo's mise-en-scène seems forcefully geared toward a sense of unease, with a heavy reliance on artificial green light, handheld cinematography, and clouds of smoke. Chouchou proceeds to hail a cab and embarks on a journey punctuated with a series of jump cuts, which fragment an already uncomfortable conversation with a sexually aggressive cab driver into a cubist pastiche. This sequence also lurches between a series of differing spatiotemporal tableaux: Chouchou's digitally compressed image on a Nokia cellphone (an oddly archaic device by the standards of Western science fiction) and the frantic scrubbing motions of Majolie in the shower, recovering from her disturbing encounter with the secretary-general. Shot length is decidedly inconsistent, as if mimicking the rhythms of Chouchou's pothole-ridden ride and the stuttered speech of the taxi driver. Even the taxi itself—a dusty 1950s Hackney cab—is a curious encroachment on the Yaoundé of 2025, suggesting a negotiated continuity with the colonial past. Lindsey Green-Simms has observed that the presence of the motorcar in colonial African cinema typically denoted the "ultimate proof that nothing was beyond the reach of technological progress" (2010, 212). When encountered in *Les saignantes*, however, the ghostly, anachronistic taxi instead becomes the symbol of breakdown and improbability, a pointed rejection of the automobile's symbolic associations with the march of futurity.

Les saignantes conforms entirely neither to science fiction's typical embrace of advanced scientific technology nor, conversely, to the Eurocentric othering of Africa as "stuck in the past." Achille Mbembe argues that "the postcolony encloses multiple *durées* made up of discontinuities, reversals, inertias, and swings that overlay one another, interpenetrate one another, and envelop one another: *an entanglement*" (2001, 14). Engaging a sense of blurred pasts, futures, and presents, *Les saignantes* distills the contingencies of the postcolony into a multivalent temporal vision replete with stylistic absurdities. As relics of outdated technology wash up unexpectedly in *Les saignantes*, fashion likewise figures decisively as a means of exploring and troubling Africa's relationships to globality and telos. As Agamben suggests, fashion is a prime vehicle for what we consider contemporary; however, it is similarly fractured by multiple temporalities and contingencies: it "constitutively anticipates itself and consequently is always also too late" (2009, 47). The means by which Majolie and Chouchou play with fashion—as a "ludic resource" (Mbembe 2001, 128) through which they can experiment with various identities—crystallizes this uncertainty and fractures the connection between futurity and "progress."

One sequence in particular stands out as an illustration of this, during which Majolie and Chouchou perform in front of a mirror to a music video-style montage of rhythmic cuts. It begins as the pair collapse into bed, exhausted at the thought of two women "that always get screwed," in Majolie's dispirited words, having to take on the regime of corrupt political elites. With characteristic humor, Chouchou counters Majolie's cynicism, asserting, "No one is going to screw me!" Exemplifying this confident resolve, Majolie and Chouchou then start to playfully dance in front of their wardrobe mirror to the bouncing electronic beat of Brenda Fassie's "Vuli Ndlela." They take turns trying on clothing, exchanging, variously, a printed T-shirt into hot pink underwear, a blue sarong, a low-cut black dress, and a fuchsia sheath. Timed to a twirl of Chouchou's hair (figure 10.3), Bekolo then cuts to face the women, deliberately overexposed and in close-up. The pair then playfully try on tinted sunglasses, body jewelry, a feather boa, and a pair of oversize gold earrings. Majolie's dancing body also changes, via a morphological visual effect, into Chouchou's, and vice versa. Toward the end of the sequence, a voice-over announces: "Mevoungu had rediscovered our integrity. . . . We were ready for the final phase!"

Here, clothing is undoubtedly part of Majolie and Chouchou's performative self-construction as glamorous and conversant with the latest trends. However, with its emphasis on mutation, inconsistency, and variety—the blurring of Majolie and Chouchou, and their uncanny doubling—*Les saignantes* overindulges fashion's appeals to contemporaneity, taking its link to futurity to a point of surreal excess. Tapping into these practices of polymorphic self-fashioning, Mbembe writes of a postcolonial subject who, drifting between local conditions of material precarity and the rampant consumerism of the globalized media, mobilizes "not just a single 'identity,' but several fluid identities which, by their very nature, must be constantly 'revised' in order to achieve maximum instrumentality and efficacy as and when required" (1992, 5). It is such that, as Mbembe writes, "fashion and pleasure" should be considered modalities of postcolonial African power in much the same way that supernatural phenomena, such as "witchcraft," are imagined to be (27). It also is important to note that fashion is in fact triangulated, in this sequence, with the women's ability to invoke the power of Mevoungu, a Cameroonian Beti rite centered

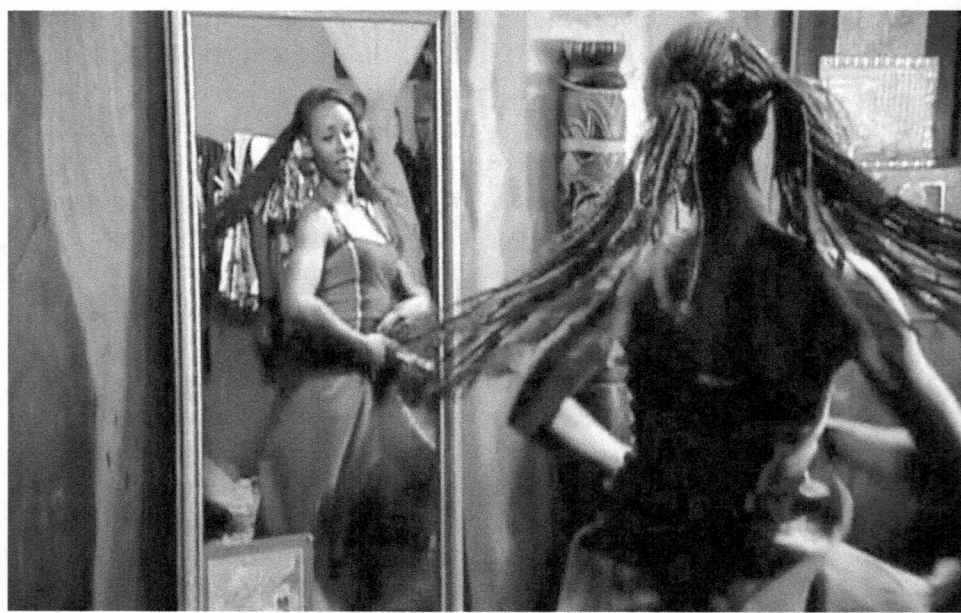

FIGURE 10.3. Chouchou performing in front of a mirror in the dress-up sequence. Film still from Jean-Pierre Bekolo (dir.), *Les saignantes*. Courtesy of Jean-Pierre Bekolo.

around the clitoris and the mythic celebration of female power. The sequence thus takes on a highly performative quality, stemming both from its symbolic investment in ritual and from Bekolo's editing techniques, which blend and distort Majolie's and Chouchou's eroticized bodies, uncoupling their femininity from the digitized projection thereof. Embodying an "ethos of masquerade" (Bastian 1996, 99; see also McRobbie 1989), Majolie and Chouchou's dress-up routine is both a celebration of their embodied agency and a playful satire of the economy of sexuality that routinely "screws" them.

Given the invocation of Mevoungu, this routine also of course serves to unsettle the Western anthropological spectrum that places "tradition" and "modernity," "civilization" and "the archaic" at opposite cultural poles. One item of clothing in particular epitomizes this temporal collision: a cowrie shell charm worn around Chouchou's waist in a girdle style, shown off to excellent effect as she playfully gyrates her hips in front of the mirror. In northern and western Africa, the conch, or cowrie, shell has long been employed as currency and as a protective talisman (Yang 2019, 160), and it is noted by anthropologists across the globe for its symbolic associations with female fecundity and menstruation (Ortner and Whitehead 1981, 143; Yang 2019). The symbolism of the moon throughout *Les saignantes* further underscores this implicit menstrual theme; it appears on-screen at key moments when Mevoungu is at work, and, as Majolie explains, hearing older women say that they had "seen the moon" meant that they were receiving their period. The cowrie girdle binds these experiences together in an expression of mythological female power wielded masterfully through the gyrating, eroticized bodies of the two *saignantes*, or "bloodettes." Moreover, in the through line between the cyclical phases of the moon, female power, fashion, and menstrual chronicity, *Les saignantes* appears, ultimately, to yield to a mythological temporality that is "chronic, cyclical, enfleshed, and subjective" (Przybylo and Fahs 2018, 217). Majolie and Chouchou's kinetically charged performance in the dress-up sequence is a synthesis of these mercurial timescapes in an embodied assertion of resistance to patriarchal power.

As Nedine Moonsamy shows in her discussion of the work of Dilman Dila elsewhere in this volume, there is a need to approach cinematic inscriptions of the abject critically insofar as they are applied to women of color, not least of all because of the risk such representations run of uncritically reinscribing colonial tropes of African women's subhumanity. Such caution should of course also be applied here, with regard to *Les saignantes'* aesthetics of menstruation and explicit sexuality. In particular, it should be emphasized that fashion, in *Les saignantes*, does not reify a biologically essentialist vision of African femininity but instead continually offers a means of perturbing the distinctions between such identities and their performance. Here again, an important connection can be made between dress, screen, and Bekolo's eclectically fashioned Cameroon of 2025. As discussed earlier, the set design of *Les saignantes* is characterized by an interest in the prosthetic (Langford 2018, 185), observable via the ubiquitous presence of electronic devices and mechanical objects, many of which are outmoded or appear uncannily out of place. This foregrounding of mechanical intervention resonates strongly with the dress-up sequence, with its emphasis on an artificially assembled, masquerading femininity, yielding a visibly "manufactured gap" between the self and the fashioned image (Doane 1991). The ubiquitous presence of abjected bodies and bodily secretions, such as menstrual blood, in *Les saignantes* works in tandem with the liminality of the women's fashioned performance to animate the uncanny "frontier between the self and the not-self," the zone in which Elizabeth Wilson (2003, 3) locates the unstable language of fashion. It is in fact precisely through this ambivalent quality of fashion—its liminal inorganicity—that Bekolo defamiliarizes the cultural conventions through which bodies are coded, as well as the "naturalized" function of technology as a seamless enhancement of human agency. Littered with objects conspicuously grafted from different timelines, Bekolo's screen is a biologically enhanced prosthesis through which Majolie, Chouchou, and the streets of Yaoundé are consciously *fashioned*.

As in Adeline Masquelier's study of the dress styles of Nigerien youth, fashion allows Majolie and Chouchou to position themselves strategically as *branché*—plugged in, connected "to circuits of information via technology" (2013, 140). She elaborates, "Being branché . . . is not about enjoying financial stability so much as it is about projecting a stylistic savoir-faire enabled by one's consumerist engagements and grasp of current fashions" (140). As in *Les saignantes*, the distinction between materiality and virtuality, clothing and performance here becomes malleable, enabling an uncoupling of fashion from its limited associations with Western cultural capital, futurity, and progress. Couched in Cameroonian ritual, this is, of course, not a film that claims to speak for "all," flattening distinctions of gender, race, and cultural context, and I am conscious that my reading should not reduce it to such. However, by framing the women's construction of gender as akin to the outfits that Majolie and Chouchou remove and recombine, *Les saignantes* asserts that its construction of African "feminine" identity is neither static nor predetermined. In the intermedial network of screen and dress, we find Majolie and Chouchou are able to fluidly dismantle and reconstruct their identities, liberating fashion from its putative Western "origins" to design a new future on their own transgressive terms.

Conclusion

As an index of contemporaneity and change, fashion has had much to contribute to Bekolo's and Sembène's visions of African postcolonial society. It envelops and connects with various other fabricated canvases—the dystopic cityscape, the (neo)colonial home—in a network of textural power. In both instances, however, the "material" through these regimes is revealed to be surprisingly dynamic and mutational. In both films, fashion acts as a portal to new geographies, transgressing cultural boundaries and erecting new ways of being in the aftermath of colonization. In *Les saignantes*, Majolie and Chouchou's fashioning of their bodies goes even further to jam the ideological matrix through which technology, capital, and social "progress" are linked. While the films diverge somewhat in their visions of societal change, a crucial constant is the significance of the female bodily surface as a locus of embodied resistance and self-articulation. *La noire de . . .* and *Les saignantes* are united by appropriations of fashion and material culture that give unique expression to this possibility, connecting individual and historical processes and rendering visible the highly corporeal means by which women have shaped the contours of African screen worlds.

By focusing on *La noire de . . .* and *Les saignantes*, I have hoped to suggest that fashion has been a part of independent African cinema since its early iterations and will continue to materially shape its relationship with the present and future. Emerging screen cultures have demanded creative theoretical approaches to the study of screen media, as scholars are faced with increasingly decentralized, globally scattered models of filmic distribution and spectatorship (see, for instance, Adejunmobi 2007; Harrow and Garritano 2019a, 2019b). My plea here is that this does not become a reason to overlook the distinctly material, often gendered practices by which social worlds are fashioned. A critical awareness of this drives us to look beyond the "political" as a predominantly male sphere of action, to consider how this realm has been powerfully shaped by African women in the material traffic between film, fashion, and screen. In my personal experience, I have also found an awareness of these material practices to be a tool of self-pedagogy, which has nourished further critique of my own assumptions about fashion, demanding that I situate it in racial and geopolitical contexts.

NOTES

1 It should be added that *La noire de . . .* and *Les saignantes* are still commensurate with the long-standing tradition of assertive, multidimensional female characters in African postcolonial cinema, even in films directed by men (see Dovey 2012, 18–19).

2 My use of the term *self-fashioning* reflects its application by Jaji "in the most literal sense" (2014, 116) to refer to the application of cosmetics and clothing. However, I am sympathetic also to its application by David Scott (1999) to refer more broadly to the embodied techniques through which subaltern subjects have resisted colonial authority.

3 I borrow this notion from Giuliana Bruno, who describes cinema's materiality as "play of fabrics" animated by "a sartorial *architexture*" (2014, 18).

4 *Larousse*, edition 2024, s.v. "bien." https://www.larousse.fr/dictionnaires/francais/bien/9151. Translation mine.

11

Nollywood Cinema and Its Housemaids' Fandom

The Case of Eldoret, Kenya

SOLOMON WALIAULA

There has been a trend in local popular culture in the town of Eldoret, Kenya, that brings together two relatively distinct social experiences: Nollywood cinema reception and the housemaid experience. The reception is ensconced within housemaids' everyday work routine. In this context, the line of distinction between Nollywood reception as leisure and as part of everyday working life is blurred. This chapter investigates the social processes that produced this cultural trend and examines its significance for the housemaids. I develop the argument that the housemaids' Nollywood fandom offers much more than leisure; it is a psychosocial tool the housemaids use to deal with the immediate needs of companionship and social identity but also becomes a medium that helps them transcend the limits of their situation and aspire to another, much more desirable world. In this sense, I consider this particular fandom as one of the ways in which Nollywood as a screen world becomes a place where people within a social category that is locally marginalized can visualize fictional representations of aspects of life they identify with. It is significant that for most of the live-in housemaids, their world is reducible to the houses in which they offer their labor—labor that sets up and freshens others to go out and encounter the "real world." It is a life lived for others, and one that represses the personal dreams of the housemaids. It is in this sense that Nollywood cinema, part of their claustrophobic, domestic reality, opens to them another world, albeit fictional. The chapter foregrounds the housemaids' social experiences before they became Nollywood fans to provide the background against which we explore the social world that produces them and leads them to Nollywood.

Methodology

This chapter draws on four months of fieldwork in Eldoret, from December 2019 to March 2020, but it also benefits from long-term media fieldwork with Nollywood audiences across western Kenya that dates back to 2012 (Waliaula 2014). As had been the case with my larger study of audiences in Eldoret (Waliaula 2019), this study benefited from my long-term exposure to and critical evaluation of patterned social practices in the everyday experience of life. The study was deductive in approach and aimed at generating grounded explanations; an open and linear exploration would not have suited this research, based as it was on personal experiences of a socially marginalized group. In this light, sampling for the study was done by drawing on extant social networks as well as snowballing. Twelve participants were engaged in this study and were all drawn from within a radius of about eight kilometers around Bondeni, my residence at the time of the research, and the immediate neighborhood that included Shauri Yako, Huruma, and Kipkarren, all within a four-kilometer radius to the west of town; only two of the participants were working in Pioneer Estate, which is about five kilometers from Bondeni, to the south of town. Methods mostly involved participant observation and unstructured interviews. In dealing with participants who also happened to be employed by my friends and close acquaintances, my positionality was a factor I needed to consider. The housemaids would be cautious with me because they considered me as being "on the same side" as their employer. In such cases, I blended their responses with critical observation. Furthermore, there was a general sense of "social difference" between me as a perceived member of the local elite and my participants as members of a socially marginalized group. In this case, I cultivated a rapport with them before conducting interviews, and I also tried to create an informal and convivial atmosphere and hoped this would make them feel comfortable and at ease with me. This is an approach that was informed by my earlier fieldwork experience in which I learned that a study of housemaids' media consumption calls for a high level of confidentiality and care between the researcher and research subjects. The language we used in the fieldwork experience was Kiswahili but also frequently mixed with Sheng, especially for housemaids who had been part of the urban experience for a relatively long time. In my analysis, I have elected to do a personal translation to English that is an approximation not necessarily capturing everything that was said, as it was in the actual language we used in the field. I should also note here that my critical engagement with my participants is made against the background of my own long-term personal involvement as a Nollywood fan and student of the same.

The Eldoret Housemaids' Social World

There is a sense in which one could perceive the social and working lives of live-in housemaids as one and the same. The housemaids' work routine dovetails with their lives, and in this way they become reducible to their domestic work. Though they are workers like any other, with a separate social identity beyond their job, housemaids in particular are expected to lose themselves in their roles as domestic laborers. Sri Lankan writer Nayla Moukarbel vividly captures this scenario in her personal reflection of her experience with one particular housemaid:

> I was a few months old when Jamileh arrived and 12 when she left. To this day, I still remember the pain and frustration I felt the moment she said goodbye. At that stage in my own life, I could not comprehend her need for a life elsewhere. For me, she simply belonged with us; she was "part of the family"; people sometimes mistook her for my big sister. I never saw her again, never knew what had happened to her, if she got married as she hoped for, if she forgot about me and us. If she was indeed 'part of the family' wouldn't she, wouldn't we, stay in touch? Or does her 'belonging', in fact, end with the job? (2009, 330)

Moukarbel's observation reveals that the housemaid in question always had two personas running side by side, but one was deliberately suppressed to enable her to conform to social expectations. The suppressed persona never died, and at the appropriate time, she discarded the housemaid dress and resumed the earlier trajectory of her life. It is thus probable that for twelve years this housemaid, like many others in her position, was predisposed to tensions and anxiety and was always in need of psychosocial care. Studies have been done on what has been described as the physical and social morbidity of housemaids (Ayenalem 2015; Jaishree and Krishnakumar 2020; Nelson and Brown 2017; Zenebe, Gebresilassie, and Assefa 2014). These studies adopt a quantitative approach to examine the prevalence of mental illness among live-in-housemaids, which they attribute to trauma that defines their everyday life. Despite the fact that these studies are based on social contexts distinct from Eldoret, their findings resonate with the local experience here. But the studies tend to be exploratory in approach and pessimistic in tone, identifying and describing illnesses associated with the work of housemaids with little focus on how the "victims" navigate this scenario. In contrast, by exploring housemaids' consumption of screen media, I seek to demonstrate how what I want to call "Nollywood care services" are constructed in the unique space of their work.

It is worth noting that the most elaborate research on housemaids' experiences of life has been based on migrant groups—women who have moved from their homes to different geographic, cultural, and social contexts and who are compelled to make a clean break with their earlier lives and dreams in exchange for a life in worlds they never really feel they belong to. The current study focuses on local women who find themselves offering domestic labor as a way of coping with the harsh realities of life. Most of them either come from very poor backgrounds, were orphaned early in life, or experience unwanted pregnancies and drop out of school early; in other words, they do not choose this work. In spite of the vital role they play as reproductive workers in households, they are generally held in low regard. Indeed, it has been observed that in general domestic work is undervalued, and this is linked to the perception of domestic work and caregiving as "unproductive."

In contexts such as Eldoret, there is almost no formal regulation of this reproductive labor market, and almost every housemaid works under informal and uncertain conditions. They see themselves as having been derailed from the main track of their life, living in an ambivalent position, from which they hope to exit and return to normal life. A countrywide survey done in 2016 revealed that the majority of housemaids (52 percent) had attained a primary (basic) level of education and missed the opportunity to attain higher levels due to financial difficulties. Many of them still yearn for a chance to continue with their education to complete the primary, secondary, and tertiary cycles. This sets them up in a world of dreams, having their feet in the present but projecting their minds and hopes onto a world of aspiration. But these young women have unhealed psychic injuries that they see as having been reconstructed in the stories that are told in Nollywood films, which in my earlier study (Waliaula 2019) I referred to as the audience's perceived personal relationships with televisual cinema. In this way, this study echoes Ien Ang's (1991) argument that audiences bring their personal social experiences, cultural affiliations, and everyday events they encounter to the reception experience and that the meanings they make out of these experiences are an outcome of the negotiation between what they see as audiences and what the screen offers.

The Evolution of Nollywood Fandom in Eldoret

The housemaid fandom of Nollywood is a popular culture that evolved from other earlier Nollywood reception cultures. In the mid to late 1990s Nollywood was introduced to Eldoret, and to many parts of Kenya, and at this time films were mainly accessed through local video shops where VHS tapes were played on medium-sized screens (Waliaula 2014). Some households also bought VHS players and could watch from the comfort of their living rooms. Local entrepreneurs also established video libraries that leased VHS tapes for a fee. The tapes were shared between households and video showrooms, and in this way Nollywood fandom grew. Locals were captivated by the stories, especially those who seemed to resonate with their sociocultural realities such as the everyday struggle with material deprivation, social tensions in marriage and family, and, perhaps most appealingly, the portraits of sorcery and witchcraft (see Waliaula 2014). But many locals did not have easy access to Nollywood then because of the scarcity of electricity and the need for a "household cinema kit," which consisted of a television and a VHS player. Young women from low-income neighborhoods were disadvantaged because they were both materially and socially marginalized from the public sphere and rarely got a chance to watch the movies in video shows, which took place within "masculine" social spheres such as barbershops (Waliaula 2014). Furthermore, household film consumption was largely a family affair, and only in rare cases were these marginalized young women able to access "household Nollywood."

In the late 1990s, however, social transformations impacted audience consumption in different African contexts. Commenting on the Ugandan experience, Dominica Dipio (2014, 91) has observed that this period overlapped with the height of privatization of the country's economy and the liberalization of airwaves that resulted in the opening of several private television stations, and that the trickle of Nigerian movies on Ugandan television in the late 1990s turned into an explosion at the turn of the millennium. Katrien Pype has also observed this phenomenon happening in Kinshasa, Democratic Republic of the Congo, and relates it to the rise of a televisual-reinforced Pentecostal church culture. She examines how the opening up of the country's mediascape in 1996, coinciding as it did with the charismatic renewal in urban centers throughout sub-Saharan Africa, led to a shift in Kinshasa's public culture, in particular its broadcast media, and she points out that the influence of West African video films was so significant at that time that it "altered the aesthetics of local television drama in Kinshasa" (2013, 199). This evangelical element in Nollywood engraved itself in spectacular narrative arcs that (re)constructed African religion and then juxtaposed it against Christianity, which was paired with modernity, mainly through imagery of material wealth, comfort, and a happy and fulfilling life (see Meyer 2002). This had significant appeal, especially to locals in Eldoret, because it not only played on a preexistent popular imaginary but also represented the metaphysical world in persuasive imagery. Nollywood films, at least the earlier ones, constructed a tantalizingly transcendental world, previously known only through myths and rumor, but that was now accessible in material film form (Waliaula 2014, 79).

By around 2008 in Kenya, Nollywood distribution and consumption experienced something of a transformation, in at least in two ways. First, Nollywood cinema was appropriated by local television and inserted into everyday programming by the leading local television houses such as Citizen TV and Kenya Television Network (KTN). Indeed, it was now popularly christened "Afrosinema." The movies occupied perhaps 50 percent of local television airtime, particularly on Citizen TV but later on the other local television stations as well. By 2010, in the lead-up to Africa's first soccer World Cup in South Africa, the satellite television industry that had previously limited itself to DStv also experienced further transformation that broadened access to Nollywood. More local "pocket-friendly" channel packages had been introduced, and the parallel GOtv was also introduced, followed later by ZUKU TV and the Chinese-owned StarTimes. These television channels had twenty-four-hour Nollywood channels, which meant that this cinema was now not only the most easily accessible entertainment option but also part of the everyday rhythm of life in most households. It was in this light that a new Nollywood fandom community emerged in Kenya, consisting of the people who spent most of their time in the house: live-in housemaids and housewives, both part of marginalized social groups in distinct ways (Waliaula 2019). This led to the "televisual turn" (Adejunmobi 2015) of Nollywood, facilitating the spread of Nollywood to large numbers of spectators and decoupling it from public leisure.

Indeed, this is not the first study to explore the local appropriation of Nollywood in different places; other studies include those of Katrien Pype (Kinshasa), Heike Becker (Windhoek), Jane Bryce (Barbados), and Giovana Santanera (Turin) (all 2013). Of particular significance to the current study is that each of these studies explores how Nollywood audiences in these locations use the reception experience to address their immediate social needs; the closest is perhaps that of Santanera, who describes Nigerian Nollywood fans in Turin, Italy, as watching Nollywood films daily "not so much to avoid the hardships of the present and reconnect themselves with an idealized homeland, but more to measure themselves against a familiar, symbolic, and discursive order to cope with feelings of disorientation in a foreign society" (2013, 246).

Rural Initiations

In the 1990s and up to the turn of the new millennium, Nollywood cinema was not the commonplace cultural form that it is today in Eldoret. It was scarce in the larger parts of rural western Kenya. The rural socialization to life is a factor in this research because it is the point of origin and socialization for most of the housemaids. I draw on the experiences of Grace, Caro, and Rehema (not their real names) to discuss the significance of rural socialization to life for the young women who eventually become housemaids and, in this case, Nollywood fans. The three all spent their childhoods in western Kenya in the late 1980s through the 1990s. I consider Grace's and Rehema's experiences as representative examples of rural girls' initiation to Nollywood, not just because the two young women ended up as committed fans of Nollywood but also because the socioeconomic circumstances surrounding their childhood and upbringing are typical of many local housemaids.

By the time of this fieldwork, I had known Grace Nafula for over six years. She was working in Pioneer Estate for my colleague and family friend. She told me that she had been orphaned at the age of four and was adopted by an aunt in Busia town, where for the first time she encountered Nollywood. She observed:

> It was only later, when I had moved to live with my aunt in Busia that I saw a television set for the first time. That was in 2005. I also watched my first Nollywood film in church. I do not remember the title, though, but I still recall the story. It was about a man that came from a very poor family. He joined a cult to become rich and ended up sacrificing almost all his family, except his sister, who was a steadfast Christian and

involved her pastor in breaking the chains that linked her brother to the forces of darkness. (Grace Nafula interview, February 10, 2020)

It turned out that this was also her initiation to Nollywood fandom, but she did not have frequent access to it and looked forward to the times when her aunt would allow her to go to church, which was rare because it turned out that her aunt had taken her in not as an adopted child to support her through school but as a domestic worker. Grace was only fourteen then. At sixteen she eloped with a local boy who worked as a night guard in Eldoret, but their marriage did not work out, and she moved out to try her luck on odd jobs, for her survival, including work as a cleaner in a small eating house in the industrial part of town. Here she reconnected with Nollywood, as there was a television screen set up for the customers' entertainment, which is common in such places. She emphasizes the positive role that Nollywood played in her life. When I asked her to mention any memorable titles, she was not in a position to do so but mentioned that Mama G (Patience Ozokwor) was her favorite character because she was "real." Grace worked at the eating house for two years, and then her employer recommended her for a housemaid job to her close friend. At the new workplace, Grace was alone in the house from 7:00 a.m. to 4:00 p.m. while everyone else was at work or school. Because of this arrangement, she faithfully followed Nollywood on the Afrosinema show on Citizen TV, particularly in the afternoon.

Rehema's case resonates with that of Grace. I knew her because during my fieldwork she worked for a household in our neighborhood. I always saw her in the evening at the main gate to our apartment block, waiting for the school bus to drop off her employer's children, who went to the same school as mine. I found out that she was a Nollywood fan by sheer accident. On one occasion, I did not see her at the main gate at the usual 4:00 p.m., when the children are dropped off. The bus driver was under instructions to only drop off the children if he saw their caregiver. On this occasion he took a gamble and dropped them off, asking me to look after them. I met Rehema rushing to the gate just after the bus had left. She thanked me for saving her day and, indeed, maybe saving her job. When I asked her why she was late, it turned out she had been so absorbed in a Nollywood film that she lost her sense of time. I advised her to be more careful to avoid similar scenarios in future. She pleaded with me not to report her to her employer. I gave her my word, and we have had a good rapport since then. We held several conversations about Nollywood, during which I learned that she had been introduced to Nollywood, rather serendipitously, during a difficult time in her life. At age fourteen, she had been pregnant and in a forced marriage with her schoolmate boyfriend, who was responsible for the pregnancy but who continued on with his schooling. Rehema observed: "His mother was a Nollywood cinema fan and had a video player, screen, and well-stocked library of Nollywood films on VHS tape. We watched many films with her, mostly in the afternoons when we were free from the domestic chores." It turned out that after delivering her baby, the marriage broke down, and Rehema was forced to move on, to work as a housemaid in Eldoret town. Her first job lasted for just three months, and she did not have access to the television at all. But her second housemaid job, which was the job she held at the time of this research, was different. She told me: "I got employed by my current employer in 2016, and I have been with them ever since. Her husband [is] a businessman in South Sudan and comes here only once in a while. My employer is also employed, and thus I am almost always alone in the house. We are subscribed to GOtv, and it has channels that are exclusively for Nollywood. I watch lots of the movies daily, because my employer has only two kids that stay in school all day" (Rehema Achieng interview, February 12, 2020).

It is evident that, for these housemaids, Nollywood is an important part of their journey from an early age to the present, a journey on which they embark from a point of disadvantage. They have adopted Nollywood into their lives, and it has become one of the ways in which they define their identity. It is also significant that they do not pay attention to particular film titles but rather look at Nollywood as one continuous story dovetailing with their own lives. Furthermore, both Grace and Rehema, and other housemaids I have talked to over the years, have developed a fragmented reception approach; they do not necessarily watch a film from start to end because usually they have to interrupt it to attend to something else in or around the house. Sometimes they walk in on an ongoing film and have to find a way to fit viewing it into their work schedule. These housemaids' stories of how they found themselves as Nollywood fans, and how they have managed to sustain themselves through it, show that their fandom does not consist of a critical reading of specific themes and characterization but rather a habitual activity that they have ritualized and consider as part of their everyday lives.

At the Nollywood School

Most Nollywood audience reception studies have established that audiences tend to consider the films as didactic and as a true account of life. Santanera quotes one of the Nigerian Nollywood spectators in Turin as follows: "Nigerian videos tell true stories. Even though they didn't happen to you, you can't say they don't happen in the real world. Sometimes they do. Otherwise, they wouldn't be on the screen. That is why Nollywood gives you an idea of things that can happen" (2013, 251). Santanera also observes that "more precisely, the audience believes that directors and scriptwriters are warning the audience about dangerous situations through the medium" (251). In my earlier study comparing Nollywood and foreign telenovela spectatorship in Eldoret, one of the participants, a young woman, observed: "If I compare, I can say Nollywood is more real and the telenovela is just fantasy . . . sometimes I watch the stories (of telenovelas) and see that a boyfriend can wake up early to make breakfast for you, in Africa that does not happen" (2019, 187). This was obviously an observation made in light of the social boundaries of her lived experience that is arguably the same social world inhabited by the typical Eldoret housemaids.

When I undertook to establish some of the specific lessons the housemaids had drawn from their fandom experiences by asking each to mention any two Nollywood films that they considered as educational, I noted a significant pattern in their responses. The lessons mentioned were connected to their immediate life experiences, and many of the films mentioned also seem to explore the social implications of poverty on extended family relationships. Judy recalled the story of the "rural housemaid" with insufficient exposure to modern technology and who fumbled when operating household electronic equipment such as the refrigerator, microwave, and television. In Judy's story, the maid was also impatient and rude to her employer and was eventually fired. Judy also mentioned the story of a disobedient young woman who got married to a much older man, against her parents' wishes. The man abandoned the young woman, and she had to return home to seek forgiveness. Dina recalled the story of a poor woman and her daughter. After the woman's husband died, his extended family sent mother and daughter away, and they moved to a slum. It happened that the child had been earmarked to be a princess, but her father died before telling her that. Her paternal grandmother tracked her down to link her up with her prince. Jealous relatives were not happy and kidnapped the daughter. The grandmother finally found the young woman and enabled her to become a princess, and she in turn got her mother out of poverty. Dina also recalled the story of two brothers; the younger brother was less successful than the elder brother and was jealous of him. The younger brother also kept bad company, and one of his friends influenced him to steal from his brother. The older brother found out about this misdemeanor but forgave him. The brother's mother was equally jealous of her older son; she did not want him to get married to his fiancée and went to consult a witch doctor to block the marriage, but the charm backfired and the young woman went mad instead, whereupon a pastor was called to pray for her. The young woman recovered and the marriage happened. Dina also told me the story of two sisters; one of them was envious of the other, and poisoned and killed her and took over her husband and tortured their children; she was later found out and fled. Dina also recounted the story of a housemaid who got involved in a romantic relationship with the husband of her employer, which got her sacked and also wrecked the marriage.

The two stories directly based on the housemaids' experience focus on the challenges of domestic work. One is concerned with the technological gap between the rural background of most housemaids and the urban contexts where they mostly get employed, a gap that is frequently held up as justification to define them as "primitive." The added attribute of rudeness could actually be accounted for; if the housemaid has no grasp of the basic technology in her new place of work, she is also likely to have to adapt to the interpersonal relationships with her employer in this space. This same point could be made of the film in which a housemaid is accused of a sexual misdemeanor. The typical housemaid has very little agency in her social relations within the house, and what may pass as a sexual relationship with the man of the house could just as well be sexual exploitation in which she is the victim, as has been explored in other studies (Ayenalem 2015) and is the story in one of the classical Nollywood films known as *Palace Maid*. In our interview session, Dina simply said the lesson she drew from this film was that a housemaid should not involve herself sexually with her employer's husband; she swore that she could never do that but also admitted she was not sure about what she would do if she were to fall victim to an employer's rogue husband. The other stories could be read as commentaries on the social costs of poverty on the family, a popular Nollywood theme. But one aspect stands out as key to the housemaid experience: the Cinderella motif. In these narratives, the orphaned young woman living in abject poverty eventually becomes a princess. The housemaids project themselves into her situation and use her experience as a source of hope for a better future. Most of the housemaids I have talked to in my fieldwork have explicitly expressed their admiration for this Cinderella narrative in Nollywood stories.

However, it is also significant that in considering their Nollywood fandom as a form of learning, the housemaids only pick up lessons they want to learn. They tend to identify with whatever connects with their own social experience and immediate living circumstances and that also promises to improve their life chances. This is comparable to my earlier findings (Waliaula

2014) that focused on manual laborers in a rural setting who, because of their proximity to local mythology around witchcraft and African religion, found Nollywood movies on witchcraft very "educational." One could argue that the housemaids' preferred Nollywood stories contain an element of the African fable. The plot and characters are constructed around specific moral lessons. Similarly, the narrative closures speak to the housemaids' immediate social conditions and dreams for the future. Nollywood may not portray the typical animal characters associated with fables, but the plots and characters tend to be melodramatically unreal (despite often being interpreted by spectators as "real"). As such, most Nollywood stories are not designed to project the social experience of human beings in their complexity. People are either very bad, evil, and wicked or purely good and innocent victims of bad people. However, this is not about people as human beings but as "everyman characters" who represent social experiences.

Affective Interpretation of Nollywood

In my fieldwork for this study and others, I have encountered housemaid fans of Nollywood who claimed to have seen their real lives portrayed in certain Nollywood narratives. Santanera, who made the same observation during her fieldwork, has written that "it is common to meet people who say that they have seen a film that tells their own story exactly" (2013, 253). In the current study I encountered two such fans, both of whom I had known for a relatively long time, but here I will focus on the experience of one of them, whom I have anonymized as Lena. When I conducted this research, Lena had been married for nine years, was running a small roadside informal eatery, and was a fan of Nollywood, especially of village- or rural-based Nollywood narratives. When I asked why that was the case, she answered, "I only watch films from which I can draw useful lessons" and then provided some examples: "Those films set in the village have relevant lessons for me, yes; even those that straddle both the village and the urban experiences are OK for me, because you will find witchcraft, poverty, envy, polygamy, and the problems associated with it such as jealousy and rivalry between co-wives, use of magic and sorcery by some of the wives to destroy the children of their co-wives. . . . I like such stories because they leave you with questions to reflect upon" (Lena Andisi interview, February 15, 2020).

I reminded Lena that the issues she had raised were also prevalent in the urban areas, even in Eldoret. She insisted that the village was more rooted in values and that perhaps if she had grown up in the village, if her parents had been purely village folk, she would not have ended up the way she did. It turned out that she had been a victim of a game of deception in which her parents arranged for her to work in a "mentorship project" at the home of family friend (a university lecturer) for just a year in return for the benefactor family's financial support for her high school studies. Four years later, she was still an "apprentice" in that household, which was basically a housemaid job, without pay. Her wages were paid directly to her parents. She observed: "I grew bitter and frustrated. The family had a big library of Nollywood films on VHS tapes. I spent most of my time alone and thus watched many of those films. At that time, I watched them to kill boredom. But later, when I had quit that job hoping to pick [up] the pieces of my life, only to be thrown back to the same conditions, I started reflecting on those Nollywood stories" (Andisi interview, February 15, 2020) It turned out that Lena had returned home to find that her parents had relocated to a village in western Kenya after the social disintegration that followed the 2007–8 presidential polls. She had to move to her elder sister's place, where she resumed domestic work once more. By this time Nollywood films had gone televisual, and she easily resumed her fandom, as she stayed indoors most of the time, helping her sister with domestic duties, hoping that her sister would help her go back to school. But she realized she had become her sister's housemaid, and there was no plan for her to return to school. It was at this point that she noticed a disturbing link between certain Nollywood stories and her life. She recalled:

I used to watch films that presented young women who underwent life experiences that were similar to mine. But within the stories, their lives turned round, yet mine did not. I had been trapped in the cycle of housemaid work. I tried to join my sister in her hairdressing business, but it did not work. I am left-handed and most of the clients lamented that it is a hand of bad fate. I had reached the very end of my tether when God turned my life around. In September 2010, I met a man in church that proposed to me and we got married two months later. This is when I looked back and realized God had used Nollywood to prepare me for my portion. The very first Nollywood film I watched was about a married couple that had challenges because they stayed with the wife's mother, who ended up taking over her daughter's husband. But the wife was a prayerful woman and she consulted her pastor to intercede for their marriage as well. It worked. Her mother got mentally deranged, drank a poisonous concoction, and died. I also remember another movie, this one I recall the title, *Days of Bondage*. There is this girl, the daughter of a single parent that also worked as a commercial sex worker. The girl did not even know her father. Her mother forced her into prostitution when she was very young. She also got a baby in the process. You see, she had been caught up in an evil trap, just like I was caught up in the exploitative housemaid job. But she miraculously met a man that loved her unconditionally and married her. I remembered many other Nollywood stories that had been about the virtue of patience and waiting for God's time. (Andisi interview, February 15, 2020)

It occurred to me that Lena had considered marriage and the Christian faith as her salvation, and she was proud of her small informal eatery because it was a source of livelihood. It was also significant that she had ended up in a business in which she could leverage her cooking and cleaning skills acquired and refined through her housemaid experience. For her, Nollywood had helped her face her situation for what it was and, in her view, to keep her positive.

Conclusion

This chapter has examined Nollywood fandom as a popular cultural practice in Eldoret featuring housemaids as the protagonists. Through the use of a fieldwork study, I explored the social experience of housemaids as reproductive domestic laborers and established that for most of them, their conditions of work and socially constructed identity are fraught with tensions and anxieties. This is occasioned by the informal nature of their work that has tended to bring together employers and employees in personal and unregulated contracts largely based on trust and goodwill. The housemaid job has also been subjected to some ambivalence in terms of its social definition as distinct and respectable work; neither employers nor employees consider it a career like any other. Existing literature on this subject shows that social prejudice against the housemaid job is related to the fact that the employees are mostly drawn from poverty-stricken backgrounds and take up these jobs out of desperation. Their job is undervalued because the workers are also undervalued. In the case of Eldoret, this study has established that most of the housemaids not only hail from humble backgrounds but that, as children, were victims of social injustices and bad fate. The literature on the global experience of housemaids has established the various physical and psychosocial ailments associated with this domestic work. On the basis of these research findings, and my observation of local trends in Eldoret, one can argue that some cinema cultures may have developed as forms of repurposed leisure. It is hoped that these findings have raised a number of critical issues around the methodological and sociocultural framing of Nollywood fandom in places such as Eldoret. In terms of methodology, this study has not only established the significance of fieldwork in studies of Nollywood audiences but also shown that positionality in such studies is crucial. It is hoped that through the use of a sociocultural frame, the study has shown that the diffusion of Nollywood from its home in West Africa to other parts of Africa, such as Eldoret, is followed by local adaptation and what I have identified as affective responses grounded in a hermeneutics of self-interest.

INTERVIEWS

Achieng, Rehema. Interview, Kipkarren, February 12, 2020.
Amakobe, Mary. Interview, Bondeni, February 10, 2020.
Amoit, Caroline. Interview, Bondeni, February 20, 2020.
Andisi, Lena. Interview, Bondeni, February 15, 2020.
Atsiaya, Judy. Interview, Shauri Yako, February 20, 2020
Awuor, Dina. Interview, Huruma, February 18, 2020.
Malesi, Rina. Interview, Huruma, February 18, 2020.
Midecha, Phyllis. Interview, Kipkarren, February 16, 2020.
Nafula, Grace. Interview, Pioneer, February 10, 2020.
Nanzala, Everline. Interview, Huruma, February 17, 2020.
Okoiti, Florence. Interview, Kipkarren, February 16, 2020
Shilaho, Esther. Interview, Bondeni, February 22, 2020.

12

Archival Films in Contemporary Archives

Fragmented Legacies of a North African Women's Film Heritage

STEFANIE VAN DE PEER

With the excitement of innovations and new directions in African cinema also comes an increasing awareness of the value of its heritage. Reflection on the past lives of storyworlds and the responsibilities of archives is more and more urgent, as pioneers who were active in the 1970s and 1980s pass on and their films as well as their collective memory are in danger of getting lost. In this self-reflexive chapter, I explore early works by three pioneering North African women filmmakers and the archival lives of their feminist work. I reflect on my own experiences with their films and their particular archival lives, with a focus on restoration practices, and the afterlives of archival films through contemporary festival networks. The self-reflexive ethos of this chapter stems from my main argument that close personal relationships and professional networks are essential to the success of a contemporary restoration project and the confirmation that exhibition remains entirely dependent on efficient distribution practices of classic films. I focus on four films by three North African women: *Fatma 75* (1976) by Selma Baccar from Tunisia; *La Nouba des femmes du Mont Chenoua* (1978) and *La Zerda ou les chants de l'oubli* (1981) by the Algerian filmmaker Assia Djebar; and *Une porte sur le ciel* (*Door to the Sky*; 1989) by the Moroccan director Farida Benlyazid. The digitization of *Fatma 75* was initiated and funded by Africa in Motion in Scotland. *La Zerda* was restored and digitized by Arsenal in Berlin and *Door to the Sky* by Exeter University in England. During the final stages of this book's production, Assia Djebar's film *La Nouba* was restored by the Cinemateca de Bologna in collaboration with the World Cinema Project. This is a hugely important step for the increasing recognition of a global women's feminist film heritage. In considering these films' individual and combined stories of archiving and preservation, I explore a way forward for historical research across diverse African screen worlds.

When UNESCO, the World Cinema Project (WCP), and Pan African Federation of Filmmakers (Fédération Panafricaine des Cinéastes or FEPACI) announced in 2017 that they would commit to restoring fifty African films with the African Film Heritage Project, they had already restored seven African films, among which four are from North Africa: *Alyam, Alyam* (1978) and *Trances* (1981, restored in 2007) by Ahmed El Maanouni from Morocco and *Al Mummia* (1969, restored in 2009) and *The Eloquent Peasant* (1969, restored in 2010) by the Egyptian director Shadi Abdel Salam. The other three films were *Touki Bouki* by Djibril Diop Mambéty (1973, restored in 2008), *Borom Sarret* by Ousmane Sembène (1963, restored in 2013), and Sembène's *La noire de . . .* (*Black Girl*; 1966, restored in 2015). Largely inspired by Martin Scorsese's personal taste, this selection points to a common issue in the history of African cinema: the Western reverence for auteurship and the canonization of male filmmakers. Although he mentions Safi Faye by name in his announcement of the African Film Heritage Project, Scorsese's WCP did not restore a single woman's film—let alone an African woman's film—until September 2021, when *Sambizanga* (1972) by Sarah Maldoror was brought back to life (Jones 2021).[1]

In 2018, I worked on the Africa's Lost Classics project with the Africa in Motion film festival. We intended to restore and digitize *Sambizanga* at that point, but the only copy of the film we could locate was stored in the New York Public Library, and we could not afford the insurance and transport costs for obtaining the copy. It was then that we realized the WCP had not yet worked on any women's films, and our project found its main mission: to restore African women's films. We worked on *Fatma 75*, *Mossane* (Safi Faye 1996), and *Flame* (Ingrid Sinclair 1996). *Fatma 75* became the success story of the project, having been screened at many film festivals worldwide, from Kurdistan to Mexico and Melbourne to Salé, since 2018. It inspired the work, two years later by another project, on *A Door to the Sky*, which now often accompanies *Fatma 75* at screenings worldwide as a duo of early North African feminist films.[2] The films in focus in this chapter—*Fatma 75*, *La Nouba*, *La Zerda*, and *Door to the Sky*—were all produced without the dominance of European funding. In my view, they need to be recognized as pioneering films not just in terms of feminist statements but also in terms of the autonomy of pan-African film production—and now, in restoration.

Through my own activist work in restoration and my related scholarship (such as this chapter), I want to contribute to the decolonization and decanonization of film studies and critique the continued European dominance over filmmaking and film restoration funding and infrastructure. Indeed, one of the major obstacles facing African filmmakers and film historians is that continued control of the audiovisual collective memory resides with institutes and multinational corporations monetizing archives and denying access to the content of these archives to those with limited means. This chapter suggests some routes to think through the new lives for those films that are either neglected or favored by European preservation and restoration projects.

Looking Back at a Maghrebi Feminist Film Heritage

Until March 2018, there was no cinematheque in Tunis. The 16mm print of *Fatma 75* had been stored at Tarak Ben Ammar's Quinta Communications–owned Gammarth Studios, just outside of Tunis. For my doctoral studies I had visited and interviewed the filmmaker Selma Baccar at length about her films, so we had a preexisting relationship. The film is a hybrid docu-fiction and an essay film that deals with the history of women's rights and feminism in Tunisia, using archival footage alongside interviews with contemporary feminist activists and a framing story about Fatma, a student doing research about feminism in Tunisia for her university studies. I knew the film had had a controversial history in Tunisia itself and was neglected abroad: after its initial world premiere in the Netherlands, where the film was also subtitled in Dutch (which was for a long time the only version of the film circulating, thus minimizing accessibility), it was largely forgotten, and while often referred to in academic work, it was never discussed in detail due to its inaccessibility (Van de Peer 2014).

When I approached Selma Baccar in early 2018 about the possibility of doing work on and making *Fatma 75* newly available through a one-year project, funded by the Arts and Humanities Research Council (AHRC) and titled

Africa's Lost Classics, one of her conditions was that we have the film restored and resubtitled in Tunisia rather than ship it to our preferred restoration facilities in the United Kingdom. She advised me that this would mean she could retain control over the quality of the restoration in collaborating with the technicians, while it would also be much cheaper for us to finance. Gammarth is only thirty minutes away from where Baccar lives, and the studio had recently invested in the infrastructure to do digitization work. It seemed quite fortuitous that these circumstances converged on our project. Likewise, in our desire to decolonize our project, this confident attitude toward the film's preservation on Baccar's part made us think about our involvement in the continued dominance of European money and infrastructure in the world of film preservation.

As such, our research group agreed with the filmmaker, and along with her assistants she took the lead and the responsibility for the restoration, working with a local facility. However, though communication with the staff in Gammarth was fluent and friendly, in the final weeks before the world premiere at the Africa in Motion film festival in Edinburgh, the staff encountered a technical problem I did not manage to clarify entirely, though I suspect it had to do with the then-newness of the infrastructure in Gammarth and the lack of technical know-how in terms of restoration. Consequently, the Gammarth team had to ship the film to their mother company in Paris, where the digitization and the creation of the new digital camera package (DCP) were finished only one day ahead of the screening.[3] We had invited the filmmaker to Edinburgh's Filmhouse for the premiere, and although the audience was small (by my estimate, around fifty people), spectators were very enthusiastic, and in the question-and-answer session after the film, many showed deep insight into and knowledge of the development of women's positions in Tunisia and the Maghreb. At this screening, Baccar agreed that the time coding of the subtitles needed improvement, and so she asked the Paris-based Quinta studio to correct the subtitling in order to ensure that the film lived up to expectations for screenings elsewhere in the world.

The film continues to tour the world's festivals to great acclaim, and all screening fees go directly to the filmmaker. But this makeshift distribution agreement is not professional enough—we own a DCP copy (as does the filmmaker), but we do not have a high-quality digital file, and as some screening venues do not have the infrastructure for DCP, there are still significant limitations to how and where the film can be shown. Baccar herself has attempted to set up a locally run distribution deal for the film so that her film's life can continue to be managed from Tunisia, acknowledging its role in Tunisian film heritage. However, this deal has encountered issues in terms of the worldwide and regional (Arab) rights the distributor can obtain. She therefore continues to have to count on our European networks and efforts to promote the film for screenings at events around the world. The festivals that do screen the film are located mostly in North and South America and in Europe and tend to be festivals that have an activist, feminist, or otherwise political identity or strand in their program. Our do-it-yourself approach to the distribution of *Fatma 75* does not reflect the importance of the film, and this is something Africa in Motion continually reflects on. The film was, after all, digitized and subtitled with European money and on a European initiative. The Tunisian Gammarth studio's issues with the restoration were quickly resolved in France, thus again confirming the inequalities in knowledge and experience between the Global North and Global South. Although the learning curve was very valuable to us, and we witness a growing recognition of the film and its significance in a global women's film heritage, the film's afterlife remains insecure, as Africa in Motion is an exhibition, not a distribution, platform.

Assia Djebar's films are the subject of much academic work, even though they have been very difficult to access. The 16mm *La Nouba* was produced in 1978 by L'Office National du Commerce et de l'Industrie Cinématographique (ONCIC, the Algerian state's National Office for the Trade and Film Industries). *La Zerda*, shot in 1982 on 16mm, was made for Radiodiffusion Télévision Algérienne (RTA; Algerian Broadcasting). Djebar, as a revolutionary and feminist activist, became a controversial figure during the Algerian Civil War in the 1990s and among the Algerian establishment and the conservative government, which runs ONCIC. With Djebar having passed away in 2015, her family has subsequently not been able to reclaim the rights to *La Nouba*. The centralization and nationalist nature of the inaccessible film archive at ONCIC— which grew out of the nationalist independence government and the National Liberation Front's filmmaking efforts—resulted in the film's relative obscurity. Nevertheless, until the 2010s, a low-quality DVD version of the film was available from Women Make Movies (WMM), a feminist production and distribution company based in New York City and founded in 1972. The company now states in its catalog that the DVD is "not recommended for exhibition. This is the only existent digital copy from the original film, which was produced by the late filmmaker."[4] So, although WMM's distribution platform made the important feminist film easily accessible on DVD for a while, the unstable materiality of the DVD format has terminated its availability. The 16mm version of the film is now the only one that remains, but to this day ONCIC's archive is difficult to access, especially with regard to films such as *La Nouba*, which had an explicitly feminist revolutionary message. We know that the 16mm copy is located in the Centre Algérien de la Cinématographie, the Algerian cinematheque. But, as Madeleine Bernstorff from Arsenal in Berlin testifies: "The Cinematheque was founded in 1964 and re-opened in 2011 after a 3-year renovation program. For over 40 years, it was a prominent place for open debate and criticism on both aesthetic and social and political themes and was regarded as a central meeting point between Maghreb and African filmmaking and cinema from the rest of world. The civil war years between 1992 and 2002 had a devastating effect on the institution, as well as on cultural life in Algeria in general" (2013).

Bernstorff celebrates how the Algerian archive's past openness created the possibility for films such as those by Djebar to see the light of day in the first place, but she mourns its contemporary gatekeeper role. Many international film festivals have attempted to screen *La Nouba* in the past two decades, but the lack of responsiveness from the archive impedes public access. Indeed, Africa in Motion screened *La Nouba* in 2007, but we used WMM's DVD. Nevertheless, there is now a new shred of hope for the film's life: in 2020, Courtisane, an experimental film festival in Belgium, miraculously succeeded in screening the film from its original 16mm copy (Debuysere 2020). As we did in 2007, Courtisane also first received a DVD copy of the film but insisted it required the 16mm celluloid copy. Due to the postponement of the festival because of the COVID-19 pandemic, the programmer continued his negotiations with the Cinematheque, and—after an entire year of intensive liaising, assisted by the Algerian embassy in Brussels and the Belgian Ministry of Culture—he finally received the 16mm copy. He told me the reels were dirty and dark, in a dire condition, and not subtitled. So, the festival screened the imperfect copy and created English soft titles (Stoffel Debuysere email, April 2020).[5] To my knowledge, this is the only occasion on which *La Nouba* was screened from its original reels.

In contrast with ONCIC's approach to archiving its film heritage, RTA's decentralized archives appear to be more accessible. After *La Zerda* was shown in the Berlinale Forum in 1983, a 16mm copy was stored at Arsenal, the Berlin-based Institute for Film and Video Art. *La Zerda*—through which Djebar recounts the story of the colonization of the Maghreb—consists entirely of archival footage (from French newsreels) repurposed by the artist-filmmaker. In an ironic juxtaposition between colonialist imagery and anticolonialist poetic voice-over, she highlights the unfair appropriation of Algerian history in French images and the bias inherent in Pathé-Gaumont's newsreel archive. The archival materials she focuses on are discarded newsreels about daily life in the Maghrebi colonies in the early twentieth century. The film employs montage to "search for the truth behind these 'images of a killing gaze', a truth which they pointedly do not show" (Arsenal 2015). The soundtrack combines traditional Zerda chants and modern experimental music to shape an enraged indictment of physical and symbolic colonial violence.

Arsenal regularly invites curators to delve into its archives and bring them to life. One of these projects, titled Visionary Archive (2013–15), focused specifically on African content in Arsenal's archives.[6] The film festival that resulted from Visionary Archive included *La Zerda* in a newly restored version of the film, with German as well as English subtitles. The film can now be rented from Arsenal in 16mm format as a DCP or QuickTime ProRes digital file. Any profits from screenings, however, remain with Arsenal. The quality and accessibility, though, have not (yet) translated into increased visibility, perhaps because the film, like *Fatma 75* and *La Nouba*, is highly political and intellectual in nature, and even if it is now accessible in terms of its availability for screenings, it may not be visible in terms of its subject matter and relative obscurity.

What *La Nouba*'s and *La Zerda*'s material and intellectual states reveal to us is cinema's self-mythologization and the ways in which academics throughout the world view feminist film heritage. Djebar's oeuvre is as self-referential as it is unique, and the way it is revered may in fact be a hindrance to its survival since its importance is likely to make the conservative government in Algiers suspicious of the film's potential impact on the Algerian population. As such, government-run archives, subject to national cultural policies, see the act of safeguarding as entirely separate from the world's interest in the films. Conversely, the survival and recovery of *La Zerda* by Arsenal's projects thirty years after its 1983 screening in Berlin is a surprise—yet one that highlights the failure to safeguard *La Nouba*. These films' archival stories also highlight the diversity in archives and archival practices of North African film: public archives are subject to political priorities as well as the deteriorating materiality of old films. The futureproofing of a Maghrebi (or any) feminist film heritage continues to test the limits of storage facilities, political priorities, and cultural counterefforts, and this has significant implications for future (North) African, global, and feminist screen worlds in general because screen worlds are connected not just geographically or technologically but also historically. If film students or young (trainee) filmmakers do not know or do not have access to their own film heritage and the legacy of those who came before them, they cannot root their work in a historiography that gives them a lived experience of legitimacy and confidence.

The original 35mm print of the Moroccan classic *A Door to the Sky* was stored at the Centre Cinématographique Marocain (CCM) facilities in Rabat. At the time, in 2019, I worked for a three-year AHRC-funded project, Transnational Moroccan Cinema, with Professor Will Higbee from Exeter University and Dr. Florence Martin. Farida Benlyazid has a good personal relationship with Dr. Martin in particular, and so we negotiated her approval of the restoration project. This personal relationship with the filmmaker was essential in the lengthy negotiation process with the CCM about the release of the film from its vaults. The CCM's reluctance became evident when it took us more than six months to arrange the shipping of the canisters. In hindsight, however, we understand the reasons for the reluctance, as this film, like *La Nouba* and *Fatma 75*, is controversial, creatively treating aspects of religion and women's spiritual emancipation. In addition, it remains the only surviving 35mm copy of a film that, though it has been neglected for decades, remains central to Morocco's film heritage. In Morocco, the state still controls production licenses, and because the CCM is dependent on a patriarchal and conservative government, it often (directly or indirectly) censors films with religious content. As there is no restoration facility in Morocco, the film was shipped to our partnering restoration facility, Dragon DI, in Wales. Because I had experience with the problematic distribution and exhibition of *Fatma 75* after the Africa's Lost Classics project, and because this project had a much larger budget for restorations, we wanted to ensure the quality and efficiency of this restoration as well as its future distribution opportunities.

The film's journey to Wales was not only delayed but was also marked by the vulnerable materiality of the 35mm film and the way it was stored and packaged. Usually, a 35mm film would be stored in metal canisters and packaged to be shipped in wooden crates, which helps with the protection of the very sensitive 35mm reels. *A Door to the Sky* arrived in plastic canisters, packaged in jute bags. One of the canisters was damaged in transit, which resulted in the film being damaged as well. So, Dragon DI not only had to rearrange the canisters in terms of their order but also had to deal with a broken canister. The film was also in a worse state (dirtier and therefore darker) than we had anticipated and needed to be cleaned carefully and thoroughly, after which the scanning process also took additional time, as the film was significantly longer than we had been told. Furthermore, the subtitling caused extra delays, as the existing Arabic and French soundtracks existed only in Word document files and needed to be transferred to .rst files.[7] The subtitles also needed detailed updating and reinterpretation. This was discovered by the team of subtitlers, who were linked to a parallel project, also based at Exeter University, titled

Subtitling World Cinema.[8] As experts in language *and* cultural translation, the team—in collaboration with the filmmaker—retranslated, for example, specific paragraphs from the Koran quoted in the film, and modernized and corrected the French subtitles which were at times incorrect or incomplete based on the Moroccan Arabic original. The age of the film also exposed different sensibilities around religion, women's roles, and the sacred heritage of the Sufi *zawiya*.[9] This revealed the relative modern sensibilities inherent to the filmmaker's feminist ethos in the 1980s as opposed to the increasingly conservative nature of modern Morocco. The finalized French subtitle tracks then needed to be time-coded and translated into English, which was entirely new for the film. Once the process of cleaning, scanning, translation, and resubtitling was finished, the filmmaker requested a few final changes in the credits, to reflect past collaborations on the film in the 1980s as well as the 2019 project funding that had made the restoration possible. This shows, in complex ways, how screen worlds are never complete or finished. Films and their histories are fluid and alive. Translation, reinterpretation, and restoration illustrate how films are always works in progress, even after they are released.

Finally, at the Berlinale in February 2020, we attempted to set up a new distribution deal for the film with an important Arab film distributor. However, after the positive negotiation initially provided us with hope for a new future for the film in the Arab world, this deal fell through as the distributor prefers contemporary cinema and does not have that much content of Moroccan origins—a reminder of the precarity of *historical* African, Arab, and global screen worlds and the human effort required to keep these older storyworlds in circulation. A much more limited distribution deal with Benlyazid's producer through the University of Exeter therefore currently manages the film's travels across the world. Through my personal and professional involvement in both projects, the film often travels with and is screened alongside *Fatma 75*, as a duo of films giving shape to a Maghrebi feminist film heritage, and from which *La Nouba* is sadly still missing.

In trying to embrace what we see as decolonization principles (for example, respecting African autonomy and independence in film restoration projects), we did consider working with the Gammarth facility in Tunisia, but the difficulty with the final delivery of *Fatma 75* made us wary. However, even in working with the highly efficient and experienced Dragon DI, the obstacles in communication between the administratively complex CCM and the shipping company, and the language barrier between CCM and the UK-based restoration facilities, also resulted in the restored film being ready just one week ahead of its world premiere at the National Film Festival in Tangiers on March 5, 2020, with the DCP having to be personally carried and delivered to the festival by one of the project researchers in order to be screened at the festival. After that, it was placed in both the private archive of the filmmaker and the public archive of the CCM.

The quality of the DCP and the digital file we have for *A Door to the Sky* is much more professional and up-to-date than the files we have for *Fatma 75*. This attests to the experience and quality control of Dragon DI and how such professionalism does justice to the film. With a much larger budget and more time on the project behind this restoration, *A Door to the Sky* is now accessible for festivals around the world, though arguably it still is not visible enough because of the lack of a robust distribution deal. Its premiere at the 2020 Tangiers festival was also fraught with disappointment, as the wider Tangerine public did not gain access to the screening, reflecting the continued sense of incompleteness of our decolonizing efforts. As Will Higbee, Flo Martin, and Jamal Bahmad show, the Tangiers festival is "domestic, inward-looking . . . destined for the people of Morocco" (2020, 164), but in reality it gives priority access to those directly affiliated with the national (establishment) film industry and to the international press. Indeed, "the festivals are by-products of the patron-state's relationship with its artists, who end up serving the political agenda of the Makhzen" (164).[10] As such, the people of Tangiers, and even its film students, did not see the premiere screening of the restored *A Door to the Sky*, depriving them of their own feminist film heritage once more. The conservative state does not, therefore, take charge of safeguarding its rich film past; it also does not make this past accessible or visible to its young filmmakers for fear of its own power and authority becoming contested. The film may be an absolute triumph and the DCP of a high-quality caliber, but it is not being distributed professionally, and its afterlife is insecure and unstable once again.

Turning Individual Legacies into a Shared Global Heritage

As these four films' archival and preservation histories show, even if accessibility may (very) slowly be improving, this does not ensure visibility, nor does it safeguard an afterlife for the films in our contemporary screen worlds. Africa in Motion owns a DCP of *Fatma 75*, and Exeter University owns both a high-quality digital file and a DCP of *A Door to the Sky*, and yet, beyond our efforts to promote and screen the films at (mostly Western) arts venues, we have not been able to secure an efficient distribution/exhibition reality for the films.[11] During the COVID-19 pandemic and lockdowns, we screened the films online through video-on-demand platforms a few times, but both filmmakers feel insecure about geo-blocking, their rights, and the appropriate fees for such online events. This is further complicated by the complexity of the preservation process, such as the location of the films and the politics around ownership; the material state of the reels as well as the changing life of the subtitles in terms of how the diegetic storyworlds have aged; the budget for the restoration/digitization and the consequent format of the restored film; and the infrastructure of the arts venues where these films can be exhibited. It thus becomes starkly clear how precarious these films' lives continue to be, even after the restoration process. On top of these political, material, financial, and ideological factors, we have the apparently essential personal relationships and the trust required for a successful restoration project in difficult circumstances exacerbated by conservative governments with vested interests in the state of the archives and their contents. This tension between, on the one hand, a decolonizing effort and self-reflexive praxis rooted in concepts of global solidarity and, on the other hand, a conservative state's suspicion of both the diegetic storyworlds and the afterlifes of feminist activist films, results, in my view, in a feminist legacy that remains linked mostly to individual, personal efforts instead of a long-term vision inherent to an aspirational global feminist film heritage.

While we learn from our (relative) failures, the frustration with a lack of distribution of African content remains acute. Bringing together thinking around official and unofficial archives, and different pathways of accessing and restoring feminist films from the Maghreb, has enabled me to reflect critically on the legacies of colonial, neocolonial, and patriarchal political priorities, cultural policies, and a neglected feminist heritage. The individual legacies of North African feminist filmmakers, whose work from the 1970s and the 1980s remains neglected and fails to enter the world's feminist film heritage due to continued shortcomings in terms of circulation and exhibition, are in danger, as the filmmakers age and pass on. While there are initiatives working toward a decolonization of the canon, the archive, and the world's screen heritage, distributors of African film need to follow suit by seeing the cultural and crucially also the commercial values of the (feminist) past. With an increasing interest in "safeguarding" a global film past comes a reflection on the significance and precarity of personal and public film archives. It is the lack of efficient distribution and exhibition opportunities for almost all African (archival) cinema that inhibits individual legacies of African (feminist) cinema to become an integral part of a shared global feminist film heritage.

NOTES

1   The Nigerian filmmaker Rahmatou Keïta told me on January 10, 2022, that she was part of the FEPACI board, which worked with WCF to identify the fifty African films pledged for restoration. She assured me efforts were made to include women's films but that the (mostly French) distributors did not want to release the rights to these films for the WCF to restore them. This very complex archival reality inspired the Egyptian filmmaker Jihan El Tahri, and many other pan-African and Arab filmmakers, to write a manifesto on the liberation of the archives of global cinema (see Dickinson et al. 2019).

2   By focusing on three North African women filmmakers, I also want to move beyond the idea of African cinema being dominated by sub-Saharan geographies. The Maghreb specifically, on the northwestern point of the continent, has often been excluded from studies of African cinema while continuously being neglected in Arab film studies. In many ways, it has become its own field of focus within Francophone cultural studies, mostly concentrated in specialist publications, events, and projects. Nevertheless, production—both historically and contemporaneously—is to such a scale and quality that it has produced numerous Cannes and Oscar "foreign" film nominations and winners. In fact, North African production has contributed to the contemporary popularity of cinema from France, as "Beur" cinema. A central aspect of this "Eurocentric" outlook in the Maghreb is its sheer proximity to Europe, described by filmmakers literally or in metaphors as the hope for a better future outlook for resource-poor Maghrebis. Filmmakers also describe the preferential attitude of many North African filmmakers toward Europe as a consequence of French funding cycles and regulations. However, through increased cross-Saharan and pan-African development collaborations, such as AfricaDoc, and through the increase in inter-African coproductions between organizations like Centre Cinématographique Marocain and sub-Saharan filmmakers (see, for example, *The Wedding Ring* [2016] by the Nigerien director Rahmatou Keïta), an interesting trend in film production and development is the explicit circumvention of European funding, something filmmakers such as Keïta are very passionate about.

3   The digital cinema package is the standard format for a high-quality digital film screening and generally is regarded as a stable and robust format that can stand the test of time better than the highly flammable and easily damaged 35mm or 16mm celluloid formats. However, not all venues have the infrastructure for DCP yet, in particular activist or noncommercial arts venues.

4   Women Make Movies (WMM), n.d., "La Nouba des femmes du Mont Chenoua," accessed January 3, 2022, https://www.wmm.com/catalog/film/la-nouba-des-femmes -du-mont-chenoua/.

5   Soft subtitles are text files that live outside of the video file but can be toggled on or off in the video player. They are often incomplete (the credits are not usually included), and the time coding, being separate from the video file, is also not normally synchronized perfectly.

6   The Visionary Archive project collaborated with Cimatheque in Cairo (an alternative to the official, national film archive in Egypt), the Bioscope Cinema in Johannesburg (an organization dedicated to independent cinema), the private archive of the pioneering Sudanese filmmaker Gadalla Gubara in Khartoum, and the National Film Institute of Guinea-Bissau.

7   An .rst file is a digital file format that contains textual data which can be linked to a timecode and a file in a nontext format. It serves as the basis for most digital subtitles.

8   For more information about Subtitling World Cinema, see the project's webpage: https://subtitlingworldcinema.com/ (accessed August 6, 2024).

9   A *zawiya* is an institution within the Sufi mysticism tradition of Islam. It functions as a place of worship and for education or shelter. In this film, the *zawiya* is a safe space for women, who can find refuge from the dominant men in their lives.

10 Makhzen, for most Moroccans, is an apparatus of state violence and domination and, at the same time, a system of representation of traditional royal power. For more information, see Daadaoui 2011.

11 The digital file we have is of very low quality, and its subtitles are the initial, imperfect ones. We have failed to secure the higher-quality corrected file from the French sister company of Quinta Gammarth.

Part IV

———

Theatrical Screen Worlds

In the Church, Cinemas, Video Halls, and Hills

13

Cinema in the Church

The Evangelical Film Worldview in Nigeria

ELIZABETH OLAYIWOLA

Nigeria has a range of dynamic and ever-evolving screen cultures. This chapter observes how evangelical films, grounded in Nigeria but with a global dimension, have created new screen and screening practices. The discussion opens with the unexpected and innovative use made of church buildings as screening spaces. I argue that these new cinema spaces and the networks they convene have influenced the mode of distribution and consumption of Nigerian screen worlds at home and abroad and can become a model for other African screen worlds. The emergence and then proliferation of church screenings offer a vivid case study of the wide possibilities and dynamic nature of African screen worlds (figure 13.1).

In contemporary Nigeria, many aspects of social, political, economic, educational, and cultural life are inextricably linked to the development and

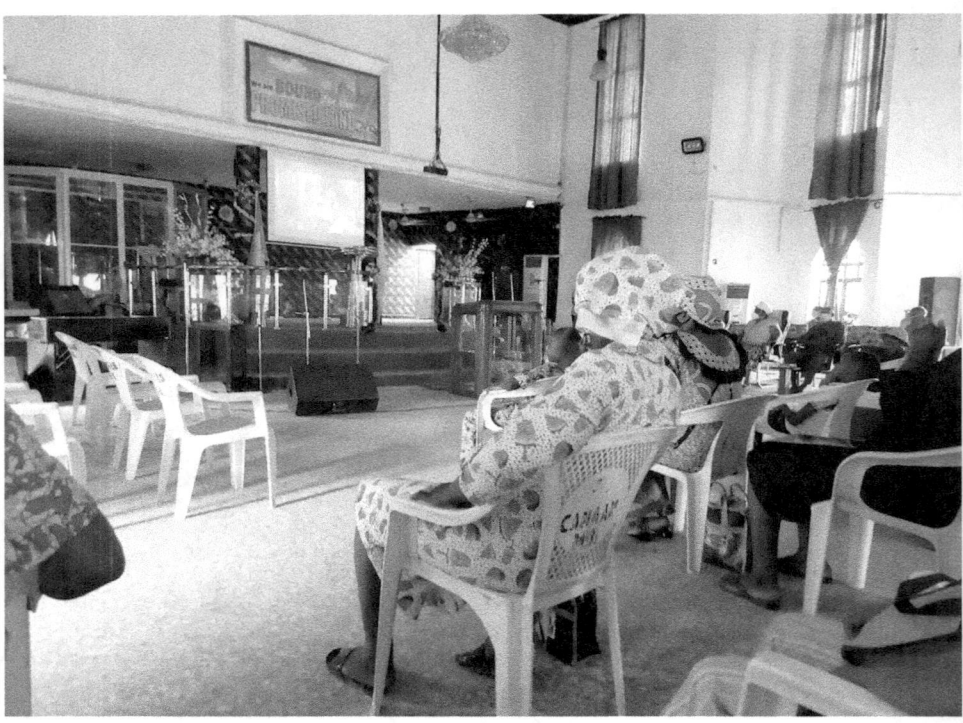

FIGURE 13.1. Church screening. Author photograph

expansion of Pentecostalism. Asonzeh Ukah (2016) makes the point that Pentecostalism as a force accounts for urban transformation in Nigeria, and indeed Africa more broadly, and Ebenezer Obadare (2018) has argued that Pentecostalism has shaped the politics of Nigeria's fourth republic. Pentecostalism's impact, however, reaches beyond politics; its influence extends to entertainment and—of greatest relevance to this volume—to cinema as well.

The theme running through this chapter is the innovation that Pentecostalism has brought to screen worlds in Nigeria. On a material level, what is interesting is how church buildings have become repurposed into screening halls. During Nigeria's affluent decades, as cultural life and entertainment flourished, several cinema halls were built. In the period following structural adjustment, however, the Nigerian economy began to contract, and cinema owners could no longer run a profitable business. During this period, many cinema halls were sold to churches, which took over the buildings for their religious services. Today this pattern has been reversed and complicated, as churches are becoming makeshift concert and cinema halls. The existing networked communities within the churches have provided the human capital to open up distribution and production opportunities. I focus here on one such evangelical filmmaker and his networks: Mike Bamiloye. Bamiloye is the founder of Mount Zion Faith Ministries International (MZFMI) and the driving force behind Mount Zion Film Productions (MZFP), the Mount Zion Institute of Christian Drama (MZI), and a range of other creative enterprises. He is the most prolific and influential of the evangelical filmmakers. Central to his creative vision is that he not only manages and leads a production company but also runs a training institute. He has mentored and trained thousands of evangelical filmmakers through the institute, which has been in existence since 1991.

It is important to situate this evangelical film tradition within Nollywood, which for many people is synonymous with Nigerian cinema. Scholars have attempted to classify various strands within Nigerian cinema and Nollywood, for example, in the use of the term *religious Nollywood*, within which there are subtypes such as Christian evangelical films. For the sake of classification (a dominant trend in Nigerian film studies), Bamiloye's art is situated firmly within the religious block of the Nigerian film industry. The use of the word *evangelical*, as opposed to merely *religious*, emphasizes the function and motive of this category of films, namely, to preach the gospel of Christ. Alongside Bamiloye's brand of evangelical films, one can also find other evangelical strands, and further distinctions can be made between subdivisions like independent and church-based evangelical films. These films are made in a range of languages, and another attempt at categorization might classify the films along language divides such as evangelical Hausa or evangelical Yoruba or a range of other languages.[1]

Leaving aside these questions of classification, what characterizes these films is the ambition to evangelize through film; this is the force that continues to drive and motivate innovation of the evangelical screen. Evangelical filmmakers first became widely known and popular in Nigeria in the 1990s when its most prolific group, Mount Zion Film Productions, was seen on a program screened by the Nigerian Television Authority (NTA). A church general overseer, after watching a stage performance, had decided to sponsor a video shooting of the performance for television transmission. I grew up watching some of these films on Nigerian television broadcasts, at church crusade grounds, and at friends' houses. By the time I started researching MZFP for my doctoral thesis in 2012, these recordings had proliferated and were widely available. I acquired over fifty titles on video compact discs and started watching them from an analytical perspective. My understanding of these faith-based products changed again in 2016 when I met the producers. This encounter and my ongoing engagement with the makers of evangelical films inform my research into the worldview of evangelical filmmakers in Nigeria.

The "Bamiloye" Brand

The group founded by Mike Bamiloye, Mount Zion Faith Ministries International, is strictly speaking a ministry, not a church, since its members belong to different churches. MZFMI does not hold Sunday or mid-week services; rather they meet regularly for scheduled activities, which include prayer meetings but also film production sessions and ongoing technical training. This clarification is important because researchers sometimes refer to the organization as a church. The MZFMI owns MZFP, the Mount Zion Christian Drama Institute (MZI), and Mount Zion Television (MZTV). There are now many evangelical film production groups in Nigeria, but in most cases, their production philosophy has been shaped by Mike Bamiloye. As far as Christian drama in Nigeria is concerned, Bamiloye (who is famously referred to as Daddy Mike) has reached the same status as the Nigerian Christian leaders who are referred to as the (general overseer or GO), a title that became famous with the flourishing of Pentecostalism in Nigeria. The GO figure represents an individualistic style of church administration as opposed to the collective council style of governance the orthodox church employs.

Bamiloye has over the years built networks that are both human and nonhuman and, through these, increased the visibility and popularity of evangelical screen cultures. MZFMI set out in 1985 with the vision to evangelize the world through film drama. At the time, Bamiloye, its founder, was a young graduate of a college of education in Ilesha, and his team members, including Gloria Obembe, who later became his wife, were all college students. The strategy for MZFMI was to start by producing church stage plays. From there, it expanded in 1990 to video productions that were broadcast on television. The MZFMI trajectory has certain similarities with the development of the well-known Yoruba theater tradition (see Barber 2000; Clark 1979). This is perhaps not surprising, as Bamiloye grew up amid that rich cultural tradition. In my interview with him in May 2016, he mentioned that as a child in primary school he watched this theater group on the screen and also participated in theater productions. MZFMI, like the Yoruba theater group before it, began to tour Nigeria with stage plays. On one such tour, the group traveled to Kano and stayed for a month, staging plays in various church halls. MZFMI also toured the neighboring countries of Ghana and Cameroon, in accordance with its self-driven evangelical intention.

Bamiloye later set up several initiatives, moving from the television screen to churches and Android screens. During the early years, his films were screened on national television and also circulated on VHS and later on video compact discs. In 2016, MZFMI's MZTV launched a channel on the CONSAT-TV cable network, a paid television option with over fifty channels that range from movies to sports and news. Today most of the MZFP catalog can be found on the YouTube channel of Damilola Bamiloye, Mike and Gloria's firstborn son. When Damilola posted *The Train: The Journey of Faith* (a two-hour biopic of Bamiloye), the film was viewed twelve thousand times on the first day and had over a million views within two weeks. Damilola's YouTube channel has more than 570,000 subscribers, and the film has been viewed millions of times as I complete this chapter in January 2022. These figures prove the success Bamiloye has had selling an evangelical worldview on-screen. Bamiloye has often stated that the evangelical filmmakers are ministers of the gospel called to preach through drama, whereas the secular participants in the sector are actors aiming to entertain. Although in recent times Bamiloye's films have come to embrace and incorporate entertainment elements, he maintains that entertainment should not be prioritized or allowed to distort the message of a film. When Bamiloye started his ministry in the mid-1980s in Nigeria, he worried that the indigenous television shows lacked a Christian worldview, so he positioned himself as the Christian alternative. In the following section, I explore how evangelical filmmakers' worldview is made manifest in their filmmaking practices and discuss how their alternative exhibition practices through church screenings have increased the visibility of Nigerian cinema.

Behind the Screen Network

Human and nonhuman networks built over the years have contributed to the visibility and popularity that evangelical films now enjoy. Understanding early on that the vision of the evangelical screen culture does not fit into mainstream Nigerian screen cultures, the makers of evangelical videos created independent networks and operational manuals of their own. Evangelical filmmakers have been able to build a national network by using the existing formal and informal religious networks. The All Nigerian Conference of Evangelical Drama Ministers, for example, is the primary coordinating body for most evangelical filmmakers and has chapters in each of Nigeria's thirty-six states, holding annual conferences at the state and national levels.

The COVID-19 pandemic lockdown led to the further flourishing of the global networks of the evangelical filmmakers. MZI training made use of the Zoom platform and thus was able to reach participants from many countries, including Estonia, Belgium, Belize, Ghana, Ireland, Egypt, the United Kingdom, Turkey, Gambia, Canada, the United States, Spain, Switzerland, India, South Korea, Australia, Italy, Germany, Uganda, Namibia, the Dominican Republic, Russia, Qatar, France, and the Netherlands. The subsequent editions expanded to include even more participants from over fifty countries. Although participants were mainly diasporic Nigerians, this popularity is still an indication of the continuous spread of the evangelical worldview through film. This spread is further evidenced through the fact that Mount Zion filmmakers and alumni are producing evangelical films in a variety of indigenous African languages—for example, Felix Bankole has made films in Hausa, Yoruba, French, Ga, Twi, Ewe, Nupe, Gurmancema, Dakarawa, Fulfulde, Bassa, Igala, and Egbira.

In addition, the evangelical filmmakers started their own film festival and awards ceremony, Gofestival, which operates independently from the mainstream awards and festivals.[2] The festival accepts only evangelical films, and one of its expressed aims is to create a system that recognizes and rewards exceptional evangelical films. The training programs have also led to the formation of an international alumni association called Mount Zion Institute of Christian Drama Alumni International Fellowship (MZIAIF). About a year after its formation, this group started the MZIAIF International Christian Film Festival, which held its first festival in October 2021—via Zoom. This festival represents yet another screen innovation made possible by the networking efforts of the evangelical filmmakers. The logo and slogans of MZFMI reveal its clear evangelical aims, namely, reaching people well beyond Nigeria to spread the gospel.

Ontology of the Evangelical Screen Worldview: "We Are God's Alternative"

Creating an alternative in response to adversity and the lack of resources is a feature of every film industry in Nigeria. The video film industry itself started in response to the lack of funding and support for celluloid filmmaking. This understanding of serving as an alternative is key to the way the evangelical filmmakers approach their work, and this has helped to open up a space for experimentation in content and exhibition. Bamiloye has become the leader of networks of evangelical filmmakers in Nigeria and beyond. Besides setting himself up as an alternative, he is also encouraging a generation of filmmakers to think of themselves as the alternative to secular filmmakers. MZI provides Bamiloye with a platform to mentor clusters of such filmmakers in Nigeria as well as in other countries, among them Cameroon, Togo, Kenya, the United States, Canada, Australia, and India. For example, in 2012 when MZFMI visited Cameroon, Bamiloye wrote in a newsletter to his disciples about the need for evangelical filmmakers to spread their influence in Cameroon and other West African countries before the secular arm of Nollywood infiltrated them: "Mount Zion has visited Cameroon twice in the latter part of last year and there received a strong burden to take hold of the land before it is invaded by secular artists with Nollywood movies, the way it happened in Ghana" (2013, 5). Bamiloye sees his work going beyond providing an alternative; he presents it as part of a battle between worldviews. The evangelical filmmakers see themselves as "God's alternative" on earth.

Bamiloye's ideological stance shares certain similarities with the fundamentalist evangelical filmmakers of the United States. James Russell argues that North American evangelical filmmakers seek "a degree of cultural isolation, seeing themselves as separate from, if not actively opposed to, mainstream media culture." The most extreme of them, he writes, "view Hollywood as an epicenter of atheistic, liberal and irreligious value" (2010, 393). In 2013, Bamiloye shared this message with his filmmaker disciples: "Bro. Ayobami Adegboyega [an MZI alumnus] has gone on a drama mission trip to the Republic of Zambia, in southern Africa to hold a drama school and a few other evangelical drama projects. We are encouraging other drama ministers to go all out and fulfil the Mandate of *Godly Alternatives*, by giving unto God Inspiring drama and movie offerings that will feed the hungry souls and quench the thirst of dry hearts" (5; emphasis added).

Bamiloye stresses the oppositional nature of his type of film, not as opposition just to secular Nollywood but also to secular film industries across the globe. Speaking about his film *Rupantar* (2014), shot in India in collaboration with the Nigerian-initiated Shiloh Global Ministries of India, he again emphasized his position as an alternative, using his distinctive language: "The movie was premiered before the entire cast and crew as a new revival wave of evangelical movies is born in India, and the old rugged cross wood invade the base of the old crusting Bollywood" (2013, 2). Bamiloye encourages his followers to exploit all media to spread their gospel, using a language of energetic activism: "Storm the television, cables, and satellite, the radio stations with audio radio drama, make short movies, short drama skits on internet for the 'You-Tubes and God-Tubes,' invade campuses and secondary school with series of film shows, take to the street, parks, town squares, with as long as a week film screening" (2). He says that each filmmaker must "reach out to the whole world as a drama prophet of this time" (2).

Bamiloye's revolutionary stance has some similarities to the Third Cinema manifesto of Fernando Solanas and Octavio Getino (1969). The military language that commands his followers to "storm" and "invade" resembles the Third Cinema school of thought, which saw film as needing to reject offering mere entertainment, instead making itself available as a revolutionary medium capable of initiating change. Like the Third Cinema filmmakers, Bamiloye also puts his movement in opposition to the mainstream industries of Nollywood, Hollywood, and Bollywood. His call has drawn various responses. For example, Adeola Jerry Oluwagbemi's film *One Street One Sound* premiered on June 21, 2019 at his alma mater, the Federal University of Agriculture Abeokuta.[3] Since then it has toured campuses and churches, mainly in western Nigeria. Chinwe Chiazor's film *Mended* (2017) had a church premiere at one of the most popular congregations in Nigeria, the Redeemed Christian Church of God (RCCG) provincial headquarters in Rivers State.[4] Bola Akande rented out movie theaters to screen her films *Broken* (2018) and *Behind the Mask* (2019).[5] And Opeyemi Akintude Ojerinde's *Stepping into Maggie's Shoes* (2020) received a full Viva film distribution deal and screened concurrently in thirty-two cinemas; it was also set to be screened at the Odeon cinema chain in London but could not due to closures during the COVID-19 pandemic.

"We Are Mini-Stars, Jesus Is the Star"

Bamiloye has mentioned on several occasions that the actors in evangelical productions are "mini-stars," not stars, and that the script is a message. A pun is employed with the use of *mini-stars* to draw on the similar-sounding word *minister*. The use of *mini-star* is also used as a self-conscious contrast with the star system of the secular mainstream production.

The evangelical film world has its own unique star system. In an interview, Segun Badejoh, the founder of Gideonite Pictures and the Gideons Drama and Film Institute, explained that the drama ministers are "mini-stars," whereas Jesus is the main star. As such, they operate differently from the glamorous stars of Nollywood, who are foregrounded as part of a business model (Tsika 2015). In contrast, evangelical films place more importance on the message of the script than on the actors. Evangelical actors are mere vessels, privileged to be used by God. According to Gloria Bamiloye, these actors still have wide fan bases within and beyond Nigeria, but she says that as they are showered with praise, they must return the praise to God (Gloria Bamiloye interview, May 2016).

A clear distinction between evangelical and secular filmmakers is this sense of calling. Most, if not all, of the evangelical filmmakers are convinced that God has called them to preach the gospel through drama. For them, their work is first and foremost a spiritual call to serve rather than a profession. Whereas a young secular filmmaker pursues professional training and probably attends a film school, the young evangelical filmmaker seeks spiritual mentorship and training. The early training offered at a typical evangelical film school consists of heavy doses of prayer and Bible study sessions. While some coproductions include Nigerian filmmakers and share star actors, evangelical filmmakers strongly discourage their actors from taking roles in the mainstream secular Nollywood industry.

One result of being ministers and not just performers is that, rather than signing a contract or bargaining for their pay, these minister-actors receive honoraria at the discretion of the producer. Jerry Olugbemi (one of MZFP's producers and a founding member and also dean of student affairs at MZI) explained in an interview that the honoraria depend on the number of appearances made and the number of days the minister-actor puts in (Jerry Olugbemi interview, May 2016). Although this may appear to be an exploitation of talent, in personal conversations these minister-actors indicate that their primary source of satisfaction comes from knowing they have been able to minister to the world with their God-given talent. Given that some of this work involves a voluntary contribution by the minister-actors, many of them still need other jobs to pay their bills. However, this approach helps to cut staff production costs, enabling completion of films on relatively low budgets.[6]

The message is the important element for a minister. Evangelical filmmakers privilege the message rather than picture and technical quality. There are notable differences between the content of the productions of the evangelical and the secular industry. Although the secular filmmakers often produce films with broad Christian traits, the narratives seldom reflect a consistent, intentional biblical interpretation. For instance, the Nollywood classic *Living in Bondage* (1992) closes with a Christian prayer, but up to that point there has been no buildup indicating an intent to tell a faith-based story. The resolution with a Christian prayer is imposed on the film to elicit the protagonist's confession and to drive the story to a close. In the film, while the pastor prays for the protagonist, Andy, to regain sanity, Andy's mother excuses herself and goes to her late daughter-in-law's grave to beg the spirit of the dead to forgive her son and set him free from madness. In the scene that follows, Andy is cured from insanity, but the source of Andy's deliverance is not clear. In contrast, the evangelical filmmakers are quite clear on such matters. In the evangelical film *Attacks from Home* (2000), Mr. Mayowa, an unbeliever who refuses to become a Christian, becomes mad as a result of a spell cast on him by a rival. A group of Christian believers pray for him, and he regains his sanity and becomes a Christian. In short, although mainstream films may incorporate certain Christian tropes to appeal to their audience, the evangelical narrative is built systematically and self-consciously on biblical doctrine. It is the ability to sermonize that sets the screen up as an agent of conviction aiming to transform unbelievers and encourage believers.

Church Screenings

Nollywood studies has been preoccupied with the effects on the Nigerian film industry of the rise of big corporations and the resultant rise of cinemas, satellite stations, and streaming services. Film exhibition in Nigeria is taking on diverse and more glamorous forms, and film releases often involve loud premieres. Kunle Afolayan's *The CEO* (2016), for example, was premiered on an Air France flight and then shown at international festivals and through theatrical runs (Agina 2019). Jonathan Haynes (2018, 13) explains how corporate backing provides big budgets, equipment, and international distribution for secular Nollywood. The evangelical filmmakers' attention to the alternative distribution networks provides an illuminating counterexample. For the evangelical filmmaker, the church can sometimes be what the corporation is for secular Nollywood.[7] The evangelical production team members, however, always focus on their aim, which is to serve a church's evangelical goal; they must fit into the larger plan to get church support.

The church may not always provide funds to make evangelical films, but it offers resources in the form of human capital, networks, and infrastructure. People outside Nigeria do not always understand Nigerians' obsession with the church. It has become a multifaceted venture, going beyond the spiritual realm to offer a wide range of uses and forms of value. Most Nigerian churches have succeeded in setting themselves up as social forces and as places where significant cultural exchange takes place. The church provides space for social activities, health talks, vocational training, human capital training of all sorts, fashion and culinary skills, and peer-group meetings. Members support each other's social functions (such as burials, and naming and wedding ceremonies) with in-kind assistance and cash. Some members of the congregation further capitalize on the presence of crowds to advertise their various products and even to meet sales targets.[8] One can raise one's economic status through the networking that the church provides. In Nigeria, prominent churches also run housing complexes and even independent water and electricity-generating plants. The RCCG, located along the Ibadan–Lagos expressway, has schools, a health center, a market, banks, and its own security and power plant. Also, typical Nigerian church services include considerable musical and dance expression, combining spiritual as well as social and cultural activities that invoke joy and thus encourage patronage. This rich and diverse set of activities creates bonds and sustains the fellowship and commitment of members, causing them in turn to invest time and funds in church projects. This shows how the church has stepped in to provide alternatives where the government has failed and has succeeded in building cultural capital (Bourdieu 1984) to its advantage.

The church, especially the Pentecostal church, is very resourceful in its use of media. Many studies have explored how religious influence has expanded beyond church walls. Birgit Meyer (2002, 2006) repeatedly states that of all religions across Africa, Christianity, especially its Pentecostal form, is the most actively engaged in media proselytization. She describes in detail how Pentecostalism in Ghana has, through various media, escaped the institutional walls to enter the public sphere. On a similar topic, Katrien Pype (2013) writes of the influence of Nigerian Pentecostal elements on the Kinshasa media space and analyzes how the genre of melodrama serves the evangelical project (Pype 2015). Both Meyer and Pype establish clearly the influence of Pentecostalism over the media sphere of Africa. As Francis Benyah (2019) usefully puts it, various media technologies are employed for the scaling up, branding, and self-packaging of churches.

The more cosmopolitan a church is, the more likely it is to use media, and most Nigerian Pentecostal churches display a cosmopolitan outlook. Asonzeh Ukah describes a Nigerian-initiated London parish, which he says is representative of the typical church setting in Nigeria: "Cosmopolitan in outlook and identity, with many members drawn from middle-class members of professions such as medicine, law, and academia. These cosmopolitan parishes use the very latest media technology in their religious services to emphasize a universalistic disposition and aspiration" (2009, 112). More than ever, the church is helping to popularize filmmaking, with many church drama groups rapidly growing into film companies. The reverend Leslie Willis Sprague has gone so far as to say that "the church that is not equipped to show motion pictures is as incomplete as a church without an organ" (quoted in Lindvall 2010, 55).

The church is thus increasingly coming to play the role that the cinema space and screen play for secular filmmakers. Church buildings have the same basic architectural features as do cinemas and are often structured as a hall with a proscenium stage. In these makeshift evangelical cinemas, the main screen is installed on the wall behind the proscenium with the audience facing it, seated in comfortable chairs. Some churches also have food court areas where a wide range of snacks and drinks are available. Although the auditorium mostly cannot become as dark as a cinema can, the acoustic quality, built for sound production, creates a cinematic experience. For example, the RCCG has become a significant collaborator in church screenings. One RCCG parish I visited in Lagos has a multimedia unit that includes engineers as well as various teams focusing on production, postproduction, sound, lighting, newscasting, and social media. The church hall has a big screen that measures about ten by ten feet and other smaller screens in the range of fifty to sixty inches. The church uses video cameras, cranes, body microphones, mixers, and extensive lighting equipment—used mainly to record sermons and for music and news production, and also for film production and exhibition when the need arises. Although the church provides space for a collective viewing, the same film may be experienced differently, depending on the quality of available technology provided for the projection of images and sound. Yet the audiences do not seem to mind, as the content of the film is the most interesting part for them.

The resilience of evangelical filmmakers in creating an alternative worldview and screening tradition, along with their creativity concerning exhibition spaces, is aiding the popularization of the evangelical film genre and increasingly opening up screen options for audiences. The notion of screen here moves away from the capitalist one of purely entertainment for profit and instead provides a religious as well as a rooted screen experience. Church screenings became a new tradition, modified from time to time, depending on the time frame and congregation type. Some years ago, screening and prayers often went together. A film would be screened for about fifteen minutes, then paused so that prayers inspired by the film's story could be shared, before the film would resume. In one such case, a series called *Idile Alayo* (2015), translated as *Joyful Home*, was screened as part of a three-day women's conference. Episode 2 of the series describes two couples. In the first, a wise wife builds a happy home; the second couple live a miserable life because the wife is presented as being slack in her wifely duties. The filmmaker paused the film in the middle of a screening and called on the women present to pray against the spirit of laxity that threatens the home. At other times, evangelical films are

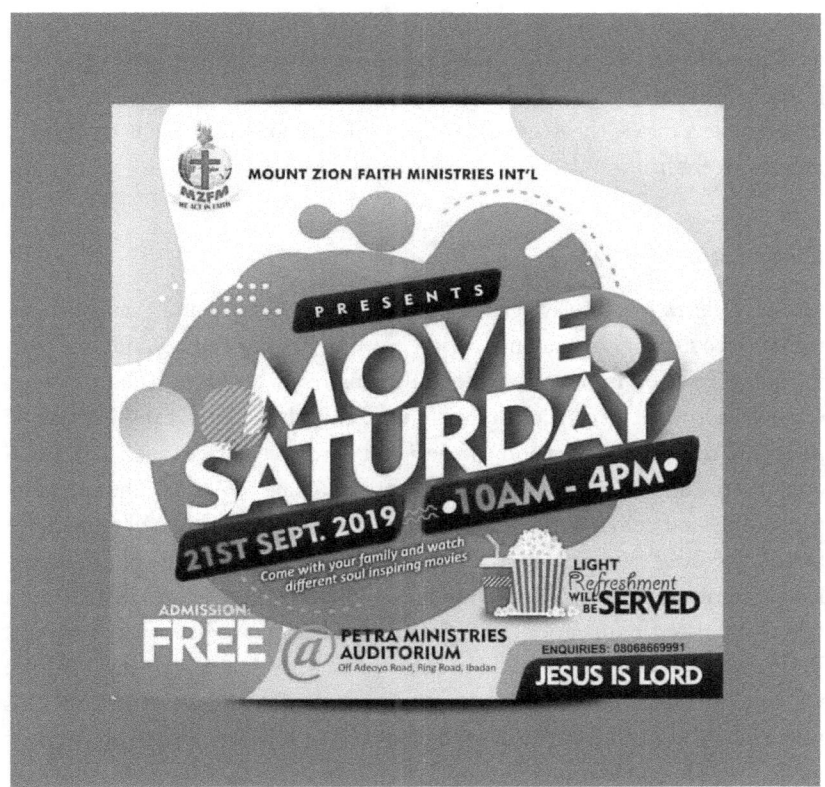

FIGURE 13.2. Promotional poster for a Mount Zion Faith Ministries International "Movie Saturday" in Ibadan, Nigeria.

screened for church outreach, followed by an altar call led by the convenor, filmmaker, or pastor.[9]

Some church screenings can be loosely organized to serve more of a social than a spiritual function, and screenings can take the form of a social outing that closely resembles a cinema experience. One example was the "Movie Saturday" event, which was organized by MZFMI and took place on September 21, 2019, in Ibadan, at which five films were shown for free (see figure 13.2). The event opened with prayers, followed by a brief speech on what the audience should expect from the films. The audience consisted of about a hundred people of all ages and from different churches. Publicity for the screening occurred mainly via phone text messages, Facebook, and Instagram. All five movies were played without interruption or interval, popcorn was served, and some of the minister-actors were also in attendance, although there were no question-and-answer sessions. The movies were played on a laptop and projected onto white fabric attached to the altar wall. The church hall was made to resemble a movie theater by boxing up the windows to prevent any rays of light from entering.

Conclusion

MZFMI defines its objective clearly: to produce a spiritual and evangelical alternative to secular cinema. In practice, however, it goes well beyond this, seeking to define itself in opposition to the mainstream. MZFMI has been able to establish a form of screen culture within the church in Nigeria and has started to export this practice beyond the national borders to places such as Cameroon, Togo, and Kenya, and even to countries outside of Africa. The spread of these films and collaborations outside Nigeria has resulted in Mike Bamiloye building global evangelical filmmaking communities, such as the North America Conference of Evangelical Drama and Film Ministers, the UK Christian Drama Ministers Association, and Mount Zion Eagles on Missions in Australia. In this way, Bamiloye, in particular, has created a revolutionary screen culture with a Christian worldview, seeking to connect with audiences who share this worldview and to convert those who do not. It is, however, worth noting that while the older generation of evangelical filmmakers are deliberate about creating an alternative cinema culture, the younger generation seem to seek inclusion in the mainstream film, a topic I will explore in future research.

NOTES

1   See Brian Larkin (2000) and Abdalla Uba Adamu (2010) for details on the Hausa film industry (Kannywood). Felix Bankole says his Hausa productions will serve as the Christian alternative to Kannywood.

2   Gofestival, the first gospel film festival in Nigeria, was founded by Olaitan Faranpojo. It is held annually in the city of Ibadan and had its first edition in 2009.

3   Adeola Jerry Oluwagbemi is the son of two of the founding members (Jerry and Feyi Oluwagbemi) of MZFMI. According to him, he was born into the ministry, and this makes him a bona fide member of MZFMI. He has served as the continuity manager for several Mount Zion productions. With his film *Countdown* (2017) (shot during his compulsory National Youth Service Corps year in collaboration with the Nigerian Christian Corpers Fellowship, Owerri branch), he decided it was time to direct and produce his own films.

4   Chinwe Chiazor is an alumna of MZI and a graduate of Lagos State University in physics. She is the producer of *Mended* (2017), directed by Ben Ope Johnson.

5   Bola Akande is the daughter of the legendary Ishola Ogunsola, popularly referred to as Dr. I Sho Pepper. She was in the cast of the Mount Zion film *Haunting Shadow* (2005).

6   In several interviews with evangelical filmmakers, when asked how they are able to fund a project, the one phrase that kept recurring was that "we are ministers and we act in faith." This comment aligns with the inscription contained in MZFMI's logo. Probing further, I learned that most projects are self-funded through personal savings, gifts from friends and churchgoers, and calling in favors for crew and post-production work.

7   MZFP's first successful production was funded by a general overseer of a church in Nigeria. The group staged *The Unprofitable Servant* (1990) in a church. Because the pastor wanted more people to see the message in the play, he funded the video version of the same play, and it was broadcast by the Nigerian Television Authority.

8   The Experience 13, an edition of the gospel concert series, was held at the Lagos stadium and had a multimedia screen that showed a variety of projects by the convener (House on the Rock). A trailer for the film *God Calling* (2018) was also screened, with a later announcement calling on the thousands in attendance to support this Christian undertaking by going to the cinema to see the film.

9   On her Facebook page, Seyi Pedro-Adetola, an evangelical filmmaker, invites churches and ministries to use her film *Oore Ofe* (*Grace*) for evangelism: "Do you need a message on salvation for evangelism? Do you need a message that talks about the grace of God for evangelism? Are you considering a less than 60 minutes movie for your outreaches? Do you need a movie for a fishing program, crusades, revival, etc.? Then, I strongly recommend this movie for you. You will be glad that you used it."

INTERVIEWS

Bamiloye, Gloria, vice president and executive producer of Mount Zion Film Productions, Nigeria. Interview conducted at the Mount Zion Drama Institute, Ile-Ife, Nigeria, May 2016.

Bamiloye, Mike, president and executive producer of Mount Zion Film Productions, Nigeria. Interview conducted at the Mount Zion Drama Institute, Ile-Ife, Nigeria, May 2016.

Olugbemi, Jerry, producer, Mount Zion Film Productions, Nigeria, and Dean of Student Affairs, MZI. Interview conducted at the Mount Zion Drama Institute, Ile-Ife, Nigeria, May 2016.

14

Tezeta in Motion

A Glimpse into a Performative Ethiopian Screen World

MICHAEL W. THOMAS AND ASTEWAY M. WOLDEMICHAEL

On a cold, autumn evening on October 19, 2019, in the shadows of London's financial district, an Amharic film made in Ethiopia, by Ethiopians—ቁራኛዬ/*Kuragnaye*/ *Enchained* (2019, dir. Moges Tafesse)—was screened at the Rich Mix Cinema in Shoreditch. The audience was largely composed of members of the Ethiopian diaspora living in the United Kingdom, and for many of them, the event offered a taste of "home" through the audiovisual and social experiences of cinema. The theatricality of the film content was amplified by the organizers, who curated elements of live performance and audience interaction during the event. Not only was there a Q&A with the film's director and leading actor directly after the screening, but there was also an actor dressed in a rural Ethiopian costume, matching the costumes worn in the film, welcoming audiences outside the auditorium and engaging with them throughout the event. The character being portrayed by this actor was a የቆሎ ተማሪ/ yekolo temari—a traditional church student, who lives off food collected by begging.

The physical presence of, and personal interaction audiences had with, such a character, rarely seen outside of rural Ethiopia, and in authentic dress complete with sheep hide and in bare feet, induced a nostalgia, or ትዝታ/tezeta, attached to memories of "home" that directly referenced the sights and sounds of the movie, thereby allowing the diegetic storyworld to spill out of the screen and into the experiences of spectators.

This chapter explores the complexities of performance, liveness, and theatricality as they relate to film, drawing on the "performative turn" (Bachmann-Medick 2016; Conquergood 2013; Rosaldo 1993) in the arts and humanities in order to conceptualize and interpret a specific cinematic event. We write as a collaboration between Asteway M. Woldemichael, the actor and theater lecturer who performed at the premiere mentioned in the vignette at the beginning of this chapter, and the film scholar, curator, and filmmaker Michael W. Thomas. Bringing into conversation our diverse experiences and perspectives of Ethiopian cultures, cinemas, and performance arts, we read the relationships between these artistic and cultural forms in the specific context of *Kuragnaye*'s screening in London.

The role Asteway played was that of a performer and central protagonist in the screening of *Kuragnaye* at the Rich Mix on October 19, 2019. Michael, however, was not present at the event and so has instead played the role of an inquisitive interpreter, a student of culture and film whose life journey over the past decade has been split between Ethiopia and the United Kingdom. Our methodology itself has thus embraced both descriptive narrative—trying to recount the contours and experiences of the Rich Mix event—and critical analysis, attempting to bring together different understandings of text, context, and performance in a way that also values our shared and different epistemological formations. *Kuragnaye*, the film at the center of the screen world we are analyzing, tells the story of a love quarrel set in the mid-1910s that is resolved through an old feudal juridical practice in Ethiopia. Highlighting the respect a mastery of language commands in Ethiopian cultures, the film shines a light on the traditions of ቅኔ/kiné, a style of Ethiopian Orthodox Christian poetry which takes four to five years of rigorous training to master. The film's climax culminates in a stylized argument in front of the newly crowned Empress Zewditu in which the victor secures the hand of the woman his heart desires through impassioned and poetic persuasion.

Kuragnaye was the first fiction feature film produced by Synergy Habesha Films and Communication, with the film distributed by the streaming service habeshaview. Habeshaview organized live screenings of *Kuragnaye* at cinemas in Europe and North America and at various film festivals as a way of reaching out to diasporic Ethiopian audiences to promote their new video-on-demand (VOD) site, launched to coincide with the film's regional premieres. Through this promotional strategy there has been a clear symbiotic relationship between the physical screening event of the film in cinemas and using these screenings to recruit VOD subscribers. The film itself, then, became an advertisement for some of the exclusive content available on habeshaview.[1]

Habeshaview was conceived, developed, and is currently directed by businesswoman Tigist Kebede (see figure 14.1, in which Tigist Kebede and Asteway M. Woldemichael can be seen together before the 2019 *Kuragnaye* screening at the Rich Mix). Founded in 2015, the company spent time securing international distribution rights for a select number of Ethiopian-centered films and setting up its app and VOD platform before it made *Kuragnaye* accessible through a pay-per-view model in January 2020, marking its full launch. As an international film distribution agent and internet portal TV (streaming) service provider, although having a rather limited catalog of four films in 2021, habeshaview focuses on attracting audiences from the Ethiopian and Eritrean diaspora communities spread across the world. Tigist Kebede has represented habeshaview as its operations director at numerous film markets and industry conferences, with the company also cosponsoring the first formal Ethiopian film delegation at the European Film Market in 2020, part of the seventieth edition of the Berlinale. With roughly thirty employees scattered around the world, habeshaview has particularly close ties with the Ethiopian diaspora community in the United Kingdom but also maintains its legal, technical, and part of its social media team in Ethiopia, Turkey, and the Netherlands, with financing and management decisions made in the United States. The global dynamics of habeshaview reflect the international distribution and streaming opportunities that the company pursues and shows how, through streaming services, African screen worlds can navigate globalized circuits of connectivity.

Habeshaview is the first VOD site geared toward Ethiopian audiences to harness the promotional potential of live event screenings in cinemas. Building on the success of the 2019 *Kuragnaye* screenings in London, in September 2021 the company also organized its annual Ethiopian Film Week that coincided with the Ethiopian New Year. Also held at the Rich Mix in London, this Ethiopian Film Week offered public screenings of the limited number of films habeshaview has the rights to distribute or exhibit, which are all available on its VOD platform; this included a repeat screening of *Kuragnaye*. The fact that a VOD platform is investing in live screening events offers an interesting example of how physical

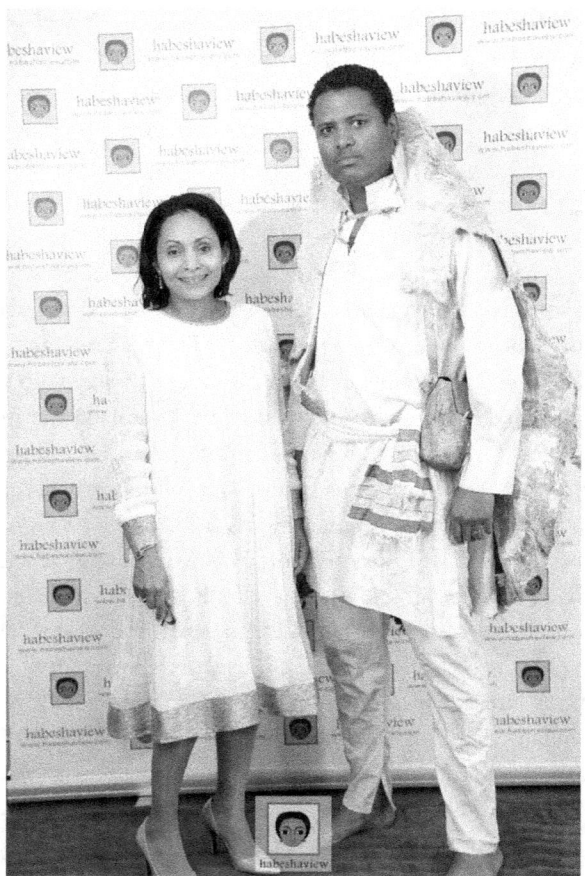

FIGURE 14.1. Habeshaview operations director Tigist Kebede (*left*) and actor Asteway M. Woldemichael (*right*) in *yekolo temari* pose on the red carpet before the *Kuragnaye* screening on October 19, 2019.

"event" screenings are increasingly being used to promote a company's online services and products. While this presents a fascinating line of inquiry for further research, our focus here is to delve deeper into the live screening itself and explore how an Ethiopian screen world materialized in a London location for a few fleeting, yet memorable, hours. We aim to do this by theorizing this event through a lens colored by an Ethiopian worldview and tinted with *tezeta*, a culturally specific sense of Ethiopian nostalgia, reading the *Kuragnaye* screening as a means of generating a particular Ethiopian screen world.

A key approach to exploring this live screening event is to situate our thinking within performance studies. A "performative turn" in certain cultural discourses has helped to reemphasize social process as the source of human creativity. By harnessing interpretative analytical styles that recognize "performance as cultural process" (Conquergood 2013, 18) and "as constitutive of culture" (19), we use a mix of people-oriented, textual, and contextual research methods to construct a triangulated approach to understanding "the generation of cultural meanings and experiences" (Bachmann-Medick 2016, 73) at a film screening event. Similarly to many of the people-oriented contributions in this volume, we are concerned specifically with how the imaginative storyworld of *Kuragnaye* has been brought to life by both on-screen and live, in-person performances. We embrace performance studies as a liminal discipline that challenges the divide between theory and practice and that allows us to better grasp temporary, fleeting experiences of screen cultures that feed into our understanding of the liveness and ever-changing nature of screen worlds.

The Performances of Kuragnaye: Context, Text, and Live Interaction

The theatricality of *Kuragnaye*—in terms of the film's plot, setting, dialogue-driven narrative, and performances by the actors—is such that the story almost feels better suited to a live stage performance. This is not surprising given the context of the film's production history and crew, who mostly hail from a theater background. Similar theatrical roots and traits are common in the domestic commercial cinema of Ethiopia, where personnel in the creative industries move freely between different mediums and sectors, with a background in theater being a common thread (see Eyerusaleam Kassahun [2018], whose comments on Ethiopian women in film also apply to men). Such is the commonality of this cross-performance pollination in theater, film, television, music, and radio that creatives and performers of all types are generally referred to by the anglicized moniker "አርቲስት/artist."

The osmosis between different creative pursuits and mediums coupled with a lack of formal film-specific training in Ethiopia mean that theater and film are closely related thematically (see Plastow 2020), narratively, and aesthetically and in the personnel they employ. Modern training in performance arts and theater flourished during the reign of Haile Selassie I (1930–74), with many early practitioners fusing backgrounds in traditional Ethiopian Orthodox church education with modern craft and techniques (Plastow 2020). Jane Plastow notes how the greats of Ethiopian theater managed to combine the sacred poetic double meanings of ሰም ወርቅ/*seminna werk* (wax and gold), as taught in the Kiné Bet (Ethiopian Orthodox Church School of Religious Poetry), with social commentary and secular topics. Such was the extent of the success of theater practitioners, particularly in the 1970s and 1980s, that these figures and their works remain central in performing arts education in Ethiopia today. *Kuragnaye* can be seen as a continuation of this movement, both because of the theatrical backgrounds of many of its cast and crew and, importantly, because of the theatrical style and structure of the film text itself. In terms of *Kuragnaye*'s structure, its narrative is constructed around scenes based on performances. The film starts with a *kïné* recital by the protagonist Gobezé as he improvises a *kïné* for his teacher and fellow *yekolo temari* in praise of Zewditu's ascension to the throne, clearly establishing the period in which the film is set (ca. 1916). As his name denotes, Gobezé is defined by his wit, a trait that not only enables him to create a *kïné* in praise of the empress but also allows him to allude to his unrequited love, Alem, whose name means "world" in Amharic. This wit and clever turn of phrase define the protagonist as he is bound to defend himself against accusations of adultery at a traditional court hearing in front of the empress during the film's climax—marking the film's final theatrical scene.

In between these opening and closing performances, Gobezé exhibits his highly regarded gift of gab in front of his peers in settings reminiscent of theatrical live performances. Gobezé happens upon Alem by chance one day and discovers that she is already married (to an older, higher-status man), but their desire for one another remains undiminished by time. After Gobezé is literally caught with his trousers down, a highly performative and premodern form of Ethiopian justice, called በላ ልበልሃ/*bela libeliha*, takes place shortly after. This method of meting out justice is one in which the members of a community gather to act as the jury while the aggrieved parties poetically argue their case; from a Western reference point, this community is reminiscent of the chorus in an ancient Greek play who act as witnesses to the action and bearers of a moral compass (figure 14.2). The performative nature of *bela libeliha* is also characterized by exaggerated gestures and a style of well-rehearsed, loud, and clear oratory not unlike what one would expect from a stage performance. Crosscut with the *bela libeliha*, Gobezé and his rival engage in another traditional Ethiopian style of performance as they exchange thinly veiled poetic barbs with an *azmari* (Ethiopian troubadour) acting as a neutral interlocutor. These four major theatrical scenes are the four main performative "acts" of the film: the first establishes our protagonist, the period and setting, and his unrequited love; the second sees the protagonist win over the people, becoming ritually enchained to his rival as they are bound to take their argument to a royal hearing; the third pits the rival suitors against each other for the first time in jest; and the performance in front of the royal court sees the rivals waging their rep-

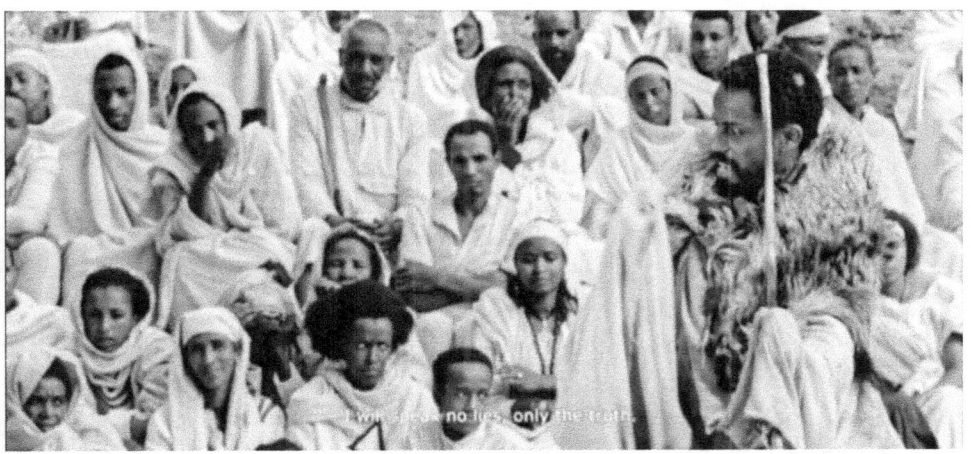

FIGURE 14.2. In *Kuragnaye*, Gobezé speaks at the *bela libeliha* with the whole community present. Screenshot

utations on the outcome of their stylized debates justifying their right to Alem's hand.

The protagonist, Gobezé, is central in the four performative acts throughout *Kuragnaye*. The character is cast as an underdog; he is young and brazen, and as is customary for a *yekolo temari*, begs in order to feed himself. The character is a performer and composer of *kiné* who fuses wit and passion through words, ultimately winning the admiration of all those who hear him speak and see him perform. The performance and gestures of Gobezé are extremely exaggerated, as one would expect. However, even when Gobezé is not performing, for example, in more introverted moments, his quivering lips, jerky head movements, darting eyes, and dramatic pauses come across as unnatural in the close-ups and medium shots that capture these gestures. This theatrical style of acting on-screen is common in the domestic commercial cinema of Ethiopia and is indicative of the theater background of most actors. Although perhaps jarring for audiences not familiar with such an acting style and often criticized by Ethiopian cultural commentators for lacking subtlety, this exaggerated style of screen acting emphasizes the theatricality of the film and can prove highly emotive if one's emotional investment in the film experience is maintained. A more powerful emotional audience response is all the more likely if the film is viewed in the context of a sold-out live screening, as was the case here with *Kuragnaye*, filled with a mainly diasporic Ethiopian audience invested in the subject matter of the film, nostalgic for "home," and eager to actively participate in the live event.

Asteway's involvement in the film screening at the Rich Mix in London in October 2019 deepened the performative and theatrical elements of *Kuragnaye*. As noted, as an actor, he was wearing full traditional *yekolo temari* dress that directly referenced *Kuragnaye*'s protagonist Gobezé (see figures 14.1 and 14.2). Although not actually performing in character as Gobezé, the manifestation of a person in the same costume as the film's protagonist effectively bridged the fictional screen world of the film and the real world for audiences who attended the screening. And, for Asteway himself, the performance carried an extra weight, occurring only a few months after he relocated to London from Wolkite, Ethiopia. The costume he wore reminded him of his home and the life he left behind there. As a lecturer in theater at an Ethiopian university, his area of academic interest is the practice of premodern performance in Ethiopia. While still living there, he wrote, directed, and managed a number of locally specific performances with various communities, which allowed him to explore and research performative aspects found in different cultural contexts in Ethiopia. When it came to the *Kuragnaye* screening in London, walking barefoot for six hours on the cold concrete floors of the Rich Mix was thus not such a hard task, as it represented a chance for Asteway to experience elements of being home in Ethiopia through nostalgic sensations. Because the wearing of animal skins is common in historical plays in Ethiopia, it was the costume in particular that also allowed Asteway to reminisce about his theater career back home. Raised in a small town southwest of Addis Ababa, Asteway grew up watching *yekolo temari* begging for food and attending their *kiné* recitals in monasteries and churches. These experiences he had of observing *yekolo temari* and their discipline helped him understand their movement and way of communicating. Far from being a promotional gimmick, Asteway's performance at *Kuragnaye* represented a chance for him to practice his craft in London for the first time, and the role allowed him to channel his childhood memories through his performance.

As recalled by Asteway, the most apparent sensations this live performance contributed to at the film's screening were those of smell and touch. The distinctive smell of the sheepskin cloak he wore was mentioned by audience members who gave feedback, and they noted the particular impact the smell and touch of this garment had on transporting them back to memories of their youth in refrains akin to a nostalgic *tezeta* as they held back tears. The material power of transposing a costume seen on-screen into the live environment of a film's screening through a living, breathing, walking, talking performer inspired instinctual responses from such audience members. These audience members became active participants within the live event as they interacted with the performer and the costume he wore. Despite the fictional, theatrical nature of the film, audience members clearly felt that Asteway represented a "real" world, and they came up to him to share their emotional responses to a performer appearing as a specific character from the film. The feelings these audience members expressed were filtered through *tezeta* as they reminisced about their "homeland" with Asteway. The interactive, performative elements of *Kuragnaye*'s screening, then, can be seen to have played a vital role in generating and transforming the cultural experience of cinema-going for diaspora Ethiopian audiences in London by heightening the sensations of *tezeta*, particularly through the ability to interact with a performer and through touching and smelling a specific Ethiopian traditional costume.

Performative Tezeta

The sense of "live" performance in our case study blurs the lines between conceptions of "media events" and "film festivals." Lindiwe Dovey differentiates these two separate screen media phenomena as follows: "The former pride themselves on the liveness (or 'real time' transmission) of the *content*, whereas the latter pride themselves on the live togetherness, rather than dispersion, of the *viewing participants*" (2015b, 14). The performer's interaction with audience members in the case of *Kuragnaye*'s screening in London had the effect of bridging the gap between these two. In this case, then, the live performer brought a part of the film's diegetic screen world into real life through his interacting with audiences and so also became part of the "live togetherness" of the "viewing participants" in the Rich Mix auditorium. In this way, although the film was still of course prerecorded, the event was able to re-create a live performative experience more akin to theater.

It is important to highlight that the cultural specificity of this performative aspect in *Kuragnaye*'s London screening has its roots in the live performances found in everyday cultural experiences in Ethiopia (Harrop and Ashagrie 1984; Zerihun 2019). Performance is an important aspect of both sacred and secular culture in Ethiopia, from the religious poetry (*kiné*), dance (*aquaquam*), and various *zema* (chants) and *mezmur* (hymns) that form a constant soundscape being emitted from the loudspeakers of Orthodox Ethiopian churches to the begging cries of *lalibela* and the musical performances of *azmari* (Ethiopian troubadours). Audience participation in performances also features in Ethiopian culture—this is evidenced in *Kuragnaye*, for example, in the sequences with the *azmari* where audience members can beckon the singer to repeat a verse of their own creation. Such collaborative acts between audience members and *azmari* are still commonly performed today. Similarly, Ethiopian cinema-going involves social interactivity between audience members and an active engagement with the content projected on the screen. Thus, the infiltration of a fictional character into the real-world screening of *Kuragnaye* is not so far removed from widespread performative aspects of culture in Ethiopia. Understanding the interaction between performer and audience in the *Kuragnaye* screening in London from an Ethiopian cultural perspective helps us foreground the event within a broader context of Ethiopian cultural expectations.

A preeminent and powerful notion in Ethiopian culture is the concept of *tezeta*, and foregrounding this notion in relation to our case study is just as important for understanding the performative aspects of Ethiopian screen worlds. *Tezeta* can be understood as a profound cultural and emotional response tied to memories of or nostalgia for Ethiopian experiences. Asteway recalls the late theater director Abate Mekuria as saying: "*Tezeta* is something that describes the soul of an Ethiopian. It is a recollection of the past, as an inspiration for the future." This *tezeta* represents "one of the metaphors characterizing Ethiopian culture" (Girma 2012, 139) that, although rooted in a musical mode, evokes "an 'active memory,' . . . that resides in the past, inflects the present, and projects itself into the future" (Mennasemay 2010, 87). Memory infused with *tezeta*, therefore, takes on a powerful and culturally specific form that, according to Mohammed Girma, "enthralls all Ethiopians irrespective of their class, gender, age, and ethnic difference" (2012, 139).

In recognizing the specificity of Ethiopian cultural feelings, we delve deeper into this concept of memory that leads us to a realm where our own positionalities and experiences affect our engagement with, in this case, an Ethiopian screen world where feelings of *tezeta* (a specific Ethiopian rendering of cultural memory) have been heightened. Asteway relates *tezeta* to a tether that ties his Ethiopian identity to his spirit and which maintains his sanity while he is living in a foreign land. Furthermore, *tezeta* expresses itself through the act of remembering, something that was strongly felt by Asteway at the *Kuragnaye* screening through the film, his performance, and his interactions, specifically with diaspora Ethiopian audiences. The diaspora community, which now includes Asteway, feels this sense of *tezeta* heightened due to their circumstances of living in a foreign land and enables people to process and reflect on deep feelings of separation, longing, loss, and loneliness. The expression of *tezeta* through music, literature, film, television, and theater reinforces a sense of belonging and Ethiopian cultural identity. In the case of *Kuragnaye*'s screening in London, the feelings of *tezeta* inspired by the sights and sounds of the film were further augmented by the presence of a live performer in the physical space of the auditorium. A sense of theatrical performance in this space heightened the "live togetherness ... of the *viewing participants*" (Dovey 2015b, 15) prior to, during, and after the film screening.

Resolution: More Than Meets the Eye

By focusing on a case study in which an Ethiopian film was powerfully enhanced by live, interactive performance, thereby bringing *tezeta* into being for audiences, we have tried to conjure a screen world that goes beyond what is simply seen on a screen. Our exploration of the connections formed between a premodern diegetic screen world and a contemporary, diasporic audience—largely due to the performative role that Asteway as an actor played at the screening, mirroring a character from the film—shows how performance itself, as a fleeting yet tangible and embodied cultural experience, significantly impacts people's experiences of screen worlds and of their Ethiopian identity. Habeshaview sets itself apart from other Ethiopian-focused VOD platforms in its organization of "offline" events that complement its "online" screen worlds. The power of live performance in such "offline" screenings can be a catalyst for audiences to actively engage with elements of screen worlds in an intimate communal atmosphere that heightens culturally specific feelings, such as *tezeta*, that cannot be reproduced to the same extent remotely. More broadly, we hope that our case study reveals how our understandings of the dynamic screen worlds of contemporary Amharic cinema and television can be enhanced through grounding them within the performing arts that are so vital to Ethiopian cultures and worldviews.

NOTE

1   Unlike the many YouTube channels that stream Ethiopian films and screen media for free (often, though not always, through pirated means), VOD platforms specializing in Ethiopian content often promote themselves as offering exclusive programming and claim to offer better distribution deals for filmmakers. The platform Sodere.com has the most content, but it is modeled more on Amazon than Netflix, with a key part of its business consisting of its online market and goods delivery service. Sodere.com emerged from a blog set up by the American-based CEO Girum Assefa in 2010. It streams domestically produced films that have been successful in cinemas across Ethiopia as well as less well-known films with lower production budgets. Other VOD platforms that target Ethiopian audiences are the Canadian-based Fuchet, which advertises itself as hosting content with an Ethiopian theme but not necessarily produced by Ethiopians. There are also two Ethiopian-based platforms, Arkwod and Avetol (both of which had soft launches in 2021), which are still in their infancy but claim to be inspired by having the best interests of the domestic Ethiopian film sector at heart.

15

Hillywood and Beyond

Forms of Spectatorship and Screen Worlds in Rwanda

ALISON MACAULAY

The meanings of decolonization, decolonizing the gaze, and decoloniality in the contexts of African film have been the topic of rich analysis and fulsome debate (Barlet 2000; Diawara 2010; Dovey 2020; Givanni 2000; Saul and Austen 2010; Tcheuyap 2011; Ukadike 1994). Lindiwe Dovey and Sendra Fernandez (2023) have explored what meaning(s) festival screenings can hold and what it might mean to move "towards decolonised film festival worlds." This chapter explores how Rwanda offers an exciting example of the productive possibilities that arise when considering festival screenings in conjunction with nonfestival theatrical screen worlds, including small-scale city cinemas and *agasobanuye* veejay (VJ, or video jockey) translations and adaptations. To begin imagining what a decolonized (or *decolonizing*) film festival world can look like, this chapter posits the importance of placing festival screenings in a geography of local film consumption that considers the spatial, historical, and political specificities at hand. The history of screen media consumption in Rwanda from the late 1990s to 2014 offers additional spaces to consider when conceiving of screen worlds and thinking through what it means to decolonize both the practice and the theorization of film, film spectatorship, and film festival worlds.

In exploring multiple articulations of theatrical screen worlds in Rwanda, this chapter focuses on how Rwandan audiences have engaged with different types of screens and screening environments in the recent past. The chapter conceives of screen worlds, specifically theatrical screen worlds, as layered spaces of participation and consumption. In each of the cases discussed—Hillywood festival screenings, small-scale city cinemas, and *agasobanuye* rooms—screen worlds are part of broader considerations and public discourses around commemoration and perceptions of class status and propriety. These specific screen worlds are representative of trends elsewhere on the continent in terms of film festival rural outreach programs and VJ translation/adaptation, and this chapter contributes to these literatures by exploring how these worlds operate in the Rwandan context. Although scholarship on the Rwandan film industry is growing (Cieplak 2008, 2009, 2010, 2017; Dauge-Roth 2010, 2017; Edwards 2018), spectatorship practices and nonfestival screen worlds remain understudied (see MacLeod 2020 for a welcome exception). In line with Haidee Wasson's (2019, 75) characterization of cinema as a "multimediated environment," this chapter highlights the degrees of variation, audience preferences, and social perceptions of theatrical-spectatorial spaces within Rwanda's ever-growing and ever-changing mosaic of screen environments.

The first half of the chapter considers outdoor mobile film festival screenings, with a 2014 screening in Rwamagana (a town outside Kigali) as part of the Rwanda International Film Festival (RFF) as a case study. Founded in 2004, RFF is the country's longest-running festival. A central component to the festival is Hillywood, which involves traveling to small towns around the country and screening a series of films on inflatable screens in large open spaces (typically stadiums or soccer playing fields) to rural Rwandan audiences. Hillywood holds a prominent position in the brief history of Rwanda's growing film industry. Jennifer H. Capraru and Kim Solga argue that the Hillywood program is "the jewel in the [Rwanda Cinema Centre]'s crown" (2013, 45). The journalist Tom Cropper claims Hillywood is what makes RFF "the world's most unique film festival" because "for many, this is the first time they will ever see a film at all, let alone one made in their local language, Kinyarwandan [*sic*]" (2009). In the documentary *Finding Hillywood* (2011), RFF interviewees also stressed first and foremost the unique experience Hillywood offers rural Rwandan popula-tions to see Rwandan films, in Kinyarwanda, on-screen. Film scholars have ex-plored the concept of the "new" when it comes to waves of industry production, technologies, and ideological directions in festival curation (Dovey 2015b; Har-row 2013; Orlando 2017; Tsika 2018). The notion that Rwandan rural audiences are entirely new to film, and that Hillywood is their first introduction, high-lights the value of contextualizing conversations about film festivals, including their meaning for audiences and their potential future decolonization, within their specific contexts and considering broader nonfestival avenues of screen media consumption in other forms of screen worlds.

Hillywood is one (albeit a major) part of a constellation of modes of screen media consumption in Rwanda. The second half of this chapter assesses other forms of theatrical screen worlds, including small-scale cinema halls and the translation/adaptation practice of *agasobanuye* that flourished in Rwanda from the late 1990s into the first decade of the twenty-first century. *Agasobanuye* in Rwanda, like other examples across the continent (Dovey 2015a; Krings 2013), refers to films, typically from Hollywood, Bollywood, and East Asia, that have been translated, either prerecorded or live, into Kinyarwanda. In both nonfes-tival alternatives, engagement with these theatrical spaces has been tied up in perceptions of class, education, and propriety. Taken together, these nonfesti-val alternatives offer exciting context for further understanding the "meaning making" of festival screenings and for conceptualizing more broadly the varied history and future of theatrical screen worlds in Rwanda and beyond.

This chapter is based on my experience as a festival employee during the RFF in 2014 and a series of oral interviews with members of Rwanda's film community in 2019. The discussion that follows is predicated on my ability to exercise a mobility tied up in layers of outsider status and privilege (as a white Canadian). My position as a location coordinator in 2014 gave me a particu-lar vantage point from which to observe, participate in, and compare screen-ing events in the city (at Kigali's Century Cinema theater) with a Hillywood screening in Rwamagana. What follows are reflections shaped by this experi-ence and engagement with festival curators, filmmakers, and industry profes-sionals from 2014 to 2019.

The Rwanda Film Festival and Hillywood

In her analysis of the 2013 Durban International Film Festival, Dovey notes that "festival and film meanings are not stable, but constantly redefined by spe-cific audiences" (2015b, 159). The 2014 RFF run was intended to be particularly meaningful: it celebrated the tenth anniversary of the festival and marked twenty years since the 1994 genocide against the Tutsi. The festival's theme for that year, "Reflection," highlighted its desire to engage with larger national processes of commemoration and remembrance. Yet, the theme applied only to its Kigali screenings—the Hillywood program offered rural audiences a different kind of meaning-making opportunity. In Kigali, RFF held screenings in a variety of locations. Some locations, like Century Cinema, the Kwetu Film Institute, and The Office (now the Impact Hub), catered to the local film community and expatriates. Others, like Club Rafiki in Nyamirambo, were geared toward Rwandans living or working nearby. Urban audiences were not monolithic, and RFF sought to program content in spaces where different segments of Kigali's population typically spent time. This approach to programming, which embedded the festival within the minutiae of Kigali's city spaces, reflected RFF 2014 artistic director Romeo Umulisa's broader ethic toward curation. Dovey's interview with Umulisa regarding RFF 2013 details how his curatorial style as an "insider/outsider," as a Rwandan-Congolese creative who split his time between Kigali and Berlin, included "the incorporation of local, Rwandan audience perspectives in the conceptualization of the festival's shape and meaning" (2015b, 154). Umulisa's 2013 curatorial methodology involved "a great deal of time discussing films with people in Kigali to gather a sense of their tastes and interests" (154). With Umulisa at the helm, RFF fostered screen worlds that were seemingly collaborative, where both audience and curator preferences informed the final experience. Umulisa planned a dynamic and international program in 2014, with different locations offering diverse segments of the Kigali population opportunities to watch both local and international content that, to varying degrees, reflected RFF 2014's commemorative atmosphere.

The 2014 Hillywood program crafted a decidedly different atmosphere for spectators in Rwamagana, highlighting the festival's capacity to create and facilitate a multitude of theatrical screen world experiences. Dovey argues that "many film festivals in Africa struggle with a disjunct between their relatively well-organized programs in central, middle-class venues, and their poorly organized or nonexistent 'outreach' programs in impoverished areas" (2015b, 141). In Rwanda, the Hillywood section was, rather than a poorly organized or nonexistent component of the city-centric festival, a significant and the most long-standing component. In Rwamagana, the spectacle of inflating the screen was by far the most effective form of advertisement for that evening's activities—the slow rise of the screen in the open air transformed what had previously been a soccer field into a theatrical space (figure 15.1). As the sun began to set, the growing audience was shown a series of music videos, such

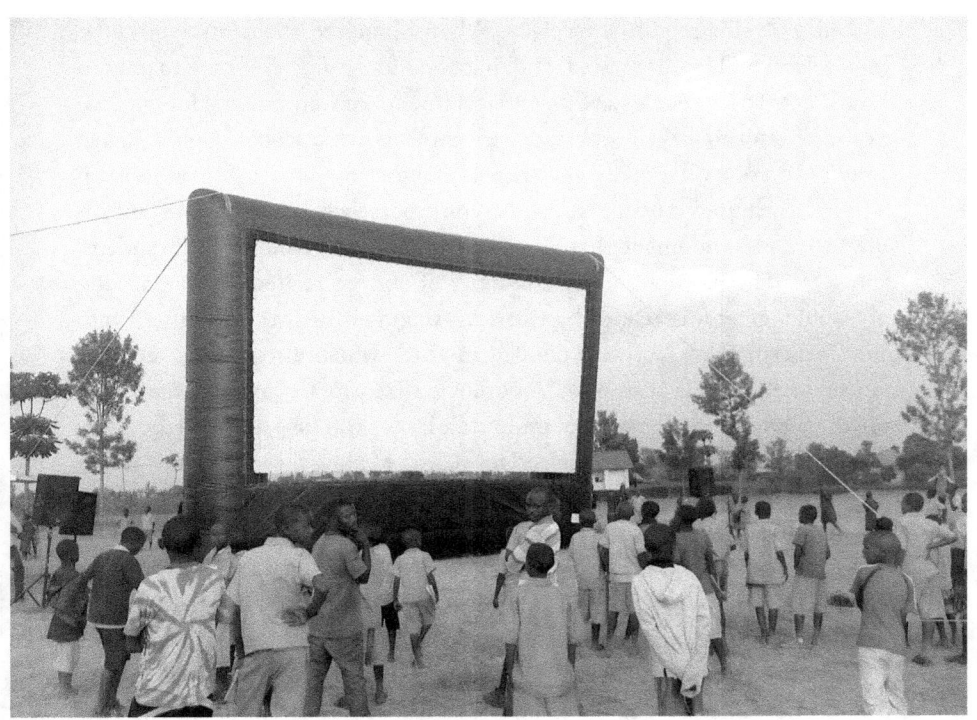

FIGURE 15.1. Preparations for an outdoor screening at Hillywood in Rwamagana, Rwanda, July 2014. Author photograph

as Iggy Azelia's "Fancy," to draw spectators and set the evening's tone of light entertainment. The feature film was a family-friendly adventure comedy, *Africa United* (2010), which follows a trio of Rwandan children who embark on a trip to South Africa so that one of the boys can try out for a youth soccer team. Although crowds began to dissipate as *Africa United* ended at around 8:30 p.m., those who stayed were shown short films by Rwandan filmmakers that dealt with themes of family relationships and domestic violence. The music videos prompted the loudest and most boisterous reactions, but audiences were perhaps at their most engaged during the short films, loudly expressing disapproval when a character behaved badly and clapping when that character faced consequences. After the short films concluded, the crowd, whose members varied in age and gender but included many school-age children, slowly dispersed as the Hillywood team deflated the screen and returned to Kigali.

The curation of the Hillywood program in 2014 was informed by perceptions of what audiences might enjoy and an awareness of how a commemoratively minded screening might be received. When I inquired about his 2014 Hillywood selection, Umulisa stated, "I didn't want any genocide-heavy themes in those areas. These people have no entertainment; we were coming for one day. We didn't want to make people sad; we wanted to make people laugh" (Romeo Umulisa interview, December 20, 2020). The purpose of the festival took on different meanings outside Kigali—commemorative reflection was substituted with entertainment that was seemingly missing from rural Rwandans' daily lives. The perception that a scarcity of options related to what spectators would enjoy was echoed by Chris Mwungura, the director of the Rwandan Christian Film Festival (founded in 2012), which also hosts screenings outside of Kigali. He reasoned, "Any movie that you are going to take [outside the city], as long as they can understand, they will love to watch it . . . but here [in Kigali] they are very selective" (Chris Mwungura interview, May 13, 2019). For some festival programmers, because mobile screenings offer a seemingly novel experience, their curatorial approach to rural audiences required a different approach. Because Hillywood was in Rwamagana for only one day, Umulisa consciously shifted the program away from reflection and reconciliation toward a more celebratory evening that featured local film.

The festival's bipartite structure provided curatorial flexibility, allowing RFF to offer different audiences distinct theatrical experiences. In the city, spectators could choose an evening of action-packed entertainment or partake in a commemorative screening event. Outside the city, Hillywood offered Rwamangana audiences an opportunity for joyful engagement with mobile cinema during a particularly significant, and difficult, year for most Rwandans. Without speaking for rural Rwandan communities, it is likely safe to assume that Hillywood screenings, which appear with little notice and with variable regularity, do not occupy a central role in their day-to-day lives. Despite the "spontaneous liveness" inherent in short festival runs, RFF crafted meaningful experiences— however temporary—for different segments of the Rwandan population, illustrating the inherent multiplicity, complexity, and flexibility of screen worlds. As the next section details, RFF screenings were not the only films accessible to Rwandan spectators, both inside and outside the city limits.

RFF Alternatives: Cinema Halls and Agasobanuye Screenings

Hillywood screenings, which offered an enjoyable experience for most and an opportunity to see local content, were one facet of Rwandan screen media consumption, though not the only theatrical screen world available to Rwandans during this period. This section moves beyond festival screenings to explore the conceptual range and depth that small-scale cinemas and *agasobanuye* screenings offer in thinking through the creation of and engagement with Rwanda's wide array of screen worlds. There has been significant change in commercial film production and distribution in Rwanda since the late 1990s, and small cinemas and live *agasobanuye* screenings have reduced their operations substantially since the mid-2010s. Yet, engaging with these now mostly defunct theatrical spaces can still actively and meaningfully inform conversations about futures of screen media consumption and the circulation of screens and screenable material.

Rwanda's film industry is still in its nascent stages, but the country has not been devoid of opportunities for screen media spectatorship. Although there were few options for film watching in Rwanda in the 1970s and 1980s (especially compared with other East African contexts; see Fair 2018), there were several cinema halls in Kigali's Nyamirambo neighborhood, including Ciné Muhima, La Ciela, and Ciné Mayaka (also known as Ciné Elmay). Muhima's founder remembers audiences as mostly young neighborhood people, but film fans from other provinces also traveled to Kigali to visit these cinemas to either watch a film or rent tapes to screen closer to home (Anonymous interview, June 24, 2019). Ciné Muhima shut its doors in 1990 with the onset of civil war, though its founder attempted to reopen at a different location in 2007 under the name Ciné Silver. However, dwindling audiences, the popularity of televised soccer, and rising operational costs forced him to rent out, and eventually sell, the theater to a local church.

Other theaters reopened after the genocide and offered Kigali residents alternatives to the popular *agasobanuye* halls that emerged in the late 1990s. As Remy Ryumugabe recalls, cinemas like Ciné Elmay were spaces to watch "independent, art house" films and were often considered by locals to be "for educated people, rich people" because there were no live translations or subtitles (Remy Ryumugabe interview, May 8, 2019). La Ciela and Ciné Elmay still exist but have stopped screening films regularly. Although they now usually stand empty except for the occasional soccer match, these theaters made a lasting impression on their frequent visitors. Ryumugabe, with codirector Ganza Moise, is currently in postproduction on a reflexive documentary called *Kinema* (for which I am executive producer), which is a poetic and nostalgic love letter to the cinema spaces they grew up with and includes footage of these once-popular cinemas that now stand empty.

If cinema halls catered primarily (though not exclusively) to Kigali residents, local *agasobanuye* screening rooms had a wider geographic reach. As Felix Sibiyo of the budding Rwanda Film Office recalled, "Actually, every Rwandan has [experience] watching *agasobanuye!*" (Felix Sibiyo interview, June 10, 2019).[1] *Agasobanuye,* a Kinyarwanda term that refers to both the screening rooms themselves and the process of translation/adaptation, came to Rwanda in 1997 by way of returning refugees, most notably Mazimpaka Jones Kennedy, who was Rwanda's first *agasobanuye* veejay (Mazimpaka Jones Kennedy interview, May 29, 2019). *Agasobanuye* films were screened in small rooms called halls or theaters, usually on VHS cassettes on small televisions mounted in the upper corner of the room. Admittance typically cost fifty to one hundred francs, providing a somewhat affordable alternative to buying a home television set or attending urban cinema screenings. *Agasobanuye* encouraged different forms of mobility—in terms of both technology and spectators. Some young Rwandans would travel up to fifteen kilometers from smaller villages into towns that had *agasobanuye* rooms to watch movies (Mutiganda wa Nkunda interview, May 8, 2019), while others traveled to larger towns to purchase VHS copies to screen in smaller locales for a modest price (Sibiyo interview, June 10, 2019). Many in Rwanda's film industry today cite *agasobanuye* screenings as their first experience with cinema. The filmmakers Shema Deve and Remy Ryumugabe happily recalled feeling like these halls "drugged" (Shema Deve interview, April 26, 2019) them and that they became "like an addict" (Remy Ryumugabe interview, May 8, 2019).

With the proliferation of *agasobanuye* screen worlds came a rich public discourse, illustrating how screen worlds fit into and shape perceptions of popular culture and entertainment in Rwanda. Children who went to *agasobanuye* were often punished by their families, sometimes even physically beaten, when they would come home late at night after a screening, skipped school to watch films, stole money to attend screenings, or watched films that were not age-appropriate due to language, violence, or sexually explicit content (Louis Udahemuka interview, June 6, 2019). As a result, there was a perception among older Rwandans that *agasobanuye* halls were "vulgar" places for young Rwandans (Sylvie Kuyisenga interview, May 5, 2019). Parental disapproval toward *agasobanuye* was tied up in socioeconomic concerns and perceptions of class—some Rwandans recalled their parents telling them that *agasobanuye* were for "street children" or for those who did not go to school (Nicole Kamanzi interview, May 5, 2019). As David Ndahiriwe notes, however, Rwandan parents were not concerned just about the content of the films but also about the general environment of the screening hall because "the people in the room, sometimes they [were] smoking" (David Ndahiriwe interview, May 6, 2019). For many young Rwandans, "it was forbidden to go there," which, perhaps unsurprisingly, gave these halls an additional allure (Aimable Imanirakiza interview, May 6, 2019). For both small-scale Kigali cinemas and *agasobanuye* halls, then, engagement with a particular screen world went beyond one's experience of the space or of the film in question, as it could impact how one was perceived by one's family and community.

The Rwandan authorities also had reservations about *agasobanuye*. The practice of translating these films was technically illegal (distinct from dubbing, which was given much more leeway). However, much like Rwandan parents, the police were primarily concerned with the assumed vulgarity associated with these adaptations—according to Kennedy, his "clean" and family-friendly approach to *agasobanuye* saved him from prosecution (Kennedy interview, May 29, 2019). To mitigate these concerns, some *agasobanuye* halls instituted age restrictions, but those eager to watch films found ways to sneak in, including bribing door attendants, or worked at cleaning the halls after screenings in exchange for admission (Deve interview, April 26, 2019). Those who did manage to sneak in had to be wary of potential raids by local police, who would be looking for children too young to be there. As filmmaker Mutiganda wa Nkunda recalls, "That is why my friends, those who were [also] minors, used to sit beside a window, the back window, so that if we heard someone say 'the police,' we would jump all the way out and [rush home]" (wa Nkunda interview, May 8, 2019). Despite the risks associated with going to these screenings, Ndahiriwe remembered, "every day you go back" (Ndahiriwe interview, May 6, 2019).

Although not entirely absent from Rwandan public life, the number of *agasobanuye*-style adaptations and screening halls has decreased significantly since their heyday. The rise in DVD piracy from 2011 to 2013 rendered both *agasobanuye* and local commercial production unprofitable, forcing many into other career paths (Kennedy interview, May 29, 2019). The increasing number of young Rwandans learning English in school, alongside the increasing ubiquity of smartphones, also rendered adaptations and translations less necessary for some viewers (Ndahiriwe interview, May 6, 2019). Despite their decreased presence in daily life, these theatrical alternatives to official film festival spaces signal Rwanda's rich tapestry of screen media engagement and the intersections between screen worlds and broader discussions of space, class, and propriety. Within the context of imagining and formulating decolonized film worlds, the Rwandan case highlights the productive possibilities of looking to the recent past to think through possible new and exciting directions for the future. These modest, though detailed, examples from Rwanda offer compelling additions to wider-ranging projects of decolonization as they showcase the importance of audiences' multiple and layered experiences with screen worlds and offer possible avenues for future studies.

Conclusion

Rwanda's local film industry is still in its early stages—since the late 1990s, filmmakers, festival curators, and businesspeople alike have responded to rapid changes in technologies, markets, and screen media content. This chapter has detailed three diverse interlocking screen worlds with which Rwandan spectators have engaged since this period—mobile open-air festival screenings, small-scale cinema halls, and *agasobanuye*. Each of these respective theatrical spaces offers insight into the myriad of methods for publicly consuming screen media in Rwanda. Beyond spectators' engagement with the screen itself, each space carries additional opportunities for meaning-making in terms of commemorating (or choosing to *not* commemorate) difficult histories, articulating or perceiving class status, and highlighting generational sensitivities to seemingly transgressive or improper spaces. In many ways representative of cases elsewhere on the continent, Rwanda gestures toward future directions in assessing varied styles of screen media consumption and the kinds of spaces to consider when imagining the decolonization of film and film studies. It remains to be seen how screen worlds, in whichever form they take, will operate in Rwanda after the COVID-19 pandemic. However, as this chapter has explored, Rwanda has no shortage of theatrical precedents from which to draw. For their part, Rwandan filmmakers have continued to produce and develop projects throughout the pandemic, ensuring that as public screening opportunities continue to return in full force, there will be no shortage of new local material to screen.

NOTE

1   The establishment of the Rwanda Film Office is an exciting development, though the office does appear to be geared primarily toward promoting and facilitating international film production in Rwanda rather than bolstering the local film community.

INTERVIEWS

Anonymous. Interview, June 24, 2019.
Deve, Shema. Interview, April 26, 2019.

Imanirakiza, Aimable. Interview, May 6, 2019.

Kamanzi, Nicole. Interview, May 5, 2019.

Kennedy, Mazimpaka Jones. Interview, May 29, 2019.

Kuyisenga, Sylvie. Interview, May 5, 2019.

Mwungura, Chris. Interview, May 3, 2019.

Ndahiriwe, David. Interview, May 6, 2019.

Ryumugabe, Remy. Interview, May 8, 2019.

Sibiyo, Felix. Interview, June 10, 2019.

Udahemuka, Louis. Interview, June 6, 2019.

Umulisa, Romeo. Interview, December 20, 2020.

wa Nkunda, Mutiganda. Interview, May 8, 2019.

16

FESPACO @ Fifty

Forms, Formats, Platforms, and African Screen Media

PIER PAOLO FRASSINELLI

In this chapter, I discuss the 2019 edition of the Pan-African Film and Television Festival of Ouagadougou (Festival panafricain du cinéma et de la télévision du Ouagadougou; FESPACO), the best-known and the second-longest-running film festival on the African continent—the oldest is the Carthage Film Festival (Journées Cinématographiques de Carthage; JCC), established in Tunis in 1966. In 2019, FESPACO celebrated fifty years since the first edition in 1969.[1] This anniversary edition presents a unique opportunity to reflect on some of the most significant recent changes in African cinemas, which have to do with the political economy of content production, distribution, and consumption; with the different spaces and platforms—screens, cinemas, film festivals, websites, and other public and private spaces—where African films are screened; and with the new forms, genres, and trends these films represent. In fact, the very categories of film and cinema are today in need of being revisited and updated to include the multiplicity of forms, formats, and platforms with which they coexist, from short clips to serials available from the internet or via online streaming; hence the need for the introduction of new categories such as "African screen media" or, in this collection, "African screen worlds" (see, among others, Adejunmobi 2016; Brown 2016; Dovey 2010; Haynes 2018). Kenneth W. Harrow and Carmela Garritano have identified "the TV screen, computer screen, or cell phone" as "the primary technology for viewing" African films. This viewing experience has radically changed not only in relation to technology but also in its spatiotemporal dimension, as African viewers watch movies "on a bus, at home in between trips to the kitchen, at restaurants or in hotels" (2019b, 13–14).

The main transformation marking the present and looming on the horizon of African cinemas is arguably the ever-more-significant role played by digital media streaming and multinationals such as Netflix, South Africa–based Naspers—owner of MultiChoice, DStv, Showmax, M-Net, and Mzansi Magic, among others—or Nigeria-based iROKOtv, which dominate this market.[2] This is not to say there are no challenges to providing online content to Africa-based audiences. They include "the difficulty of accessing fixed line broadband, low bandwidth, high data costs, lack of online payment options, and an inability or unwillingness to pay for content" (Dovey 2018, 97). Despite a recent slowing of subscriber growth, Netflix has over 200 million paid subscribers worldwide, but in 2020 only 1.4 million of these subscribers were on the African continent (AFP Relaxnews 2020). Traditional linear free-to-air television continues to be the privileged means of accessing audiovisual content across Africa, where connectivity and the cost of data stand in the way of newer digital screen viewing. Still, content acquisition and, increasingly, production for online streaming and watching are fast-growing industries on and for Africa.

In South Africa, before the arrival of the COVID-19 pandemic, MultiChoice was planning to produce fifty-two local movies and twenty-nine dramas in 2020. DStv and Showmax doubled their number of South African users between 2018 and 2019 and are locally bigger than Netflix (de Villiers 2019), which has announced that it is planning to invest considerably more into the African continent. Productions include South Africa's first original series, *Queen Sono* (2020), a fast-paced action spy drama featuring the South African actress Pearl Thusi in the lead role; Nosipho Dumisa's *Blood and Water* (2020); and Malawi's *The Boy Who Harnessed the Wind* (2019), directed by and starring Chiwetel Ejiofor. In Egypt, the arrival of Netflix is revolutionizing content production with heavy investment in local TV drama (Fouad 2019). Netflix has also acquired the rights to a growing selection of Nigerian films, thereby contributing to promoting the phenomenon of New Nollywood, a "director's cinema of higher quality films" (Haynes 2018, 7) than the earlier low-budget, straight-to-VHS or straight-to-DVD Nollywood movies that are being featured with increasing frequency at African and international film festivals (see chapter 3 of this volume).

Nigerian films available as of February 2021 in South Africa from Netflix include Oluseyi Asurf Amuwa's *Hakkunde/In Between* (2017; screened at FESPACO 2019) and the New Nollywood director and producer Kunle Afolayan's *The Figurine* (2009; screened at FESPACO 2011 but relegated to the video category), *October 1* (2014), *The CEO* (2016), and *Mokalik* (2019). Likewise, the current Netflix selection of South African films showcases such genre-crossing and critically acclaimed films as Gavin Hood's adaptation of Athol Fugard's novel *Tsotsi* (2005; winner of the 2006 Academy Award for Best Foreign Language Film and nominated for the Golden Globe for Best Foreign Language Film in 2006) and Neill Blomkamp's Johannesburg-set science fiction movie *District 9* (2009; winner of four Academy Awards and seven British Academy Film Awards). This corporatization and "Netflixation" of African film production and distribution are bypassing and redefining old divisions between auteur and commercial cinema.[3] All these changes could also be felt at the 2019 edition of FESPACO, a festival that historically has represented the other side of African cinemas, the place where art house and auteur films were promoted. New convergences are taking place, realigning different sectors and creating new tensions and synergies. As the Nollywood scholar Jonathan Haynes suggests, the "division between the African cinema and Nollywood-studies paradigms, always unfortunate if perhaps initially inevitable, makes progressively less sense as everyone works with similar digital equipment and Nollywood has begun to produce films of more or less equal technical quality and professionalism, which appear in the same festivals" (2018, 24). Indeed, the transformations brought about by the diffusion of new forms, formats, and platforms invite us to revisit but crucially also take us beyond the old, by now well-known, debate on Nollywood versus auteur African cinema.

Popularly known by its acronym, FESPACO celebrated its fiftieth birthday from February 23 to March 2, 2019.[4] This was the twenty-sixth edition of the festival, which is part of the first generation of film festivals on the African continent that focus on African and African diasporic cinemas. Its first edition took place in February 1969, and the shorthand name FESPACO dates back to 1972, when the main prize, the Etalon de Yennenga—which would later become the Etalon d'or de Yennenga—was introduced (Bayala 2019). In the words of Michel Ouédraogo, the former director of the Ouagadougou festival, FESPACO "was created in a context in which the African states had recently acquired their independence and they wanted to express their sovereignty and their identity" (cited in Dovey 2015b, 95). The history of FESPACO, a political film festival aiming to bring African cinema to African audiences since its inception, has continued to be marked by its relationship with the socioeconomic and political context from which the festival emerged. Not only is it sponsored by the Burkinabé government, making it literally a "state" issue (Dupré 2012), but its fortunes are determined by local and regional politics (see Aveh 2020, 121–25).

FESPACO 2019 has been described as an attempt to "resurrect" the festival in the face of the challenges and decline of the previous decade (Barlet 2020), which included local and regional political instability, underscored in 2019 by the militarized environment in which the festival took place. The whole area of the festival had a heavy presence of armed men in military uniforms carrying AK47s while the government talked up its security measures on national media. Since 2016, al-Qaeda's presence in the Sahel spread to Burkina Faso with attacks on a restaurant and hotel, followed by several others (Chutel 2019). To mark its jubilee edition, FESPACO 2019 was themed "Mémoir et avenir des cinémas africains" ("Memory and Future of African Cinemas"). The festival was accompanied by a two-day colloquium (February 25–26) organized by the Burkinabé veteran filmmaker Gaston Kaboré titled "Confronter notre mémoire et forger l'avenir d'un cinéma panafricain dans son essence, son économie et sa diversité" ("Confronting Our Memory and Shaping the Future of a Pan-African Cinema in Its Essence, Economy, and Diversity"). The emphasis on pan-Africanism reflects an important dimension of FESPACO, highlighted by the award since 1987 of the Paul Robeson Prize for films from the global Black diasporic community (Dovey 2015b, 102), which in 2019 went to the Brazilian director Joel Zito Araújo's *Meu amigo Fela* (*My Friend Fela*; 2019). As Gaston Kaboré and Michael Martin emphasize in the introduction to the 2020 special issue of *Black Camera* dedicated to the festival, "FESPACO's defining mission is to unapologetically recover, chronicle, affirm, and reconstitute the representation of the African continent and its global diaspora of peoples, thereby enunciating in the cinematic, all manner of Pan-African identity, experience, and the futurity of the Black World in the project of worldmaking" (2020, 5–6).

In addition to competitions for the various prizes, FESPACO 2019 also presented a retrospective featuring the previous winners of the first prize, the Étalon d'or de Yennenga for best film, which were shown at pop-up outdoor cinemas throughout the city—organizers added the winner of the 2001 Jury

Prize, Dany Kouyaté's *Sia, la rêve du python* (*Sia, the Dream of the Python*; 2001), to the winners of the main prize. Organized by the digital network Cinéma Numérique Ambulant, the free screenings were well attended by festivalgoers and Burkinabés sitting on their scooters or plastic chairs, which provided evidence of the popular dimension that has long defined FESPACO and continues to set it apart from many other film festivals (Dupré 2020). But if the canonized past of African cinema seemed ripe for celebration, its present and future looked distinctly uncertain. Ouagadougou is where Ousmane Sembène and the other doyens of African cinema used to congregate at a special table at the Hôtel Indépendance (Diawara 2010, 24) before the hotel was set aflame in 2014. One of the questions every edition of FESPACO is now expected to answer is who and where are Sembène's heirs.

The veteran Cameroonian filmmaker Jean-Pierre Bekolo, often seen as just such an heir (see Grieve, this volume), was at FESPACO 2019 with *Les armes miraculeuses* (*Miraculous Weapons*). This beautifully shot, delicate character study and vaguely surreal political meditation is set in 1960s apartheid South Africa in the small Free State town of Vrede, where two French women, the Black owner of a bed and breakfast and a political prisoner, discuss freedom, Jean-Paul Sartre, and the poetry of negritude under the watchful eye of apartheid state security. The film won the Ecobank Foundation's Ousmane Sembène Prize; otherwise, younger filmmakers won the lion's share of awards and critical attention. The top prize was awarded to the Rwandan director Joel Karekezi for *La miséricorde de la jungle* (*The Mercy of the Jungle*; 2019). A lavishly filmed, gripping story, it brings the audience deep into the jungle on the border of Rwanda and Congo, where two soldiers battle for survival during the Second Congo War. The film also won best actor prize for costar Marc Zinga, while the prize for best actress went to Samantha Mugatsia for her nuanced performance in Wanuri Kahiu's Kenyan queer romance, *Rafiki*, which has already made history for being selected at Cannes after being banned in its home country.[5] The fact that these younger filmmakers and actors are present bodes well for the future. But questions still linger about the prospects and direction of the festival and its packaging of African cinemas.

The first question has to do with how FESPACO has had to face the adjustments required to come to terms with the challenges posed by digital production and distribution technologies. For several years, FESPACO struggled to accommodate video filmmakers shooting in digital formats, their work having become impossible to ignore. First, in 2009, a separate competition for "TV/Video Films" was introduced. This ill-judged and anachronistic move, out of step with technological, economic, and aesthetic developments in African screen media, "came to a head at FESPACO 2013, when several films selected for the official competition were suddenly disqualified because the organizing committee discovered they were not on 35mm celluloid film" (Dovey 2015b, 105). Since 2015, films shot digitally have become eligible for the festival's main prize, which up to that point had been reserved for celluloid films only (see Aveh 2020, 122–23).

These technological innovations also signal the generic and aesthetic shifts that are affecting FESPACO. At the 2019 edition, the two movies that received the warmest reception among the screenings I attended were not the kind of film one normally associates with the "auteur" tradition of the festival. One was the Ivorian film *Résolution* (2019), directed by Marcel Sagne, an urban, upper-middle-class drama of domestic violence and physical abuse perpetrated against a successful CEO and her son by a violent husband. Its earnest denunciation of gender violence had the audience loudly voicing its disapproval at the physical brutality inflicted on the female protagonist and cheering her resolution, after an unconscionable amount of abuse suffered, to finally stand up to her brutal husband, which was followed by the arrest of the perpetrator and a women's march against gender violence. The film earned the director a standing ovation when she arrived after the screening. Some film critics, however, were less impressed. The French journalist and African film critic Olivier Barlet, for instance, took issue with how the film "reproduces the dominant narratives available on all the world's channels—emotion is replaced by either violence or sentimentalism, characters are stereotypes, and thought is impossible when complexity is absent" (2020, 333). This critique targets not only the film in question but, as the reference to "all the world's channels" indicates, much of contemporary commercial production, including on the African continent.

The second screening I attended that received the viewers' loudest approval was *Hakkunde/In Between*. It is the first Nigerian publicly crowdfunded movie by the Africa Magic Viewers' Choice Awards award-winning director and producer Oluseyi Asurf Amuwa. This Nollywood-style comic tale of a self-made man who makes money by selling cow dung to farmers as a prodigious fertilizer also got the audience laughing and applauding for much of the film. As I was standing in the usual long queue before entering the festival's main venue, Ciné Burkina, for the screening, I struck up a conversation with a film enthusiast from Lagos, who complained that Nigerian cinema has been snubbed by FESPACO for much too long. The filmmaker Imruh Bakari states that the emergence of Nollywood presented an instance "in which it became apparent that FESPACO's institutional ability and capacity was out of step with the changing reality of African film culture" (2020, 296). As Ajao Aderinsola also argues, "While pioneers like Ola Balogun might have found it a useful platform for discourse, exhibition and collaboration, FESPACO's dominantly francophone pose and overt predilection for 35mm would, for many years, exclude most films and filmmakers from an Anglophone Nigeria." Fast-forwarding to 2019, Aderinsola states, "Not much has changed" (2019, 35). *Hakkunde* was the only Nigerian entry to the main competition. Still, its inclusion and success with audiences are not insignificant. In his commentary on FESPACO 2019, Aboubakar Sanogo meditates on the "curatorial practices intended to potentially transform African film and film-festival practice." Among these, he singles out "the entrance, for the first time in the entire history of the festival, of a Nollywood film in the official feature competition: Oluseyi Asurf's debut feature, *Hakkunde/In Between*." Sanogo goes on to note that this "was a landmark event for African cinema" in that it "formalized [the] beginning of a fruitful conversation between its so-called popular and auteurist traditions. Clearly the festival that bills itself as home of 'all of African cinema' could hardly continue keeping at bay the films that are most watched by Africans both on the continent and in the diaspora" (2020, 175–76).

The other issue that stood out at the fiftieth-anniversary edition of FESPACO was the contestation surrounding how the festival's history and present are gendered. One can verify this by taking a stroll in Ouagadougou's Rue de cineastes, the filmmakers' avenue, where the statues of the fathers of African cinema and previous awardees of FESPACO's main prize are lined up. Headed by Ousmane Sembène, they parade the festival's patriarchal lineage: Sembène, Dikoungue Pipa, Souleymane Cissé, Lancine Kramo Fadiga, Drissa Ouédradogo, Gaston Kaboré. A look at FESPACO winners of the main prize, the Étalon d'or de Yennenga—which ironically celebrates the horse of Princess Yennenga, the mother of the Mossi ethno-nation—confirms how male-dominated its world is. In the first fifty years of existence and twenty-six editions, no woman won the main prize. In 2019, out of a selection of 124 films in competition and 79 not in competition, women represented a small portion of the directors participating: only 29 in competition—4 long feature films, 6 long documentaries, 7 short feature films, 6 short documentaries, 3 animation films, 3 school projects—and 9 films not in competition. Still, women, who in Africa and the world get less funding and less access to the film market than their male counterparts, were outnumbered but not silent. Initiatives included the meeting titled "Where Are the Women?" on February 25 and another roundtable organized by the Non-Aligned Filmmakers Collective on February 27 on the place of women in African cinema (see El Echi and Aïssatou 2019; Ellerson 2020).

An appendix to this debate was the huge audience success at the festival of the Burkinabé filmmaker Apolline Traoré's *Desrances* (2019), whose scheduled and widely advertised festival screenings were sold out, with long queues and many people unable to enter the cinemas, so that an additional screening at the Institut Français's spacious outdoor cinema had to be arranged. This is by no means unusual at FESPACO, where local films tend to be the most popular with Burkinabé audiences and often attract the largest crowds (Dovey 2015b, 101). In this case, the success of the film and the fanfare around it were compounded by Traoré's self-candidature as the first female director to win the Étalon, which ended in disappointment, complete with a harsh reception by critics who underscored the weakness of the film's plot, characterization, and motifs; its straying "into the implausible and the sentimental"; and "a pervasive use of spectacle to hook the audience" (Barlet 2020, 334; see also Polato 2019, 57).

Here, too, we have a tangible example of how the audience of FESPACO is constituted by different groups, who at the 2019 edition clashed with one another over the value and aesthetics of African cinema. This is in turn symptomatic of the ongoing changes brought about by digital platforms and the streaming market I have been discussing, whereby commercial imperatives and the pervasive turn to genre are redefining African cinema in ways that disrupt its traditions and modes of scholarly analysis and reception (Frassinelli 2021). These same disruptions also affect our interpretation of a film festival such as FESPACO, where our analysis and evaluation need to come to terms with complex dynamics and multiple audiences. As Lindiwe Dovey and Estrella Sendra Fernandez (2023) argue, academics who study film festivals in Africa must question our own positionality as mobile scholars who can more or less easily access these festivals (thanks to our access to funding, flights, and visas)—vis-à-vis, in this case, the local audiences who continue to lend FESPACO its distinctive popular dimension, especially if compared with other prominent African film festivals, such as the Durban International Film Festival, that are increasingly becoming "industry events" defined by the participation of a high number of (international) practitioners and industry representatives and a lack of (local) popular audiences.

From this perspective, perhaps the biggest challenge faced by FESPACO has to do with the forms of attention that the seventh art requires. The festival was very well attended. The main venue, Ciné Burkina, was usually packed. However, part of the audience seemed incapable of focusing on the film they had ostensibly come to watch instead of the tiny screens of their cell phones, which kept flickering and occasionally ringing. I wondered why there were no preshow announcements asking the audience to turn off their phones, possibly because these announcements tend not to work anyway (see Piepenburg 2015). This is in fact a global issue. The new digital environment has brought about habits of intermittent viewing, or what Laura Mulvey calls "narrative disintegration": ways of skipping, repeating, and browsing videos on digital devices that are at odds with the experience of sitting through a whole film in the darkened room of a cinema (2006, 27–29).

If it is to survive and thrive, African cinema must adapt to today's audiences, digital devices, and forms of distraction, which means opening up to new platforms, formats, and forms. The Nigerian video industry has already started producing short films and clips that are easier and cheaper to stream on phones, while Nollywood fans have taken to uploading very short excerpts and scenes to YouTube in a process of remediation (see also Sendra, this volume). Maybe, as Jason Njoku, the CEO of iROKOtv has put it, "the future is on android" (cited in Haynes 2018, 6). As we have seen, some of the most important changes in contemporary audiovisual screen production and consumption are related to technological innovation, especially internet penetration and the diffusion of digital and social media, which has prompted the suggestion that the focus of cinema and screen studies must now turn to "the 'supersmall' screen of the smartphone" (Dovey 2018, 98).

As the changes introduced by FESPACO in recent years illustrate, new media forms, formats, platforms, modes of production, circulation, and consumption call for new ways of cataloging and curating the content that makes up the fast-changing and diverse contemporary African screen media, as well as for new interpretive categories and paradigms for making sense of them. Jonathan Haynes (2019) argues that the popular arts paradigm of early Nollywood, which was undoubtedly commercial but in an informal way at variance with Euro-American models of the culture industry, needs to be supplemented with new ones that account for the emergence of a new capitalist mode of production and distribution, which is quickly expanding beyond Nollywood and incorporating a growing share of the film industry across the African continent (see also Haynes 2018, 5–7). Key among these innovations are the arrival of multinational corporations, which have taken over distribution and increasingly production of content; the shift to digital streaming platforms; the investment in and promotion of television serials as a new popular form; and the emergence of the smartphone as an increasingly important new platform for watching clips and films. That the 2019 edition of FESPACO provided an opportunity to register these changes testifies both to its enduring relevance and to the challenges it faces.

NOTES

1 I have no space in this chapter to discuss the history of the festival. This is outlined in several of the articles included in the special issue of the journal *Black Camera* 12, no. 1 (2020), issued to mark the occasion of the festival's fiftieth edition.

2 I am not including the quantitatively massive phenomenon of piracy in this discussion because it is beside the focus of this chapter but also because of the difficulties in assessing and studying its scale, reach, and impact on African cinemas (see Dovey 2018; Haynes 2019).

3 Even though this would seem an anachronistic dichotomy, some of the scholars working on African cinema either continue to get stuck in it (see, for instance, Prabhu 2014) or carry on identifying African cinema with its auteur tradition (see, for instance, Williams 2019).

4 A first version of my account of FESPACO 2019 appeared in *The Conversation* on March 18, 2019. See Frassinelli 2019.

5 This also speaks to one of the problems with FESPACO: that some of the films in competition have been shown elsewhere and, as in this case, are already well known. Half of the films selected for the 2019 edition had already been shown at festivals and in cinemas (Barlet 2020, 321). As Farah Polato notes, "At present, the films in competition may have participated in other festivals: as a result, a consistent portion of them has already been seen, on occasion repeatedly, elsewhere. When they arrive at the biennial Ouagadougou festival their attractiveness for industry operators and distributors has been accordingly diminished" (2019, 51). Here and elsewhere, translations from languages other than English are mine.

Part V

———

Transnational Screen Worlds

Music Video in Africa, Beyond, and Back

17

Music Video and the Transnationalism of Nigerian Screen Media

Watching Falz's "This Is Nigeria"

FEMI EROMOSELE

The year is 2006, Lagos. I am in the sitting room with my siblings, waiting patiently for Soundcity to come on *TV*. I mutter a silent prayer electricity won't go out before the show is done. Since it revamped into an hour-long program, it has become almost the highlight of the day. We all agree the show has a superior song selection to regular *TV*, but what we really mean is that the videos are better, more lush, and when Nigerian acts are screened alongside international ones, it is sometimes difficult to tell them apart.

Fast-forward.

2019, Johannesburg. A friend in India texts to ask if I know the musician Falz. I do. Really funny guy, I say. She tells me she prefers his "This Is Nigeria" to the original, "This Is America," by Childish Gambino. I have no idea what she is talking about. Buried in my thesis, it has been a while since I watched *TV* or followed anything on social media. I search on YouTube and find Falz's video. Childish Gambino's too. There are several "This Is" wherevers queued up on the list. I start from the top.

This vignette I begin with evokes a narrative of multimedia consumption in Nigeria and offers a useful perspective for exploring contemporary developments in the country's visual culture. It highlights the place of technology in shaping filmic forms in the country as well as their insertion or otherwise into global networks of circulation. Since the early decades of the twenty-first century, computer and phone screens have become as important as the television as a medium of audiovisual consumption. Sophisticated applications, video streaming sites, and social media platforms have changed the way screen media is made and accessed. They not only significantly shift audience configuration but also inform the kind of relationship cultural texts are capable of having with others outside their immediate contexts of production. I use here the music video "This Is Nigeria" by the Nigerian musician Falz as a case in point. Released in 2018, it is a version among many of Childish Gambino's (Donald Glover's) "This Is America."[1] The video "broke the internet"—to use the words of a friend in Nigeria—for the contentions it generated within the country and the recognition it garnered internationally. Admittedly, the idea of "breaking" as a measure of popularity is relative and often relies on the perception of a video's uptake within a networked group of interested viewers. As of December 2021, Falz's video had about 20 million views on YouTube, beside Childish Gambino's 810 million, indicating the superior reach of the latter's influence. However, Falz's video seems to have also drawn the attention of those who would normally not view Nigerian content. The aim of this chapter is to examine the ways that audiovisual productions in the digital age, especially the music video, can help us to contemplate the transnationality of Nigerian screen media. I argue that the significance of the music video in this regard rests on the way its ambiguous properties allow it to travel easily across different places and different screens. This portability brings it to a common space—music shows and online video streaming platforms—where it interacts with productions from other climes and where the use of playlists creates a nonhierarchical relationship that captures audiences of dissimilar cultures. To address all these, I begin by engaging with some key points in the scholarship on Nigerian media's transnationality and then home in on the music video and the specific case of "This Is Nigeria."

Nigerian screen culture has become, in recent years, a fertile ground for academic research by scholars from diverse disciplinary backgrounds. Much of this scholarship emerges in the study of Nollywood, the English-language film industry based in southern Nigeria, and provides a starting point to contemplate how other screen products might be analyzed. The industry's popularity is partly predicated on its escape from the confines of the national border, making it capable of influencing cinematic trends in countries as diverse as Tanzania (Böhme 2013; Krings 2010, 2013) and Barbados (Bryce 2013). The essays in the edited volume *Global Nollywood* by Matthias Krings and Onookome Okome (2013) trace this phenomenon across the different sites of consumption in Africa and beyond. The issues that emerge from their reflections are diverse and point to the way Nollywood resists homogenization; as Nollywood deals with the opportunities and limitations of an increasingly interconnected world, it interacts with diverse cultures, economies, and sociopolitical arrangements in the places it travels. The relationship to technology and its influence on modes of dissemination constitute a significant nexus for these conversations.

Central to the discourse of Nollywood's transnationalism is its embeddedness or lack of it in global and mainstream networks of cultural production. The informality of its emergence and sustenance is identified as responsible for its characteristic position. Largely funded by individual entrepreneurs and small cooperatives in its early years, Nollywood blossomed outside government intervention and global capital. The availability and affordability of the video format enabled filmmakers to circumvent the conditions that halted the celluloid tradition of the 1970s and 1980s and reach viewers for whom, owing to the deterioration of security and of cinema facilities in the country, the small screen had become the primary mode of audiovisual enjoyment (Haynes 2016; Haynes and Okome 1998; Jedlowski 2016; Okome 2007; Onuzulike 2007). The relative lack of regulation and inconsistent enforcement of copyright laws also meant that the products could be easily pirated nationally and internationally. Constituting an alternative network of dissemination, piracy became pivotal to Nollywood's connection with the rest of the world, prompting Alessandro Jedlowski, in "From Nollywood to Nollyworld," to classify it specifically as a "pirate transnationalism" (2013a, 34).

Nollywood evolves at a bewildering pace, quickly rendering analytical categories as just described insufficient or in need of modifications. The "*exclusion* from dominant global networks" that Jade Miller (2012, 118; emphasis in original) identifies as characteristic of Nollywood becomes "partial embeddedness" (Adejunmobi 2014). Seeking admission into global circuits of cinematic production, some Nigerian movie directors have turned to theatrical releases and the high-production-value films they demand. This is also primarily commercially motivated, as the glut in the movie industry in the first decade of the twenty-first century drastically reduced profits and forced stakeholders to seriously consider its diaspora audience as a source of revenue. Where satellite television providers like DStv in Africa and OBE and BEN TV in the United Kingdom used to be the major means for disseminating Nollywood products to a diasporic audience through formal channels, the proliferation of internet platforms, video-sharing sites, and streaming mobile apps has also begun to play a very significant role in this regard.[2] The 2010s saw the rise of streaming services such as Afrinolly, iBAKAtv, iROKOtv, and others. For a monthly subscription, viewers get access to hundreds of titles across genres. Even in terms of funding, filmmakers are turning to online platforms of crowdfunding—which necessarily extend beyond national borders—though with limited success (Ebelebe 2017).

The transformations brought about by big media corporations have changed not just the landscape of Nollywood productions but also the scholarship around it. Less emphasis now rests on Nigerian screen media as predominantly reliant on informal networks, as the pirated CDs and VCDs that used to be the primary means of disseminating made-in-Nigeria films and videos to a diasporic audience have become much less relevant since the advent of video-on-demand platforms (see Adejunmobi 2019; Simon 2021). However, the configuration of its transnational audience seems to be generally understood as unchanged, limiting the transnationalism ascribed to the industry. In Moradewun Adejunmobi's 2014 essay, she describes Nollywood's transnationalism as "affinitive" in the sense that it consists of people who "'who are like us' rather than an instance of making marginalised cultures attractive to mainstream publics in Western societies" (87). The idea one gets is that the ability to connect to a global mainstream audience at the level of content and technological expertise, in addition to modes of distribution, constitutes a marker for successful transnationalism (see Adejunmobi 2007). Though global media corporations like Netflix and Amazon Prime now offer selected premium Nigerian content, the aim is less about making that content attractive to a global mainstream than reaching Africans in the diaspora (Simon 2021). The music video extends this audience to significantly include viewers who share neither racial nor cultural identities with the artists.

The Music Video in Nigeria

The music video is a somewhat amorphous animal, a ghost capable of partaking in several conversations simultaneously. In its early beginnings, the ambiguity of the medium resulted in a predictably variegated approach to its study. Some scholars drew on film studies, ignoring, for the most part, the lyrical or musical elements. Others focused on the musical and ignored the visual. A third approach, like E. Ann Kaplan's (1987), seemed to bypass this dichotomy, emphasizing the medium's affinity with a postmodern culture (Hearsum and Inglis 2013). Recent scholarship has sought a more holistic approach through attention to both visual and aural aspects. Carol Vernallis's (2004, 2013) work is significant in this regard, following Andrew Goodwin's attempt, in *Dancing in the Distraction Factory* (1992), to account for elements of the visual and musical as well as embeddedness within a larger structure of star iconography. New digital and communicative technologies have further influenced the emergence of new genres incorporating diverse forms, necessitating even more interdisciplinary modes of analysis (Burns and Hawkins 2019; Osborn 2021; Vernallis 2013).

Music video is at once an advertisement for a song and its singer, an artifact of star iconography, and a cultural text with its own claims about the human experience. It draws on cinematic aesthetics and creates its own interpretation of aural experience. Because its viability and innovations are tied to the availability of technology, ideas about what it ought to look or be like are constantly challenged as new technologies emerge and shape how it is made, disseminated, and consumed (Vernallis 2013, 11). The music video is certain to remain a "problematic and controversial media entity" (Arnold et al. 2017, 1), seeing as it "reside[s] at the crossroads of musical genres and styles, visual genres and styles, lyrical narratives and messages, artistic subjectivities and cultural representations, new media technologies, as well as participatory culture and social media" (Burns and Hawkins 2019, 3). Its formal elements and varying objectives pull it in different directions, with the consequence that some aspects get emphasized above others, depending on where and when it is encountered. For example, watching Falz on TV in my living room is a different experience from watching him on YouTube while I am riding on a bus. It is a different experience watching him via a link from a friend rather than encountering him as an option on a preset playlist. It is different in 2018, when the song to which the video refers is the rave, from what it will be several years later when Falz has made more music and the song is tagged "old school." The music video can take on features attached to the moving image as well as those of the music, such that, at different times, the viewer can associate the video with a filmic tradition or a musical one, or both simultaneously. One might, for example, be fascinated by the use of certain filmic techniques, like the long take in "This Is Nigeria," popularized in films like *Birdman* (2014; dir. Alejandro G. Iñárritu), or the similarities of its sonic properties with other versions of "This Is America," including the original. The significance of this is in how the videos bend to a variety of uses and contexts in ways that enhance their mobility.

It is crucial that music videos are not usually sold as primary products. Gone are the days when the only way to enjoy them outside a TV broadcast was by purchasing DVDs and box sets by artists or video directors. As free content on TV stations and internet sites, they are both unattractive to pirates and less encumbered by the restrictions of purchasing power. Anyone with a TV or access to YouTube can enjoy them, at no obvious charge. Because of their small size, they can be easily downloaded and transferred across devices. This complicates the dominant thinking around the transnationality of Nigerian screen media, which dwells largely on media as commodity, as products meant to be directly generative of profit. Such understanding underwrites the founding assumptions in the literature. In Adejunmobi's analysis of Nollywood, its status as a "commercial [form] of transnational cultural productivity" (2007, 1) distinguishes it from African cinema typically associated with directors from Francophone West Africa, most notably Sembène Ousmane. While the latter can pass as a "global ethnic," Nollywood may still be restricted by that need to be profitable. But what if the screen media text does not need informal structures of piracy or lucrative cinema and video-on-demand deals to travel? This question can shift how we see the trajectory of Nigeria's cultural influence in Africa and beyond. For one, it shows how extensive circulation can be an end in itself, thus giving more impetus to the spread of the visual text. This can also influence the choice of subject matter so that a more provocative stance can be more beneficial than conservatism. A political topic that resonates with more people may prove more advantageous for circulation than playing it safe with censorship regimes.

Artistes in Nigeria are more likely to pay for the dissemination of their videos than to expect payment. The skeletal structure of the country's music industry since the early 1990s has meant that promotion and publicity for albums rest on the musician or their private labels. Before the proliferation of digital media, this involved making deals with audiovisual "pirates" or informal distributors in Lagos (the Alaba International Market in particular) who position themselves as "marketers" and "promoters." The distributors produce mixtapes with selected tracks from up-and-coming artistes alongside those of recognized stars. This helps to generate familiarity with new artistes and "sell" them as stars of the caliber of those they are mixed with (Simmert 2020; Tade and Akinleye 2012). A similar strategy is used with music videos. Artistes pay TV stations and video jockeys (unofficially) to ensure constant rotation of their songs on various charts and playlists. Though YouTube and other internet

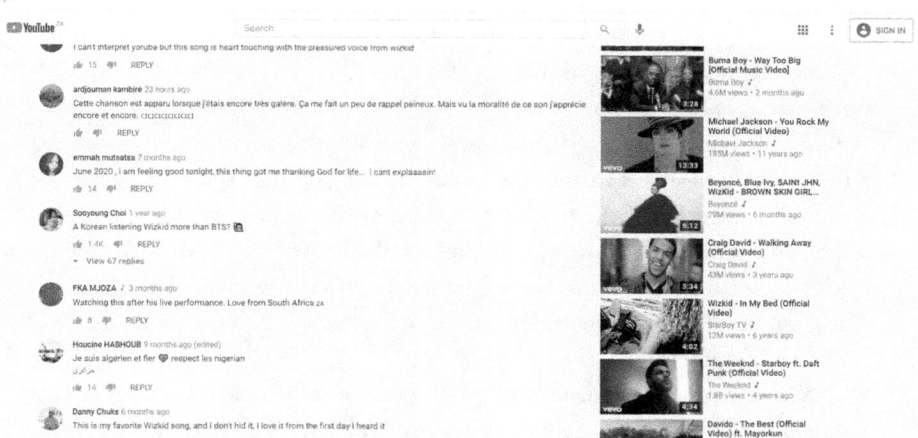

FIGURE 17.1. A queued list of videos related to Wizkid's "Ojuelegba" generated by YouTube's algorithm. Visible here are Davido, Burna Boy, and Wizkid alongside Michael Jackson, Beyoncé, Craig David, and The Weeknd. Screenshot

platforms are changing how this arrangement works, terrestrial and satellite broadcasting outfits remain relevant, especially among those without access to the internet. Television stations in Nigeria, such as AIT, ONTV, Soundcity, and Trace, still mediate public access to new music and visuals. While specific shows operate on a regional logic—screening kinds of videos by the national or geographic location of the star—others are organized by musical genre, such that a single playlist can feature videos from South Africa, the United States, Kenya, and so on. In this way, different videos, by virtue of an organizing rubric dictated by their musical component, are brought into conversation. This is a common practice with music video channels (local and international) and streaming sites. The playlist becomes a technology of leveling that presents the diverse artistes and their cultures as parallel alternatives.

One can identify something similar in the way Nollywood films on global platforms like Netflix appear alongside others from around the world. However, there seems to be a degree of hierarchization not to be found in the playlist logic of most music video channels and streaming platforms. Noah Tsika writes that many Nollywood movies on Netflix "sit as free streaming options and not as titles to be rented or purchased individually" (2016, 115), signaling the perception that certain kinds of production are more valuable than others. On music video channels, all videos are somewhat more parallel. Classification is driven by generic consideration and television programming. A show dedicated to party tunes, for example, will feature videos of whatever songs are considered favorites—or likely to become so—at parties or clubs at that point in time, regardless of their provenance. On sites like YouTube the algorithm curates playlists based on a person's past watching experience or by generic contiguity in a way that brings regionally disparate productions next to each other. This is further facilitated by the fact that such sites are more inclusive in terms of the production value of the videos uploaded, meaning that any work can potentially become available even to those only familiar with a global mainstream. Such conditions create the kind of connections and potentials for transnational conversations we see achieved with "This Is Nigeria" (figure 17.1).

As already mentioned, a recurrent point in the scholarship is that Nigerian screen media transnationality is affinitive (Adejunmobi 2014; Ajibade 2013), meaning that while its cultural influence reaches across national and continental boundaries, it simply resonates with "like people" in other climes and does not constitute an attraction to a "mainstream" audience. This is a sentiment already evident in Jedlowski's earlier observation that diasporic communities have been "the main vehicles for transnational circulation of Nigerian videos" (2013a, 26). The music video paints a different picture. Its attraction to a mainstream audience is not only the moving image but also the music it carries. Those whose musical tastes go beyond the categories promoted by more visible labels in Western countries find in the music video a veritable means of accessing these sounds from elsewhere. Music thus becomes as much a reason to seek out a video as a video promotes the music. The increasing collaboration between Nigerian musicians and international acts is a testament to this transnational influence that is not affinitive. For example, Burna Boy appears alongside the British singer and rapper Ed Sheeran and Stormzy in "Own It"; and alongside Chris Martin, lead singer of the group Coldplay, in "Monsters You Made." Davido collaborates with the American Chris Brown on "Blow My Mind," and Wizkid features in Beyoncé's "Brown Skin Girl." These sorts of projects reveal active participation in a global mainstream in ways that expand the audience base of already popular acts in the United States and do the same for Nigerian cultural producers.

The point here is that the connectivity afforded by new and social media means that multimedia cultural texts can potentially congregate in a common pool accessible to all kinds of viewers. The generic features of the music video, which, unlike film, do not necessarily differ according to the region of production, ensure a familiarity of codes across cultures and spaces. The aesthetic configurations of Nollywood, Bollywood, Hollywood, or French cinema are fairly distinguishable. Music videos, on the other hand, circulate in a space where directors often aim for readability within very limited time by drawing on common codes: jump cuts, close-ups of star's faces, choreography, and so on. Despite the difficulty of pinning down what a music video is, one knows it when one sees it. Tracking its dissemination through common video-sharing sites, one may, with some qualification, agree with Gina Arnold's summation regarding South Korean Psy's "Gangnam Style" that, in an era dominated by such platforms, "Western and non-Western video standards are now blending into a mushy stew of standardized pop sounds that have nothing to do with their countries of origin" (2017, 246). I say "with some qualification" because, while techniques and formal elements may be quite generic, it is possible to conjecture a music video's origin through its content, like dance, costume, and the like. Viewers of Falz's video can guess the region his story emanates from through familiarity with the culture and social-political milieu of the place.

The preceding discussion enables us to think of screen worlds in the encompassing sense of the convergence of multiple worlds onscreen, multiple screens in the world, and multiple genres of screen. Through the process of connectivity mentioned earlier, different worlds, cultures, are captured with different kinds of cameras (phones, DSLRs, professional video cameras), in different genres (film, music videos, DIY online videos), and further dispersed through different kinds of screens (TV, phones, laptops, tablets) accessing content in largely concentrated platforms. The music video's form—as a mix of other media with its own recognizably unique aesthetic—primes it perfectly to interact with these conditions. It is simultaneously a process of convergence and dispersal. In such a milieu, certain sounds and acts become options within a mainstream and do not necessarily exist outside of it. To illustrate, when I told a senior scholar in the field about my research, he narrated how his children (American-born and raised in the United States) were quite surprised to learn that Wizkid is Nigerian. Also, the person who texted me from India about Falz's video is neither African nor of African descent. What this often entails for cultural productions is a generic designation that combines formal, racial, and regional markers to make them recognizable in Western media. Such nomenclature, like the recently popular "Afrobeats," creates visibility for cultural products outside their domains of emergence and offers them as alternatives to genres like pop, rock, and hip-hop that predominate in Europe and America (see Osiebe 2020).

"This Is Nigeria"

Falz's "This Is Nigeria" was released in May 2018 to popular acclaim. Despite its pointed criticism of Nigerian society, it seemed to find a comfortable place in the musician's iconography, which until then had been built largely on his capacity for comic impressions. My first encounters with Falz on social media were of his hilarious mimicry of mannerisms common to Yoruba speakers of English as (an improperly learned) second language. But Falz, trained as a lawyer and the son of Femi Falana, a renowned Nigerian lawyer and human rights activist, is no stranger to social critique. His previous works have taken on issues ranging from sexual harassment to fraud and the capitalist inclinations of Nigerian Christian clergy. Falz's propensity for outspoken criticism may be seen by some as an inevitable result of his background. In this sense, "This Is Nigeria" expresses his individual vision and message. The video wears a different face, depending on who is looking, enacting different versions of itself. To the international viewer, it is a Nigerian version of Childish Gambino's "This Is America," reprising the latter's recognizable themes of violence and the indifference of a population lulled into stupor by popular entertainment. The average Nigerian viewer, on the other hand, is likely to be aware of these themes but also keenly attuned to the layers of references in the video. They can place it within Falz's star image and a tradition of sociopolitical criticism they recognize as local. It is unsurprising that Falz is often compared to Fela Kuti and not to any other renowned activist figure outside the country, since, for most Nigerians, Fela is emblematic of the sort of music that is unapologetically political. The abundant allusions in the video have occasioned some blog attempts to make it legible to non-Nigerian viewers (see, for example, Akingbe and Onanuga 2020; Unah 2018). For the benefit of the reader who is unfamiliar with the text, I will proceed with a description, hopefully avoiding arduous repetition.

The video opens with Falz, holding a stereo on his left shoulder, listening to a broadcast. What we hear is the voice of his activist father, Femi Falana, condemning the endemic corruption in Nigeria. The stereo is old and of antiquated technology, the cassette. The camera slowly pulls out from Falz's back. He is wearing striped yellow and red pants. *Okadas* (commercial motorcycles) move back and forth in front of him while two men fight on the side. There is a man in Fulani garb, smiling and playing what looks like a guitar. He suddenly stops, walks ahead, picks up a machete, and motions to behead a man on his knees. The camera moves away, deeming the sight too gory for the viewer. The image is clearly that of normalized chaos and violence, a situation in which killing is as mundane as pleasantly enjoying a guitar tune. In the background,

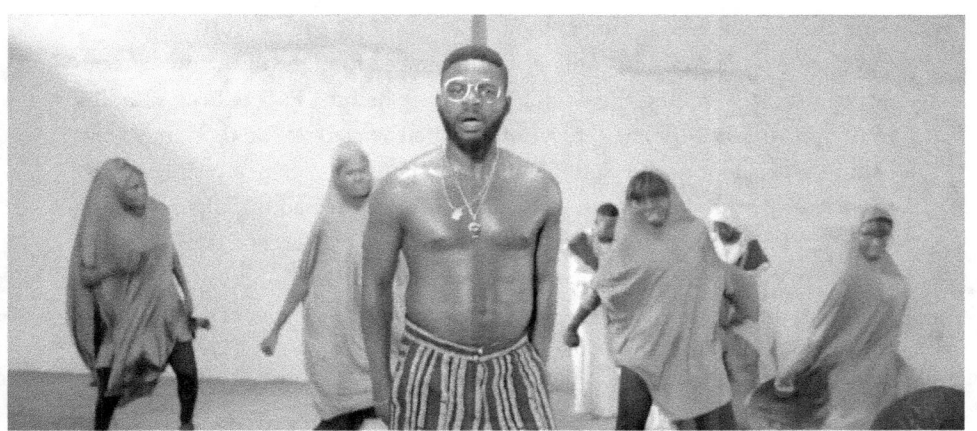

FIGURE 17.2. Falz dances and sings while dancers in hijab do the *shaku shaku* dance in the music video "This Is Nigeria." Screenshot

the movements have intensified. Another man is vandalizing something with a cutlass. Two *okadas* nearly collide; a *keke* (commercial auto rickshaw) goes past. The camera follows Falz as he approaches, now without the stereo, dancing and singing, "This is Nigeria. Look how I'm living now. Everybody be criminal." He unceremoniously steps over the dead body as a journalist takes photographs and another man tries to drag the body away.

The atmosphere of normalized violence is further intensified as four dancers in hijab appear behind Falz, doing the *shaku shaku* dance in synchrony (figure 17.2).[3] This is a clear reference to the Chibok girls abduction, which, as Falz indicates in an interview on *Hello Nigeria* (now on YouTube), could have been dealt with swiftly if the government had not chosen to skirt the issue. The camera moves left to take in a woman crouching and holding currency notes, as a snake comes toward her. From the lyrics, we learn this is "Madam Philomena" Chieshe of the Joint Admission Matriculation Board, who blamed missing 36 million naira from her office on a money-eating snake. Falz returns to the center of the frame, with the dancers standing arms akimbo. They dash away at the words "police station dey close by six, security reason o!" The camera focuses on two young men high on syrup, a reference to the growing concerns about substance abuse among Nigerian youth. A young man celebrates as he holds a check for ₦25,000,000 for winning Big Sister Nigeria. A flamboyantly dressed man, standing with a skimpily dressed woman, holds a container marked "ballot box," representing politicians who brazenly hijack electoral processes.

In one of the video's three observable cuts, Falz parts a curtain and the camera moves to where a woman is being prayed for. One of the men gropes her chest. He is pulling the demon out of her breasts, Falz tells us, alluding to the prevalence of sexual predation among the clergy. The dancers appear behind him again. As the camera pulls out, there are two men trying to start electric generators. Everyone scatters when men dressed in Fulani clothing show up. Like the earlier beheading, the scene is a reference to the violent clashes in Northern Nigeria between farmers and Fulani herdsmen. To the right, a young man sits with a woman on each side of him and a laptop in front of him. He lavishly throws money in the air. He is a *yahoo boy*, the face of the Nigerian stereotype abroad as a nation of scammers and fraudsters. The camera catches Falz exchanging pleasantries with a group of friends as the police arrive and begin to harass them. The lavishly dressed man from earlier shows up and offers the police a bribe to let off one of the young men—possibly a relative. The others are left at the mercy of the police. Falz sneaks away and ends the singing in medium shot. As the music stops abruptly, a man in uniform is reading a speech. Like a broken record, he is unable to get past the word *transmission*, giving the impression that he is probably not literate enough in English to read. The beat and music return, along with the nondiegetic layering of Femi Falana's voice condemning exploitation by pastors. The voice and beat fade, the camera moves out slowly, taking in the warehouse where the scenes have been acted out. Falz is standing on a car, making protest signs behind the actors. His hands are raised with clenched fists, Fela style. The last addition to the frame as the video fades is of a Nigerian flag with a gaping tear in the middle. The white in the Nigerian flag symbolizes peace. Torn, it becomes symbolic of a nonexistent or fragile peace.

Weeks after "This Is Nigeria" was released, it was banned by the Nigerian Broadcasting Corporation, which cited the "vulgarity" of the line "everybody be criminal" (Forrest 2018). The Muslim Rights Concern also threatened to sue the musician for depicting violence by Fulani men and featuring dancers wearing hijab while dancing *shaku shaku*, which it referred to as "drug related" (Unah 2018).[4] Of most significance, however, is the manner in which the video sparked a heated conversation over social media, with many lauding Falz's efforts. Despite the ban from Nigerian terrestrial airwaves, the song continued to pile up views on the internet, especially on YouTube, where it was freely available for viewing and download.

The viral status of "This Is Nigeria" was buoyed in part by the endorsement of the American rapper and music entrepreneur P. Diddy on social media and the fact that it resonated well with an international audience. It is in some ways reminiscent of the Azonto dance craze analyzed by Jesse Weaver Shipley (2013), which, begun in 2011 in Ghana, spread quickly throughout Africa and among Ghanaians in the diaspora, riding on the affordances of digital technology. The trend, Weaver argues, allowed Ghanaians abroad to connect with a sense of home and those back at home to perform a cosmopolitan subjectivity. Falz's "This Is Nigeria" does something slightly different by simultaneously courting Nigerian and non-Nigerian audiences. The conditions of existence of the music video I have mentioned—the common access points, generic aesthetics, its affiliation to music, and its detachment from the currents of direct profit—enabled it to participate in a global phenomenon initiated by Childish Gambino. It is therefore an illuminating case study of the transnationality of Nigerian music video. As an analogy, it shows how a particular template (the music video) can be written on in a way that not only stays in communication with a wider audience but also remains resolutely local. In other words, the music video faces outward and inward simultaneously, capable of traveling despite (and perhaps exactly because it is) staying at home. It is a form that enables cross-cultural consumption. "This Is Nigeria," understood as an illustration, takes a global conversation about social ills and translates it into relatable phenomena for the artiste's immediate audience.

A search on YouTube for Childish Gambino's video queues up Falz's and vice versa, connecting the viewer not just to the similarity of the videos but also to the resonances in the political issues they raise. As Fred Khumalo comments, watching both videos together, one is "taken into the heart of a conversation between the children of the Transatlantic slave trade and their cousins in Africa" (2018). Importantly, these sorts of transnational conversations cannot be stifled by the peculiar aversion of postcolonial African governments to criticism. While many music videos are indeed no more than a celebration of spectacle, when they do take on the hue of critique, they can evade the obstructions that assail music and films in the form of censorship and bans. In the current technological climate, banning a video on Nigerian airwaves is hardly a guarantee that it will be relegated to oblivion or forced to circulate through "unofficial channels." Rather, it might very well spur its popularity. The censorship regimes of the international music channels and online platforms that the videos go through greatly differ from those enforced by the national government. As such, videos that have been blacklisted on national airwaves may still be available on YouTube and other online platforms, and their notoriety within the national space could become the catalyst for appealing to a more transnational audience.

Conclusion

This chapter has been concerned with examining "This Is Nigeria" as a productive instance of the transnationality of Nigerian audiovisual productions. I argue that music videos, by their multimedia composition and movement against the current of direct profit, add to our understanding of Nigerian media beyond ideas of "pirate transnationalism," as Jedlowski calls it. Their transnationality is not simply affinitive either. The videos are consumed by people who are neither Africans nor of African descent. The popularity of Nigerian music in recent times, under the categorization of Afrobeats, draws in viewers who are first and foremost listeners. What this means for further research is more attention to the interconnections between screen media and contemporary music. As much as the movement of media corporations like Netflix into Nigeria exposes its productions to a wider audience, this might not yet be representative of the full range of the global influence of Nigerian media. The diverse—and more frequently portable—screens that enable contemporary engagement with visual media are also music devices. "In the new world of viral video," Gina Arnold says, "videos are of supreme importance for the circulation of music, replacing radio as a mainstream source of music discovery" (2017, 248). Watching becomes a way of listening. An evaluation of the transnational audience of Nigerian screen media also will need to reckon with those who *listen* to screen media or are directed to them through encounters facilitated by platforms that congregate videos of varying provenance.

NOTES

1 Though this online phenomenon has tended to be referred to as "parody," I consider such nomenclature highly inaccurate in capturing the kind of cultural work the video performs. Rather than a mere spoof or mimicry of Gambino's video, it is a formal appropriation and one that, for some, outdoes its original in the magnitude of social issues it takes on. I use "version" to include other iterations of the video and not to imply its accuracy.

2 Digital Satellite Television (DStv) is a direct broadcast satellite service owned by MultiChoice, a South African company. The company caters to subscribers in sub-Saharan Africa. Original Black Entertainment (OBE) was a British television station that operated between 2003 and 2011. Bright Entertainment Network (BEN TV) is also a British television station providing broadcast services to Africans living in Europe.

3 This is a Nigerian hip-hop dance that became popular in 2018.

4 The Fulani are predominantly Muslim.

18

Rolling to "A-Free-Ka"

*Seeing and Hearing the Transmedia Screen Worlds
of Kahlil Joseph's "Cheeba"*

JOE JACKSON

Since 2010, Kahlil Joseph, an accomplished artist across a broad range of visual
practices, has created a variety of short films, music videos, advertisements,
and installations. His projects draw from manifestations of African cultures—
developing ideas from Sierra Leonean literature, expanding interpretations
of the Yoruba deity Oshun, quoting the Senegalese film master Djibril Diop
Mambéty—while expressing the contemporary condition of the diaspora in
a variety of contexts. His collaborators include the musicians Beyoncé, Kendrick Lamar, FKA Twigs, Flying Lotus, and Sampha as well as the fashion
labels Vans and Kenzo and the telecommunications company O2, earning
widespread praise across a variety of international audiences and globalized
contexts. This chapter focuses on the screen text "Cheeba" (2010), one of Joseph's earliest works hitherto neglected by media scholarship. By examining

the transatlantic flows nuancing the aesthetics of "Cheeba" alongside the diasporic undercurrents that shape Los Angeles's overlapping film and music scenes, the chapter draws out the screen text's sophisticated relationships with the African continent, exploring how the project constructs in both audial and visual terms "A-Free-Ka," a fundamental concept underpinning the musical work of Joseph's collaborator Shafiq Husayn.

Negotiating the Smoke: Sights and Sounds of "A-Free-Ka" in "Cheeba"

"Cheeba," one of Joseph's earliest music videos, was described by a reviewer as feeling "like a short film, or a montage in a movie" for its abstract, cinematic style (Tewksbury 2010). The music video's song is the first single from multi-instrumentalist Shafiq Husayn's debut solo project En' A-Free-Ka (2009), featuring the soulful vocals of the singer-songwriter and producer Bilal. Husayn—one-third of Sa-Ra Creative Partners and a collaborator with the likes of Egyptian Lover, Afrika Bambaataa, and Erykah Badu—often works on psychedelic music projects shaped by belief in spirituality, diasporic relationships with continental Africa, and multilayered understandings of the self. In typical fashion he states that his album about "A-Free-Ka" is an attempt to articulate "freedom of the mind" in the form of a soundtrack, exploring the myriad ways in which "freedom is reflected in the music" (Husayn 2009). In the same way that "Cheeba" glides across genre boundaries by combining in polymorphous fashion Bilal's neo-soul singing with gentle funk sounds and soft echoes of bluesy horns, Joseph's smooth camera movements and fluid transitions link visual representations of an underground recording studio, unspecified spaces in France, and a roller-skating rink in Los Angeles.[1] The director's vision of "A-Free-Ka" is liberated from strict spatiotemporal boundaries and moves beyond the African continent, thus engendering gentle, contemplative sensations as means of conveying in audiovisual terms the fluidity and freeness (or "A-Free-Ness") of the song's heterogeneity as well as the screen text's negotiation of various media formats.

Joseph adopts subtle green filters and lighting during the screen text's roller-skating rink scenes, indirectly evoking hazy sensations connected to the psychoactive effects of *cheeba*, a transnational slang term for cannabis or marijuana, rooted in the Spanish word for "young goat" or "kid" (*Merriam-Webster Dictionary* 2019). Complex sensations of strangeness and dreaminess established by the green lens filter are thus accentuated by innocuous posers sedated in the smoking area and the romantic affection of sensual dancers grinding together rink-side. By capturing such feelings through visual depictions of the dancing roller skaters partaking in dynamic recreational activities, "Cheeba" combines Husayn's mesmerizing singing with hallucinatory moving images to communicate feelings of lightness and detachment experienced while under the influence of a cannabinoid "high." The complex feelings of surrealness and time-warping spirituality engendered by Joseph's visuals are rooted in the percolating sounds of Husayn's song, which, in turn, subtly echo the tradition of enhanced spirituality communicated by Rastafarian Nyabinghi rhythms.[2] Margins of time and space, past and present, become interwoven and entangled through the music video's homage to the liberating qualities of the borderless, cheeba-saturated visualizations of "A-Free-Ka," forming a polymorphic "transmedia screen world" that likewise fluctuates at genre boundaries and spatiotemporal borders.

Since the marijuana plant spread from the vast fields of its native homes in Central Asia as a paste-like form in Ethiopian pottery and the travel bags of wandering Sufis in Egypt, the hallucinogenic properties of tetrahydrocannabinol have been extracted through smoking pipes and consuming edible formats for ritualistic, recreational, and medicinal purposes in various parts of the world (Clarke and Merlin 2013; Rubin 1976). Certain depictions of cheeba in American popular music cultures deviate from the spiritualistic and contemplative values of introspection associated with early usages of the plant, extracting childish humor from the degradation of one's quality of life as a result of cannabis overconsumption in a fashion similar to Cheech Marin and Tommy Chong's feature-length film *Up in Smoke* (1978) and Afroman's music video "Because I Got High" (2000). In contrast, the lyrics in "Cheeba" explore the ways in which a mysterious, nameless female figure permits "ancient routes to glory" in the present moment, establishing timeless flows between the mystical entity's origins and her present manifestations by emphasizing how "she sets [him] free" through a state of profundity as natural and awe-inspiring as "the sun and sea." Husayn's abstract lyrics may therefore refer to a variety of things: the Muse, a figure we briefly see protecting her son in the music video's earlier scenes; cheeba, the plant with the power to grant the roller skaters new dimensions of introspection and understanding, moving across African, American, and European territories in the same way that the Spanish term's original slang meaning for "young goat" traversed and transformed over national territories; or, indeed, music *writ large*, the sounds and styles from different generations and genres that uplift the jazz community and inspire Husayn's *En' A-Free-Ka* album.

In this nostalgic homage to the multitudinous local, regional, and global factors that shape Husayn's creative output and Los Angeles's contemporary social configurations, Joseph imbues notions of globalization with solemn respect for past and future movements of Black families in the music video's establishing shots. Sampling En' A-Free-Ka's multistylistic track "Le'Star" (2009) in the screen text's introductory moments, nostalgic accordion sounds and extracts of a French lamentation are set to black-and-white footage of a woman with a packed suitcase conveying her struggles to a tiny child. The young boy—a physical manifestation of Husayn's spiritual lineage, emblematizing members of the African diaspora from previous generations—stares innocently into his worried mother's eyes as she sighs: "La famille ava pas, / Je n'ai pas d'argent." By infusing the language of colonizers into both En' A-Free-Ka's title and the parent's complaint, the backdrop of the locked door that frames the mother and child as she sorrowfully acknowledges absent family members symbolizes the restrictions, or closed opportunities, endured by the African diasporas during and after the height of imperialism, wherein family units are broken, loved ones separated from relatives, and close groups forced by circumstance to disperse and relocate to new, oftentimes alien, areas. However, after recognizing the severity of her plight, the mother continues to speak: "Mon pseudo-copain n'est pas la, / Alors je t'attends, / Viens me chercher." Embracing the possibility that a change in her fortunes is forthcoming as she softly utters this optimistic invitation, an airplane's underbelly soars overhead, gently shifting the diegetic, transmedia screen world of "Cheeba" away from the undisclosed Francophone setting by landing, instead, in contemporary Los Angeles.

Although the French word en hearkens back to the colonial language of past oppressors, in ancient Egyptian the word ka means "the ethereal shape of the man [representing] the personality as a kind of astral body . . . the idealised self" (Carus 1905, 420), thereby imbuing the linguistic construction of Husayn's album title En' A-Free-Ka with emphasis on the liberation of one's spirituality through discursive constructions of "Africa" and "A-Free-Ka" without denying the existence of imperialism's prevailing legacies. While the introductory scenes establish connections between "A-Free-Ka," Europe, and the United States in order to emphasize the forces of displacement that characterize the grand trajectories of the African diasporas' historical movements, the final words of hope at the understated climax of the mother's lament communicate her dignity and composure in the face of enforced familial dissolution, an unswayable desire to control her destiny in spite of the nefarious colonial frameworks conspiring to displace and disempower by closing significant doors on her innocent son's future.

Mimicking the fluidity with which Husayn's heterogeneous collage of sounds and musical styles fluctuates and flows, the depiction of Afrodiasporic characters moving effortlessly between continents and epochs in "Cheeba" emphasizes the mother's focus on the liberating aspects of her situation rather than the limitations imposed by the effects of colonialism's brutal structures. The components of "Cheeba" thus communicate the album's core concepts—the myriad formulations of freedom and liberation that may empower the geographic and indeed spiritual movements of the African diasporas—by articulating in audiovisual terms the smoothness with which Husayn's production skills effortlessly blend gentle, trembling brass instruments, serene keys and synthesizers, and hypnotic percussion sounds with Bilal's soulful vocals. Although Bilal's "neo-soul" comparisons place him in the company of the esteemed artists Erykah Badu and D'Angelo, his impassioned croons also echo James Brown's gospel-inspired soul music and the pining blues sound of Louis Armstrong, thereby propelling Husayn and Bilal's musical experimentations into exciting new territories through the music video's sonic labyrinths of contesting and competing styles and sounds. Indeed, Bilal's tender, trembling voice harmonizes with the song's smooth, soulful combinations of horns, electronic keys, and metronomic percussion in order to exemplify the "unabashedly sentimental" feelings of heartfelt emotion that came to define the very "soul" of soul music (Landau 1976, 210). The music video thus captures in visual terms the rupturing of one's sense of time and space while under soul music's mesmerizing spell, forming a montage of disparate locations and time frames to create the impression of a spaceless, timeless soul singer lost in the heat of the moment and the passion of the performance.

Diasporic Flows of LA's Jazz-Rap Fusion

Today, Los Angeles is experiencing a revival period for its jazz heritage through a fashioning of new music that draws from the city's widespread popularity of gangsta rap. Jazz music evolved in New Orleans from a three-stroke pattern known in Afro-Caribbean and Latino cultures as a tresillo (Peñalosa and Greenwood 2010; Sublette 2008); hip-hop emerged in New York through the popularity of Jamaican outdoor sound-system cultures (Brunson 2011); and both jazz *and* hip-hop were nuanced by the call-and-response patterns of slave songs from the plantations (DeVeaux 1991; Hamlet 2011). Joseph—through collaborations with a range of contemporary Los Angeleno jazz/hip-hop musicians, including Flying Lotus, Kendrick Lamar, Thundercat, and, the subject of this chapter, Shafiq Husayn—has thus produced interdisciplinary audiovisual projects that mirror the intergenerational and transatlantic energies of Los Angeles's contemporary jazz/hip-hop fusion scene. While the contemporary jazz scene's divergent roots extend back to the prime years of Central Avenue when "all races and classes gathered in the clubs" there to listen to jazz and rhythm and blues (Isoardi 1998), the new fusion of musical legacies merges the city's heritage of inclusive, desegregated jazz with the militant, anti-institutional energy of West Coast rap, cultivating the countercultural properties of Black Atlantic music's roots by exploring the overlapping lineages between old and new jazz musicians *as well as* old and new hip-hop pioneers. The saxophonist Kamasi Washington, a key figure at the heart of Los Angeles's new fusion movement, observes: "We've now got a whole generation of jazz musicians who have been brought up with hip-hop. We've grown up alongside rappers and DJs, we've heard this music all our life. We are as fluent in J Dilla and Dr Dre as we are in Mingus and Coltrane" (cited by J. Lewis 2016). The countercultural elements of Los Angeles's gangsta rap movement are thus channeled into the jazz/hip hop sounds of the new scene, forming a series of sonic markers whose liminal statuses and polygenericism echo the double consciousness of African diasporas.

Joseph's music video for "Cheeba" features black-and-white vignettes of joyous dance moves in a recording studio at an improvised jamming session. The dancers wear "retro" suits and dresses reminiscent of socializers from a paradigmatic Central Avenue jazz club in downtown Los Angeles, thereby intensifying the retrospective, soul-meets-blues qualities of the music video's heterogeneous sound by communicating the musical diversity associated with the region's jazz music peak, when the area was a hedonistic space flouting both physical and sonic forms of segregation and separation. Oftentimes coupled with a gritty lens effect to create the impression of low-quality film stock's material decomposition, the worn, grainy texture of the recording studio's black-and-white footage compounds the retrospective, nostalgic styles of the enthralled participants' classic formal attire, transforming "Cheeba" into a pastiche of glamorous lounges, fizzing cocktails, and polished shoes plucked from the backdrop of a dizzying Langston Hughes or F. Scott Fitzgerald novel. The raucous energy of Central Avenue's community and its "nonstop, vibrant club scene" are thus channeled into the video's smoky underground studio as sweat drips from entranced band members' heads, wine and whiskey glasses clinking as dancers cool themselves with ornate fans (Isoardi 1998).

At the same time, the area's decline and eventual destruction in the Watts riot fires in 1965 are captured by the tone of reminiscence pervading the hazy black-and-white footage, communicating the complex, overlapping sensations of happiness *and* regret engendered by the recollection of Los Angeles's former vibrancy as a haven of Black jazz music. Joseph's music video here merges a series of America's most popular recreational activities into an unlikely dialogue, juxtaposing recording studio scenes against footage of the modern multipurpose entertainment complex equipped with roller-skating rink and bowling alley, thereby channeling the liberty and swagger of the Roaring Twenties' social libertarianism and economic prosperity within a popular yet unglamorous venue from a section of present-day Los Angeles struggling to resist waves of inflated building prices.

At their peaks the Bloods claimed Compton's Skateland USA, and the Crips were associated with World on Wheels; thus, the setting of "Cheeba" possesses an undercurrent of territorial gang affiliations. Although "Cheeba" hints at the city's rap roots through the presence of a grainy low-fidelity hip-hop beat, Joseph's audiovisual depictions of suited, stylish dancers in an underground recording studio emphasize the history of Los Angeleno jazz music over the city's "gangsta rap" heritage. However, in the aftermath of the 1965 riots, the jazz clubs were disfigured or destroyed, leaving "decaying buildings and rubble-filled lots, some surrounded with chain-link fencing, [which] seemed to contain few secrets . . . a terribly aged outpost" (Isoardi 1998).

The gradual downturn of World on Wheels in its later years is implied by Joseph's framing of the recreational facility in relation to the ghostly memory of Central Avenue's once-thriving jazz scene, suggesting in a forlorn manner that a similarly problematic fate reminiscent of the jazz clubs' progressive transformation—and eventual decline—could likewise deprive the city of its iconic multipurpose rink. Indeed, the music video's merging of the city's forgotten jazz club legacies with its declining entertainment facilities proved an astute observation. Despite offering fifty-two years of service to the local community and even surviving the civil unrest of the 1992 Los Angeles riots "that left its neighbours burned out hulks," World on Wheels, the setting for "Cheeba," closed in 2013 after its owner, AMF Bowling Worldwide, filed for bankruptcy for the second time, citing "a cash crunch" as well as "[failure] to find a buyer for the business" (Griffin 2013).

Los Angeleno Rebels: Transcontinental Undercurrents of LA Filmmaking

The transatlantic flows of musical influences in "Cheeba" are mimicked by the film–music video hybridization's visual components. The main setting, Los Angeles, is of course the home of Hollywood, the central region of the city that became shorthand for the American film industry due to its national and, eventually, worldwide recognizability. However, a group of African American and African students who studied at UCLA's film school program between the late 1960s and early 1990s felt troubled by the unrealistic and problematic representations of Black peoples' lives that were circulated by Hollywood's prevalent filmmaking cultures. Inspired by the rebellious, countercultural spirit of Los Angeleno civil protesting (the Watts Riots in 1965 and the Rodney King riots of 1992) that brought attention to law enforcement's violence toward African American citizens and the inhospitable living conditions for the city's Black communities, the UCLA graduates started to produce and direct a series of works that retaliated "against the form and content of the [Hollywood] tradition they were being taught" (Snead 1994, 117).

Although these artists were independent in the sense that they made their films based on individualized perspectives and singular artistic visions, their contributions to what contemporaneous LA Rebellion filmmaker Ben Caldwell describes as "emancipating the image" and decolonizing their filmic content demonstrate a shared preoccupation with representing and treating Black people and their communities' lives and concerns with levels of dignity, respect, and care that were otherwise absent in the works of their cinematic counterparts from Hollywood (cited in Field, Horak, and Stewart 2015, 1). As such, the group of LA-based filmmakers formed a type of pan-African solidarity that took inspiration from the anticolonial Third Cinema movement, originating in Latin America before moving into Africa through such filmmakers as Sarah Maldoror and Joaquim Lopes Barbosa as Angola, Mozambique, and many other nations struggled for liberation against imperial forces throughout the 1960s and 1970s, thereby capturing the transatlantic flows on which Black Atlantic (counter)cultural expression is grounded (Buchsbaum 2015).

This particular moment in Black independent filmmaking history has been retrospectively named the LA Rebellion for the ways in which filmmakers rejected conventionalized Hollywood filming and editing techniques in favor of a style of cinema that "set about *recoding* black skin on screen" (Snead 1994, 115; emphasis in original) through what was perceived as "the revolutionary act of humanizing Black people on screen" (Field, Horak, and Stewart 2015, 1). Charles Burnett, for example, independently directed, edited, and shot a feature-length drama called *Killer of Sheep* (1978). In drawing from the tradition of Senegalese cinema by reimagining the mask from Ousmane Sembène's *La noire de . . .* (1966) and referencing the moments of animal slaughter from Djibril Diop Mambéty's *Touki Bouki* (1973), *Killer of Sheep* emphasized the transatlantic connections underpinning LA Rebellion filmmaking. Although in 1977 Burnett submitted an earlier version of the film to UCLA as part of the thesis project for his master of fine arts degree, Paul Dallas argues that the official release of *Killer of Sheep* to the public "heralded the emergence of a new Black independent cinema in America" through its merging of music and moving images to create a neorealist portrayal of life for the family of an African American slaughterhouse worker (2017, 139).

In 2010, Joseph reenacted a scene from *Killer of Sheep* in his short film *Belhaven Meridian*. During the original scene, a determined, resilient wife confronts two gangsters who are attempting to recruit her husband for a violent task before remonstrating her partner on their porch for being tempted to use his "fists" rather than his "brains" to solve their financial issues. Alessandra Raengo and Lauren Cramer of Georgia State University's *liquid blackness* research group thus acknowledge that the spirits of experimentation *and* political awareness foregrounded by the filmmakers of the LA Rebellion shape and nuance Joseph's contemporary work, thereby bringing "film studies and film education, artistic space and praxis, popular culture, and the experimental and avant-garde into a fluid exchange" (2020, 139). While Joseph's direct reference to the doorstep scene from *Killer of Sheep* attempts to generate a filmic lineage between Burnett and his own work in 2010, a range of personal and professional relationships further emphasize the crossroads and crosscurrents across cultures and generations that link Joseph's contemporary projects to the LA Rebellion filmmaking movement. Haile Gerima, an Ethiopian filmmaker who earned a bachelor of arts degree and a master of fine arts degree from UCLA during the LA Rebellion period, trained Joseph's close friend and filmmaking collaborator Arthur Jafa (as well as their mutual friend, collaborator, and cinematographer Malik Sayeed).

By introducing the works of UCLA Rebellion filmmakers Burnett and Julie Dash to his then-student Jafa—who, in turn, proceeded to mentor and collaborate with Joseph, as well as the Ghanaian-British filmmaker Jenn Nkiru—Gerima's tutelage exemplifies the intergenerational relationships that connect Joseph's new media works with many of the key independent filmmakers associated with the LA Rebellion. In turn, an explicitly Afrodiasporic approach to forming diegetic transmedia screen worlds through the sophisticated amalgamation of sonic and visual frequencies gained a cohesive yet incomplete structure in the early 1990s through the theorizations of Joseph's close friend and collaborator Jafa.[3]

BVI Aesthetics and Beyond: Toward New Intercultural and Transmedia Vernaculars

Manthia Diawara argues that the LA Rebellion filmmakers "were using films in a very powerful manner . . . they had a Black aesthetic that one could compare to Black music—you know, the Blues, the vernacular" (cited in Diawara 2006, 10).

Indeed, Jafa poses the ambition to create a new style of cinema wherein "Black images vibrate in accordance with certain frequential values that exist in Black music" (1992, 254). He argues that classical Western music traditions emphasize the precision and clarity of specific tonalities dictated by a single commanding rhythm, whereas traditional African music heritages include a broader range of tonal formations coordinated by "polyrhythms" which sometimes possess as many as four rhythms at once. The uneven call-and-response bends and stretches of later Afrodiasporic musical forms—trembling blues bars, wobbling jazz notes—are indebted to the free-form, improvisational structures and energizing, communalizing functions central to continental African music and its associated rituals. The theorization of Black Visual Intonations, or a BVI mode of expression, thus attempts to bridge the gap between the sonic and the visual, between Black music and Black moving images, in a way that mimics "the tendency in Black music to 'worry the note'—to treat notes as indeterminate, inherently unstable sonic frequencies rather than the standard Western treatment of notes as fixed phenomena" (254). Jafa therefore strives to translate Afrocentric musical features in audiovisual terms, seeking aesthetic breakthroughs attached to the musical heritage of Afrodiasporic communities.

Jafa's manifesto is largely predicated on using the irregular speeds of a "nonmetronomic camera rate" to replicate musical rhythms (255). Jafa originally claims to have designed 372 "alignment patterns" or "fixed frame replication patterns" that might be used to create the visual equivalences of "samba beats, reggae beats, all kinds of things" (254), relying heavily on visual aspects of sound-image amalgamations at the expense of the sonic. While focusing on the possibilities of experimental editing structures, by his own admission Jafa's original hypotheses do not establish for certain whether visions for BVI aesthetics may successfully transition from "theoretical possibilities" into recognizable audiovisual features that manifest in artistic form (253). Jafa has not directly updated his original manifesto in twenty-seven years; thus, the practical guidelines behind his original theorizations are out of sync with his and Joseph's contemporary realizations of the BVI audiovisual aesthetic. However, "certain possibilities in Black cinema" (254) are starting to materialize through the ways in which Jafa's and Joseph's works form transmedia screen worlds by hybridizing film and music video formats.

Although irregular and improvisational editing techniques play important roles in Joseph's and Jafa's recent artworks, their manifestations of the BVI aesthetic do not rely exclusively on the visual aspects of the filmmaking process. Throughout their respective artworks, moving images shift and react to certain musical moments of the accompanying soundtracks. The tempo and harmonic reverberations of a song's sonic frequencies drive the music *and* the filmic content of Joseph's and Jafa's audiovisual creations, uniting sounds and moving images in affective proximity as a complex yet cohesive whole.[4] For example, in Jafa's Underground Museum installation *Love Is the Message, The Message Is Death* (2016), a barrage of moving images set to Kanye West's gospel-themed track "Ultralight Beam" (2016) jump between fleeting glimpses of Afrodiasporic cultures. The rise-and-fall or call and response pattern of the song is mimicked when sounds and conversations that correspond to the video montage's footage resonate at moments of solemn reflection and peaceful quietness within "Ultralight Beam," thereby avoiding clashes with West's singing and the heavenly cries of the celestial choir. Audial *and* visual elements of the installation herein combine to capture moments of the sincere and sophisticated mood emanating from West's track. Simultaneously, these combinations unlock new dimensions for the song, demonstrating the power of audiovisual hybridity when music is positioned in relation to a series of evocative moving images. Rather than wholly capturing the aesthetics of "Cheeba" in a fixed, concrete fashion, BVI theorizations instead offer promising starting points from which to explore and experiment with transcontinental combinations of music and moving images from "A-Free-Ka," transcultural Los Angeles, and beyond.

Conclusion(s): "A-Free-Ka" and the Audiovisual

By discussing an underexamined screen text created at the beginning of the artist's career, this chapter argues that Joseph's "Cheeba" challenges simplistic definitions of media forms by oscillating at films' and music videos' distinguishable media or "screen world" borders. In turn, these interdisciplinary, transcontinental aesthetics create transmedia screen worlds, articulating cultural convergence as elements of the Global North and Global South overlap and interact. "A-Free-Ka," the key concept behind Shafiq Husyan's debut studio album *En' A-Free-Ka*, is marketed indirectly through the amalgamation of neo-soul crooning, repetitive Rastafarian Nyabinghi drumbeats, and hallucinogenic movements between provincial France and the busy heart of Los Angeles in the music video. Black visual intonations, meanwhile, fluctuate across the boundaries of film and music video, oscillating between African cultural contexts and contemporary American locations. The complexities of overlapping sonic and visual jazz, soul, and Rastafarian influences in "Cheeba" echo how significations associated with notions of "Africa" and

"African diaspora" may freely transform from subject to subject, person to person, generating intricate networks of meaning and (mis)understanding. The emphasis on plurality within the intersecting crossroads of cultural markers in "Cheeba" challenges any interpretations that are totalizing or singular, counteracting the threat of racial essentialism's (pseudo)scientific grounds by reenergizing the semantic freedom of the terms *A-Free-Ka* and *A-Free-Kan diaspora* as their meanings continuously shift and constantly fluctuate in different settings and situations.

Joseph's transmedia aesthetics—oscillating somewhere between audiovisual representations of "A-Free-Ka" and Jafa's Black Visual Intonations—operate in tandem with Husayn's music-writing abilities and Bilal's captivating vocal deliveries, generating polymorphous diegetic transmedia screen worlds wherein conventional boundaries of time and space are ruptured and, instead, new possibilities and configurations are formed through music, sound, and moving images. A collaborative working environment or synergetic transmedia screen world likewise emerges in the nondiegetic or "real" space beyond the fictional realms of "Cheeba." According to Jafa, Black Visual Intonations—the combined phonic and visual materialization of Afrodiasporic music, the audiovisual encapsulation of "Black voices" in both musical *and* discursive senses—are exemplified by oscillating, oftentimes uneven combinations of sound, music, and moving images. Mimicking paradoxical sensations of the simultaneous liminality and fixity of Afrodiasporic positionalities within our contemporary networked environment, Joseph's "Cheeba" epitomizes a pioneering contemporary form of audiovisual artistry that draws from the polyrhythmic and multitonal roots of continental African music to "audio-visualize" and thereby communicate sophisticated sensations and feelings associated with the African diaspora's experiential dynamics and the navigation of concurrent cross-cultural affiliations.

Since the original notions of Black visual intonations were theorized by his friend and collaborator Arthur Jafa, it seems fitting that Joseph's multifaceted diegetic *and* nondiegetic transmedia screen worlds are based on precepts of collaboration. Although Joseph is assigned as the director for "Cheeba," the project frequently channels and foregrounds the talents and artistic personas of his colleagues Shafiq Husayn and Bilal Oliver, exemplifying how future waves of artists may work together effectively when shifting across visual *and* audial modes of communication. The collaborative constructions of interdisciplinary, transcontinental screen worlds in "Cheeba" thus offer fruitful avenues for new generations of filmmakers, musicians, and beyond. By subverting rigid compartmentalizations for audiovisual expression while, at the same time, challenging strict, reductive systemizations of humanity's cultural flows, such artistic developments enhance our understandings of the cultural pluralism underpinning Afrodiasporic screen cultures across the globe. Contemporary formations of "A-Free-Ka" and its transmedia screen worlds therefore present fresh opportunities to broaden our outlooks, helping us decolonize the mind as we see *and* hear the ways Africa's diaspora shapes and nuances contexts and settings beyond the African continent.

NOTES

A portion of this chapter initially appeared in *Kahlil Joseph and the Audiovisual Atlantic: Music, Modernity, Transmedia art* (New York: Bloomsbury Academic, 2024), part of the New Approaches to Sound, Music, and Media book series edited by Holly Rogers, Lisa Perrott, and Carol Vernallis. Republication here is courtesy of Bloomsbury Academic US, an imprint of Bloomsbury Publishing Inc.

1 Bilal's captivating vocal delivery has resulted in certain commentators categorizing his style within the framework of "neo-soul," which, broadly defined, marks the amalgamation of R&B and hip-hop with aesthetic attributes extracted from soul music of the seventies (Huff 2012; Okoth-Obbo 2017). However, the singer has repeatedly refuted rigid systemization of his singing technique, arguing that his classically trained falsetto merges and blurs genre boundaries, thereby extending beyond any fixed definitions.

2 The term *Nyabinghi* was originally adopted by a secretive anticolonial society in East Africa, rumored to have been led by the Ethiopian monarch Haile Selassie I (Edmonds 2003; Tafari 1980). Although the time and location of the first Nyabinghi Assembly organized by Rastafarians remain contested, it is vital to note that these congregation sessions celebrate important dates in the Rastafari calendar explicitly tied to the religion's African origins, such as the birth of Haile Selassie I or the anniversary of his first visit to Jamaica to commemorate African Liberation Day. A group of oftentimes unappointed or unelected organizers from the Rastafarian faith known as an Assembly of Elders dictate proceedings at Nyabinghi congregations, wherein cyclic, hypnotic drumbeat rhythms build walls of sound in tandem with traditional chants, heightening the spirituality of those in attendance (Barnett 2005; Kiyaga-Mulindwa 2005). Smoking cheeba may form a key aspect of the religious ceremonies as elders encourage the discovery of one's "inner consciousness" through an altered state of perception (Edmonds 2012, 49). Thus the Rastafarian roots of Nyabinghi Afro-rhythms in "Cheeba" are visually represented through the green lens's subtle allusions to the cannabinoid "high" warping and reshaping the experiences of the roller skaters in present-day Los Angeles.

3 Arthur Jafa's work *Love Is the Message, The Message Is Death* (2016) has been screened at Joseph's family business, the Underground Museum; and Joseph co-produced and partly shot Jafa's experimental "docu-poem" *Dreams Are Colder Than Death* (2014).

4 In numerous interviews, Jafa cites the influence of John Akomfrah's notion of "affective proximity." Echoing Sergei Eisenstein's montage theory, Jafa describes "affective proximity" as the process "when two things come together . . . [an image] demanding to be emancipated from the context in which it found itself and placed next to where it was supposed to go" in order to generate a new effect (Jafa 2016). Akomfrah in turn states: "To begin to force many ways of being and living, I must work with the premises of the cinematic. . . . Organizing new spectacularity, new configurations, or what constitutes moving images—multiplicity, overlap, affective proximity, and subjectivity are very important" (Akomfrah and Canela 2018).

Afterword 1

The Political Worlds of African Screen Media

ALESSANDRO JEDLOWSKI

It is a difficult task to react to a collection of essays of the size, depth, and quality of *Contemporary African Screen Worlds*. This volume presents a wide range of innovative studies in the field of African screen media, which, in my view, is set to importantly influence the scholarly debate in this field for the coming years. Particularly fertile is the editors' decision to open up the debate about African cinema to a few original theoretical and methodological orientations, which make it possible to take into account the important transformations happening on the ground, moving away from conventional definitions of cinematic practices and aesthetics in order to produce more dynamic and original analysis of the constantly evolving African screen worlds. In this sense, the volume's focus on small and supersmall screens; on the impact of technological innovation on processes of media production and distribution; on the growing role of female entrepreneurs and artists; on the analysis of the material dimensions of processes of media production, circulation, and consumption; and on decolonial theory and its potential for renewing our understanding of how screen media are imagined, produced, and consumed by Africans will certainly contribute by encouraging new research projects and debates in the future. Taking these fascinating materials as a starting point, in the following pages, I will formulate a few reflections that are aimed at pointing out further directions for future research.

The analysis of the economic and political transformations introduced by technological innovation and processes of economic transnationalization are at the heart of numerous contributions presented in this volume. A nuanced picture emerges here, which highlights both the processes by which international corporations such as Naspers and Netflix carelessly extract profits from African screen media industries and the ways in which local entrepreneurs and artists manage to profit from these companies' presence to introduce important innovations, increase their economic capital, and develop international careers. Less visible is the position of the state in relation to these transformations. Are, for instance, local authorities profiting from technological innovation to further control the contents that are produced and the uses that the audiences make of them? Are they finding ways to better monitor and extract the (potential) fiscal revenues that the exponential increase in media production, circulation, and consumption across the continent has produced? Or, rather, are the audiences and producers benefiting from the massive involvement of international companies to circumvent the censorship and control strategies that many African governments try to enforce on their citizens? If the neoliberal reforms of the 1980s and 1990s made us believe that the age of nation-states' centralized authority had come to an end, the new millennium has brought the state regulatory and repressive apparatus back into the picture, in Africa as elsewhere in the world. I think that, despite the tendency to associate technological innovation with global connectivity and borderless flows of information and contents, we should pay more attention to how African states (or, better, those of the ruling regimes) are able to orient and shape the outcomes of technological innovation so as to protect and achieve their interests.

A few contributions in the volume seem to confirm the optimistic belief in the liberating and democratizing possibilities connected to the introduction of new media technologies in Africa. However, if the technological penetration of new media technologies might have opened new possibilities, the commercial strategies adopted by media platforms have also importantly participated in shaping them in specific ways, which have important political impacts in terms of the processes of formation and transformation of African public spheres. Platforms such as iROKOtv and Netflix, but also StarTimes and DStv, for instance, make explicit attempts at differentiating and fragmenting their publics according to their purchasing power (on the basis of packages that include channels and content of varying degrees of quality depending on the price). In this context, the universalization of the access to processes of media production and distribution allowed by technological innovation (linked, among other things, to the massive dissemination of low-cost Chinese-made technological devices, capable of democratizing access to these goods everywhere in Africa) is played out in parallel with ongoing transformations in the way capitalism operates, which are oriented toward locking consumers into "silos" that connect users of the same technology or the same platform to each other while isolating them from other consumers who have chosen other options (see Srnicek 2017). These processes, their political impact, and their cultural consequences need, in my view, to be further explored so as to develop a more complex and nuanced appraisal of the impact of this new screen media era on African audiences and media professionals, as well as on the processes of (un)making African public spheres.

In-depth analysis of local understandings and uses of technological innovation, including the study of the African concepts and terminologies that are adopted on the ground by audiences and media practitioners to describe specific technologies and products, is pivotal for opening up our epistemological approaches and making us grasp the African agency involved in shaping these processes. Temitayo Olofinlua's analysis of the Yoruba terminology for different media technologies is in this sense an instructive example of the potential that a "decolonial" approach to the study of African screen media carries for the future of media theory at large. But Olofinlua's research also hints at an interesting paradox. Her chapter focuses on the analysis of MTV Shuga Naija, a television series carrying sex education messages, that targets youth audiences and makes use of sophisticated strategies of social media and audience engagement to build an online community around the show. The program is designed and produced by an international, mainly Western, production team. At first sight, its developmental, message-oriented structure recalls the style of "communication for development" NGO programs and, further back in the past, colonial documentaries aimed at "educating" the colonial subjects on pressing health issues and modern sexual behaviors. Within this context, Olofinlua's decision to focus on this show without necessarily problematizing its genre's genealogy is particularly interesting to me. In my view, her decision to do so in a chapter that underlines the importance of studying African epistemologies to better understand African screen worlds and put at center stage the agency of African audiences in shaping not only media reception but also processes of media production and circulation obliges us to complicate our understanding of what a decolonial approach might be.

Olofinlua implicitly suggests that in order to decolonize African screen media theory we have to conduct two, partially contradictory but fundamentally intertwined intellectual efforts. On the one hand, we have to thoroughly research African epistemologies, concepts, and terminologies to penetrate the complexity of how Africans make sense of screen media today. On the other hand, we have to do this while moving away from (or, at least, beyond) the issue of "authenticity," so as to be able to include in our analysis cultural forms and genres that might have a complex genealogy connecting them to the colonial experience, as well as media programs that, while imagined and produced by Western media companies, are relevant for large numbers of African spectators. This reminds me of the way in which Kwame Anthony Appiah discusses the aesthetic ambiguities of the Yoruba statuette titled *Man with a Bicycle*: "What we should learn from it is the imagination that produced it. *Man with a Bicycle* is produced by someone who does not care that the bicycle is the white man's invention: it is not there to be Other to the Yoruba Self; it is there because someone cared for its solidity; it is there because it will take us further than our feet will take us; it is there because machines are now as African as novelists . . . and as fabricated as the kingdom of Nakem" (1991, 357). What this tells us, in my view, is that the right balance between researching African epistemologies to renew our approach to the study of African screen worlds, and avoiding the creation of problematic essentializations based on distorted understandings of cultural authenticity, is hard to find, and much work needs to be done in this direction to make such complexity more visible and productive.

The concept of "screen worlds" that the editors place at the center of this collection is, in this sense, a very important suggestion. This concept clearly sets two important and ambitious objectives for the collection (and for the research project that is behind it): on the one hand, to subvert the implicit assumptions contained in the concept of "world cinema," in which the use of the singular (*world* rather than *worlds*) has positioned African and other "non-Western" filmmaking traditions at the margins of a mainly Euro-American and Anglophone canon; on the other hand, to open up our research agenda to the study of the multiple transmedia forms that inhabit the everyday practices of screen media producers and consumers across Africa. If the variety and relevance of the case studies from different regions of the continent included in this volume perfectly show the complexity and diversity of screen cultures that exist across Africa and their global relevance, the predominance of essays focusing on cinematic forms shows that the volume still mirrors some of the ambiguities of the field of studies to which it belongs—a field in which the existing tension between the study of "cinematic worlds" and "screen worlds" is not entirely explored, and research on the latter often ends up being swallowed up by studies about the former. As a result, in the landscape of the existing scholarship, studies about cinematic and televisual forms (such as FESPACO-like author cinema and Nollywood-like film and TV series) are still very much at the center of the picture, while other audiovisual forms that participate in the broad ecology of screen media across the continent remain almost invisible. Obviously, this volume could not balance this disparity by itself. But what it does is already very relevant: it clearly points to the directions we need to follow in order to renew our field of study so as to make it closer to the experiences of screen media producers and consumers on the ground while simultaneously making it more apt to the elaboration of global media and film theory.

Afterword 2

Africa's Contemporary Screen Media Era and Questions of Autonomy

MORADEWUN ADEJUNMOBI

In the contemporary screen media era in Africa, as advanced in this volume, Africans interact with screen media cultures that are dynamic, fragmented, multiply connected, decentered, and more accessible than the screen media cultures of previous eras. All of these attributes have implications for how audiovisual stories are told and accessed using different media.

Continuing with a trend already evident in the preceding chapters, I will illustrate these assertions by referring mainly to developments emanating from Nigeria, though the directions I highlight are evident in many other countries on the continent. To start with, the screen media landscape in this age is dynamic in the sense that both producers of screen media content and viewers are adapting relatively quickly to the emergence of new screen media options. These include social media apps that function as important adjuncts for interacting with viewers and attracting new viewers to individual performers or audiovisual narratives. Secondly, and to the extent that individual viewers and groups of viewers are seldom engaging with the same content as everyone else in their communities, the screen media cultures of this age can be described as fragmented. Even in instances where one family's primary access to audiovisual storytelling is through a television set, it is not unlikely that their neighbors will be watching narratives in a different language or have subscriptions to a different pay TV service. Both small-scale producers of narratives and bigger media corporations have a commercial incentive to cater to as many differentiated tastes and preferences as possible.

Furthermore, the array of media narrative formats is more complex than at the beginning of the twenty-first century. In addition to well-known narrative types like feature films and documentaries, as well as televisual serials and series of varying durations, there has also been an explosion of audiovisual narrative forms like comedic skits and adaptations of entire foreign films or of clips from foreign films. To get a sense of the significance of these other narrative categories in contemporary African screen media culture, consider, for example, that at the time of writing, skits from the popular *Mark Angel Comedy* series on YouTube, ranging from three to ten minutes in duration on average, regularly attracted more than a million viewers per episode. With at least one new episode released every week, *Mark Angel Comedy* was reaching between two and four million views every month. At the time of writing, the *Mark Angel Comedy* channel on YouTube had over seven million subscribers. With a limited though growing number of cinema screens, even the highest-grossing Nigerian films are unlikely to reach as many people during an initial theatrical run as these skits do on YouTube.

Long-form and short-form fictional storytelling are only two of many audiovisual forms present in contemporary African screen media cultures. Additional audiovisual forms obviously include music videos but also other kinds of user-generated content, such as solo dance performances, travel and lifestyle videos, cooking demonstrations for meals from different African cultures, and idiosyncratic performances like the Senegalese duo Xuman and Keyti's *Journal rappé* (the news in rap), among many others. What we have, in effect, is a crowded screen media culture with no dominant form. In this setting, very few media professionals can afford to work exclusively with only one medium, which explains why pursuing multiple connections between different media is a characteristic of the contemporary screen media era in Africa. Indeed, the multiplatform strategy that Dennis-Brook Prince Lotsu describes for the Ghanaian filmmaker Peter Sedufia, circulating skits on WhatsApp but also making feature films for screening in local theaters and at film festivals, is now fairly typical in some African settings. Other performance professionals, like comedians in particular, will often circulate their skits on YouTube but also on Instagram, Twitter (renamed X in 2023), and Facebook at the same time. Content creators like the Nigerian Tayo Aina, or the Ghanaian Wode Maya, for example, who upload short African travel narratives videos on YouTube, will also often make their videos available on several other platforms as well.

In this new era, and despite the challenges with piracy that the DVD/VCD market pose for filmmakers everywhere on the continent, the supply of—and the demand for—DVDs/VCDs with locally produced narratives has not entirely cratered in several countries. For a subsection of Africans, DVDs remain more affordable and accessible than a subscription to a pay TV service or payment for digital data. As Jade Miller intimates, the hope that most Africans will soon access audiovisual storytelling mainly through digital media is one that is still awaiting fulfillment. In this respect, she concludes that "online distribution initiatives are extremely long term at best and will serve the diaspora first and foremost, before Nigerian audiences, the core of Nollywood's audiences" (2021, 273). At the same time, an increasing number of African feature films are migrating to a streaming service. For producers, and even actors, a streaming portal offers the best opportunity for accruing earnings by those who have invested their skills and capital in the making of a film. The streaming services offering access to African audiovisual storytelling come in different configurations. Some, like AfrolandTV, are not Africa-based but are Africa-centered in terms of their catalog. Others, like iROKOtv, are Africa-based and Africa-centered in terms of their content. However, the viability of these Africa-centered streaming services is not guaranteed, as the high-profile failures of platforms like Kwesé and Afrostream indicate. Finally, some streaming services like Netflix and Tubi TV that are playing a growing role in the global circulation of African audiovisual narratives are not Africa-based, nor are they Africa-centered when it comes to their programming.

Currently, Netflix, with a potential to shape African audiovisual narratives, might appear to pose the greatest challenge for maintaining some degree of autonomy in African audiovisual storytelling. However, and though Netflix may have become the ultimate destination for the highest-grossing films at the Nigerian box office, this does not mean that the entirety of the Nigerian film market is headed toward Netflix. Even if Netflix were to win the African streaming wars, it would still be reaching only a fraction of Africans who regularly interact with screen media. In this respect, the screen media cultures of the current era are quite decentered. Furthermore, and as remarked by Amanda Lotz, Ramon Lobato, and Julien Thomas, "Some evidence already exists that Netflix recognizes that it cannot gather a base of subscribers by serving up only US content or by creating 'placeless' or delocalized stories and characters" (2018, 38). Indeed, the streaming portals seeking to lure as many African (and African diasporic) viewers as possible to their platform now see the provision of highly localized narratives and content as the key to success. For example, and to win over viewers in Kenya, the South Africa–based streaming service Showmax created a Kenyan television series using Kenyan actors (Dovey 2018) and later partnered with its parent company, MultiChoice, to stream the popular television show *Big Brother Naija*, evidently with a view to recruiting Nigerian and West African subscribers. It is also noteworthy that Netflix appears to rely on proxy and localized assessments for many of its Nollywood selections. Most of the Nigerian films that eventually migrated to Netflix were initially successful at the Nigerian Box Office. This is the case for films like *The Wedding Party* (2016) or *Merry Men: The Real Yoruba Demons* (2018). For streaming services today, as has been the case for much of pay TV in Africa since the early twenty-first century, culturally distinct narratives represent a highly desirable commodity. The possibility that Netflix could flatten and homogenize all African productions to suit global taste preferences does not appear to constitute the greatest danger for African autonomy in contemporary screen media culture. Rather, and since authors and producers of audiovisual narratives are now more dependent on streaming services for profitable distribution of their work, they are vulnerable not so much to edicts emanating from a corporation but to both inadvertent and deliberate miscues of algorithmic culture. The pernicious effects of reliance on speciously designed algorithms to drive traffic to videos are already visible on ad-supported platforms like YouTube where Nollywood videos featuring thumbnails with sexual images quickly rack up thousands of views.

In this media landscape, film festivals might still serve as guardians of artistic independence and talent, but they matter mostly to the extent that they facilitate movement of films to different kinds of streaming services. Thus, the trajectory of Abba Makama's *The Lost Okoroshi* (2019) reveals yet an additional pathway to inclusion in Netflix programming. This film owes its presence on Netflix not to the Nigerian box office but to its screening at several international film festivals, such as the Toronto International Film Festival, the Berlin Critics' Week, and the British Film Institute Film Festival, among others. Unfortunately, some film festivals on the African continent are still organized for a world in which screen media in its entirety is synonymous with cinema and live exhibition. For example, writing in this volume about the 2014 Hillywood film festival in Rwanda, Alison MacAulay observes that curation "was informed by perceptions of what audiences might enjoy and an awareness of how a commemoratively minded screening might be received." Similarly, the Pan-African Film and Television Festival of Ouagadougou (known as FESPACO), the most prestigious film festival on the continent, continues to be informed by a seeming lack of awareness of the nature of contemporary African screen media cultures as fragmented, decentered, multiply connected, and accessible. This is despite the fact, as Pier Paolo Frassinelli remarks in this volume, that at FESPACO 2019, the theatrical experience was often marred by the flickering and ringing of smartphones during the screening of films.

It is notable that only two of the Nollywood films that have thus far migrated to Netflix appear to have ever been screened at FESPACO, namely, *Hakkunde* (2017) and *The Figurine* (2009). While the fact of being screened at FESPACO was undoubtedly beneficial to both films, selection for screening at FESPACO appears to be less and less important for triggering increased circulation of an African film. *Hakkunde*, for example, made the rounds of other film festivals as well as award events in and outside Africa that have been playing a growing role in generating critical acclaim for Nigerian films. These include the Africa International Film Festival in Nigeria and the Nollywood Week film festival in Paris, among others. Furthermore, Netflix was not the only streaming service to acquire *Hakkunde* for its programming. At the time of writing, the film could also be viewed on Amazon Prime and Tubi TV and had been screened on MUBI.

As a matter of fact, films that win awards at FESPACO generally seem much less likely to be present in many corners of this fragmented and decentered screen media culture than the films that did not win or were not considered for official selection at FESPACO. For the kinds of African filmmakers whose work might be selected for consideration at FESPACO, artistic and ideological independence often means separating their films not just from commercial exhibitors but also in a sense from the new technologies of film distribution. As a result, their films can become inaccessible artifacts, celebrated from afar, but often absent from contemporary African screen media cultures. By contrast, Nollywood-style storytelling is present everywhere, though it is vulnerable to manipulation by commercial forces. As is clear from current trends, aesthetic independence without control over the means of distribution is limited at best. It is thus in the realm of distribution of African audiovisual narratives that the fiercest battles are currently being waged for audience share in the first instance, but also for the preservation of a degree of autonomy for African artists and producers.

Filmography

Ademinokan, Daniel, dir. *Gone*. Blue Pictures. 2021.

Adepoju, Yemi, and Isaac Femi-Akintunde, dirs. *The Train: The Journey of Faith*. Mount Zion Film Productions. 2020.

Adetiba, Kemi, dir. *King of Boys: The Return of the King*. Kemi Adetiba Visuals. 2021.

Adetiba, Kemi, dir. *The Wedding Party*. EbonyLife Films. 2016.

Adorkor, Eyram, dir. *Dzigbeza*. 2016.

Afolayan, Kunle, dir. *The CEO*. 2016.

Afolayan, Kunle, dir. *Citation*. Golden Effects Pictures. 2020.

Afolayan, Kunle, dir. *The Figurine*. Golden Effects Pictures. 2009.

Afolayan, Kunle, dir. *Mokalik*. 2019.

Afolayan, Kunle, dir. *October 1*. 2014.

Afroman. "Because I Got High." Music video. Directed by Michael Alperowitz. 2000.

Agyapong, Isaac, dir. *Forkboyz*. 2019.

Ahuja, Hamisha Daryani, dir. *Namaste Wahala*. Forever 7 Entertainment. 2020.

Akande, Bola, dir. *Behind the Mask*. 2019.

Akande, Bola, dir. *Broken*. 2018.

Akinmolayan, Niyi, dir. *Prophetess*. Anthill Studios/Filmone Entertainment. 2021.

Amarteifio, Nicole, dir. *Before the Vows*. 2018.

Ansah, Kwaw, dir. *Love Brewed in the African Pot*. 1981.

Araújo, Joel Zito, dir. *Meu amigo Fela*. 2019.

Asamoah, Kofi, dir. *Amakye and Dede*. 2016.

Asamoah, Kofi, dir. *John and John*. 2017.

Asamoah, Kofi, dir. *Kalybos in China*. 2015.

Asampana, Evelyn, dir. *Anamkena*. Family Entertainment. 2019.

Asurf, Oluseyi, dir. *Hakkunde/In Between*. Asurf Films. 2017.

Austen-Peters, Bolanle, dir. *The Man of God*. BAP Productions. 2022.

Baccar, Selma, dir. *Fatma 75*. 1976.

Bamiloye, Mike, dir. *Haunting Shadow*. Mount Zion Film Productions. 2005.

Bamiloye, Mike, dir. *Rupantar*. Mount Zion Film Productions. 2014.

Bandaele, Biyi, and Kenneth Gyang, dirs. *Blood Sisters*. 2022.

Bekolo, Jean-Pierre, dir. *Les armes miraculeuses (Miraculous Weapons)*. 2017.

Bekolo, Jean-Pierre, dir. *Les saignantes*. Quartier Mozart Films. 2005.

Benlyazid, Farida, dir. *Une porte sur le ciel (Door to the Sky)*. 1989.

Beti, Ellerson, dir. *Sisters of the Screen: African Women in the Cinema*. Women Make Movies. 2002.

Beyoncé. "Brown Skin Girl." Music video. Directed by Beyoncé and Jenn Nkiru. 2020.

Blomkamp, Neill, dir. *District 9*. 2009.

Bradbeer, Harry, and Tim Kirkby, dirs. *Fleabag*. 2016–19.

Brown, Chris, and Davido. "Blow My Mind." Music video. Directed by Edgar Esteves. 2019.

Burnett, Charles, dir. *Killer of Sheep*. 1978.

Chiazor, Chinwe, dir. *Mended*. 2017.

Chisembele, Dominic, dir. *The Lawyer*. Muvi Television Limited. 2008.

Dila, Dilman, dir. *Cursed Widow Blues*. 2017.

Dila, Dilman, dir. *How to Start a Zombie Apocalypse*. 2017.

Dila, Dilman, dir. *No Letting Go*. 2017.

Djebar, Assia, dir. *La nouba des femmes du Mont Chenoua*. L'Office National du Commerce et de l'Industrie Cinématographique. 1978.

Djebar, Assia, dir. *La Zerda ou les chants de l'oubli*. Radiodiffusion Télévision Algérienne. 1981.

Dougherty, Libby, dir. *Panic Button*. 2014.

Dovey, Lindiwe, dir. *From One Woman to Another: The Screen Worlds of Bongiwe Selane*. 2023.

Dumisa, Nosipho, dir. *Blood and Water*. 2020.

Ejiofor, Chiwetel, dir. *The Boy Who Harnessed the Wind*. 2019.

Ellerson, Beti, dir. *Sisters of the Screen*. 2002.

El Maanouni, Ahmed, dir. *Alyam, Alyam*. 1978.

El Maanouni, Ahmed, dir. *Trances*. 1981.

Emma, Ikenna, dir. *Palace Maid*. 2009.

Falz. "This Is Nigeria." Music video. Directed by Geezy (Iyobosa Rehoboth). 2018.

Faye, Safe, dir. *Mossane*. 1996.

Frimpong-Manso, Shirley, dir. *Adam's Apples*. Sparrow Pictures. 2011.

Frimpong-Manso, Shirley, dir. *The Perfect Picture: 10 Years Later*. Sparrow Pictures. 2019.

Frimpong-Manso, Shirley, dir. *Potato Potahto*. Sparrow Pictures. 2017.

Frimpong-Manso, Shirley, dir. *Potomanto*. Sparrow Pictures. 2013.

Gambino, Childish. "This Is America." Directed by Hiro Murai. 2018.

Greene, Tim, dir. *Skeem*. 2011.

Gulabrai, Ramesh Jai, dir. *Bad Luck Joe*. 2018.

Gulabrai, Ramesh Jai, dir. *Life*. 2017.

Gyang, Kenneth, dir. *Oloture*. EbonyLife Films. 2019.

Hood, Gavin, dir. *Tsotsi*. 2005.

Husayn, Shafiq. "Cheeba." First single from *En' A-Free-Ka*. Music video. Directed by Kahlil Joseph. 2010.

Husayn, Shafiq. *En' A-Free-Ka*. Album. 2009.

Husayn, Shafiq. "Le'Star." Track 14 on *En' A-Free-Ka*. 2009.

Imanuke, Chief, and Bismark Idan, dirs. *Hashtag Series*. 2021.

Iñárritu, Alejandro G., dir. *Birdman*. 2014.

Jafa, Arthur, dir. *Dreams Are Colder Than Death*. 2014.

Joseph, Kahlil, dir. *Belhaven Meridian*. 2010.

Kahiu, Wanuri, dir. *Rafiki*. 2018.

Karekezi, Joel, dir. *La miséricorde de la jungle (The Mercy of the Jungle)*. 2018.

Kasum, Kayode, dir. *Kambili: The Whole 30 Yards*. 2020.

Kasum, Kayode, dir. *Quam's Money*. 2020.

Keïta, Rahmatou, dir. *The Wedding Ring*. 2016.

Kouyaté, Dany, dir. *Sia, la rêve du python (Sia, the Dream of the Python)*. 2001.

Lamis, Louis, dir. *Kejetia and Makola*. 2017.

Lediga, Kagiso, and Tebogo Malope, dirs. *Queen Sono*. 2020.

Makama, Abba, dir. *The Lost Okoroshi*. Osiris Film and Entertainment. 2019.

Maldoror, Sarah, dir. *Sambizanga*. 1972.

Mambéty, Djibril Diop, dir. *Touki Bouki*. 1973.

Manuvor, Horla, Jr., dir. *Camouflage*. 2021.

Manuvor, Horla, Jr., dir. *Inside Life*. 2021.

Manuvor, Horla, Jr., dir. *What's Up*. 2016.

Marin, Cheech, and Tommy Chong, dirs. *Up in Smoke*. 1978.

Martin, Chris. "Monsters You Made." Music video. Directed by Meji Alabi. 2020.

McBaror, Toka, dir. *Dark October*. Filmone Production. 2023.

McBaror, Toka, dir. *Merry Men: The Real Yoruba Demons*. Corporate World Entertainment/FilmOne. 2018.

Mekwunye, Ekene dir. *One Lagos Night*. Bukana Motion Pictures / Riverside productions. 2021.

Minghella, Anthony, Charles Sturridge, and Tim Fywell, dirs. *The No. 1 Ladies' Detective Agency*. BBC, HBO. 2009.

Moleya, Thabang, dir. *Happiness Is a Four-Letter Word*. 2016.

Montsho, Mmabatho, dir. *Emoyeni*. Fireworx Media, Ngonyama Kapital. 2018.

Montsho, Mmabatho, dir. *The Groom's Price*. 2017.

Montsho, Mmabatho, dir. *Thula's Vine*. Coal Stove Productions. 2017.

Mount Zion Film Productions. *Attacks from Home*. 2000.

Mount Zion Film Productions. *The Unprofitable Servant*. 1990.

Mwape, Owas Ray, dir. *Chenda*. Owas Crystal Films. 2015.

Ndlovu, Duma. *Muvhango*. Word of Mouth Productions. 1997.

New Heritage Baptist Church, dir. *Idile Alayo* (Happy Family). 2015.

Nkelemba, Nozipho, dir. *Mmino wa Modimo (God's Hymns)*. 2017.

Nnaji, Genevieve, dir. *Lionheart*. Entertainment Network. 2018.

Nworah, Chinenye, dir. *Shanty Town*. 2023.

Ojerinde, Opeyemi Akintude, dir. *Stepping into Maggie's Shoes*. 2020.

Okonkwo, Kenneth, and Francis Agu, dirs. *Living in Bondage*. 1992.

Okwo, Mildred, dir. *La Femme Anjola*. Audrey Silva Company. 2021

Oluwagbemi, Adeola Jerry, dir. *Countdown*. Mount Zion Productions. 2017.

Oluwagbemi, Adeola Jerry, dir. *One Street One Sound (OSOS)*. Mount Zion Productions. 2019.

Paterson, Debs, dir. *Africa United*. 2010.

Phiri, Angel, dir. *Mushala*. Muvi Television Limited. 2019.

Sagne, Marcel. *Résolution*. StudioCanal. 2019.

Sakala, Henry J., dir. *LSK Heroes*. Muvi Television Limited. 2014

Sakala, Henry J., dir. *Street Circles*. Muvi Television Limited. 2013.

Sakala, Henry J., dir. *When the Curtain Falls*. Muvi Television Limited. 2009.

Salam, Shadi Abdel, dir. *Al Mummia*. General Egyptian Cinema Organisation/ Merchant Ivory Productions. 1969.

Salam, Shadi Abdel, dir. *The Eloquent Peasant*. Arab Egyptian Films. 1969.

Sasore, Bodunrin, dir. *God Calling*. Heart in Motion Pictures. 2018.

Sedufia, Peter, dir. *AloeVera*. Canal+, Gravelroad Distribution. 2020.

Sedufia, Peter, dir. *Hi-MUMMY*. 2014.

Sedufia, Peter, dir. *Keteke*. 2017.

Sedufia, Peter, dir. *Master and 3 Maids*. OldFilm Productions. 2016.

Sedufia, Peter, dir. *Percher*. 2013.

Sedufia, Peter, dir. *Sidechic Gang*. 2018.

Sedufia, Peter, dir. *The Traveller*. 2014.

Sedufia, Peter, and Kofi Asamoah, dirs. *Away Bus*. 2019.

Sembène, Ousmane, dir. *Borom Sarret*. 1963.

Sembène, Ousmane, dir. *La noire de . . . /Black Girl*. 1966.

Sibbuku, Frank N., dir. *Mpali*. Zambezi Magic Production. 2018–.

Sibbuku, Frank N., dir. *Njila: The Phase*. Zambezi Magic. 2016–2019.

Sibbuku, Frank N., dir. *Njila: The Phase*. Zambezi Magic. 2019.

Sibbuku, Frank N., dir. *The Red Bag*. Muvi Television Limited. 2014.

Sibbuku, Frank N., dir. *The Vanguards*. Muvi Television Limited. 2010.

Sinclair, Ingrid, dir. *Flame*. 1996.

Stormzy featuring Ed Sheeran and Burna Boy. "Own It." Directed by Nathan James Tettey. Music video. 2019.

Sy, Kalista, dir. *Maîtresse d'un homme marié (Mistress of a Married Man)*. Marodi TV. 2019–20.

Sy, Kalista, dir. *Yaay 2.0*. Kalista Productions. 2022.

Tafesse, Moges, dir. *Kuragnaye/Enchained*. Synergy Habesha Films. 2019.

Thompson, Lawrence, dir. *Kabanana*. Picture Perfect Productions/Zambia National Broadcasting Corporation. 2001–2004.

Thompson, Lawrence, dir. *Makofi*. Zambezi Magic Production. 2021.

Thompson, Lawrence, dir. *Turn of Fortune*. Centripetal Media. 2019.

Towey, Chris, and Leah Warshawski, dirs. *Finding Hillywood*. 2013.

Traoré, Apolline, dir. *Desrances*. Orange Studio, Les Films Selmon, and Araucania Films. 2019.

Tutu, Mpho Osei, dir. *Zone 14*. Bomb Film/The Bomb Shelter. 2018.

Ugah, Adze, Thabang Moleya, Amanda Lane, Catherine Stewart, and Neil Sundstrom, dirs. *Jacob's Cross*. Bomb Film/The Bomb Shelter. 2007–13.

Vundla, Mfundi. *Generations*. 1993.

Weaver, Lloyd, dir. *I Need to Know*. Nigerian Television Authority Network. 1997–2002.

West, Kanye. "Ultralight Beam." Track 1 on *The Life of Pablo*. 2016.

References

Adamu, Abdalla Uba. 2010. "Islam, Hausa Culture, and Censorship in Northern Nigerian Video Film." In *Viewing African Cinema in the Twenty-First Century: Art Films and Nollywood Video Revolution*, edited by Mahir Saul and Ralph Austen, 11–25. Athens: Ohio University Press.

Adejunmobi, Jonathan Adegoke. 1974. "The Development of Radio Broadcasting in Nigeria, West Africa." Master's thesis. North Texas State University. Accessed December 10, 2020. https://digital.library.unt.edu/ark:/67531/metadc663486/m2/1/high_res_d/1002773656-Adejunmobi.pdf.

Adejunmobi, Moradewun. 2007. "Nigerian Film as Minor Transnational Practice." *Postcolonial Text* 3 (2): 1–16.

Adejunmobi, Moradewun. 2011. "Nollywood, Globalization and Regional Media Corporations in Africa." *Popular Communication* 9 (2): 67–78. https://doi.org/10.1080/15405702.2011.562101.

Adejunmobi, Moradewun. 2014. "Evolving Nollywood Template for Minor Transnational Film." *Black Camera* 5 (2): 74–94.

Adejunmobi, Moradewun. 2015. "African Film's Televisual Turn." *Cinema Journal* 54 (2): 120–25.

Adejunmobi, Moradewun. 2016. "African Media Studies and Marginality at the Center." *Black Camera* 7 (2): 125–39.

Adejunmobi, Moradewun. 2019. "Streaming Quality, Streaming Cinema." In *A Companion to African Cinema*, edited by Kenneth W. Harrow and Carmella Garritano, 219–43. New York: John Wiley and Sons.

Adepoju, Adunola. 2005. "Sexuality Education in Nigeria: Evolution, Challenges and Prospects." Understanding Human Sexuality Seminar Series 3. Lagos: Africa Regional Sexuality Resource Centre. Accessed December 10, 2019. http://www.arsrc.org/downloads/uhsss/adepoju_sexed.pdf.

Aderinsola, Ajao. 2019. "Un demi-siècle en dents de scie/A Checkered Half-Century." *Awotele: La revue the ciné panafricaine* 12:34–35.

Adom, Kwame. 2016. "Tackling Informal Entrepreneurship in Ghana: A Critical Analysis of the Dualist/Modernist Policy Approach, Some Evidence from Accra."

International Journal of Entrepreneurship and Small Business 28 (2/3): 216–33. https://doi
.org/10.1504/IJESB.2016.076640.

AFP Relaxnews. 2020. "Netflix Doubles Down on Efforts to Tap African Market." *IN-
QUIRER.net*, October 10. https://business.inquirer.net/309352/netflix-doubles-down
-on-efforts-to-tap-african-market#ixzz6v6dA3W2c.

AfriqueITNews. 2013. "Marodi.tv, futur concurrent de Youtube en Afrique?" October 6.
https://afriqueitnews.com/interviews/marodi-tv-futur-concurrent-youtube-en
-afrique/.

Agamben, Giorgio. 2009. "What Is the Contemporary?" In *What Is an Apparatus? And
Other Essays*, translated by David Kishik and Stefan Pedatella, 39–54. Stanford, CA:
Stanford University Press.

Agina, Añulika. 2019. "Cinema-Going in Lagos: Three Locations, One Film, One
Weekend." *Journal of African Cultural Studies* 32 (2): 131–45. https://doi.org/10.1080
/13696815.2019.1615871.

Agina, Añulika. 2021. "Netflix and the Transnationalization of Nollywood." From *New
Filmic Geographies*, edited by Suzanne Enzerink. *Post 45*, April 13. https://post45.org
/2021/04/netflix-and-the-transnationalization-of-nollywood/.

Agina, Añulika. 2022. "Nigerian Film Audiences on the Internet: Influences, Preferences and Contentions." In *Routledge Handbook of African Popular Culture*, edited by
Grace Musila, 237–59. London: Routledge.

Agina, Añulika, and Vinzenz Hediger. 2020. "Nollywood and Netflix's Burgeoning
Relationship." *Nation Online*, December 1. https://thenationonlineng.net/nollywood
-and-netflixs-burgeoning-relationship/.

Ajibade, Babson. 2013. "Nigerian Videos and Their Imagined Western Audiences: The
Limits of Nollywood's Transnationality." In *Global Nollywood: The Transnational Di-
mensions of an African Video Film Industry*, edited by Matthias Krings and Onookome
Okome, 264–84. Bloomington: Indiana University Press.

Akingbe, Niyi, and Paul Ayodele Onanuga. 2020. "'Voicing Protest': Performing Cross-
Cultural Revolt in Gambino's 'This Is America' and Falz's 'This Is Nigeria.'" *Contemporary Music Review* 39 (1): 6–36. https://doi.org/10.1080/07494467.2020.1753473.

Akomfrah, John, and Juan Canela. 2018. "John Akomfrah 'Purple' at Museo Nacional
Thyssen-Bornemisza, Madrid: John Akomfrah in Conversation with Juan Canela."
Mousse Magazine, February 20. https://www.moussemagazine.it/magazine/john
-akomfrah-juan-canela-2018/.

Akwei, Ismail. 2017. "Sex Education in Schools Sparks Debate in Conservative Nigeria." *Africa News*, accessed July 7, 2021. https://www.africanews.com/2017/08/15/sex
-education-in-schools-sparks-debate-in-conservative-nigeria/.

Alexander, Neta. 2016. "Catered to Your Future Self: Netflix's 'Predictive Personaliza-
tion' and the Mathematization of Taste." In *The Netflix Effect: Technology and Entertainment in the 21st Century*, edited by Kevin McDonald and Daniel Smith-Rowsey,
81–98. London: Bloomsbury.

Al-Hassan, Ramatu, and Xinshen Diao. 2007. "Regional Disparities in Ghana: Policy
Options and Public Investment Implications." IFPRI Discussion Paper No. 00693.
Accra: International Food Policy Research Institute.

Allman, Jean Marie. 2004a. "Fashioning Africa: Power and the Politics of Dress." In *Fashioning Africa: Power and the Politics of Dress*, edited by Jean Marie Allman, 1–10. Bloomington: Indiana University Press.

Allman, Jean Marie. 2004b. "'Let Your Fashion Be in Line with Our Ghanaian Costume': Nation, Gender, and the Politics of Clothing in Nkrumah's Ghana." In *Fashioning Africa: Power and the Politics of Dress*, edited by Jean Marie Allman, 144–65. Bloomington: Indiana University Press.

Andrade-Watkins, Claire. 1996. "France's Bureau of Cinema–Financial and Technical Assistance, 1961–1977: Operations and Implications for African Cinema" [1990]. Rpt. In *African Experiences of Cinema*, edited by Imruh Bakari and Mbye Cham, 112–27. London: British Film Institute.

Andrews, Samuel Samiái. 2020. "Netflix Naija: Creative Freedom in Nigeria's Emerging Digital Space?" *The Conversation*, March 19. https://theconversation.com/netflix-naija-creative-freedom-in-nigerias-emerging-digital-space-133252.

Ang, Ien. 1991. *Desperately Seeking the Audience*. London: Routledge.

Apata, Kolade, and Lukuman Azeez. 2019. "Motivations for Engaging in Radio Phone-In Programmes among Radio Users in Osogbo." *New Media and Mass Communication* 81:36–44. https://www.iiste.org/Journals/index.php/NMMC/article/view/48348.

Appiah, Kwame Anthony. 1991. "Is the Post- in Postmodernism the Post- in Postcolonial?" *Critical Inquiry* 17 (2): 336–57.

Appiah, Kwame Anthony. 2006. *Cosmopolitanism: Ethics in a World of Strangers*. London: Penguin.

Arnold, Gina. 2017. "Why Psy? Music Videos and the Global Market." In *Music/Video: Histories, Aesthetics, Media*, edited by Gina Arnold, Daniel Cookney, Kirsty Fairclough, and Michael N. Goddard, 245–54. New York: Bloomsbury.

Arnold, Gina, Daniel Cookney, Kirsty Fairclough, and Michael N. Goddard. 2017. "Introduction: The Persistence of the Music Video Form from MTV to Twenty-First Century Social Media." In *Music/Video: Histories, Aesthetics, Media*, edited by Gina Arnold, Daniel Cookney, Kirsty Fairclough, and Michael N. Goddard, 1–13. New York: Bloomsbury.

Arsenal. 2015. "La zerda et les chants de l'oubli." Accessed January 4, 2022. http://films.arsenal-berlin.de/index.php/Detail/Object/Show/object_id/1282/lang/en_US#.

Au Sénégal. 2018. "Les web TV veulent changer le visage médiatique au Sénégal." December 5. https://www.au-senegal.com/les-web-tv-veulent-changer-le-visage-mediatique-au-senegal,15532.html?lang=fr.

Auslander, Philip. 2008. *Liveness: Performance in a Mediatized Culture*. Abingdon, UK: Routledge.

Aveh, M. Africanus. 2020. "FESPACO—Promoting African Film Development and Scholarship." *Black Camera* 12 (1): 117–28.

Ayenalem, Seblewongiel. 2015. "Causes and Consequences of Sexual Abuse and Resilience Factors in Housemaids Working in Addis Ababa: A Qualitative Inquiry." *Ethiopian Journal of Social Sciences* 1 (1): 24–38.

Bâ, Saër Maty, and Kate E. Taylor-Jones. 2012. "Affective Passions: The Dancing Female Body and Colonial Rupture in Zouzou (1934) and Karmen Geï (2001)." In *De-Westernizing Film Studies*, edited by Saër Maty Bâ and Will Higbee, 53–66. New York: Routledge.

Bachmann-Medick, Doris. 2016. *Cultural Turns: New Orientations in the Study of Culture.* Berlin: De Gruyter.

Bakari, Imruh. 2020. "Towards Reframing FESPACO." *Black Camera* 12 (1): 289–300.

Bamiloye, Mike. 2013. "African Drama Missions." *Mount Zion Faith Ministries Newsletter*, 1–12.

Banda, Fackson. 2009. "Zambia—Teaming Up for Public Interest Communication." In *Beyond Broadcasting: The Future of State-Owned Broadcasters in Southern Africa*, edited by Guy Berger, 45–68. Windhoek: Fesmedia Africa and FES.

Banerjee, Abhijit, Eliana La Ferrara, and Victor Hugo Orozco-Olvera. 2019. "The Entertaining Way to Behavioral Change: Fighting HIV with MTV (English)." Policy Research Working Paper No. WPS 8998, World Bank Group, Washington, DC. Accessed December 10, 2019. http://documents.worldbank.org/curated/en /518151568049461993/The-Entertaining-Way-to-Behavioral-Change-Fighting-HIV -with-MTV.

Banks, Mark, and Justin O'Connor. 2021. "A Plague upon Your Howling: Art and Culture in the Viral Emergency." *Cultural Trends* 30 (1): 3–18.

Barber, Karin. 1982. "Popular Reactions to the Petro-Naira." *Journal of Modern African Studies* 20 (3): 431–50.

Barber, Karin. 1987. "Popular Arts in Africa." *African Studies Review* 30 (3): 1–78.

Barber, Karin. 1997. "Preliminary Notes on the Audience in Africa." *Africa: Journal of the International African Institute* 67 (3): 347–62.

Barber, Karin. 2000. *The Generation of Plays: Yorùbá Popular Life in Theater*. Bloomington: Indiana University Press.

Barber, Karin. 2022. "Foreword." In *Routledge Handbook of African Popular Culture*, edited by Grace Musila, xv–xx. Abingdon: Routledge.

Barlet, Olivier. 2000. *African Cinemas: Decolonizing the Gaze*. London: Zed Books.

Barlet, Olivier. 2020. "FESPACO 2019: Moving toward Resurrection." *Black Camera* 12 (1): 320–36.

Barnard, Alan. 2000. *History and Theory in Anthropology*. Cambridge: Cambridge University Press.

Barnett, Michael. 2005. "The Many Faces of Rasta: Doctrinal Diversity within the Rastafari Movement." *Caribbean Quarterly* 51 (2): 67–78.

Bastian, Misty L. 1996. "Female 'Alhajis' and Entrepreneurial Fashions: Flexible Identities in Southeastern Nigerian Clothing Practice." In *Clothing and Difference: Embodied Identities in Colonial and Post-colonial Africa*, edited by Hildi Hendrickson, 97–132. Durham, NC: Duke University Press.

Bayala, Marie-Laurentine. 2019. "FESPACO: The Locomotive Driving Burkinabe Cinema for 50 Years." *Awotele: La revue ciné panafricaine* 12:9.

BBC World Service Trust. 2009. *Ten Stories of Change*. London: BBC World Service Trust. https://assets.publishing.service.gov.uk/media/57a08b5440f0b64974000ac2 /trust_at_10_web.pdf.

Becker, Heiki. 2013. "Nollywood in Urban Southern Africa: Nigerian Video Films and Their Audiences in Cape Town and Windhoek." In *Global Nollywood: The Transnational Dimensions of an African Video Film Industry*, edited by Matthias Krings and Onookome Okome, 179–98. Bloomington: Indiana University Press.

Benstock, Shari. 2006. "Afterword." In *Chick Lit: The New Woman's Fiction*, edited by Suzanne Ferriss and Mallory Young, 253–56. London: Routledge.

Benyah, Francis. 2019. "Church Branding and Self-Packaging: The Mass Media and African Pentecostal Missionary Strategy." *Journal of Religion in Africa* 48 (3): 1–24.

Bernstorff, Madeleine. 2013. "Let a Hundred Living Archives Bloom!" *Arsenal Berlin*. Accessed January 4, 2022. https://www.arsenal-berlin.de/en/living-archive/projects/living-archive-archive-work-as-a-contenporary-artistic-and-curatorial-practice/individual-projects/madeleine-bernstorff.html.

Bhabha, Homi. 1994. *The Location of Culture*. London: Routledge.

Bisschoff, Lizelle. 2012. "The Emergence of Women's Film-making in Francophone Sub-Saharan Africa: From Pioneering Figures to Contemporary Directors." *Journal of African Cinemas* 4 (2): 157–73. https://doi.org/10.1386/jac.4.2.157_1.

Bisschoff, Lizelle. 2017. "The Future Is Digital: An Introduction to African Digital Arts." *Critical African Studies* 9 (3): 261–67. https://doi.org/10.1080/21681392.2017.1376506.

Bisschoff, Lizelle, and Stefanie Van de Peer. 2020. *Women in African Cinema: Beyond the Body Politic*. New York: Routledge.

Blaser, Mario, and Marisol de la Cadena. 2018. "Introduction: Pluriverse: Proposals for a World of Many Worlds." In *A World of Many Worlds*, edited by Marisol de la Cadena and Mario Blaser, 1–22. Durham, NC: Duke University Press.

Böhme, Claudia. 2013. "Bloody Bricolages: Traces of Nollywood in Tanzanian Video Films." In *Global Nollywood: The Transnational Dimensions of an African Video Film Industry*, edited by Matthias Krings and Onookome Okome, 327–46. Bloomington: Indiana University Press.

Boni, Marta. 2017. "Introduction: Worlds, Today." In *World Building: Transmedia, Fans, Industries*, edited by Marta Boni, 9–27. Amsterdam: Amsterdam University Press.

Bourdieu, Pierre. 1984. *Distinction*. London: Routledge and Kegan Paul.

Bourdieu, Pierre. 1994. "Structures, Habitus and Practices." In *The Polity Reader in Social Theory*, edited by Polity Press, 95–110. Cambridge: Polity Press.

Brown, Matthew H. 2016. "African Screen Media Studies: Immediacy, Modernization, and Informal Forms." *Black Camera* 7 (2): 140–58.

Bruno, Giuliana. 2014. *Surface: Matters of Aesthetics, Materiality, and Media*. Chicago: University of Chicago Press.

Brunson, James, III. 2011. "Showing, Seeing: Hip-Hop, Visual Culture, and the Show-and-Tell Performance." *Black History Bulletin* 74 (1): 6–12.

Bryce, Jane. 2013. "TEN 'African Movies' in Barbados: Proximate Experiences of Fear and Desire." In *Global Nollywood. The Transnational Dimensions of an African Video Film Industry*, edited by Matthias Krings and Onookome Okome, 223–44. Bloomington: Indiana University Press.

Buchsbaum, Jonathan. 2015. "Militant Third World Film Distribution in the United States, 1970–1980." *Revue Canadienne D'Études Cinématographiques / Canadian Journal of Film Studies* 24 (2): 51–65.

Buckland, Warren. 2020. "The Wes Anderson Brand: New Sincerity across Media." In *Transmedia Directors: Artistry, Industry and New Audiovisual Aesthetics*, edited by Carol Vernallis, Holly Rogers, and Lisa Perrott, 19–34. New York: Bloomsbury.

Bud, Alexander. 2014. "The End of Nollywood's Guilded Age? Marketers, the State and the Struggle for Distribution." *Critical African Studies* 6 (1): 91–121.

Bud, Alexander. 2019. "In Search of the Nigerian Pastoral: Nollywood and the Nigerian Creative-Industrial System." PhD diss., The Open University.

Bud, Alexander. 2021. "Squandermania or Nigerian Urban Renaissance? Houses, Hotels and Nollywood in an African Creative Economy." *Anthropologie & développement* 52:29–49.

Burns, Lori, and Stan Hawkins. 2019. "Introduction: Undertaking Music Video Analysis." In *The Bloomsbury Handbook of Popular Music Analysis*, edited by Lori A. Burns and Stan Hawkins, 1–10. New York: Bloomsbury Academic.

Capraru, Jennifer H., and Kim Solga. 2013. "Performing Survival in the Global City: Theatre ISOKO's *The Monument*." In *Performance and the Global City*, edited by D. J. Hopkins and Kim Solga, 40–60. New York: Palgrave Macmillan.

Caputi, Jane, and Lauri Sagle. 2004. "Femme Noire: Dangerous Women of Color in Popular Film and Television." *Race, Gender and Class* 11 (2): 90–111.

Carus, Paul. 1905. "The Conception of the Soul and the Belief in Resurrection among the Egyptians." *The Monist* 15 (3): 409–28.

Chávez, Christopher A., and Ashley Cordes. 2018. "Selling Subversion: *An African City* and the Promise of Online Television." *Television and New Media* 19 (3): 191–207. https://doi.org/10.1177/1527476417712458.

Christensen, Clayton M., Michael E. Raynor, and Rory McDonald. 2015. "What Is Disruptive Innovation?" *Harvard Business Review*, December. https://hbr.org/2015/12/what-is-disruptive-innovation.

Chukwuezi, Barth. 2001. "Through Thick and Thin: Igbo Rural-Urban Circularity, Identity and Investment." *Journal of Contemporary African Studies* 19 (1): 56–66.

Chutel, Lynsey. 2019. "One of Africa's Most Influential Film Festivals Has Survived DVDs and Now Terrorism." *Quartz Africa*, February 21. https://qz.com/africa/1556071/fespaco-burkina-faso-film-festival-celebrates-50-years/.

Cieplak, Piotr A. 2008. "Hooray for Hillywood." *Sight and Sound* 18 (7): 9.

Cieplak, Piotr A. 2009. "Image and Memory: An Interview with Eric Kabera." *French Cultural Studies* 20 (2): 199–208.

Cieplak, Piotr A. 2010. "Alternative African Cinemas: A Case Study of Rwanda." *Journal of African Media Studies* 2 (1): 73–90.

Cieplak, Piotr. 2017. *Death, Image, Memory: The Genocide in Rwanda and Its Aftermath in Photography and Documentary Film*. London: Palgrave Macmillan.

Clark, Ebun. 1979. *Hubert Ogunde: The Making of Nigerian Theatre*. Oxford: Oxford University Press.

Clarke, Robert, and Mark Merlin. 2013. *Cannabis: Evolution and Ethnobotany*. Berkeley: University of California Press.

CNRA. 2019. "DÉCISION N°0001 / Traitement plainte contre le téléfilm 'La Maîtresse d'un homme marié.'" March 30. http://www.cnra.sn/do/decision-n0001-traitement -plainte-contre-le-telefilm-la-maitresse-dun-homme-marie/.

Conquergood, Dwight. 2013. *Cultural Struggles: Performance. Ethnography, Praxis*. Edited by E. Patrick Johnson. Ann Arbor: University of Michigan Press.

Cooley, Heidi Rae. 2014. "It's All about the Fit: The Hand, the Mobile Screenic Device and Tactile Vision." *Journal of Visual Culture* 3 (2): 133–55.

Courtois, Cédric, and Pieter Verdegem. 2016. "With a Little Help from My Friends: An Analysis of the Role of Social Support in Digital Inequalities." *New Media and Society* 18 (8): 1508–27. https://doi.org/10.1177/1461444814562162.

Craik, Jennifer. 2003. "The Cultural Politics of the Uniform." *Fashion Theory* 7 (2): 127–47.

Cropper, Tom. 2009. "Hillywood Dreams." *New Internationalist*, November 6. https:// newint.org/features/special/2009/11/06/hillywood-dreams.

Cunningham, Stuart, and Jon Silver. 2013. *Screen Distribution and the New King Kongs of the Online World*. New York: Palgrave Pivot.

Curtin, Michael, and Kevin Sanson, eds. 2016. *Precarious Creativity: Global Media, Local Labor*. Berkeley: University of California Press.

Daadaoui, Mohamed. 2011. *Moroccan Monarchy and the Islamist Challenge*. New York: Palgrave Macmillan.

Dallas, Paul. 2017. "Kahlil Joseph on Sound, Silence and Spirituality." *Extra Extra: Nouveau Magazine Erotique* 9:134–53.

DataReportal. 2020. "Digital 2020: Senegal." February 18. https://datareportal.com /reports/digital-2020-senegal.

Dauge-Roth, Alexandre. 2010. *Writing and Filming the Genocide of the Tutsis in Rwanda: Dismembering and Remembering Traumatic History*. Lanham, MD: Lexington Books.

Dauge-Roth, Alexandre. 2017. "Conferring Visibility on Trauma within Rwanda's National Reconciliation: Kivu Ruhorahoza's Disturbing and Salutary Camera." In *Scars and Wounds: Film and Legacies of Trauma*, edited by Nick Hodgin and Amit Thakkar, 77–100. London: Palgrave Macmillan.

Debuysere, Stoffel. 2020, "Out of the Shadows: The Pioneering Work of Atteyat Al-Abnoudy, Assia Djebar, Jocelyne Saab, Heiny Srour." Courtisane Festival. Accessed January 3, 2022. https://www.courtisane.be/en/section/out-of-the-shadows-0.

De Kosnik, Abigail. 2013. "Fandom as Free Labor." In *Digital Labor: The Internet as Playground and Factory*, edited by Trebor Scholz, 98–111. New York: Routledge.

de Valck, Marijke. 2014. "Supporting Art Cinema at a Time of Commercialization: Principles and Practices, the Case of the International Film Festival Rotterdam." *Poetics* 42 (February): 40–59. https://doi.org/10.1016/j.poetic.2013.11.004.

DeVeaux, Scott. 1991. "Constructing the Jazz Tradition: Jazz Historiography." *Black American Literature Forum* 25 (3): 525–60.

de Villiers, James. 2019. "Multichoice Plans to Make 52 Local Movies the Next Year— And Saw Streaming Subscriber Double." News24, June 22. https://www.news24.com /news24/bi-archive/multichoice-netflix-showmax-dstv-dtsv-now-local-movies -streaming-service-naspers-2019-6.

Diallo, Ibrahima. 2016. "'Wiri Wiri,' la série sénégalaise qui a détrôné les telenove-las dans les foyers dakarois." *Le360afrique.com*, December 20. http://afrique.le360 .ma/senegal/culture/2016/12/20/8396-wiri-wiri-la-serie-senegalaise-qui-detrone-les -telenovelas-dans-les-foyers-dakarois-8396.

Diawara, Manthia. 2006. "Troubling the Waters: A Conversation with Manthia Di-awara." Interview by Audret McCluskey. *Black Camera* 21 (1): 1–2, 9–10.

Diawara, Manthia. 2010. *African Film: New Forms of Aesthetics and Politics.* Munich: Prestel.

Dickinson, K., N. Djedouani, J. El Tahri, A. Essafi, O. Haddouchi, S. Jubara, M. Mau-rer, M. Nasr Eldien, E. Rongen-Kaynakçi, R. Salti, and M. Yaqubi. 2019. "Liberate the Image" Manifesto. Documentary Convention, Leipzig, Germany, April 2019. https://documentary-convention.org/archive-manifesto-liberate-the-image/.

Dieng, Rama, ed. 2021. *Féminismes africains, une histoire décoloniale.* Paris: Présence Africaine.

Dila, Dilman. 2017a. "Cursed Widow Blues." Uploaded by Dilstories. YouTube. Ac-cessed December 19, 2018. https://www.youtube.com/watch?v=4gOnhZbZOKU.

Dila, Dilman. 2017b. "How to Start a Zombie Apocalypse." Uploaded by Dilsto-ries. YouTube. Accessed December 19, 2018. https://www.youtube.com/watch?v =SnJob5gW9Bo.

Dione, Ibrahima. 2019. "Senegal: Where Local Soap Operas Outshine Foreign Tele-novelas." APA News, September 11. http://apanews.net/en/news/senegal-where-local -soap-operas-outshine-foreign-telenovelas.

Dipio, Dominica. 2014. *Gender Terrains in African Cinema.* Pretoria: Unisa Press.

Doane, Mary Ann. 1991. "Film and the Masquerade: Theorising the Female Spectator." In *Femmes Fatales: Feminism, Film Theory, Psychoanalysis*, 17–32. New York: Routledge.

Dovey, Lindiwe. 2010. "African Film and Video: Pleasure, Politics, Performance." *Journal of African Cultural Studies* 22 (1): 1–6.

Dovey, Lindiwe. 2012. "New Looks: The Rise of African Women Filmmakers." *Feminist Africa* 16:18–36.

Dovey, Lindiwe. 2015a. "'Bergman in Uganda': Ugandan Veejays, Swedish Pirates, and the Political Value of Live Adaptation." In *The Politics of Adaptation: Media Convergence and Ideology*, edited by Dan Hassler-Forest and Pascal Nicklas, 99–113. New York: Palgrave Macmillan.

Dovey, Lindiwe. 2015b. *Curating Africa in the Age of Film Festivals.* New York: Palgrave Macmillan.

Dovey, Lindiwe. 2015c. "Through the Eye of a Film Festival: Toward a Curatorial and Spectator Centered Approach to the Study of African Screen Media." *Cinema Journal* 54 (2): 126–32. https://doi.org/10.1353/cj.2015.0005.

Dovey, Lindiwe. 2018. "Entertaining Africans: Creative Innovation in the (Inter-net) Television Space." *Media Industries* 5 (2): 94–110. http://dx.doi.org/10.3998/mij .15031809.0005.206.

Dovey, Lindiwe. 2020. "African Film Festivals in Africa: Curating 'African Audiences' for 'African Films.'" *Black Camera* 12 (1): 12–47.

Dovey, Lindiwe. 2023. "Intermediality in Academia: Creative Research through Film." *Arts* 12 (4): 1–12. https://www.mdpi.com/2076-0752/12/4/169.

Dovey, Lindiwe. 2025. "Transforming Documentary Film Cultures in East Africa: Judy Kibinge and Docubox." In *Women and Global Documentary*, edited by Najmeh Moradiyan Rizi and Shilyh Warren, 27–50. London: Bloomsbury.

Dovey, Lindiwe, and Estrella Sendra Fernandez. 2023. "Towards Decolonised Film Festival Worlds." In *Rethinking Film Festivals in the Pandemic Era and After*, edited by Marijke de Valck and Antoine Damiens. New York: Palgrave Macmillan. E-book.

Dupré, Colin. 2012. *Le Fespaco, une affaire d'État(s)*. Paris: L'Harmattan.

Dupré, Colin. 2020. "FESPACO Film Festival." *Black Camera* 12 (1): 282–86.

Dy, Angela Martinez, Susan Marlow, and Lee Martin. 2017. "A Web of Opportunity or the Same Old Story? Women Digital Entrepreneurs and Intersectionality Theory." *Human Relations* 70 (3): 286–311. https://doi.org/10.1177/0018726716650730.

Ebelebe, Ugo Ben. 2017. "Reinventing Nollywood: The Impact of Online Funding and Distribution on the Nigerian Cinema." *Convergence: The International Journal of Research into New Media Technologies* 25 (3): 1–13. https://doi.org/10.1177/1354856517735792.

Edmonds, Enis Barrington. 2003. *Rastafari: From Outcasts to Culture Bearers*. Oxford: Oxford University Press.

Edmonds, Ennis Barrington. 2012. *Rastafari: A Very Short Introduction*. Oxford: Oxford University Press.

Edwards, Matthew, ed. 2018. *The Rwandan Genocide on Film: Critical Essays and Interviews*. Jefferson, NC: McFarland.

Edwards, Paul N., Lisa Gitelman, Gabrielle Hecht, Adrien Johns, Brian Larkin, and Neil Safier. 2011. "AHR Conversation: Historical Perspectives on the Circulation of Information." *American Historical Review* 116 (5): 1393–435.

Ekwok, Lawrence. 2017. "Women as Tireless Goddesses, Super-humans and Geniuses in the African Alternative Cinema." *International Journal of Information and Communication Sciences* 2 (5): 68–74.

El Echi, Sadar, and Ly Aïssatou. 2019. "Regard au féminin." *Le pays* (Burkina Faso), March 1.

Ellerson, Beti. 2000. *Sisters of the Screen: Women of Africa on Film, Video and Television*. Trenton, NJ: Africa World Press.

Ellerson, Beti. 2015. "Teaching African Women in Cinema: Part One." *Black Camera* 7 (1): 251–61.

Ellerson, Beti. 2016. "Teaching African Women in Cinema: Part Two." *Black Camera* 7 (2): 217–33.

Ellerson, Beti. 2020. "Fifty Years of Women's Engagement at FESPACO." *Black Camera* 12 (1): 246–54.

Entwistle, Joanne. 2000. *The Fashioned Body: Fashion, Dress, and Modern Social Theory*. Cambridge: Polity Press.

Ezepue, Ezinne. 2020. "The New Nollywood: Professionalization or Gentrification of Cultural Industry." *SAGE Open* 10 (3): 1–10.

Fabian, Johannes. 2014. *Time and the Other: How Anthropology Makes Its Object*. New York: Columbia University Press.

Fair, Laura. 2018. *Reel Pleasures: Cinema Audiences and Entrepreneurs in Twentieth-Century Urban Tanzania*. Athens: Ohio University Press.

Fanon, Frantz. 2008. *Black Skin, White Masks*. London: Pluto Press.

Ferreira, Thinus. 2015. "DStv Adds New Channel for Southern Africa Viewers." Channel24. Accessed March 23, 2020. https://www.channel24.co.za/TV/News/DStv-adds-new-channel-for-Southern-Africa-viewers-20150701.

Ferriss, Suzanne, and Mallory Young. 2006. *Chick Lit: The New Woman's Fiction*. London: Routledge.

Field, Allyson, Jan-Christopher Horak, and Jacqueline Najuma Stewart. 2015. *L.A. Rebellion: Creating a New Black Cinema*. Berkeley: University of California Press.

FilmOne Entertainment. 2020. "Cinema Count: Angolophone West Africa." *Nigeria Box Office Year Book 2020*. Accessed August 13, 2024. http://books.filmhouseng.com/books/kumi/#p=12.

Forman, Murray. 2011. "'Represent': Race, Space and Place in Rap Music." *Popular Music* 19 (1): 65–90.

Forrest, Adam. 2018. "This Is Nigeria Parody Banned in Nigeria." *Independent*, August 16. https://www.independent.co.uk/news/world/africa/this-is-nigeria-ban-video-falz-childish-gambino-a8494861.html.

Fouad, Ahmed. 2019. "Will Netflix Boost Stagnant Local TV Industry?" *New African* 597:58–59.

Frassinelli, Pier Paolo. 2019. "Africa's Top Film Festival Celebrates 50 Years: What's to Celebrate, and Learn." *The Conversation*, March 18. https://theconversation.com/africas-top-film-festival-celebrates-50-years-whats-to-celebrate-and-learn-113393.

Frassinelli, Pier Paolo. 2021. "Joburg without Joburg: The Black South African Romcom." *Social Dynamics: A Journal of African Studies* 47 (1): 37–52.

Freeland, Cynthia A. 2018. *The Naked and the Undead: Evil and the Appeal of Horror*. London: Routledge.

Ganti, Tejaswini. 2012. *Producing Bollywood: Inside the Contemporary Hindi Film Industry*. Durham, NC: Duke University Press.

Garritano, Carmela. 2008. "Contesting Authenticities: The Emergence of Local Video Production in Ghana." *Critical Arts* 22 (1): 21–48. https://doi.org/10.1080/02560040802166219.

Garritano, Carmela. 2013. *African Video Movies and Global Desires: A Ghanaian History*. Athens: Ohio University Press.

Gibson, James J. 1979. *The Ecological Approach to Visual Perception*. Boston: Houghton Mifflin.

Gibson, Sarah. 2018. "The Landscapes and Aesthetics of Soap Opera: Townships, Television and Tourism." *Journal of African Cinemas* 10 (1–2): 95–110. https://doi.org/10.1386/jac.10.1-2.95_1.

Girma, Mohammed. 2012. *Understanding Religion and Social Change in Ethiopia: Toward a Hermeneutic of Covenant*. Basingstoke UK: Palgrave Macmillan.

Givanni, June, ed. 2000. *Symbolic Narratives / African Cinema: Audiences, Theory and the Moving Image*. London: British Film Institute.

Gleason, Benjamin. 2018. "Thinking in Hashtags: Exploring Teenagers' New Literacies Practices on Twitter." *Learning, Media and Technology* 43 (2): 165–80. 10.1080/17439884.2018.1462207.

Goodwin, Andrew. 1992. *Dancing in the Distraction Factory: Music Television and Popular Culture*. Minneapolis: University of Minnesota Press.

Goyal, Pawan. 2014. "Hashtags on Twitter: Linguistic Aspects, Popularity Prediction and Information Diffusion." Presentation to Department of Computer Science and Engineering, Indian Institute of Technology, Kharagpur, India, July 24–28. Accessed December 5, 2019. https://cse.iitkgp.ac.in/~pawang/courses/SC14/lec3.pdf.

Gqola, Pumla. 2010. *What Is Slavery to Me? Postcolonial / Slave Memory in Post-apartheid South Africa*. Johannesburg: Wits University Press.

Green-Simms, Lindsey. 2010. "The Return of the Mercedes: From Ousmane Sembène to Kenneth Nnebue." In *Viewing African Cinema in the Twenty-First Century: Art Films and Nollywood Video Revolution*, edited by Mahir Saul and Ralph A. Austen, 209–24. Athens: Ohio University Press.

Griffin, Cynthia E. 2013. "Midtown Bowl Closing Its Doors after 52 Years." *Our Weekly Los Angeles*, June 20. http://ourweekly.com/news/2013/jun/20/midtown-bowl-closing -its-doors-after-52-years/.

Guerrero, Lisa A. 2006. "'Sistahs Are Doin' It for Themselves': Chick Lit in Black and White." In *Chick Lit: The New Woman's Fiction*, edited by Suzanne Ferriss and Mallory Young, 87–101. London: Routledge.

Gueye, Marame. 2019. "Senegal's Fear of Outspoken Women." *Africa Is a Country*, January 4. https://africasacountry.com/2019/04/senegals-fear-of-outspoken-women.

Guma, Prince Karakire. 2017. "Feminism: How Women in Uganda Are Shaping the Way We Think about Sex and Politics." In *Research on Gender and Sexualities in Africa*, edited by Jane Bennett and Sylvia Tamale, 133–51. Dakar: Council for the Development of Social Science Research in Africa (CODESRIA).

Hall, Peter Geoffrey. 1998. *Cities in Civilization*. New York: Pantheon Books.

Hallam, Elizabeth, and Tim Ingold. 2007. *Creativity and Cultural Improvisation*. Oxford: Berg.

Hamlet, Janice D. 2011. "Word! The African American Oral Tradition and Its Rhetorical Impact on American Popular Culture." *Black History Bulletin* 74 (1): 27–31.

Harding, Frances. 2007. "Appearing Fabu-lous: From Tender Romance to Horrifying Sex." *Film International* 5 (4): 10–19.

Harrop, Peter, and Aboneh Ashagrie. 1984. *A Preliminary Investigation of Dramatic Elements within Traditional Ceremonies among the Anuak, Majengo, Nuer and Shanko Nationalities of Illubador Administrative Region*. Addis Ababa: Addis Ababa University Press.

Harrow, Kenneth W. 2013. *Trash: African Cinema from Below*. Bloomington: Indiana University Press.

Harrow, Kenneth W., and Carmela Garritano. 2016. "Women in 'African Cinema' and 'Nollywood Films': A Shift in Cinematic Regimes." *Journal of African Cinemas* 8 (3): 233–48.

Harrow, Kenneth W., and Carmela Garritano. 2019a. *A Companion to African Cinema*. Hoboken, NJ: Wiley-Blackwell.

Harrow, Kenneth W., and Carmela Garritano. 2019b. "Introduction: Critical Approaches to Africa's Cinema, from the Age of Liberation and Struggle to the Global, Popular, and Curatorial." In *A Companion to African Cinema*, edited by Kenneth W. Harrow and Carmela Garritano, 1–20. Hoboken, NJ: Wiley-Blackwell.

Harzewski, Stephanie. 2011. *Chick Lit and Postfeminism*. Charlottesville: University of Virginia Press.

Haynes, Jonathan. 2010. "A Literature Review: Nigerian and Ghanaian Videos." *Journal of African Cultural Studies* 22 (1): 105–20. https://doi.org/: 10.1080/13696810903488645.

Haynes, Jonathan. 2016. *Nollywood: The Creation of Nigerian Film Genres*. Chicago: University of Chicago Press.

Haynes, Jonathan. 2017. *Nollywood: The Creation of Nigerian Film Genres*. Ibadan, Nigeria: Bookcraft.

Haynes, Jonathan. 2018. "Keeping Up: The Corporatization of Nollywood's Economy and Paradigms for Studying African Screen Media." *Africa Today* 64 (4): 3–29. https://doi.org/10.2979/africatoday.64.4.02.

Haynes, Jonathan. 2019. "Between the Informal Sector and Transnational Capitalism: Transformations of Nollywood." In *A Companion to African Cinema*, edited by Kenneth W. Harrow and Carmela Garritano, 244–68. Hoboken, NJ: Wiley-Blackwell.

Haynes, Jonathan, and Onookome Okome. 1998. "Evolving Popular Media: Nigerian Video Films." *Research in African Literatures* 29 (3): 106–28.

Hearsum, Paula, and Ian Inglis. 2013. "The Emancipation of Music Video: YouTube and the Cultural Politics of Supply and Demand." In *The Oxford Handbook of New Audiovisual Aesthetics*, edited by John Richardson, Claudia Gorbman, and Carol Vernallis. New York: Oxford University Press. E-book.

Higbee, Will, Flo Martin, and Jamal Bahmad. 2020. *Moroccan Cinema Uncut: Decentred Voices, Transnational Perspectives*. Edinburgh: Edinburgh University Press.

Hilson, Gavin, Richard Amankwah, and Grace Ofori-Sarpong. 2013. "Going for Gold: Transitional Livelihoods in Northern Ghana." *Journal of Modern African Studies* 51 (1): 109–37. https://doi.org/10.1017/S0022278X12000560.

Huff, Quentin B. 2012. "A Joy to Experience: Neo-Soul Singer Bilal Oliver." *Pop Matters*, January 22. https://www.popmatters.com/152722-featuring-bilal-2495902134.html?rebelltitem=1#rebelltitem1.

Hootsuite. 2020. *Digital 2020 Global Overview Report*. Accessed November 18, 2024. https://marketingdigital.blog/wp-content/uploads/2020/01/datareportal20200130gd001digital2020globaldigitaloverviewjanuary2020v01-200130025629-1_compressed.pdf.

Husayn, S. 2009. "Shafiq En' A-Free-Ka." Bandcamp: Shafiq Husayn. October 6. https://shafiqhusayn.bandcamp.com/album/shafiq-en-a-free-ka.

Independent Broadcasting Authority. 2020. "About Us." Accessed April 2, 2020. https://www.iba.org.zm/about-us/.

Ingold, Tim. 1993. "The Temporality of the Landscape." *World Archaeology* 25 (2): 152–74.

Ingold, Tim. 2007. "Introduction." In *Creativity and Cultural Improvisation*, edited by Elizabeth Hallam and Tim Ingold, 45–54. Oxford: Berg.

Ingold, Tim. 2008. "When ANT meets SPIDER: Social Theory for Arthropods." In *Material Agency: Towards a Non-anthropocentric Approach*, edited by Carl Knappett and Lambros Malafouris, 209–15. Boston: Springer.

Ingold, Tim. 2010. *Bringing Things to Life: Creative Entanglements in a World of Materials*. NCRM Working Paper 5/10, ESRC National Centre for Research Methods, Manchester, UK, July 2010.

Ingold, Tim. 2013. *Making: Anthropology, Archaeology, Art and Architecture*. Abingdon, UK: Routledge.

Ingold, Tim. 2015. *The Life of Lines*. Abingdon, UK: Routledge.

Ingold, Tim, and Cristián Simonetti. 2022. "Introducing Solid Fluids." *Theory, Culture & Society* 39 (2): 3–29. Published online September 13.

Iordanova, Dina. 2012. "Digital Disruption: Technological Innovation and Global Film Circulation." In *Digital Disruption: Cinema Moves On-Line*, edited by Dina Iordanova and Stuart Cunningham, 1–31. Fife, Scotland: University of St Andrews.

Isoardi, Steven. 1998. "Foreword." In *Central Avenue Sounds: Jazz in Los Angeles*, edited by Clare Bryant, Buddy Collette, William Green, Steven Isoardi, Jack Kelson, Horace Tapscott, Gerald Wilson, and Marl Young, xv. Berkeley: University of California Press.

Izugbara, Chimaraoke O. 2011. "Sexuality and the Supernatural in Africa." In *African Sexualities: A Reader*, edited by Sylvia Tamale, 533–58. Cape Town: Pambazuka Press.

Jafa, Arthur. 1992. "69." In *Black Popular Culture*, edited by Gina Dent, 249–54. Seattle: Bay Press.

Jafa, Arthur. 2016. "Arthur Jafa in Conversation with Hans Ulrich Obrist: Los Angeles, 2016." Serpentine Galleries Archive. Accessed March 24, 2021. https://www.serpentinegalleries.org/files/downloads/arthur_jafa_in_conversation.pdf.

Jaishree, S., and S. Krishnakumar. 2020. "The Rhetoric and Reality of Women in the Unorganised Sector—A Study on Housemaids in Chennai." *Studies in India Place Names* 40 (48): 238–45.

Jaji, Tsitsi. 2014. *Africa in Stereo: Modernism, Music, and Pan-African Solidarity*. Athens: Ohio University Press.

Jancovich, Mark, ed. 2002. *Horror, The Film Reader*. London: Routledge.

Jedlowski, Alessandro. 2012. "Small Screen Cinema: Informality and Remediation in Nollywood." *Television and New Media* 13 (5): 431–46.

Jedlowski, Alessandro. 2013a. "From Nollywood to Nollyworld: Processes of Transnationalization in the Nigerian Video Film Industry." In *Global Nollywood: The Transnational Dimensions of an African Video Film Industry*, edited by Matthias Krings and Onookome Okome, 25–45. Bloomington: Indiana University Press.

Jedlowski, Alessandro. 2013b. "Nigerian Videos in the Global Arena: The Postcolonial Exotic Revisited." *Global South* 7 (1): 157–78.

Jedlowski, Alessandro. 2016. "Studying Media 'from' the South: African Media Studies and Global Perspectives." *Black Camera* 7 (2): 174–93.

Jedlowski, Alessandro. 2017. "African Media and the Corporate Takeover: Video Film Circulation in the Age of Neoliberal Transformations." *African Affairs* 116 (465): 671–91. https://doi.org/10.1093/afraf/adx017.

Jedlowski, Alessandro. 2018. "What Netflix's Involvement in Nigeria's Massive Film Industry Really Means." *The Conversation Africa*, December 31. https://theconversation.com/what-netflixs-involvement-in-nigerias-massive-film-industry-really-means-108832.

Jedlowski, Alessandro. 2019. "African Videoscapes: Southern Nigeria, Ethiopia, and Côte d'Ivoire in Comparative Perspective." In *A Companion to African Cinema*, edited by Kenneth W. Harrow and Carmela Garritano, 293–314. Hoboken, NJ: Wiley-Blackwell.

Jedlowski, Alessandro, and Cacilda Rêgo. 2018. "Latin American Telenovelas and African Screen Media: From Reception to Production." *Journal of African Cultural Studies* 31 (2): 135–50. Published online November 26.

Jenkins, Henry. 2006. *Convergence Culture: Where Old and New Media Collide*. New York: New York University Press.

Jenkins, Henry. 2012. *Textual Poachers: Television Fans and Participatory Culture*. 2nd ed. New York: Routledge.

Jenkins, Henry, Sam Ford, and Joshua Green. 2013. *Spreadable Media: Creating Value and Meaning in a Networked Culture*. New York: New York University Press.

Jeune Afrique. 2013. "Le sénégalais Marodi.tv remporte le VentureOut Challenge pour l'Afrique." November 4. https://www.jeuneafrique.com/15009/economie/le-s-n-galais -marodi-tv-remporte-le-ventureout-challenge-pour-l-afrique/.

Jones, Kent. 2021. "Notes on Film and Restoration." Film Foundation, September 9. https://www.film-foundation.org/sarah-maldoror-kj.

Julien, Eileen. 2015. "The Critical Present: Where Is 'African Literature'?" In *Rethinking African Cultural Production*, edited by Frieda Ekotto and Kenneth Harrow, 17–28. Bloomington: Indiana University Press.

Justo, Alicia. 2020. "La serie que rompe clichés sobre la mujer senegalesa." *Wiriko*, April 21. https://www.wiriko.org/wiriko/la-serie-que-rompe-cliches-sobre-la-mujer-senegalesa/.

Kaboré, Gaston J. M., and Michael T. Martin. 2020. "Introduction." *Black Camera* 12 (1): 5–9.

Kaplan, E. Ann. 1987. *Rocking around the Clock: Music Television, Postmodernism and Consumer Culture*. New York: Methuen.

Kassahun, Eyerusaleam. 2018. "Women's Participation in Ethiopian Cinema." In *Cine-Ethiopia: The History and Politics of Film in the Horn of Africa*, edited by Michael W. Thomas, Alessandro Jedlowski, and Aboneh Ashagrie, 119–39. East Lansing: Michigan State University Press.

Keeling, Kara. 2007. *The Witch's Flight: The Cinematic, the Black Femme, and the Image of Common Sense*. Durham, NC: Duke University Press.

Kemp, Simon. 2020. "Digital 2020: Nigeria—Datareportal—Global Digital Insights." DataReportal, February 18. https://datareportal.com/reports/digital-2020-nigeria.

Kemp, Simon. 2021. "Digital in Ghana: All the Statistics You Need in 2021—DataReportal—Global Digital Insights." DataReportal, February 11. https:// datareportal.com/reports/digital-2021-ghana.

Khady. 2019. "Maitresse d'un homme marié—Review." *Senegalese Twisted* (blog), November 1. https://senegalesetwisted.com/maitresse-dun-homme-marie/.

Khiun, Liew Kai, and Sangjoon Lee. 2020. "'Transmedia and Asian Cinema' Editors' Introduction." *Asian Cinema* 31 (2): 147–49.

Khumalo, Fred. 2018. "'This Is Nigeria': Childish Gambino's 'America' Has Found an Echo in Africa." *Sunday Times*, June 10. https://www.timeslive.co.za/sunday-times /lifestyle/2018-06-09-childish-gambinos-america-has-found-an-echo-in-africa/.

Kifouani, Delphe. 2022. "'L'intimité des femmes à l'épreuve du petit écran sénégalais': *Maitresse d'un homme marié*, trame des ruptures ou modèle spectaculaire?" *Revue AKOFENA* 6 (4): 79–88.

Kimeria, Ciku. 2019. "How a Senegalese Soap Opera Went Viral across Africa by Giving Women an Authentic Voice." *Quartz Africa*, May 17. https://qz.com/africa/1621913 /senegal-s-mistress-tv-soap-sparks-feminist-controversy.

Kiyaga-Mulindwa, David. 2005. "Nyabingi Cult and Resistance." In *Encyclopedia of African History*, edited by Kevin Shillington, 3. New York: Fitzroy Dearborn.

Klein, Jessica. 2019. "MTV's Revolutionary African Show. 'Shuga' Has Made a Real Difference in the Fight against HIV." *Fast Company*, January 1. https://www.fastcompany.com/90422484/mtvs-revolutionary-african-show-shuga-has-made-a-real-difference-in-the-fight-against-hiv.

Klenk, Nicole. 2018. "From Network to Meshwork: Becoming Attuned to Difference in Transdisciplinary Environmental Research Encounters." *Environmental Science and Policy* 89:315–21.

Kolawole, Mary. 2004. "Re-conceptualizing African Gender Theory: Feminism, Womanism and the Arere Metaphor." In *Re-thinking Sexualities in Africa*, edited by Signe Arnfred, 251–68. Uppsala, Sweden: Nordiska Afrikainstitutet.

Kozlowski, L. 2012. "The Future of Film." *Forbes*, August 3. https://www.forbes.com/sites/lorikozlowski/2012/08/03/the-future-of-film/#5cd1495579d2.

KPMG. 2020. "Minister of Finance Issues Order on Significant Economic Presence by Non-Nigerian Companies." KPMG TL Series (issue 4). https://assets.kpmg/content/dam/kpmg/ng/pdf/tax/kpmg-in-nigeria-fgn-issues-cit-(significant-economic-presence)-order-2020.pdf.

Krings, Matthias. 2010. "Nollywood Goes East: The Localization of Nigerian Video Films in Tanzania." In *Viewing African Cinema in the Twenty-First Century: Art Films and Nollywood Video Revolution*, edited by Mahir Saul and Ralph A. Austen, 74–91. Athens: Ohio University Press.

Krings, Matthias. 2013. "Karishika with Kishwahili Flavour: A Nollywood Film Retold by a Tanzanian Video Narrator." In *Global Nollywood: The Transnational Dimensions of an African Video Film Industry*, edited by Matthias Krings and Onookome Okome, 306–26. Bloomington: Indiana University Press.

Krings, Matthias, and Onookome Okome, eds. 2013. *Global Nollywood: The Transnational Dimensions of an African Video Film Industry*. Bloomington: Indiana University Press.

Kwansah-Aidoo, Kwamena, and Joyce Osei Owusu. 2012. "Challenging the Status Quo: A Feminist Reading of Shirley Frimpong-Manso's Life and Living It." *Feminist Africa* 16:53–70.

Kwansah-Aidoo, Kwamena, and Joyce Osei Owusu. 2017. "A Contemporary, Empowered Female Figure? Towards a Feminist Reading of Frimpong-Manso's *Life and Living It* and *The Perfect Picture*." *Journal of African Cinemas* 9 (1): 55–73. https://doi.org/10.1386/jac.9.1.55_1.

Landau, J. 1976. "Otis Redding." In *The Rolling Stone Illustrated History of Rock and Roll*, edited by J. Miller, 210–13. New York: Rolling Stone Press.

Langford, Rachael. 2018. "Resistant Representations? Genre and Gender in Francophone African Film." *Transnational Cinemas* 9 (2): 181–96.

Larkin, Brian. 2000. "Hausa Dramas and the Rise of Video Culture in Nigeria." In *Nigerian Video Films*, edited by Jonathan Haynes, 209–41. Athens: Ohio University Press.

Larkin, Brian. 2004. "Degraded Images, Distorted Sounds: Nigerian Video and the Infrastructure of Piracy." *Public Culture* 16 (2): 289–314.

Larkin, Brian. 2008. *Signal and Noise: Media, Infrastructure, and Urban Culture in Nigeria*. Durham NC: Duke University Press.

Larkin, Brian. 2019. "The Grounds of Circulation: Rethinking African Film and Media." *Politique africaine* 1:105–26.

Lewis, Desiree. 2011. "Representing African Sexualities." In *African Sexualities: A Reader*, edited by Sylvia Tamale, 199–216. Cape Town: Pambazuka Press.

Lewis, Desiree, and Gabeba Baderoon, eds. 2021. *Surfacing: On Being Black and Feminist in South Africa*. Johannesburg: Wits University Press.

Lewis, John. 2016. "The New Cool: How Kamasi, Kendrick and Co Gave Jazz a New Groove." *Guardian*, October 6. https://www.theguardian.com/music/2016/oct/06/new-cool-kamasi-kendrick-gave-jazz-new-groove.

Lindvall, Terry. 2010. *Sanctuary Cinema: Origins of the Christian Film Industry*. New York: New York University Press.

Lobato, Ramon. 2010. "Creative Industries and Informal Economies: Lessons from Nollywood." *International Journal of Cultural Studies* 13 (4): 337–54. https://doi.org/10.1177/1367877910369971.

Lobato, Ramon. 2016. "The Cultural Logic of Digital Intermediaries: YouTube Multi-channel Networks." *Convergence: The International Journal of Research into New Media Technologies* 22 (4): 348–60. https://doi.org/10.1177/1354856516641628.

Lobato, Ramon. 2019. *Netflix Nations*. New York: New York University Press.

Lobato, Ramon, and Amanda D. Lotz. 2020. "Imagining Global Video: The Challenge of Netflix." *Journal of Cinema and Media Studies* 59 (3): 132–36.

Lothian, Alexis. 2015. "A Different Kind of Love Song: Vidding Fandom's Undercommons." *Cinema Journal* 54 (3): 138–45.

Lotz, Amanda. 2017. *Portals: A Treatise on Internet-Distributed Television*. Ann Arbor: University of Michigan Press.

Lotz, Amanda. 2020. "In Between the Global and the Local: Mapping the Geographies of Netflix as a Multinational Service." *International Journal of Cultural Studies* 14 (2): 1–21.

Lotz, Amanda, Ramon Lobato, and Julien Thomas. 2018. "Internet Distributed Television Research: A Provocation." *Media Industries* 5 (2): 35–47.

Mabry, Rochelle A. 2006. "About a Girl: Female Subjectivity and Sexuality in Contemporary 'Chick' Culture." In *Chick Lit: The New Woman's Fiction*, edited by Suzanne Ferriss and Mallory Young, 191–206. London: Routledge.

MacLeod, George. 2020. "Jacqueline Kalimunda's Interactive Love Stories: Transmedia Documentary in Present-Day Rwanda." *Research in African Literatures* 51 (1): 109–32.

Makungu, Kenny. 2004. *The State of the Media in Zambia: From the Colonial Era to 2003*. Lusaka: Media Institute of Southern Africa, Zambian Chapter.

Mambwe, Elastus. 2013. "The Use of New Media in Journalism and New Dissemination in Zambia: The Case of the Internet." University of Zambia. https://doi.org/10.13140/RG.2.2.21834.41922.

Mambwe, Elastus. 2021. "Review of Mushala, Angel Phiri (2019), 120 Mins, Zambia: Muvi Television." *Journal of African Cinemas* 13 (1): 91–93. https://doi.org/10.1386/jac_00049_5.

Mann Global Health Report. 2016. Marketing Case Study Series. MTVShuga Case Study. Accessed December 1, 2019. https://mannglobalhealth.com/wp-content/uploads/2019/08/MTV-Shuga-Case-Study-FINAL.pdf.

Marks, Laura U. 2000. *The Skin of the Film: Intercultural Cinema, Embodiment, and the Senses*. Durham, NC: Duke University Press.

Marks, L. U., and Radek Przedpelski. 2021. "Bandwidth Imperialism and Small-File Media." In *New Filmic Geographies*, edited by Suzanne Enzerink. *Post 45*, April 13. https://post45.org/2021/04/bandwidth-imperialism-and-small-file-media/.

Masquelier, Adeline. 2013. "Forging Connections, Performing Distinctions: Youth, Dress, and Consumption in Niger." In *African Dress: Fashion, Agency, Performance*, edited by Karen Tranberg Hansen and D. Soyini Madison, 138–52. London: Bloomsbury.

Massood, Paula J., Angel Daniel Matos, and Pamela Robertson Wojcik, eds. 2021. *Media Crossroads: Intersections of Space and Identity in Screen Cultures*. Durham, NC: Duke University Press.

Mbembe, Achille. 1992. "The Banality of Power and the Aesthetics of Vulgarity in the Postcolony." *Public Culture* 4 (2): 1–30.

Mbembe, Achille. 2001. *On the Postcolony*. Berkeley: University of California Press.

McCall, John C. 2004. "Nollywood Confidential." *Transition* 95:98–109.

McDonald, Kevin, and Daniel Smith-Rowsey. 2016. Introduction. In *The Netflix Effect: Technology and Entertainment in the 21st Century*, edited by Kevin McDonald and Daniel Smith-Rowsey, 1–12. London: Bloomsbury. https://doi.org/10.5040/9781501309410.ch-001.

McKay, Andy, and Eric Osei-Assibey. 2017. "Inequality and Poverty in Ghana." In *The Economy of Ghana Sixty Years after Independence*, edited by Ernest Aryeetey and Ravi Kanbur, 279–98. Oxford: Oxford University Press. https://doi.org/10.1093/acprof:oso/9780198753438.003.0017.

McReynolds, Phillip. 2005. "Zombie Cinema and the Anthropocene: Posthuman Agency and Embodiment at the End of the World." *CINEMA* 7:149–68.

McRobbie, Angela. 1989. *Zoot Suits and Second-Hand Dresses: An Anthology of Fashion and Music*. Basingstoke, UK: Macmillan.

McRobbie, Angela. 2015. *Be Creative: Making a Living in the New Culture Industries*. Cambridge: Polity Press.

Mehta, Ritesh. 2017. "'Hustling' in Film School as Socialization for Early Career Work in Media Industries." *Poetics* 63:22–32. https://doi.org/10.1016/j.poetic.2017.05.002.

Mennasemay, Maimire. 2010. "Towards a Critical Theory of Ethiopian Education." In *Education, Politics and Social Change in Ethiopia*, edited by Paulos Milkias and Messay Kebede, 67–98. Los Angeles: Tsehai Publishers.

Merriam Webster Dictionary. 2019. "Cheeba." Accessed January 5, 2020. https://www.merriam-webster.com/dictionary/cheeba.

Meyer, Birgit. 2002. "Pentecostalism, Prosperity and Popular Cinema in Ghana." *Culture and Religion* 3 (1): 67–87.

Meyer, Birgit. 2003. "Visions of Blood, Sex and Money: Fantasy Spaces in Popular Ghanaian Cinema." *Visual Anthropology* 16 (1): 15–41. https://www.tandfonline.com/doi/abs/10.1080/08949460309595097.

Meyer, Birgit. 2006. "Impossible Representations: Pentecostalism, Vision, and Video Technology in Ghana." In *Religion, Media, and the Public Sphere*, edited by Birgit Meyer and Annelies Moors, 290–324. Bloomington: Indiana University Press.

Meyer, Birgit, ed. 2010. *Aesthetic Formations: Media, Religion, and the Senses*. Basingstoke, UK: Palgrave Macmillan.

Meyer, Birgit. 2015. *Sensational Movies: Video, Vision, and Christianity in Ghana*. Oakland: University of California Press.

Mignolo, Walter, and Catherine Walsh. 2018. *On Decoloniality: Concepts, Analytics, Praxis*. Durham, NC: Duke University Press.

Miller, Jade. 2012. "Global Nollywood: The Nigerian Movie Industry and Alternative Global Networks in Production and Distribution." *Global Media and Communication* 8 (2): 117–33.

Miller, Jade. 2016. *Nollywood Central*. London: British Film Institute / Palgrave.

Miller, Jade. 2021. "VOD: Formal Challengers for Nollywood's Informal Domestic Market." In *Digital Media Distribution: Portals, Platforms, Pipelines*, edited by Paul McDonald, Courtney Brannon Donoghue, and Timothy Havens, 259–76. New York: New York University Press.

Mingant, Nolwenn, and Cecilia Tirtaine. 2012. "Global Film and Television Industries Today: An Analysis of Industrial and Cultural Relations." *InMedia* 1. https://doi.org/10.4000/inmedia.111.

Miselo, Terrence. 2017. "Who Wins the MultiChoice ZAFTA's This Saturday?" *Daily Nation*, March 29. Accessed September 2019. https://dailynationzambia.com/2021/03/who-wins-the-multichoice-zaftas-this-saturday/.

Mistry, Jyoti, and Antje Schuhmann, eds. 2015. *Gaze Regimes: Film and Feminisms in Africa*. Johannesburg: Wits University Press.

Mortey, Gershon. 2018. "Photos: Joy Prime Launches New Sitcom, Master and 3 Maids." Adomonline.com. Accessed June 18, 2021. https://www.adomonline.com/photos-joy-prime-launches-new-sitcom-master-and-3-maids/.

Motsaathebe, Gilbert, and Sarah H. Chiumbu, eds. 2021. *Television in Africa in the Digital Age*. New York: Palgrave Macmillan.

Moukarbel, Nayla. 2009. "Not Allowed to Love? Sri Lankan Maids in Lebanon." *Mobilities* 4 (3): 329–47.

Moukouti Onguédou, Georges. 2014. "[In]flujo de las telenovelas latinoamericanas en África: Popularización, efectismo y corolarios." *Belphégor: Littératures populaires et culture médiatique* 12 (1). https://journals.openedition.org/belphegor/463#quotation. Published online December 1.

Mudimbe, Valentino Y. 1988. *The Invention of Africa: Gnosis, Philosophy, and the Order of Knowledge*. Bloomington: Indiana University Press.

Muhanguzi, Florence Kyoheirwe. 2015. "'Sex Is Sweet': Women from Low Income Contexts in Uganda Talk about Sexual Desire and Pleasure." *Reproductive Health Matters* 23 (46): 62–70.

MultiChoice Africa. 2015. "Zambezi Magic Commissioning Brief." Accessed February 8, 2019. https://zambezimagic.dstv.com/news/zambezi-magic-original-films.

Mulvey, Laura, 2006. *Death 24× a Second: Stillness and the Moving Image*. London: Reaktion Books.

Musila, Grace, ed. 2022. *Routledge Handbook of African Popular Culture*. London: Routledge.

National Communications Authority. 2020. "Industry Market Statistics: Mobile Data Subscription for January to August 2020." Accra: National Communications Authority. Accessed November 25, 2020. https://www.nca.org.gh/assets/Uploads/Data -v2. . . . August-2020.pdf.

National Film and Video Foundation (NFVF). 2018. *Gender Matters in the South African Film Industry*. Johannesburg: National Film and Video Foundation. http://www.dac .gov.za/sites/default/files/NFVF%20SWIFT%20Gender%20Matters%20in%20 the%20SAFI%20Report.pdf.

Ndlela, M. N. 2013. "Global Television Formats in Africa: Localizing Idol." In *Global Television Formats: Understanding Television across Borders*, edited by Tasha Oren and Sharon Shahaf, 242–59. New York: Routledge.

Ndlovu, Musa. 2003. "The South African Broadcasting Corporation's Expansion into Africa: South African Media Imperialism?" *Communication* 29 (1–2): 297–311. https:// doi.org/10.1080/02500160308538033.

Negus, Keith, and Michael Pickering. 2004. *Creativity, Communication and Cultural Value*. London: Sage.

Nelson, Ediomo-Ubong E., and Aniekan S. Brown. 2017. "Rural Poverty and Urban Domestic Child Work: Qualitative Study of Female House Maids in Uyo, Nigeria." *International Journal of Social Sciences* 11 (1): 59–68.

Newell, Stephanie, and Onookome Okome, eds. 2014. *Popular Culture in Africa: The Episteme of the Everyday*. London: Routledge.

Nigerian Communications Commission. 2019. "NCC Hinges Nigeria's 122 Million Internet Users' Protection on Effective Governance." July 12. https://www.ncc.gov .ng/stakeholder/media-public/news-headlines/614-ncc-hinges-nigeria-s-122-million -internet-users-protection-on-effective-governance.

Nwaolikpe, Onyinyechi. 2018. "Communicating HIV/AIDS to Adolescents in South-West Nigeria: The Case of MTV *Shuga* Series." *IOSR Journal of Humanities and Social Science* 23 (1): 36–45. http://www.iosrjournals.org/iosr-jhss/papers/Vol.%2023%20 Issue1/Version-1/E2301013645.pdf.

Nyairo, Joyce. 2015. *Kenya@50: Trends, Identities and the Politics of Belonging*. Nairobi: Contact Zones NRB.

Obadare, Ebenezer. 2018. *Pentecostal Republic: Religion and the Struggle for State Power in Nigeria*. London: Zed Books.

Obono, Koblowe. 2011. "Media Strategies of HIV/AIDS Communication for Behaviour Change in Southwest Nigeria." *Africana Journal* 5 (2). http://africanajournal.org /media-strategies-hivaids-communication-behaviour-change-south-west-nigeria/.

Ohia, N. 2016. "Mothers' Attitude to Giving Sexuality Education as a Check to Sexual Abuse of Primary School Girls in South-East Nigeria." *Journal of Educational and Social Research* 6 (1): 133–40. https://doi.org/10.5901/jesr.2016.v6n1p133.

Okafor, Endurance. 2020. "Nigeria's Internet Users Surge over 14% in 2020." *Business-Day*, July 2. https://businessday.ng/technology/article/nigerias-internet-users-surge -14-in-year-to-may-2020/.

Okome, O. 2007. "Nollywood: Spectatorship, Audience and the Sites of Consumption." *Postcolonial Text* 3 (2). https://www.postcolonial.org/index.php/pct/article/view/763.

Okoth-Obbo, V. 2017. "Where Neo-Soul Began: 20 Years of Erkyah Badu's Baduizm." *Pitchfork*, February 10. https://pitchfork.com/thepitch/1440-where-neo-soul-began -20-years-of-erykah-badus-baduizm/.

Onuzulike, Uchenna. 2007. "The Birth of Nollywood: The Nigerian Movie Industry." *Black Camera* 22 (1): 25–26.

Orlando, Valérie K. 2017. *New African Cinema*. New Brunswick, NJ: Rutgers University Press.

Ortner, Sherry B., and Harriet Whitehead, eds. 1981. *Sexual Meanings: The Cultural Construction of Gender and Sexuality*. Cambridge. New York: Cambridge University Press.

Osborn, Brad. 2021. *Interpreting Music Video: Popular Music in the Post-MTV Era*. New York: Routledge.

Osei-Bempong, Kirsty. 2017. "Keteke: Shaping Ghanaian Film Excellence." *New Black Magazine*, November 14. https://thenewblackmagazine.com/2024/01/13 /httpwww-thenewblackmagazine-comview-aspxindex4017/.

Osiebe, Garhe. 2020. "Methods in Performing Fela in Contemporary Afrobeats, 2009– 2019." *African Studies* 79 (1): 88–109.

Paulson, Cole. 2012. "Marketers and Pirates, Businessmen and Villains: The Blurred Lines of Nollywood Distribution Networks." *St Antony's International Review* 7 (2): 51–68.

Peñalosa, David, with Peter Greenwood. 2010. *The Clave Matrix: Afro-Cuban Rhythm: Its Principles and African Origins*. Redway, CA: Bembe.

Phiri, Isaac. 2010. "Groping for a New National Communication Policy in Zambia." *African Communication Research* 3 (1): 185–206.

Piepenburg, Erik. 2015. "Theaters Struggle with Patrons' Phone Use During Shows." *New York Times*, July 10. https://www.nytimes.com/2015/07/11/theater/theaters-struggle -with-patrons-phone-use-during-shows.html.

Piot, Sarah, Jack Okell, and Bar Hariely. 2017. Compass. https://www.thecompassforsbc .org/sbcc-spotlights/mtv-shuga.

Plastow, Jane. 2020. *A History of East African Theatre*. Vol. 1, *Horn of Africa*. London: Palgrave Macmillan.

Polato, Farah. 2019. "Tra connessioni e disconnessioni: Riflessioni a partire dai cinquant'anni del FESPACO." *From the European South* 4:45–60.

Prabhu, Anjali. 2014. *Contemporary Cinema of Africa and the Diaspora*. Malden, MA: Blackwell.

Pratt, Lande N. 2015. "Good for 'New Nollywood': The Impact of New Online Distribution and Licensing Strategies." *International Journal of Cultural and Creative Industries* 3 (1): 70–84. http://www.ijcci.net/index.php?option=module&lang=en&task =pageinfo&id=187&index=9.

Przybylo, Ela, and Breanne Fahs. 2018. "Feels and Flows: On the Realness of Menstrual Pain and Crippling Menstrual Chronicity." *Feminist Formations* 30 (1): 206–29.

Pype, Katrien. 2013. "Religion, Migration, and Media Aesthetics: Notes on the Circulation and Reception of Nigerian Films in Kinshasa." In *Global Nollywood. The Transnational Dimensions of an African Video Film Industry*, edited by Matthias Krings and Onookome Okome, 199–222. Bloomington: Indiana University Press.

Pype, Katrien. 2015. "The Heart of Man: Pentecostal Emotive Style in and beyond Kinshasa's Media World." In *New Media and Religious Transformations in Africa*, edited by R. I. J. Hackett and B. F. Soares, 116–36. Bloomington: Indiana University Press.

Quartier Mozart Films. 2005. "Les Saignantes Synopsis." http://quartiermozart.blogspot.com/.

Radermecker, Anne-Sophie V. 2021. "Art and Culture in the COVID-19 Era: For a Consumer-Oriented Approach." *SN Business and Economics* 1 (4): 1–14.

Raengo, Alessandra, and Lauren Cramer. 2020. "The Unruly Archives of Black Music Videos." *JCMS: Journal of Cinema and Media Studies* 59 (2): 138–44.

Rice, Tom. 2016. "'Are You Proud to Be British?': Mobile Film Shows, Local Voices and the Demise of the British Empire in Africa." *Historical Journal of Film, Radio Television* 36:331–51.

Ritman, Alex. 2020. "Nigerian Producer, Mo Abudu on Striking Netflix's First Multititle African Deal: 'As a Continent, We've Remained so Quiet' (Exclusive)." *Hollywood Reporter*, September 25. https://www.hollywoodreporter.com/news/general-news/nigerian-producer-mo-abudu-on-striking-netflixs-first-multi-title-african-deal-as-a-continent-weve-remained-so-quiet-exclusive-4066612/.

Rombes, Nicholas. 2017. "Mobile Viewing." In *Cinema in the Digital Age*, 84–85. New York: Columbia University Press.

Rosaldo, Renato. 1993. *Culture and Truth: The Remaking of Social Analysis (With a New Introduction)*. Boston: Beacon Press.

Ross, Kristin. 1995. *Fast Cars, Clean Bodies: Decolonization and the Reordering of French Culture*. Cambridge, MA: MIT Press.

Ross, Sharon Marie. 2008. *Beyond the Box: Television and the Internet*. Oxford: Blackwell.

Rovine, Victoria L. 2004. "Fashionable Traditions: The Globalization of an African Textile." In *Fashioning Africa: Power and the Politics of Dress*, edited by Jean Marie Allman, 189–211. Bloomington: Indiana University Press.

Rubin, Vera. 1976. *Cannabis and Culture*. Frankfurt: Campus Verlag.

Russell, James. 2010. "Evangelical Audiences and 'Hollywood' Film: Promoting *Fireproof* (2008)." *Journal of American Studies* 44 (2): 391–407.

Sane, Maïmouna. 2019. "Que les gens arrêtent de dire que la série doit son succès aux scandales." *Seneplus*, July 11. https://www.seneplus.com/people/que-les-gens-arretent-de-dire-que-la-serie-doit-son-succes-aux.

Sanogo, Aboubakar. 2020. "Cine-Agora Africana: Meditating on the Fiftieth Anniversary of FESPACO." *Black Camera* 12 (1): 171–83.

Santanera, Giovana. 2013. "Consuming Nollywood in Turin, Italy." In *Global Nollywood: The Transnational Dimensions of an African Video Film Industry*, edited by Matthias Krings and Onookome Okome, 245–63. Bloomington: Indiana University Press.

Saul, Mahir, and Ralph A. Austen, eds. 2010. *Viewing African Cinema in the Twenty-First Century: Art Films and the Nollywood Video Revolution*. Athens: Ohio University Press.

Sawadogo, Boukary. 2019. *West African Screen Media: Comedy, TV Series and Transnationalization*. Ann Arbor: Michigan State University Press.

Schoonover, Karl, and Rosalind Galt. 2016. *Queer Cinema in the World*. Durham, NC: Duke University Press.

Scott, David. 1999. *Refashioning Futures: Criticism after Postcoloniality*. Princeton, NJ: Princeton University Press.

Scott, David. 2014. "The Tragic Vision in Postcolonial Time." *PMLA* 129 (4): 799–808.

Sembène, Ousmane. 1961. "La Noire De . . . " *Présence Africaine* 36:90–102.

Sembène, Ousmane. 1974. *Tribal Scars and Other Stories*. Translated by Len Ortzen. Portsmouth, NH: Heinemann.

Sembène, Ousmane, and Guy Hennebelle. 1998. "Ousmane Sembène: For Me, the Cinema Is an Instrument of Political Action, But . . . " In *Ousman Sembène: Interviews*, edited by Annett Busch and Max Annas, 7–17. Jackson: University Press of Mississippi.

Sendra, Estrella. 2018a. "'Displacement and the Quest for Identity in Alain Gomis's Cinema' in Close-Up 'Filming the Fall: Plurality, Social Change and Innovation in Contemporary Senegalese Cinema.'" *Black Camera: An International Film Journal* 9 (2): 360–90.

Sendra, Estrella. 2018b. "Situando el cine francófono africano en Colombia: La isla de Gorée en el cine senegalés." In *Catálogos razonados: Muestra Afro*, edited by M. Giraldo Barreto, J. A. Rodríguez, and J. A. Bogotá, 76–99. Bogotá: Cinemateca Distrital, Gerencia de Artes Audiovisuales.

Sendra, Estrella. 2020. "Women and Sexuality in African Cinema." In *The International Encyclopaedia of Gender, Media and Communication*, edited by Karen Ross, Ingrid Bachmann, Valentina Cardo, Sujata Moorti, and Cosimo Marco Scarcelli, 1569–74. Hoboken, NJ: Wiley-Blackwell. https://doi.org/10.1002/9781119429128.iegmc246.

Sendra, Estrella. 2021. "Banlieue Films Festival (BFF): Growing Cinephilia and Filmmaking in Senegal." In "Film Festivals and Their Socio-Cultural Contexts," special issue, *Aniki: Portuguese Journal of the Moving Image* 8 (1): 245–72. https://aim.org.pt/ojs/index.php/revista/article/view/734.

Seneweb News. 2019. "'Maîtresse d'un homme marié': Mame Mactar Guèye porte plainnte contre Marodi TV et . . . " March 20. https://www.seneweb.com/news/Audio/laquo-maitresse-d-rsquo-un-homme-marie-r_n_277027.html.

Shapp, Allison. 2014. "Variation in the Use of Twitter Hashtags." Qualifying paper, New York University. Accessed December 1, 2019. https://s18798.pcdn.co/shapp/wp-content/uploads/sites/18562/2020/09/Shapp_QP2_Hashtags_Final.pdf.

Shipley, Jesse Weaver. 2013. "Transnational Circulation and Digital Fatigue in Ghana's Azonto Dance Craze." *American Ethnologist* 40 (2): 362–81.

Simmel, Georg. 1973. "Fashion." In *Fashion Marketing*, edited by Gordon Wills and David Midgley, 171–91. London: Allen and Unwin.

Simmert, Tom. 2020. "Pirates or Entrepreneurs? Informal Music Distributors and the Nigerian Recording Industry Crisis." *African Identities* 8 (3): 329–45. https://doi.org/10.1080/14725843.2020.1779026.

Simon, Godwin Iretomiwa. 2021. "Adapting to Context: Creative Strategies of Video Streaming Services in Nigeria." *Convergence*, May 18. https://doi.org/10.1177/13548565211017389.

Simons, Jan. 2009. "Pockets in the Screenscape: Movies on the Move." Paper presented at MiT 6, Stone and Papyrus, Storage and Transmission. MIT, April 24–26.

Smith, Daniel Jordan. 2005. "Legacies of Biafra: Marriage, 'Home People' and Reproduction among the Igbo of Nigeria." *Africa* 75 (1): 30–45.

Smith, Daniel Jordan. 2017. *To Be a Man Is Not a One-Day Job: Masculinity, Money, and Intimacy in Nigeria*. Chicago: University of Chicago Press.

Smith, Stacy L., Marc Choueiti, and Katherine Pieper. 2014. "Gender Bias without Borders: An Investigation of Female Characters in Popular Films across 11 Countries." Funded by the Geena Davis Institute on Gender in Media, Rockefeller Foundation and UN Women. Accessed June 29, 2021. https://seejane.org/wp-content/uploads/gender-bias-without-borders-full-report.pdf.

Snead, James. 1994. *White Screens / Black Images: Hollywood from the Dark Side*. London: Routledge.

Sobande, Francesca. 2020. *The Digital Lives of Black Women in Britain*. New York: Palgrave Macmillan.

Solanas, Fernando, and Octavio Getino. 1969. "Toward a Third Cinema." *Cinéaste* 4 (3): 1–10.

Sound Check. 2021. "Interview: Producer Shafiq Husayn on His Psychedelic Upcoming Album and Collaborations with Erykah Badu, Hiatus Kaiyote." *Afropunk*, July 16. https://afropunk.com/2014/01/interview-producer-shafiq-husayn-on-his-psychedelic-upcoming-album-collaborations-with-erykah-badu-hiatus-kaiyote/.

Spencer, Lynda Gichanda. 2019. "'In Defence of Chick-Lit': Refashioning Feminine Subjectivities in Ugandan and South African Contemporary Women's Writing." *Feminist Theory* 20 (2): 155–69.

Srnicek, Nick. 2017. *Platform Capitalism*. London: John Wiley and Sons.

Statista. 2020. "Internet Users in Nigeria." Accessed July 7, 2024. https://www.statista.com/statistics/183849/internet-users-nigeria/.

Statista. 2021. "Number of Active Social Media Users in Ghana 2017–2021." Accessed January 14, 2022. https://www.statista.com/statistics/1171445/number-of-social-media-users-ghana/.

Steedman, Robin. 2017. "Nairobi-Based Female Filmmakers and the 'Creative Hustle': Gender and Film Production between the Local and the Transnational." PhD diss., SOAS University of London.

Steedman, Robin. 2019. "Nairobi-Based Female Filmmakers: Screen Media Production between the Local and the Transnational." In *A Companion to African Cinema*, edited by Kenneth W. Harrow and Carmela Garritano, 315–35. Hoboken, NJ: Wiley-Blackwell.

Steedman, Robin. 2023. *Creative Hustling: Women Making and Distributing Films from Nairobi*. Cambridge, MA: MIT Press.

Steel, W. F. 2017. "Formal and Informal Enterprises as Drivers and Absorbers of Employment." In *The Economy of Ghana Sixty Years after Independence*, edited by Ernest Aryeetey and Ravi Kanbur, 192–206. Oxford: Oxford University Press. https://doi.org/10.1093/acprof:oso/9780198753438.003.0012.

Steinberg, Marc. 2012. *Anime's Media Mix: Franchising Toys and Characters in Japan*. Minneapolis: University of Minnesota Press.

Stringer, Julian. 2001. "Global Cities and the International Film Festival Economy." In *Cinema and the City: Film and Urban Societies in a Global Context*, edited by Mark Shiel and Tony Fitzmaurice, 134–44. Oxford: Blackwell.

Sublette, Ned. 2008. *The World That Made New Orleans: From Spanish Silver to Congo Square*. Chicago: Chicago Review Press.

Szalai, Georg. 2020. "Netflix Unveils Nigerian Original Series, Three Films." *Holly- wood Reporter*, September 21. https://www.hollywoodreporter.com/tv/tv-news/netflix -unveils-nigerian-original-series-three-films-4064352/.

Tade, Oludayo, and Babatunde Akinleye. 2012. "'We Are Promoters Not Pirates': A Qualitative Analysis of Artistes and Pirates on Music Piracy in Nigeria." *Interna- tional Journal of Cyber Criminology* 6 (2): 1014–29.

Tafari, I. Jabulani. 1980. "The Rastafari—Successors of Marcus Garvey." *Caribbean Quarterly* 26 (4): 1–12.

Táíwò, Olúfẹ́mi. 2022. *Against Decolonisation: Taking African Agency Seriously*. London: Hurst.

Tamale, Sylvia. 2020. *Decolonization and Afro-Feminism*. Ottawa: Daraja Press.

Tcheuyap, Alexie. 2011. "African Cinema(s): Definitions, Identity and Theoretical Con- siderations." *Critical Interventions* 5 (1): 10–26.

Teer-Tomaselli, Ruth, Herman Wasserman, and Arnold S. de Beer. 2007. "South Africa as a Regional Media Power." In *Media on the Move: Global Flow and Contra-Flow*, edited by Daya Kishan Thussu, 136–45. London: Routledge, 2007.

Tewksbury, D. 2010. "Roll Bounce: Visionary Producer Shafiq Husayn Debuts New Video." *LA Weekly*, April 7. https://www.laweekly.com/roll-bounce-visionary -producer-shafiq-husayn-debuts-new-video.

Thackway, M. 2003. *Africa Shoots Back: Alternative Perspectives in Sub-Saharan Francophone African Film*. Oxford: James Currey.

Thiong'o, Ngũgĩ wa. 1986. *Decolonising the Mind: The Politics of Language in African Litera- ture*. Nairobi: Heinemann Kenya.

Thiong'o, Ngũgĩ wa. 2012. *Globalectics: Theory and the Politics of Knowing*. New York: Co- lumbia University Press.

Trotter, David. 2013. *Literature in the First Media Age: Britain between the Wars*. Cam- bridge, MA: Harvard University Press.

Tsika, Noah. 2015. *Nollywood Stars: Media and Migration in West Africa and the Diaspora*. Bloomington: Indiana University Press.

Tsika, Noah. 2016. "Introduction: Teaching African Media in the Global Academy." *Black Camera* 7 (2): 94–124.

Tsika, Noah. 2018. "Nollywood Chronicles: Migrant Archives, Media Archeology, and the Itineraries of Taste." In *A Companion to African Cinema*, edited by Kenneth W. Harrow and Carmela Garritano, 269–89. Hoboken, NJ: John Wiley and Sons.

Tuhiwai Smith, Linda. 1999. *Decolonizing Methodologies: Research and Indigenous Peoples*. London: Zed Books.

Turkewitz, Julie. 2019. "Bold Women. Scandalized Viewers. It's 'Sex and the City,' Sen- egal Style." *New York Times*, August 22. https://www.nytimes.com/2019/08/22/world /africa/senegal-mistress-of-a-married-man.html.

TV5MONDE. 2019. "'Maîtresse d'un homme marié' Marème et Djalika invites du JTA." YouTube, December 6. https://www.youtube.com/watch?v=hovJouJayMc.

Uduku, Ola. 1996. "The Urban Fabric of Igbo Architecture in South-eastern Nigeria in the 1990s." *Habitat International* 20 (2): 191–202.

Ugor, Paul. 2009. "Small Media, Popular Culture, and New Youth Spaces in Nigeria." *Review of Education, Pedagogy, and Cultural Studies* 31 (4): 387–408. http://dx.doi.org/10.1080/10714410903133012.

Ukadike, Nwachukwu Frank. 1994. *Black African Cinema*. Berkeley: University of California Press.

Ukah, Asonzeh. 2009. "Reverse Mission or Asylum Christianity? A Nigerian Church in Europe." In *Africans and the Politics of Popular Culture*, edited by Toyin Falola and Augustine Agwuele, 104–32. Rochester, NY: University of Rochester Press.

Ukah, Asonzeh. 2016. "Building God's City: The Political Economy of Prayer Camps in Nigeria." *International Journal of Urban and Regional Research* 40 (3): 524–40. https://doi.org/10.1111/1468-2427.12363.

Unah, Linus. 2018. "Not Everyone Is Happy with Nigeria's Viral Version of 'This Is America.'" NPR, June 1. https://www.npr.org/sections/goatsandsoda/2018/06/01/615805868/a-nigerian-rappers-take-on-donald-glover-s-this-is-america.

Van de Peer, Stefanie. 2014. "Forgotten Women, Lost Histories: Selma Baccar's *Fatma 75* (1976) and Assia Djebar's *La Nouba* (1978)." In *Africa's Lost Classics. New Histories of African Cinema*, edited by David Murphy and Lizelle Bisschoff, 64–72. Oxford: Legenda.

Van Deursen, Alexander J. A. M., and Jan A. G. M. van Dijk. 2014. "The Digital Divide Shifts to Differences in Usage." *New Media and Society* 16 (3): 507–26. https://doi.org/10.1177/1461444813487959.

Van Slooten, Jessica Lyn. 2006. "Fashionably Indebted: Conspicuous Consumption, Fashion and Romance." In *Chick Lit: The New Woman's Fiction*, edited by Suzanne Ferriss and Mallory Young, 219–38. London: Routledge.

Veblen, Thorstein. 1970. *The Theory of the Leisure Class*. London: Allen and Unwin.

Verhoeff, Nanna. 2012. *Mobile Screens. The Visual Regime of Navigation*. Amsterdam: Amsterdam University Press.

Vernallis, Carol. 2004. *Experiencing Music Video: Aesthetics and Cultural Context*. New York: Columbia University Press.

Vernallis, Carol. 2013. *Unruly Media: YouTube, Music Video, and the New Digital Cinema*. New York: Oxford University Press.

Vernallis, Carol, Holly Rogers, and Lisa Perrott. 2020. "Introduction: Intensified Movements." In *Transmedia Directors: Artistry, Industry and New Audiovisual Aesthetics*, edited by Carol Vernallis, Holly Rogers, and Lisa Perrott, 1–16. New York: Bloomsbury.

Vourlias, Christopher. 2019. "Huahua Media Signs on for First China-Nigeria Co-Production." *Variety*, November 6. https://variety.com/2019/film/news/huahua-media-china-nigeria-coproduction-filmone-entertainment-ayo-makun-1203395111/.

Waliaula, Solomon. 2014. "Active Audiences of Nollywood Video-Films: An Experience with a Bukusu Audience Community in Chwele Market of Western Kenya." *Journal of Africa Cinemas* 6 (1): 71–83.

Waliaula, Solomon. 2019. "Televisual Cinema and Social Identities: The Case of Nollywood and Latin American Telenovelas in Eldoret, Kenya." *Journal of African Cultural Studies* 21 (2): 180–95.

Wara, Habibata. 2019. "More Than 2,000 Security Agents Involved." *FESPACO News*, February 23, 6.

Wasson, Haidee. 2012. "In Focus: Screen Technologies." *Cinema Journal* 51 (2): 141–71.

Wasson, Haidee. 2019. "The Networked Screen: Moving Images, Materiality, and the Aesthetics of Size." In *Fluid Screens, Expanded Cinema*, edited by Janine Marchessault, 74–95. Toronto: University of Toronto Press.

Wells, Juliette. 2006. "Mothers of Chick Lit: Women Writers, Readers and Literary History." In *Chick Lit: The New Woman's Fiction*, edited by Suzanne Ferriss and Mallory Young, 47–70. London: Routledge.

Wendl, Tobias Maria. 2007. "Wicked Villagers and the Mysteries of Reproduction: An Exploration of Horror Videos from Ghana and Nigeria." *Postcolonial Text* 3 (2): 1–22.

Werner, Jean-François. 2006. "How Women Are Using Television to Domesticate Globalization: A Case Study on the Reception and Consumption of Telenovelas in Senegal." *Visual Anthropology* 19 (5): 443–72.

White, Patricia. 2015. *Women's Cinema, World Cinema: Projecting Contemporary Feminisms.* Durham, NC: Duke University Press.

Willemen, Paul. 2005. "For a Comparative Film Studies." *Inter-Asia Cultural Studies* 6 (1): 98–112.

Williams, James S. 2019. *Ethics and Aesthetics in Contemporary African Cinema.* London: Bloomsbury.

Wilson, Elizabeth. 2003. *Adorned in Dreams: Fashion and Modernity.* London: I. B. Tauris.

Women Make Movies (WMM). n.d. "La Nouba des femmes du Mont Chenoua." Accessed January 3, 2022. https://www.wmm.com/catalog/film/la-nouba-des-femmes -du-mont-chenoua/.

Wood, Robin. 2002. "The American Nightmare: Horror in the 70s." In *Horror, The Film Reader*, edited by Mark Jancovich, 25–32. London: Routledge.

Yamoah, Michael. 2014. "The New Wave in Ghana's Video Film Industry: Exploring the Kumawood Model." *International Journal of ICT and Management* 2 (2): 155–62.

Yang, Bin. 2019. *Cowrie Shells and Cowrie Money: A Global History.* London: Routledge.

Yeboah, Johnson, and George Dominic Ewur. 2014. "The Impact of WhatsApp Messenger Usage on Students' Performance in Tertiary Institutions in Ghana." *Journal of Education and Practice* 5:157–64.

Yoshimoto, Mitsuhiro. 2013. "A Future of Comparative Film Studies." *Inter-Asia Cultural Studies* 14 (1): 54–61.

Young, Katherine. 2019. "Hindi Film Songs and Musical Life in Tamale, Northern Ghana, 1957–Present." PhD diss., Royal Holloway, University of London.

Zenebe, Milete, Azeb Gebresilassie, and Huruy Assefa. 2014. "Magnitude and Factors Associated to Physical Violence among House Maids of Mekelle Town, Tigray, Northern, Ethiopia: A Cross Sectional Study." *American Journal of Nursing Science* 3 (6): 105–9.

Zerihun Birehanu. 2019. "Performing the Nation: Incorporating Cultural Performances into Theatre in Ethiopia." In *African Theatre* 18, edited by Chukwuma Okoye, 100–120. Woodbridge, UK: James Currey.

Contributors

MORADEWUN ADEJUNMOBI is a professor in the African American and African Studies Department at the University of California, Davis, with an interest in African literature, African popular culture, and Nollywood. She has previously taught at the University of Botswana and the University of Ibadan. She is the author and coeditor of several books. Her research on Nigerian film, media, and performance has appeared in *Popular Communication*, *Cultural Critique*, *Black Camera*, *Cambridge Journal of Postcolonial Literary Inquiry*, and *Cinema Journal*, among others.

AÑULIKA AGINA is an associate professor of media studies and the program director of the MSc media and communication at the Pan-Atlantic University Lagos, where she teaches and researches Nigerian film, media industries, cinema-going cultures and Nollywood women. She has held research fellowships in South Africa, Germany, and the United Kingdom, working on the African Screen Worlds: Decolonising Film and Screen Studies project to investigate Nigerian screen cultures. She wrote, produced, and directed a documentary on film exhibition titled *Behind My Nollywood Screen* (2022), an official selection at the iRepresent International Film Festival in Lagos. She has co-edited three books and published her research in reputable journals.

ALEXANDER BUD is a core member of the Open University project, Trans-local Migration and Creative Industries in the Global South. Having worked extensively with creative communities in Lagos, Igboland, Benin City, and London, his interests include film and television, carpentry and fabrication, tailoring and fashion, houses and hotels, wedding and event industries, and printing and artisanal advertising. Alex received his BA from The Queen's College, University of Oxford; MSc from Edinburgh's Centre of African Studies; and PhD from the Open University's Centre for Development, Policy and Practice.

LINDIWE DOVEY is a professor of film and screen studies at SOAS University of London and was the Principal Investigator of the project African Screen Worlds: Decolonising Film and Screen Studies (2019–2025), funded by the European Research Council. She is a film researcher, teacher, curator, and filmmaker. She recently directed the feature-length documentary films *Out of the Box: The Screen Worlds of Judy Kibinge* (2023, Kenya/UK) and *From One Woman to Another: The Screen Worlds of Bongiwe Selane* (2023, South Africa/UK), which have had invited screenings at film festivals, universities, and other spaces in Kenya, South Africa, Senegal, the UK, and the USA. They are available for viewing on the Screen Worlds website (www.screenworlds.org).

FEMI EROMOSELE is a research associate at the Centre for the Advancement of Scholarship, University of Pretoria. His research interests include African literature, medical humanities, and African popular culture.

PIER PAOLO FRASSINELLI died in 2022; he was working on an African cinema project at the University of Stellenbosch at the time. His home base was the University of Johannesburg, South Africa, and he retained his connections with colleagues in Italy. Frassinelli's research interests included cultural and media studies, critical and decolonial theory, and African cinema. His authored works include the book *Borders, Media Crossings and the Politics of Translation: The Gaze from Southern Africa*.

ALEXANDRA GRIEVE is a junior research fellow at St John's College, University of Oxford. She is a film scholar trained in South Africa, where she received her BA in film and media production from the University of Cape Town. Her doctorate research explored dress and material culture in African and Afrodiasporan cinema. Her current research interests are situated across disciplines and include filmmaking in Africa and its diasporas, global postcolonial filmmaking, and embodiment in cinema.

JONATHAN HAYNES wrote *Nollywood: The Creation of Nigerian Film Genres*, cowrote (with Onookome Okome) *Cinema and Social Change in West Africa*, and edited *Nigerian Video Films*, and, in 2012, a special issue of the *Journal of African Cinemas*. He is a professor emeritus of English at Long Island University in Brooklyn, New York. Educated at McGill University and Yale University and a former Guggenheim Fellow, he taught as a Fulbright senior scholar at the University of Nigeria-Nsukka, Ahmadu Bello University, the University of Ibadan, and the University of Lagos.

JOE JACKSON is a lecturer in communications and media (multimedia production) at London College of Communication, University of the Arts London. He studied at University College London (BA) and SOAS University of London (MA, PhD). Joe is a member of and promotes media content for the Screen Worlds collective. His first book is titled *Kahlil Joseph and the Audiovisual Atlantic: Music, Modernity, Transmedia Art* (2024).

ALESSANDRO JEDLOWSKI is an associate professor in African studies at the Bordeaux Institute of Political Studies (Sciences Po Bordeaux) and a media anthropologist by training. His research focuses mostly on African screen media industries (in particular, the Nigerian Nollywood), media and migration, and South-South cultural circulations. He has published widely on these topics in edited collections and international journals, such as *Television and New Media, Theory, Culture and Society*, and *African Affairs*.

DENNIS-BROOK PRINCE LOTSU (PhD) is an early career researcher with a cross-disciplinary practice that spans strategic communications, new media, digital cultures, and screen production. He is currently a casual academic with the School of Communication and Arts, the University of Queensland, where he teaches media design and media platforms courses while completing a monograph that explores the interplay between violence and affect in the films of the Ghanaian American filmmaker Leila Djansi. Previously, he held academic positions at the Royal Melbourne Institute of Technology, the National Film and Television Institute, and Christian Service University College.

ALISON MACAULAY received her PhD in history from the University of Toronto in 2022. Her dissertation, "Filming History: Visual Representations of Rwanda, 1916–2014," was awarded the 2023 John Bullen Prize from the Canadian Historical Association. Her research, funded by the Social Sciences and Humanities Research Council of Canada, focuses on the history of film in Rwanda and film as a method of historical knowledge production. Alison holds a postdoctoral fellowship with the University of Toronto Mississauga. She also coproduces projects with Kiruri MFN, a film production company based in Kigali, Rwanda.

ELASTUS MAMBWE is a lecturer and researcher in the Department of Media and Communication Studies at the University of Zambia in Lusaka. His research interests lie in media industries, screen studies, and mass communication. He completed his PhD at the Centre for Film and Media Studies at the University of Cape Town, South Africa. He is a member of the South African Communications Association (SACOMM).

NEDINE MOONSAMY is an associate professor in the English department of the University of Johannesburg. She is writing a monograph on contemporary South African fiction and otherwise conducts research on science fiction in Africa. Her debut novel, *The Unfamous Five*, was shortlisted for the Humanities and Social Sciences Fiction Award (2021), and her poetry was shortlisted for the inaugural *New Contrast* National Poetry Award (2021).

ELIZABETH OLAYIWOLA is a senior lecturer in the Department of Broadcast, Film, and Multimedia at the University of Abuja, Nigeria and a Fatema Mernissi postdoctoral fellow at the Africa Institute, Sharjah, UAE. She has distinguished herself as a Nollywood scholar, focusing on the unique culture of Nigerian evangelical filmmaking.

TEMITAYO OLOFINLUA is a creative writer and editor, with an MA in English literature from the University of Lagos. Her essays have won several awards, including the Paula Chinwe Okafor Prize for Creative Non-fiction (2019). She currently works as the creative director of Stories Click, a content studio in Birmingham, United Kingdom.

RASHIDA RESARIO is a senior lecturer in the Theatre Arts Department, School of Performing Arts, University of Ghana. Her research interests include creative industries and creative labor, arts-based research, the interaction of cultures through performance, and gender in performance. Her work has been published in journals such as *International Journal of Cultural Studies*; *Media, Culture and Society*; *Cultural Trends*; *Information, Communication and Society*; *Journal of Contemporary African Studies*; and *Geoforum*. She is currently a co-principal investigator in the collaborative research project, Advancing Creative Industries for Development in Ghana, funded by the Danish International Development Agency (DANIDA).

ESTRELLA SENDRA is a lecturer in culture, media, and creative industries education (festivals and events) at King's College London. Her main research interests are film and creative industries in Senegal, with a particular focus on festivals. She was the coprincipal investigator of the project Decolonizing Film Festival Research in a Post-Pandemic World, funded by the Government of Canada's New Frontiers in Research Fund (NFRFR-2021-00161, 2022–24). She is an advisory board member of the ERC-funded research project African Screen Worlds: Decolonising Film and Screen Studies led by Lindiwe Dovey. In 2024, she was awarded the King's Research Impact Awards (International Collaboration) for her collaborations with festivals and film programs curating African cinemas.

ROBIN STEEDMAN is a lecturer in creative industries at the University of Glasgow. She is interested in African creative and cultural industries and in questions of diversity and inequality in media production, distribution, and viewership. Her work has been published in journals such as *Poetics, Information, Communication and Society, Cultural Trends, Environment and Planning A, Geoforum*, and *International Journal of Cultural Studies*. Her first book is *Creative Hustling: Women Making and Distributing Films from Nairobi*.

MICHAEL W. THOMAS is a lecturer in film and screen studies at SOAS University of London and a postdoctoral research fellow in Ethiopian screen worlds on the project African Screen Worlds: Decolonising Film and Screen Studies (2019–25), funded by the European Research Council. His most well-known research is on the popular film culture of Ethiopia, but he maintains a broad interest in film and screen cultures from various regions throughout the world. He is the author of *Popular Ethiopian Cinema: Love and Other Genres* and the writer/director of the documentary *Cine-Addis* (2023).

STEFANIE VAN DE PEER is reader in film and media at Queen Margaret University in Edinburgh, Scotland. She specializes in feminist film history with a particular interest in Arab and African film cultures. She has published widely on the subject, most recently with the edited collection *Transnational Arab Stardom* and in the forthcoming *Stretching the Archive: Global Women's Film Heritage*.

SOLOMON WALIAULA holds a PhD in literary and cultural studies from Moi University, Kenya. He is an associate professor in literary and cultural studies at Maasai Mara University in Kenya and currently a senior research fellow at the Department of Anthropology and African Studies at Johannes Gutenberg University of Mainz, Germany. He has been a research associate at the Department of African Literature at the University of Witwatersrand, South Africa. His current project is on cinema and narration in East Africa. His research interests are in popular culture and cultural studies with a particular focus on electronic media audiences. His research has been generously funded at different stages by Deutscher Akademischer Austauschdienst (DAAD), Alexander Von Humboldt, and the Fritz Thyssen Foundation.

ASTEWAY M. WOLDEMICHAEL, a senior lecturer in theater arts, has spent the past decade undertaking teaching, scholarly research, administrative roles, and directing stage productions at Wolkite University and Addis Ababa University. He recently produced "Tirania Ko Koysani," an indigenous multimedia theater collaboration with Ethiopia's Mursi Tribe and SOAS University of London. He has also written and directed the forthcoming short film እንጀራ አለ? (*Enjera Ale?*). In the realm of journalism, he is currently a UK correspondent for Voice of America Amharic. He is also serving as a communications lead trainer for Dods Training, United Kingdom.

Index

Nigerian Television Authority (NTA), 22–23, 26, 219, 231n7

Nigezie Studios, 104

Njila: The Phase (television program; 2016–19), 82

Njoku, Jason, 58, 63, 265

Nkelemba, Nozipho, 131, 134–36

Nkiru, Jenn, 291

Nkrumah, Kwame, 140

Nkunda, Mutiganda wa, 253

Nnaji, Genevieve, 54, 57

No Letting Go (dir. Dila), 170

No. 1 Ladies' Detective Agency, The (dirs. Minghella, Sturridge, and Fywell), 122

Nollywood: disruption by Netflix, 6, 54, 56, 58, 61, 70–71; distribution models, 57–58, 65; and evangelical film, 219–20, 222–23; housemaid fandom, 185–86, 189–96; legacy of, 139–40, 270–71; meshworks of, 94–95, 108; popularity of, 84, 303; relationship to piracy, 91–92; and small screen media, 41; and stardom, 224; style of, x, 79, 96, 259, 305; transnationality of, 270–76. *See also* Nigeria; televisual turn

Nollywood Houses, 96–103, 109, 113

Nollywood studies, xii, 5, 67, 91–93, 226, 259

Nommo Awards, 154

Non-Aligned Filmmakers Collective, 263

nostalgia, 234, 236, 239–42

Nworah, Chinenye, 71

Nyairo, Joyce, 9

Nyanja language, 77, 82

Nzila, Mwiza, 82

Obadare, Ebenezer, 218

Obembe (Bamiloye), Gloria, 220

objectification, 172, 176

Oboli, Omoni, 62, 63

October I (dir. Afolayan), 259

Ogunsola, Ishola, 231n5

Ogunyemi, Chikwenye, 43

Ojerinde, Opeyemi Akintude, 224

Ojo, Iyabo, 103

"Ojuelegba" (Wizkid), 275

Okafor, Kenechukwu, 101

Okell, Jack, 24

Okome, Onookome, 271

Okonkwo, Benson, 98, 100

Okorie, Chiamaka, 98

Okwo, Mildred, 60

Olayiwola, Elizabeth, ix, 11, 14

Oliver, Bilal, 284, 287, 294, 295n1

Olofinlua, Temitayo, x, xiii–xiv, 2, 8, 9, 11, 12–13, 299

Olugbemi, Jerry, 225

Oluwagbemi, Adeola Jerry, 224, 230n3

Omotoso, Akin, 63, 133

One Lagos Night (dir. Mekwunye), 61–62

online community, 21–22, 26–32, 46–50. *See also* fandom

ONTV, 275

Onuzo, Chinaza, 64–65

Oore Ofe (dir. Pedro-Adetola), 231n9

Opoku-Agyeman, Priscilla, 115

Original Black Entertainment (OBE), 272, 282n2

Orozco-Olvera, Victor Hugo, 25

Ortzen, Len, 172

Osei, Sika, 120

Oshin, Tope, 26, 28

Oshun, 283

Othering, 133, 168, 176, 178, 300

Ouédraogo, Michel, 259

Ousmane Sembène Prize, 261

Out of the Box (dir. Dovey), 137n1

Oye, Piccolo, 99–100

Ozokwor, Patience, 192

Palace Maid (dir. Emma), 195

Palata, Mingeli, 81

Pan African Federation of Filmmakers (FEPACI), 202, 212n1

Pan-African Film and Television Festival of Ouagadougou (FESPACO), x, xii, 39, 116, 257–66, 300, 304–5

pan-Africanism, 12, 203, 212nn1–2, 260, 290

Panic Button (dir. Dougherty), 131, 133–35

Pathé-Gaumont, 206

patriarchy, 153–56, 159–66, 173, 177, 181, 208, 211, 263. *See also* gender

Patricks, Hilary, 106–8

Paul Robeson Prize, 260

P. Diddy, 280–81

Pedro-Adetola, Seyi, 231n9

Pentecostal church, ix, 118, 160, 190, 218, 220, 227–28. *See also* religion